How Migrant Labor Is Changing Rural China

One of the most dramatic and noticeable changes in China since the introduction of economic and social reforms in the early 1980s has been the mass migration of peasants from the countryside to urban areas across the country. Itinerant workers have left villages and farms in large numbers to take advantage of opportunities offered in cities by the new, lively climates of the economic boom. Migrant labor has been both the backbone of economic development and the bane of urban governments as they seek to cope with the burden of growing and unsettled populations. The impact of the migration phenomenon on urban areas and the national economy has been an active area of concern for scholars of Chinese society. In this book, Rachel Murphy provides the first study of the new implications of the boomerang effect – the return flows of the migrants, their earnings, and information – that is beginning to change the Chinese countryside.

Murphy's in-depth fieldwork in rural China offers a rich basis for her findings about the impact of migration on many aspects of rural life: inequality; the organization of agricultural production; land transfers; livelihood diversification; spending patterns; house building; marriage; education; the position of women; social stability; and state–society relations. She investigates the little-studied phenomenon of entrepreneurship by returned migrants, their contribution to rural industrialization and rural town construction, and their role in political lobbying. Her analysis focuses on the human experiences and strategies that precipitate shifts in national and local policies for economic development; she also examines the responses of migrants, nonmigrants, and officials to changing circumstances, obstacles, and opportunities. This pioneering study is rich in original source materials and anecdotes and also offers useful, comparative examples from other developing countries.

Rachel Murphy is a British Academy Post-Doctoral Research Fellow in Development Studies and a Research Fellow in Social Sciences at Jesus College, Cambridge.

Cambridge Modern China Series

Edited by William Kirby, Harvard University

Other books in the series:

Warren I. Cohen and Li Zhao, eds., *Hong Kong under Chinese Rule: The Economic and Political Implications of Reversion*

Tamara Jacka, *Women's Work in Rural China: Change and Continuity in an Era of Reform*

Shiping Zheng, *Party vs. State in Post-1949 China: The Institutional Dilemma*

Michael Dutton, ed., *Streetlife China*

Edward Steinfeld, *Forging Reform in China: The Fate of State-Owned Industry*

Wenfang Tang and William Parish, *Chinese Urban Life under Reform: The Changing Social Contract*

David Shambaugh, ed., *The Modern Chinese State*

Jing Huang, *Factionalism in Chinese Communist Politics*

Xin Zhang, *Social Transformation in Modern China: The State and Local Elites in Henan, 1900–1937*

Edmund S. K. Fung, *In Search of Chinese Democracy: Civil Opposition in Nationalist China, 1929–1949*

Susan H. Whiting, *Power and Wealth in Rural China: The Political Economy of Institutional Change*

Xiaoqun Xu, *Chinese Professionals and the Republican State: The Rise of Professional Associations in Shanghai, 1912–1937*

Yung-chen Chiang, *Social Engineering and the Social Sciences in China, 1919–1949*

Joseph Fewsmith, *China Since Tiananmen: The Politics of Transition*

Mark W. Frazier, *The Making of the Chinese Industrial Workplace: State, Revolution, and Labor Management*

Thomas G. Moore, *China in the World Market: Chinese Industry and International Sources of Reform in the Post-Mao Era*

Stephen C. Angle, *Human Rights and Chinese Thought: A Cross-Cultural Inquiry*

How Migrant Labor Is Changing Rural China

RACHEL MURPHY

Jesus College, University of Cambridge

CAMBRIDGE
UNIVERSITY PRESS

PUBLISHED BY THE PRESS SYNDICATE OF THE UNIVERSITY OF CAMBRIDGE
The Pitt Building, Trumpington Street, Cambridge, United Kingdom

CAMBRIDGE UNIVERSITY PRESS
The Edinburgh Building, Cambridge CB2 2RU, UK
40 West 20th Street, New York, NY 10011-4211, USA
477 Williamstown Road, Port Melbourne, VIC 3207, Australia
Ruiz de Alarcón 13, 28014 Madrid, Spain
Dock House, The Waterfront, Cape Town 8001, South Africa

http://www.cambridge.org

First published 2002

Printed in the United Kingdom at the University Press, Cambridge

Typeface Times 10/13 pt.   *System* AMS-T$_{\!E}$X   [FH]

A catalog record for this book is available from the British Library.

Library of Congress Cataloging in Publication data
Murphy, Rachel, 1971–
How migrant labor is changing rural China / Rachel Murphy.
p.   cm. – (Cambridge modern China series)
Includes bibliographical references and index.
ISBN 0-521-80901-0 – ISBN 0-521-00530-2 (pb.)
1. Migrant labor – China.   I. Title.   II. Series.

HD5856.C5 M87   2002
331.5′44′0951 – dc21   2001043434

ISBN 0 521 80901 0 hardback
ISBN 0 521 00530 2 paperback

Contents

List of Exhibits		*page* x
Acknowledgments		xii
Glossary		xv
Poem: "I Work in the City"		xvii
Map: People's Republic of China		xviii
Map: Jiangxi Province		xx
Introduction		1
	The Fieldwork	3
	Theoretical Approach	6
	Outline of the Study	7
1	Values, Goals, and Resources	10
	1.1 Modernization and Structuralist Evaluations	11
	1.2 Moving beyond Dichotomies: Values, Goals, and Resources	17
	1.3 Petty Commodity Producers and Livelihood Diversification	23
	1.4 Temporary and Permanent Return	25
	1.5 Conclusion	27
2	China, Jiangxi, and the Fieldwork Counties	28
	2.1 Historical Background	29
	2.2 Restructuring the Countryside in Communist China	32
	2.3 Migration from Wanzai, Xinfeng, and Yudu	36
	2.4 Why Do Internal Migrants in China Retain Links with Their Villages?	42
	2.5 Improving Population Quality: Returnees as Emissaries of Modernity	44
	2.6 Rural Livelihood Diversification	47
	2.7 Conclusion	50
3	Resource Redistribution and Inequality	52
	3.1 Researching the Impact of Migration on Rural Inequality	53
	3.2 Migration, Household Composition, and Inequality	57

3.3 The Role of Migration in Increasing Opportunities for
    Off-Farm Employment   67
3.4 Migration, Land, and Inequality   72
3.5 Conclusion   85

4   Migration, Remittances, and Goals   88
4.1 Education   92
4.2 The Life-Cycle Goals of House Building and Marriage   103
4.3 Migration and Consumer Goods   114
4.4 Conclusion   117
4.5 Education Appendix   118

5   Recruiting Returnees to Build Enterprises and Towns   124
5.1 Return and Entrepreneurship at the National Level   124
5.2 Returnees to Xinfeng and Yudu   127
5.3 Coaxing the Phoenix to Lay Eggs in the Nest   136
5.4 Conclusion   143

6   The Enterprises and the Entrepreneurs   144
6.1 The Enterprises: Scale, Type, and Ownership   144
6.2 What Kind of Phoenix Lays an Egg?   154
6.3 Reasons for Return   161
6.4 Women Returnee Entrepreneurs   169
6.5 Conclusion   175

7   Entrepreneurs, Socioeconomic Change, and Interactions with
    the State   177
7.1 Investment   177
7.2 Improving the Political Environment for Business   180
7.3 Absorbing Surplus Labor   184
7.4 "Modern" Managers   188
7.5 Integrating Natal Communities into a National Market
    Economy   190
7.6 Building Towns in the Countryside   191
7.7 Conclusion   194

8   Returning Home with Heavy Hearts and Empty Pockets   196
8.1 Unemployed Returnees   196
8.2 Illness and Injury   200
8.3 Pregnancy and Child Care   202
8.4 Marriage and Family   203
8.5 Problems of Readjustment   211
8.6 Conclusion   214

9   Conclusion   216
9.1 Resource Distribution   217
9.2 Goals and Remittance Usage   219

9.3 Return Migrant Entrepreneurship   220
9.4 Closing Thoughts   224

Notes   225
Bibliography   251
Index   277

Exhibits

TABLES

2.1: Economic indicators of the fieldwork counties compared with the national and provincial averages and migrant destination areas, 1997   *page* 38

3.1: Household categories   58

3.2: Value of per-mu grain yields and pig production for 31 households   82

5.1: Returnee business creation in Xinfeng and Yudu   128

6.1: Number of enterprises surveyed, by type and scale   146

6.2: Average monthly wage (in yuan) of interviewees prior to their return   162

7.1: Investment in returnee firms, and percentage of investment brought from the city   179

7.2: Job creation by returnee enterprises visited by the author   184

GRAPHS

3.1: Number of migrants in 129 households by number of adult laborers in household   60

3.2: Economic categorization of 129 households by number of adult laborers in household   61

3.3: Breakdown of economic categories of 129 households by number of migrant members in household   62

3.4: Breakdown of economic categories of 129 households by household involvement in migration and local off-farm employment   70

3.5: Per-capita allocation of land within the *zu* in Qifeng and Tuanjie villages, and percentage of labor that has migrated from the *zu*   75

3.6: Breakdown of economic categories of 129 households by area of arable land farmed by household   78

4.1: Breakdown of individual education levels from 138
households, by migration status 98
4.2: Breakdown of individual education levels from 138
households, by age and sex 119
4.3: Enrollments of males and females as a proportion of total
enrollments at Gaocheng Middle School 120
4.4: Percentage of students not re-enrolling for the following year
at Gaocheng Middle School 121
4.5: Percentage of students in Wanzai county not re-enrolling for
the following year 122
6.1: Duration of returnee absence, and scale and type of returnee
businesses 156
6.2: Age of entrepreneurs on return, and scale and type of returnee
businesses 158
6.3: Level of education of returnees, and scale and type of their
businesses 159

PHOTOGRAPHS AND ILLUSTRATIONS

Qualitative selection effects of migration 15
Household evaluation plaque 56
Young migrants dressed in their city clothes returning for Spring
Festival, Qifeng village 90
Attempt of local cadres in Tuanjie to discourage truancy, (i) 94
Attempt of local cadres in Tuanjie to discourage truancy, (ii) 95
Migrant recruitment poster 101
Migrant and nonmigrant neighbors, Tuanjie village, Wanzai 106
Qingshi Township Furniture Factory, Yudu county 150
Precious Pearl Toy and Clothes Factory, Xinfeng county 151
Returned migrants in Jiading town, Xinfeng 170
Returned migrants providing a livelihood for other villagers 187
Guidelines for migrating Party members 199
Cartoons: "She and I have no common language," says the returned
migrant 210

Acknowledgments

This book has its origins in a Ph.D. dissertation in the Faculty of Social and Political Sciences, Cambridge, which I commenced in October 1995. Since then I have incurred many debts of gratitude.

The first is to my supervisor, Peter Nolan, for his continual support and guidance, and for his valuable feedback during the researching and writing of the dissertation.

Tim Wright taught me as an undergraduate student and has continued to be an invaluable source of advice and encouragement. I am grateful to him for his careful reading of various drafts of the manuscript and his immensely helpful suggestions throughout.

I wish to thank the two anonymous reviewers at Cambridge University Press for their helpful suggestions on revising the manuscript. I am also very grateful to the Cambridge Modern China Series editor, William Kirby, the Cambridge editor Mary Child, and her assistant Mike Green. I would also like to thank the production controller, Cathy Felgar, as well as Matt Darnell for his meticulous copyediting.

Jeremy Riley read the manuscript with infinite patience and kindness and made valuable suggestions. Many thanks are due to Jeff Vernon, who carefully read the dissertation at various stages and contributed helpful ideas. Christine Minas and Godfrey Yeung gave valuable comments for which I am most grateful. I am also grateful to Christine for her editorial suggestions on some chapters in the present manuscript.

Delia Davin and Beverley Hooper gave helpful comments on an earlier version of Chapters 5–7. Geoff Harcourt and Paul Martin read substantial portions of the present manuscript and made valuable comments.

I am grateful to Professors Robert Ash, Geoff Hawthorn, and John Sender for their support and encouragement, and also to Anne and John Harrison for a rapid and thorough proofreading of the manuscript.

I gave two invited talks at which the participants were generous with their questions, comments, and encouragement. These were: "Return Migrant Entrepreneurship and Local State Corporatism," presented at the Foreign and Commonwealth Office One Day Conference on China: Critical Junctures, 9 March

1998; and "Migration, Consumption and Rural Inequality," presented at the Rural Development Seminar Series, Institute for Development Studies, The Hague, 31 July 1998. Thanks in particular to Jos Mooij, Bridget O'Laughin, and Max Spoor for their advice at this seminar.

I would like to thank James Alexander, Eric Breton, Nicole Craddock, Christine Minas, Firouzeh Sabri, Mukund Unavane, Jeremy Riley, and Jeff Vernon for their friendship and moral support throughout my work toward a Ph.D.

In China, my debts are too numerous to mention, but I shall try nonetheless. My fieldwork in China was hosted and arranged through the Shanghai Academy of Social Sciences, which provided wonderful moral and logistical support. Zhao Nianguo, a scholar at the Shanghai Academy of Social Sciences, made the arrangements for my fieldwork visit to Wanzai. He was rusticated there during the Cultural Revolution and was warmly remembered by people in the county. Xie Xiaowei of the Jiangxi Academy of Social Sciences, a former deputy leader in the county, also helped in making the initial contacts in Wanzai. In Wanzai, my fieldwork would not have been possible without the support of the very open and pragmatic leadership in the county. In Qifeng and Tuanjie villages, Wu Shuji and Zhou Zhuren helped me enormously. I know that I was an imposition in their already busy lives, and I thank them for their kindness and help. Mr. Guo, the principal of Wanzai Middle School, assisted my integration into the Wanzai community, and his friendship with leaders in Fengcheng enabled me to make a research visit to Rongtang town, Fengcheng. I am also grateful to officials in Gaocheng township for providing the census sheets and for their help in explaining the socioeconomic conditions in the township.

My thanks to Mr. Lai Jidong of the Yudu Labor Export Company in Shanghai and the Shanghai Academy of Social Sciences for arranging my fieldwork visit to Yudu, and to the Yudu workers at the Shanghai docks, who were welcoming and generous in sharing their experiences with me. Thanks are also due to Mr. Zhang Weidong and Mr. Xu for agreeing to host me in Yudu. Guo Guopeng was an efficient and patient guide who sacrificed much of his own time to accompany me and facilitate my research in Yudu.

My fieldwork in Xinfeng was arranged through an exchange award from the Australian and Chinese Academies of Social Sciences (CASS), which entrusted the Jiangxi Academy with the practical arrangements. A short research visit to Fengxin county was also facilitated through this award. I am very grateful to both academies, to Mr. Liu and Mr. Fan of the Jiangxi Academy of Social Sciences, and to Mr. Lu from the Xinfeng County Overseas Chinese Affairs Office. I would also like to thank Barry Glissold and Sue Rider at the Australian Academy of Social Sciences. Finally, I am grateful to the many people who assisted my fieldwork through a variety of kindnesses and to all those people who talked with me.

None of this research would have been possible without the generous financial support of Trinity College, Cambridge. Thanks to my tutor, Dr. Chris Morley, for ensuring that funds in China were always sufficient and for helping with my queries over the course of the fieldwork. The staff at the graduate tutor's office in Trinity College – Dr. Morley, Hazel Felton, and Sheila Roberts – have always been incredibly warm and helpful. I am also grateful for support from an Overseas Research Students Award.

Within the Faculty of Social and Political Sciences at Cambridge, I would like to thank the graduate secretaries Joy Labern and Silvana Dean for their help. Jesus College, Cambridge, has provided me with a cheerful and supportive environment in which to revise the manuscript. I am also very grateful for the support of the British Academy.

Last, but not least, thanks to Mum, Dad, and Bill for their love and encouragement.

Although the book has been infinitely enriched and strengthened by the help and kindness of others, the responsibility for the final product and the views expressed lies with me.

I am grateful to Cambridge University Press for permission to use material from my article, "The Impact of Migration on Inter-household Inequality in the Countryside: A Case Study of Wanzai, Jiangxi," *China Quarterly* 165 (December 2000), pp. 965–82. I wish to thank Carfax Publishing for permission to use part of my article, "Return Migrant Entrepreneurs and Local State Corporatism: The Experience of Two Counties in South Jiangxi," *Journal of Contemporary China* 9 (2000), pp. 231–48. I would also like to thank Taylor and Francis Publishing for permission to use part of my article, "Return Migrant Entrepreneurship and Economic Diversification in South Jiangxi, China," *Journal of International Development* 11 (1999), pp. 661–72. I am grateful to Blackwell Publishers for permission to use material from my chapter, "Return Migration, Entrepreneurship and State-Sponsored Urbanisation in Rural Jiangxi," in John R. Logan (Ed.), *The New Chinese City: Globalisation and Market Reform* (Oxford: Blackwell, 2001), pp. 229–44 (a revised and expanded version of material published in the two journal articles listed previously).

Finally, I wish to thank the magazine *Dagong zu* [Workers' Group; previously entitled *Wailaigong*] for permission to reproduce two cartoons from *Wailaigong* [Migrant Worker] 11 (1997), pp. 44–5. I would especially like to thank the artist, Wei Lai, for her permission to reproduce these two cartoons.

Glossary

cadre   A person in a position of authority, such as a departmental head or a government or Party administrator.

dagong   The colloquial term for selling one's labor to a boss; to work.

fen   Unit for the measure of land; 1 mu is divided into 10 fen.

hukou   The *hukou* registration system divides the population into urban residents and the agricultural population.

jin   A unit for the measure of weight; a "catty," where 1 catty = 0.5 kg.

laoban   Colloquial term for a boss.

mu   Unit for the measure of land; 1 mu = 0.1647 acres = 0.0667 hectares.

phoenix   The word *feng,* phoenix, refers to an accomplished or successful person. For example: *feng mao ji mei,* worthy son of a high officer; *qi feng teng jiao,* a rising name in literature.

population quality (*renkou suzhi*)   A term used by the Chinese state and Chinese policy-makers that incorporates the aspects of (1) eugenics and physical quality, (2) cultural quality (level of education), and (3) ideological quality (politically correct thought and moral behavior). Improving "population quality" is a key component of the national population policy, as enshrined in the slogan "control population increase, improve population quality."

rural collectives   Township and village enterprises owned by the rural residents at the township or administrative level.

xiang   Township. The *xiang* is an administrative unit, a rural jurisdiction at the same level as towns. The townships replaced the former people's communes in 1983. Townships fall under the jurisdiction of counties or city districts and are subdivided into administrative villages.

xiaokang lou   A "comfortable living building" – that is, a two-story house with sturdy walls and concrete floors and glass in the windows.

yuan   Unit of Chinese currency, where £1 roughly equals 13 yuan and $US1 roughly equals 8 yuan (1997 exchange rates).

zhen   Town. The *zhen* is an administrative unit, a small urban area on the same administrative level as townships. Towns fall under the direct jurisdiction of the county.

zu Group. A village is made up of groups, each comprising about 30 to 50 households and 100 to 150 people. The village committee allocates tasks to group leaders who help with disseminating government policy, mediating disputes, improving rural incomes, and organizing labor for the construction of township and village projects. In my fieldwork villages, the clusters of houses in which the members of each *zu* lived were spatially separated, with paddy fields in between, and it could take anywhere from five to fifteen minutes to walk from one *zu* to the next.

I Work in the City

Extracted verses from a poem by Yu Chengda

Another dawn blowing dust in my face
In a strange city, I unload my bundle of dreams.
The skyscrapers are taller and denser than the trees of home.
The bright neon lights are like leaves,
Like drops of acid dew in the moonlight,
Which cannot moisten my chaffed lips ....

Here I must bid farewell to a rhythm of life
Which is as slow as the yellow cow plowing.
I must speed ahead as fast as a car
To chase the moment
And build a life from reinforcement steel, and concrete,
And drops of sweat ....

At the end of every month,
Neither wind nor rain stops us from going to the post office,
To remit notes of money which are thin but not heavy,
And wipe away the longing and poverty of home ....

We will meet without prior appointment
At a common spot with our luggage rolled up
Returning down a familiar path
And our hearts will be clear
That in the distance
Autumn and farming await us.

Source: Zhongguo nongcun qingnian [Rural Youth of China] 2 (1996), p. 29. Translation: Rachel Murphy.

The People's Republic of China

The main fieldwork counties discussed in this book are Xinfeng, Yudu, and Wanzai. Their locations are indicated on the map by arrows.

Other places in Jiangxi mentioned in this book are Ganzhou city (the administrative center of Ganzhou prefecture), Yichun city (the administrative center of Yichun prefecture), Nankang city, Fengcheng county, and Fengxin county. These locations are indicated on the map with a black square.

All of these places are in italic.

Map of Jiangxi province showing the main fieldwork counties

Introduction

S INCE the early 1980s, over 100 million Chinese farmers have left their native villages to work as itinerant laborers and traders in the cities. They form the largest peacetime movement of people in history. To the consternation of the state, there are even more potential migrants; officials estimate that an additional 130 million rural people lack sufficient land or employment to guarantee their livelihoods.[1] The majority of migrants are from poor rural areas of the interior provinces, which are predominantly agricultural and have low levels of economic diversification. These migrants are highly visible in the cities: at railway and bus stations, on construction sites, in markets, on street corners, and in queues at postal money transfer counters. A rich body of literature discusses the situation of the migrants in the cities. However, far less is known about the impact of out-migration, remittances, and return on those living in the countryside.[2]

The impact of rural–urban labor migration on the Chinese countryside is dramatic not only because of the vast numbers of people who are affected, both directly and indirectly, but also because it is a relatively new phenomenon. Owing to economic planning and restrictions on mobility during the Maoist era (1955–1978),[3] Chinese villages were isolated for more than twenty years. Since then there have been fundamental changes, including the rise of labor and commodity markets. It is becoming clear that migration establishes linkages between rural and urban areas, allowing return flows of people, skills, capital, commodities, and information. Migration therefore has immense potential to transform the countryside, particularly those areas that are relatively distant from cities and other agents of information transfer and change.

Through migration and return flows, rural households and villagers operate within a social and economic environment that encompasses the village and the city. The rural households and the migrants depend on both urban wages and the security provided by subsistence farming. Structural features of the political economy[†] – for example, low wages, job insecurity, social prejudice, and

---

[†] I use the term *political economy* to mean patterns of resource allocation and aggregate economic activity as determined by social and political arrangements. These arrangements include

legal restrictions on rural mobility – prevent the integration of migrants into cities. At the same time, the psychological and economic security offered by the home village underpins the belief of migrants and their families that a permanent return to the countryside is inevitable. This conviction causes migrants to maintain a stake in the origin community by sending money, letters, and gifts and by making regular visits home.

Since 1995, approximately one third of the "floating migrant population" from China's interior provinces have been returning from cities to resettle in their native homes. Return migration is influenced by a range of factors, including urban unemployment, illnesses and industrial accidents, and obligations to family in the village, as well as marriage, pregnancy, deaths, and other life-cycle events. Some migrants return home with the intention of re-migrating as soon as they have dealt with a certain matter in the village. Others return home and take steps to resettle with the intention of staying permanently. Most of these individuals return to farming the land, although some work locally off the farm or even set up businesses. Of course, those returning for temporary visits may end up remaining in the village, and those who intend to resettle may eventually re-migrate.

The state, at its various levels, formulates policies aimed at maximizing the benefits of migration while minimizing the negative consequences. It envisages a role for migration and return flows that involves enriching human resources in the countryside and promoting local economic development. Rural households are urged to use their remittances for the purposes of agricultural production. Furthermore, the state makes strenuous efforts to direct migrant resources toward rural industrialization and rural "townization." These rural enterprises and towns form part of a national modernization agenda designed to ameliorate the sharp divide between the village and the city, absorb surplus rural labor, improve rural livelihoods, and stem the exodus of farmers to the cities. However, as shown in Chapter 1, migration scholars are generally skeptical about the capacity of returnees to innovate elsewhere in the world. The state also attempts to minimize the negative consequences of migration through initiatives to mitigate the destabilizing impact of unemployed migrants who periodically return *en masse*, interventions to protect the welfare of injured or ill migrants, and administrative measures to control the fertility of migrants.

the nature of political power, government policy, the organization of production, the class structure of society, the position of women, and prevailing ideologies and moral values. In this book I am primarily concerned with arrangements shaping the unequal relationship between people from rural versus urban and agricultural versus industrial sectors.

THE FIELDWORK

In order to examine how labor migration and return flows are changing the Chinese countryside, I conducted seventeen months of fieldwork in China. My fieldwork encompasses the whole environment in which migrants and their families operate, from the home villages through rural towns and county seats to the destination areas. This is because it is impossible to understand labor mobility and social change by conducting observations that are narrowly circumscribed in time and place.

Because the focus of the study is on the impact of migration on the origin areas, I conducted most of the fieldwork in the counties of Wanzai (Yichun prefecture) and Xinfeng and Yudu (Ganzhou prefecture), all located in the hill country of Jiangxi province. This in-depth qualitative research has enabled me to investigate the social, economic, and spatial structures within which migration and return take place. As de Haan notes, the causes of labor migration and the outcomes for the origin areas depend on context.[4] The comparisons facilitated by working in three counties prevent the assumption that particular features of the observed processes are universal, and they allow generalizations about the impact of return flows on origin areas to be made with greater confidence.

I conducted the fieldwork in Wanzai county from December 1996 to March 1997 inclusive, making additional visits in early September 1997, late December 1997, and February 1998 and then returning to the county briefly in December 2000. Longer-term migration from Wanzai did not commence until the early 1990s, so I was able to observe social and economic change in villages that were in the initial stages of participation in urban labor markets. A substantial part of my time in Wanzai was spent interviewing 138 rural households, 102 of which had migrant members. This provided material for examining the impact of migration and the return flow of money, commodities, and ideas on interhousehold inequalities, the reorganization of agricultural production, and rural spending patterns. Wanzai officials permitted me to live in the villages for three to four days a week and asked village cadres to help me with conducting the interviews. The cadres accompanied me for most of the formal interviews in Wanzai, and their presence greatly assisted my entry into village society. Similarly, researchers who have conducted fieldwork in other developing countries have stressed the invaluable assistance of local guides.[5]

I chose Xinfeng and Yudu as fieldwork sites because they have received widespread media publicity in China for the role of returned migrants in creating businesses. The primary interviewees in these counties are 85 returnee entrepreneurs. Migration from Xinfeng and Yudu commenced in the early 1980s, so there has been sufficient time to produce a return flow of entrepreneurial migrants. Although there are similarities between the two counties, the differences between them in terms of natural resources, infrastructure, local policy, and the occupational specialization of the migrants have led to differences in the types of enterprises established by returnees.

Research in Xinfeng was organized through an exchange between the Australian and Chinese Academies of Social Sciences (CASS) in June 1997; CASS entrusted the Jiangxi Academy to help with arranging the fieldwork. Academy scholars Mr. Liu and Mr. Fan helped enormously in the interviews, opening up new avenues of inquiry, contributing ideas, and acting as valuable mediators between myself and county officials.

Yudu county was chosen through a fortuitous series of events. After reading articles in the Shanghai evening paper about the role of the Yudu government in using labor export as a tool for poverty relief, I contacted the Yudu Labor Export Company in Shanghai and asked to talk to some of their workers. They welcomed me and allowed unaccompanied access to the dock workers' dormitories. Many of the workers related to me stories of returnee entrepreneurs to their county. The leaders of the labor export company and the Shanghai Academy of Social Sciences were helpful in establishing contact with officials in Yudu county to arrange the fieldwork visit, which lasted from late September to early December 1997. In Yudu I also interviewed households in Jiaocun village (in Xinbei township), which was the home of several migrant dock workers whom I talked with in Shanghai. Officials in Yudu were generous in granting my request to live in the countryside. I either commuted to the villages from the county guesthouse or, in more remote townships, stayed in the local government offices. Hosts used a sheet at the window, a flask, an enamel basin, and a plank bed to fashion a homely room out of offices. This arrangement allowed for informal interaction with township and village cadres. Throughout my time in Yudu I was accompanied by an official from the Office of Overseas Chinese Affairs. He was well known and liked in the Yudu countryside; as his official job did not involve sensitive work like collecting taxes, his presence at the interviews and his knowledge of the county were tremendously helpful.

Return migrant entrepreneurship is by no means common to all of rural China. Where relevant, I illuminate the distinguishing features of return migration to Xinfeng and Yudu with comparative evidence drawn from localities where, despite substantial out-migration, the incidence of returnee entrepreneurship has been minimal. This material was gathered when I lived in Wanzai and other rural areas in Yichun prefecture (the first two weeks of July 1997 in Fengxin county; the month of April 1997 in Fengcheng county).

The interviews with the rural households and returned migrants were semi-structured in that I started with basic questions about migration and livelihoods and then allowed the conversation to evolve. As Jan Breman observed, successful interviews never work in exactly the same way. This is because each new informant offers the opportunity to test the validity and relevance of the information already obtained while also permitting the researcher to add new elements to it.[6] Since interviewees were generally reluctant to discuss money, these questions were left until the end.

Researchers have argued against producing a pen and notebook during interviews because they might impede communication.[7] However, as many of the interviews were public events with my official guides sometimes taking their own notes, the respondents were always conscious of being interviewees. Hence there was no disadvantage to producing my notebook. On the contrary, interviewees helped to record the information by writing down the Chinese characters for place names and special terms that I did not understand.

I supplemented the information from the interviews with participant observations recorded in a personal journal of impressionistic accounts of the fieldwork. For example, I regularly watched the county television news and wrote down relevant information. I also traveled on the long-distance buses between the counties and the coast. These journeys provided me with the opportunity to chat with migrants about their feelings as they left for the city or returned home.

During the course of this fieldwork I have spoken with a range of people who are involved in or affected by rural–urban migration. These include migrants returning for Spring Festival or other life-cycle events, labor exporters and recruiters, post office personnel, credit cooperative managers, bus depot managers, journalists and academics, and officials at the levels of prefecture, county, township, and village. Other perspectives on the migration process come from interviews conducted with migrants and municipal authorities in Shanghai from September to October 1996, in August 1997, and during subsequent brief visits. I also made two brief visits to Nanhai at the end of 1997 to get a sense of the factory districts and to chat with migrant workers.

The interview material is integrated with the analysis of primary Chinese documents. County- and township-level data include government surveys of labor export, local government policy reports and work summaries, the county almanacs, and local gazettes. Additionally, Chinese academic journals as well as national and provincial newspapers provide a background for the interpretation of the micro-level data. The present study is the outcome of my efforts to integrate these numerous conversations, observations, and documents. This multifaceted and multilocal approach is necessary for studying the macro processes of labor migration and socioeconomic change.

THEORETICAL APPROACH

The concerns and assumptions that frame the empirical inquiry are made explicit through a critical review of the broader migration literature in Chapter 1. The discussion begins by analyzing modernization and structuralist theories; these two approaches to migration divide economies and spaces into modern urban cores and traditional rural peripheries, and they are influential in shaping policies pertaining to migration and origin areas in China and elsewhere. An analysis of these core–periphery theories is valuable for understanding the resource characteristics of origin and destination areas and for presenting contrasting perspectives on the role and outcomes of migration and return in distributing these resources. They also elucidate the macro-level processes and rural–urban interactions that both shape and are shaped by the livelihood strategies of villagers. These approaches – their insights and weaknesses – provide a useful starting point for the alternative framework developed here.

The book focuses on the interactions among social actors, values, goals, and resources. For now I offer only a brief explanation of these four concepts. *Social actors* are individuals and collective entities such as households or the state. *Values* are the meanings that these actors give to attributes and actions; they inform *goals* (i.e., what people want to do, become, feel, or own) and also define acceptable pathways to those goals. *Resources* are the tangible materials and the intangible sources of support that social actors obtain and deploy in attaining their goals. Social actors form and pursue goals by using and reconstituting values and structures of resource distribution.

Various kinds of interactions among actors, values, goals, and resources are important when analyzing how migration is changing the countryside. Social actors use migration and return to exploit opportunities created by the state's modernization agenda in order to pursue their own goals. This involves circumventing the structural features of the political economy that restrict their capacity to attain goals. In particular, they struggle with urban employers, rural cadres, and family members to acquire and deploy cultural and economic resources from both the countryside and cities. Through migration, values and resources from the city interact with values internal to the village, giving migrants and returnees a broadened "perspective"[8] that informs subsequent goals. At the same time, by enabling individuals to obtain more resources, migration affords them greater leverage in their bargaining with family members and other actors in rural society. Many are using their resources and pursuing their objectives in ways that are socially and economically transforming the countryside. Through the continual feedback among actors, values, goals, and resources, migration and return become institutions within the village – institutions in which both migrants and nonmigrants participate.

My attention to actors, values, goals, and resources is a response to recommendations of migration scholars to combine the macro-level study of labor mobility with micro-level research into individuals pursuing opportunities while struggling against structural constraints.[9] By considering the longer-term formation of goals and the role of social actors in using and reproducing the values and resources in their environment, this research method is a way of moving beyond models that explain migration as a short-term response to environmental stimuli. The framework is also an attempt to avoid the tendency of reducing the dramatic human experience of migration to the sorts of abstract models that characterize much of the existing literature. Accordingly, the following chapters offer an explanation of change that centers on the interdependency between (1) the aspirations, hardships, and strategies of the migrants, returnees, their family members, and cadres, and (2) the wider cultural, political, and economic environment.

OUTLINE OF THE STUDY

The study is organized into chapters as follows. Chapter 1 reviews the relevant literature and develops the theoretical framework already discussed. Chapter 2 lays out the geographical and institutional setting of the research. This serves two purposes: first, to introduce the reader to Wanzai, Xinfeng, and Yudu; second, to consider the changing position of petty commodity producers in Jiangxi province and the fieldwork counties within the context of nationwide transition. The discussion focuses particularly on the historical and structural environment in which the farmers use migration and return as strategies for acquiring resources and attaining goals; the ways in which these strategies precipitate shifts in state programs for socioeconomic development at county, provincial, and national levels; and the responses of rural people to those shifts.

Chapters 3 and 4 draw on material from household surveys conducted in two villages in Gaocheng township, Wanzai county. Chapter 3 explores the impact of migration on resource allocation and inequality and on the ways in which migration precipitates a redistribution of money, labor, and land within households, among households, and between the rural populace and the local state. In particular, the chapter examines how migration influences three existing areas of inequality: resource acquisition by families and resource distribution within families; access to off-farm earning opportunities as a result of differential access to local social and political networks; and the allocation of land and the income and burdens associated with farming. Chapter 4 considers how villagers use the resources generated by migration to achieve goals that include improving their material well-being and participating more fully in the social life of both the village and the city. The analysis focuses on the uses of remittances for education, house building and marriage, and consumer goods. It explores the ways in which the values within rural society that inform spending patterns are continually adapted to evolving social and economic contingencies, with many of them being triggered by migration. Together these chapters elucidate the role of migration in increasing the bargaining power of social actors in their pursuit of goals by enabling them to obtain resources outside the home community.

Chapters 5 to 7 are based on material gathered in Xinfeng and Yudu counties and examine the involvement of returned migrants in business. Chapter 5 considers the local state as a social actor, examining its efforts to direct the resources generated by return migration toward goals that include modernization, town construction, and rural enterprise creation. It describes the local state campaign to encourage return migrant entrepreneurship and the strategies used, such as invoking values of loyalty to the home town and offering intending entrepreneurs preferential access to local resources – for example, land in towns, credit, and raw materials. The chapter also explains the local state's enthusiasm for harnessing returnee resources in terms of the career ambitions of grass-roots cadres themselves. Chapter 6 is concerned with the characteristics of both the returnee entrepreneurs and their enterprises. Examining the characteristics of the entrepreneurs – for example, the duration of their time spent in the cities, age, level of education, gender, and reasons for return – provides insight into their control over resources from both the city and home. It also elucidates how the returnees' control over resources influences their capacity to pursue entrepreneurship, with implications for the size and type of business that they establish on their return. Chapter 7 focuses on how returnees use their urban experiences and resources to bargain with the local state in ways that improve the local policy environment and the local infrastructure; it also examines how these negotiations make the home economy more conducive to business creation.

Chapter 8 draws on material from all three counties to examine the plight of migrants who are forced to return home because of ill fortune in the cities or binding obligations at home. The discussion considers the reintegration problems that they face after a sojourn in the cities has exposed them to new values and new ways of life but has failed to provide them with the resources needed to attain their goals. It examines how returnees use their broadened perspectives to struggle against the values and social arrangements that they find oppressive, and it also considers local state responses to migrants who face hardship or who create wider social problems on their return to the village. Finally, Chapter 9 evaluates the main findings of the empirical study in light of the theoretical issues outlined in Chapter 1.

This book was written in response to the fact that the impact of migration and return flows on the countryside has received little attention in the literature on migration, development studies, and Chinese studies. This omission is critical when one considers that change in the countryside has as much significance for the future of China as events in the cities. The present study also offers insight into the lives of people in regions in China that have received little scholarly attention.

In conducting the research I have inevitably influenced and filtered what I saw and heard, and in writing the manuscript I have selected some sources of information and quotes while judging others to be less relevant. My efforts to explain what is arguably the most important source of change in rural China is therefore as much as an expression of my own perceptions and the imperatives of a social science project as it is an account of the countryside in transition.

I hope that these pages convey the ingenuity, kindness, humor, and individuality of those people who shared their experiences with me.

1

Values, Goals, and Resources

THIS book explores how labor migration is changing rural China and proceeds by examining the interactions among values, goals, resources, and social actors. *Values* are the meanings that people ascribe to attributes and actions. They are expressed in the norms and rules governing appropriate behavior in society, and they inform both goals and acceptable pathways to those goals. *Goals* are the things that people want to do, become, own, or feel; they are achieved by obtaining and deploying resources. *Resources* include both material resources (e.g., cash and commodities) and abstract resources such as contacts, information, and prestige. All these resources are distributed according to culturally embedded rules stipulating which people are entitled to what quantities of which resources under what conditions. *Social actors* are individuals or collective entities such as households. These actors usually attempt to deploy resources in ways that enable them to obtain more resources for attaining further goals. They are generally knowledgeable about society's values and distributional structures and reconstitute them as they use this knowledge to form and attain goals.[1] This means that each social actor continually stimulates interaction among values, goals, and resources. These interactions contribute to changes in the values and resources available within society to inform further goals, changes that both enable and constrain subsequent actions. Migration and return migration are strategies pursued by social actors for attaining goals; they involve the use and reproduction of particular values and mechanisms of resource distribution.

Values embedded in society underpin an expectation among both migrants and family members (remaining in the origin areas) that the migrant will return home once sufficient resources have been accumulated to attain their goals. Family and friends in the village sustain the return orientation of the migrants by providing resources to support out-migration, by conferring prestige on those who achieve their life goals at home, and by stressing values such as filial piety, love of the native place, and collective welfare. Ties between family in the origin village and fellow villagers who have already migrated furbish intending migrants with resources such as information, accommodation, and access to particular destination areas and occupational sectors. Family in the village also provide the migrants with security in the event of failure in the cities. Ideally, for their part, the migrants honor a moral duty to contribute resources for strengthening their families socially and economically. They also use their resources in the village to achieve goals pertaining to life-cycle events such as marriage, building a house, educating children, setting up a business or career, and saving funds for old age. These values, goals, and practices afford people in the home community some control over the migrants and the resources that their labor generates.[2]

Return migration is sustained not only through values but also through a whole bundle of economic remittances in the form of money, commodities, and equipment as well as "social remittances" such as letters, information, skills, and ideas. Individual migrants often bring these resource bundles home in person when they visit or resettle. Alternatively, migrants send money, gifts, and information via the postal and banking systems or entrust them to returning fellow villagers. Through material remittances migrants contribute to the livelihood diversification of their rural households. This means that households do not rely solely on agriculture for their livelihood but instead minimize their risks and raise their returns to available labor by incorporating various income sources into the household budget. By sending remittances and maintaining contact with family members, migrants demonstrate their continuing membership in their households and keep the door open for future reintegration into the origin community. The flow of people and remittances between origin and destination areas, together with the continual deployment and redeployment of resources within a framework of shared values and obligations, creates single economies and societies that are spatially dispersed.

Migration and return shape and are shaped by the ways in which social actors both form goals and negotiate in obtaining and deploying resources to achieve them. These actors include migrants, returnees, the elderly (whose labor makes the migration of other household members socially possible), dependants of migrants, labor brokers, local farmers who cultivate migrants' land, local government officials, indigenous entrepreneurs, transport operators, and labor recruiters. Examining the ways in which different social actors manipulate resources facilitates an understanding of how migration and return are changing the social, economic, and political institutions of sending areas. Yet before exploring the interactions between values, goals, and resources, I shall examine conventional theories of labor migration for insights into the resource characteristics of origin and destination areas and for contrasting perspectives on the role and outcomes of migration and return in distributing these resources.

1.1 MODERNIZATION AND STRUCTURALIST EVALUATIONS

Modernization and structuralist theories of migration have been influential in both academic and policy-making circles since the 1950s and 1960s, and this influence continues in various forms to the present day. Each theoretical category dichotomizes economies and spaces into modern urban cores and traditional rural peripheries.[3] In general, these geographical concepts of core and periphery also describe a nationwide pattern of uneven development favoring the coastal regions over the interior provinces, though within these regions cities are advantaged over the countryside.

For modernization scholars, development is a process involving the spatial redistribution of labor from low-productivity peripheries to high-productivity cores as well as the diffusion of resources from the latter to the former. They adapt the work of Lewis[4] to argue that migration contributes to modernization because cheap rural labor allows industry to accumulate capital that is directed toward industrial expansion, further propelling the demand for migrant labor. In this explanation, only "surplus" or "zero value" labor migrates; once the supply of surplus labor is depleted from the countryside and urban labor markets become saturated with workers, rural wages rise and urban wages fall in accordance with supply and demand.[5] While this is happening, capital is said to flow from the high- to low-wage sectors, further reducing differences in wage rates. In this model, labor mobility finally adjusts itself in response to the equalization of rural and urban wage rates with a general move toward equilibrium.

Much of the research influenced by this modernization perspective consists of micro-level studies of equilibrating processes. Broadly referred to as the neoclassical literature, this research assumes an economy that functions in isolation from social and economic factors and examines the decision-making of rational individuals as they weigh the costs and benefits of working in different regions and economic sectors. Todaro adjusts the standard neoclassical model to account for the fact that migrants may find themselves unemployed or working for a pittance once in the destination area. He explains that migrants base their mobility decisions on incomplete information and on the mere *expectation* that urban locations offer higher material rewards for their labor.[6]

In later studies, scholars have noted that migration does not involve simply a "one off" adjustment of the individual to intersectoral wage differences and that rational individuals seek not only to raise returns to their labor but also to minimize their risks. These realizations have led to interpretations of migration as a family-based strategy mediated by an implicit contract. In these models, the intrafamilial contract is underpinned by altruism and "enlightened self-interest," ensuring that the benefits of migration are distributed to household members in turn. For example, remittances compensate the family for previous investment in the education of the migrant. And in the absence of institutional insurance arrangements, urban wages also provide the rural household with protection against drought, pests, and other risks inherent in "low immunity ... traditional agriculture"[7] as well as a backup that facilitates experimentation with riskier crops. In turn, by remitting to the rural family, the migrant gains livelihood insurance, sustained rights to a future inheritance,[8] and enhanced social assets and prestige that enable a future dignified return to the native place.[9] In identifying rural–urban migration as a cause of surplus labor in the cities and in recommending rural development as a way of expanding rural employment opportunities and reducing the risks inherent in agriculture, many scholars approximate the structuralist position of associating migration with disequilibrium.

Although many modernization scholars recognize that equilibrium fails to occur in the real world, they nonetheless contend that – at an aggregate level – the migration strategies of individuals and households improve the distribution of labor and other resources both within and among regions.[10] To give an example of redistribution within regions, out-migrants are said to assist not only themselves but also those who remain behind because they alleviate pressure on the land, leading to higher productivity per head and facilitating technical innovation in farming.[11] With regard to redistribution between regions, migration is credited with accelerating the diffusion of cultural and economic resources from cores to peripheries. These core–periphery interactions are said to promote human capital accumulation and the adoption of modern attitudes among rural people,[12] resulting in their "lesser accommodation of poverty"[13] and the development of an entrepreneurial mentality and an achievement-based work ethos.[14] In sum, from a modernization perspective, return flows to origin areas more than compensate for the outflow of "surplus" labor.

In contrast, structuralist theories argue that exchanges between core and periphery can never function as a balancing mechanism because they are fundamentally unequal.[15] These inequalities are the result of histories of uneven capitalist expansion and colonial exploitation, adverse terms of trade in agricultural and industrial goods, and government policies affecting regional patterns of investment. Migration is denounced as both the child and parent of inequality because it helps to sustain the spatial and sectoral inequalities that propel movement from origin areas.[16] The continuous movement of labor and other resources between origin and destination areas is described in the general migration literature as "circulation."[17] This means that rural–urban migrants regularly return home to help during busy farming seasons, for life-cycle celebrations, and when sick, injured, pregnant, unemployed, or just too old to work; they also remit money and commodities to support their rural families and substitute for their physical presence. For structuralists, circulation occurs because capitalist centers employ labor at wages that are less than the cost of reproducing labor power. In this model, circulation is common when agriculture fails to guarantee the subsistence of all household members and, at the same time, urban incomes are insufficient to allow migrants to settle in the cities either alone or with their families. Because the rural family provides support systems, the wage sector escapes the burden of providing the welfare needed by migrants.[18] Thus, migrant labor generates wealth for the cores while peripheries shoulder the burden of reproducing this labor.

Although remittances are integral to circulation, structuralists argue that these resources are monopolized by the migrants and their immediate families,[19] self-ishly directed toward house building and conspicuous consumption rather than toward agriculture and community welfare.[20] Scholars point out that the tendency of rural inhabitants to use remittances for consumption purposes reflects the underdevelopment and lack of investment opportunities that propelled the initial out-migration.[21] Structuralists further contend that remittances provide a "stop gap" measure enabling farmers to live above subsistence level, thereby "maintaining current inequalities" and preventing the implementation of more fundamental measures that direct resources away from cities and toward agricultural production.[22]

Origin areas are said to lose more than they gain from migration because, in the words of one Chinese economist, "it is not only 'zero value' labor that migrates."[23] Several Chinese scholars explicitly refer to Lewis when arguing that, even if those who migrate are "surplus" in a quantitative sense, the qualitative selection effect of migration means that it is the young and skilled who move out – with detrimental consequences for developing rural enterprises.[24] Research conducted in other parts of the world similarly suggests that migration may exert a negative effect on local production because the loss of skilled workers decreases employment opportunities for others.[25] Moreover, in a situation where large numbers of able people are leaving, other villagers perceive that the city offers their only hope for advancement, propelling further out-migration. Chinese scholars contend that – even though out-migrants may be numerically surplus at a national or regional level – at the household and village levels, "nonsurplus" labor often leaves and so creates labor shortages and subsequent declines in agriculture, the maintenance of public works, and domestic welfare. These scholars state that, contrary to the Lewisian formulation, out-migration may act as a disincentive to investment in the home area and may thereby precipitate a downward spiral.[26]

Structuralists tend to evaluate negatively the potential for returned migrants to compensate for the outflow of quality labor from origin areas. They scorn the modernization idea that returned migrants use human capital gains to promote economic development at home. Explanations for the failure of returnees to innovate include the tendency for migrants to be relegated to low-paying and unskilled jobs in the cities, the perception that only failed migrants return, the lack of investment opportunities in backward areas, and the incompatibility between urban production processes and the rural setting.[27] Far from improving human capital, migration is implicated (by some structuralists) in the deskilling of rural people in that years of drudgery in the destination areas make

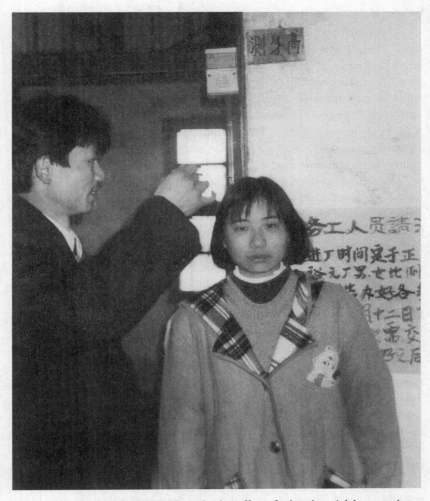

This photograph shows the positive selection effect of migration. A labor recruiter
measures the height of a potential migrant. Recruiters also check for other
indications of "quality" – for example, the dexterity of the fingers and the
ability to speak Mandarin.

them forget the farming techniques and crafts that they used to practice at home.
Other studies report the apathy of national governments toward returnees and
the resentment of local authorities toward innovators.[28] Finally, returnees are
said to be negatively selected – with only the old, ill, and untalented going back
home and forming a disadvantaged stratum in rural society.[29]

Although a few returnees do create businesses, structuralists contend that
their impact on the origin areas is at best neutral. Some studies assess pes-
simistically the cosmetic contributions of shops, hotels, and pubs established

by returned migrants in the saturated tertiary sectors of rural areas in Europe and some developing countries.[30] Other scholars, writing about former colonies, argue that migrants returning as petty traders or embryonic capitalist planters hiring paid labor exacerbate "a degenerated agrarian capitalism, corrupted and poor."[31] Returnee enterprises are generally said to do no more than provide an outlet for spending remittances, usually on urban commodities, thereby perpetuating the dependence of peripheries on cores.

Many Chinese intellectuals based in universities and government think-tanks embrace facets of both the modernization and structuralist positions. Their recommendations inform national policy-making on labor migration and rural development, thereby shaping patterns of resource deployment in the countryside. On the one hand, Chinese scholars concur with the structuralist position that government intervention is needed to redress fundamental inequalities in the political economy and that the "balancing" forces of the market are not sufficient for the regulation of migration. On the other hand, they endorse the modernization view that, if managed correctly, migration may be a low-cost way of generating resources useful for rural development. Rural–urban migration studies conducted in other parts of the world suggest that origin areas that benefit more from the developmental potential of return flows tend to have higher levels of rural development, better infrastructure,[32] a more diversified economic base, land that is more fertile, distributional mechanisms and resource bases that provide more opportunities for acquiring property, a local government supportive of investment and innovation, and a social structure fluid enough to permit upward mobility.[33] Aware that conditions in the origin areas are important in shaping the developmental outcomes of migration, Chinese scholars have argued that grass-roots officials should intervene in their local economies to harness return flows so that the countryside can build up infrastructure in ways that attract further gains from migration.[34] As subsequent chapters reveal, although grass-roots officials in China seek to direct migration resources toward a local modernization agenda, social actors are still able to pursue their own goals. Some of these goals conform to the official modernization objective, but other goals bring rural producers into conflict with the local state over the deployment of resources.

Case studies in countries other than China find that government-sponsored credit and training schemes targeting potential returnee entrepreneurs or migrant investors tend to be disappointing. These studies refer to international rather than internal migration;[35] many discuss the aftermath of mass repatriation, where origin governments expect returnees to solve their own reintegration problems through self-employment but take few measures to improve the local business environment. One problem with support schemes for intending returnee entrepreneurs is that financing is usually offered for large manufacturing projects whereas the socioeconomic backgrounds and capital restrictions of migrants limit them to small service-sector enterprises.[36] Another problem is that government-organized investment projects frequently fail because of the migrants' distrust of the government[37] and, in some instances, because of corruption. The few returnee support schemes that do exist are found to be unsystematic;[38] although some schemes generate results, these tend to be less than anticipated. Finally, returnee incentive schemes funded by governments in the host countries usually flounder because the economic benefits from re-settlement subsidies and low-interest loans fail to match the economic incentives of working in host-country labor markets.[39] Despite the overall lack of government success in creating conditions that support returnee participation in enterprise creation or encourage migrants to invest at home, parallels with official–returnee interactions in the Chinese countryside can be found in Jordan, where better-endowed returnees from the Gulf have been lobbying for a more liberal business environment and the government has been relatively responsive.[40] Later chapters will demonstrate that the actions of local officials partially explain why, in light of the general failure of returnee innovation and related government efforts in other parts of the world, migrants in many parts of rural China nevertheless have contributed to local economic development.

1.2 MOVING BEYOND DICHOTOMIES: VALUES, GOALS, AND RESOURCES

The modernization and structuralist approaches offer contrasting perspectives on the causes of migration and return and on the outcomes of resource redistribution in the origin areas. Although these approaches yield valuable insights, three weaknesses detract from their usefulness. Two of these weaknesses pertain to the role of dichotomies in restricting and simplifying the explanation of how migration is changing the countryside: the core–periphery dualism already mentioned, and the dichotomy separating analysis into micro and macro levels. A third weakness stems from the tendency of modernization and structuralist theories to understate the noneconomic dimension of the migration process. Each of these limitations is discussed in turn, together with suggestions for moving beyond them.

The enduring influence of the first dichotomy – between modern core and traditional periphery – means that migration and return flows tend to be viewed as forces that are external to peripheries. Modernization research discusses how return flows make traditional societies more modern,[41] whereas structuralist studies consider how migration undermines the socioeconomic fabric of traditional communities while providing the resources for maintaining archaic production methods, buttressing traditional power structures, and reinforcing ritualized methods of status attainment.[42] Similarly, the impact of returnees on the countryside is classified as either innovative and modernizing (e.g., bringing back ideas that challenge the traditional order) or conservative (e.g., buying land in order to live a traditional life). These interpretations, which are very much a product of the strong development policy focus of the migration studies field, plot the movement of different dimensions of origin areas along a continuum of traditional and underdeveloped at one end and modern and developed at the other, thereby limiting explanations of change.

The reification of modern core and traditional periphery also leads to the idealization of resources and values within origin and destination. So, in seeing mutual aid as a characteristic of traditional societies, both conflict in rural communities and cooperation among urban residents are ignored.[43] As another example, the idea that "traditional" migrant women from origin areas are emancipated through exposure to the modern host society disregards the role of modernization in perpetrating oppressive dimensions of gender relations and also glosses over differences among both origin societies and migrant women.[44] As shown in Chapter 4, changes precipitated by migration often defy classification as either modern or traditional and instead represent the adaptation of existing social practices to new contingencies, many of which are brought about through migration.

The second dichotomy is concerned with the level of analysis. Modernization studies examine migration decision-making at the individual and household levels, whereas structuralist research explores the relationships between migration patterns and macro-level shifts in political economy. By neglecting the interactions between the micro and macro levels, modernization and structuralist analyses offer only a partial perspective.

Regardless of whether the theoretical focus is on individual responses to economic incentives or on macro-level changes in the political economy, the resulting research tends to overlook the noneconomic characteristics of origin and destination, the nonlabor qualities of migrants, and the contingent nature of the migration process. In seeing migration and return as phenomena determined predominantly by economic and environmental stimuli, migration and return are assumed to be processes that are external to the agency and subjectivity of social actors. In reality, migration and return are strategies used by individuals for pursuing goals that are formed through continuous socialization, and migration itself becomes one of the factors in the socialization process. Furthermore, individuals form and pursue goals by using and reproducing the cultural values, social arrangements, and distributional mechanisms that constitute their environment, so they both create and respond to their environment.

Some scholars have attempted to overcome the limitations of the micro and macro dichotomy by conducting community-based studies that integrate different levels of analysis. These studies consider the social, political, and economic characteristics of origin areas and potential destinations – sometimes conceptualized for simplicity as "push" and "pull" factors – and the responses of different decision-makers to the characteristics of different places. *Push* factors usually include increases in the costs of farm inputs, inefficient credit markets, underdeveloped infrastructure, unfavorable environmental conditions, high population-to-land ratios, underemployment arising from technical innovation,[45] inequitable patterns of land distribution resulting from local class relations or inheritance customs, restrictive traditional values, and oppressive family relationships.[46] *Pull* factors can include demands for labor with certain attributes, higher urban wages, the lure of an exciting new environment, opportunities for increased freedom, and better facilities and entertainment. A further "pull" factor is the presence of fellow villagers and relatives in the destination area who assist the new arrival with finding accommodation and employment.[47] The operation of this factor is known as *chain migration,* whereby previous migrants draw fellow villagers to a particular destination area and a particular occupational sector.

A push–pull perspective can also be used to explain return migration. As examples, "push" factors would include job insecurity, poor living conditions, social discrimination, and legal restrictions on urban residence. "Pull" factors refer to expanded employment or investment opportunities in the origin areas,[48] access to land or opportunities for acquiring property, high labor demands sustained by low-technology cultivation methods, and the presence of family and kin. Yet, as Rhoda points out, it is not always easy to distinguish push from pull in the countryside because, in the absence of economic development and local job creation, improvements in infrastructure such as roads and schools may propel further out-migration.[49]

Some studies fall broadly within the neoclassical cluster in that they consider the interactions between push–pull factors, individual or household characteristics, and rational decision-making. Individual characteristics include age, gender,[50] marital status, stage of the life cycle,[51] level of education, and skills; household characteristics include demographic composition, stage of the development cycle, size of the family landholding, and socioeconomic standing. One such study among seasonal migrants in China finds that the specific demands of destination labor markets pull individuals with particular attributes, whereas household characteristics shape demands for agricultural labor and thereby determine who is pulled back home, when, and for how long.[52] The study further reveals that inhabitants of townships with more local earning opportunities are not as responsive to the pull of outside labor markets. Another category of neoclassical research focuses less on push–pull factors and more on how the attributes of individuals and their personality traits affect their sociopsychological perceptions of "place utility" and the intervening obstacles to migration.[53] Still other studies belong within a broadly structuralist cluster in that they explain how labor circulation is shaped by capitalist exploitation, traditional relations of production (including family and class-based exploitation), and resulting changes in social relations of production and demands for cash and labor in both origin and destination.[54]

The best of this research stresses that origin areas are integrated with urban networks through transport systems, proximity to towns, local marketing structures, and the mutual aid and information networks established through previous migration and that this integration produces environmental stimuli that are more complex than a bifurcated push and pull.[55] Recognition of rural–urban integration, together with ongoing debates about whether the micro or the macro is the most appropriate level of investigation, have led some researchers to designate "articulatory migration networks" as the unit of analysis. For these scholars, networks refer to the various levels and spheres of social, economic, and cultural relationships – spanning both origin and destination – that engage in different facets of an ever-changing "bipolar" world.[56] For other scholars, migration networks are the medium through which individual or household decision-makers with particular characteristics respond to shifts in combinations of push and pull caused by macro-level socioeconomic transition.[57] Some scholars also point out that effects of shifts in push and pull on household and individual decision-making are moderated by chain migration and the role of social networks in providing resources such as information, employment, and food.[58]

In trying to overcome the core–periphery and micro–macro dichotomies, this book retains the discussed insights on multilevel analysis, the ways in which social networks both shape and are shaped by the migration process, and the feedback mechanism between migration strategies and socioeconomic change in both origin and destination. However, unlike much of the existing literature, this book redresses the tendency of analytical frameworks to subordinate the agency and subjectivity of social actors to environmental factors.[59] In particular, the goals and strategies of those who have remained in or have returned to the countryside – and the ways in which they reproduce and change their social environment – require further scholarly attention.

Focusing on the interactions among values, goals, and resources is a way of making the agency and subjectivity of social actors (as well as changing combinations of environmental factors) central to the explanation of how migration is changing rural China. This is because the agency of social actors is only meaningful if interpreted within a wider social, cultural, political, and economic context. Understanding the broader environment in which social actors form goals and struggle to obtain and deploy resources involves recognizing that individuals are positioned within households and that households are embedded within a wider network of extended family, kin, community, and patron–client ties.[60] These multiple levels of socioeconomic organization affect the cultural values and power relations that underpin struggles over the distribution of resources within households (e.g., along age and gender lines) as well as the range of resources that households are able to harness from the wider society. In focusing solely on economic rationality, modernization theories overlook the fact that individuals and households seldom make decisions in isolation from wider social groups. In contrast, the perspective adopted in this book is that social groups define rationality by specifying the characteristics of a respectable person or family and thereby create shared values; hence, what is "economically rational" can be "culturally specific."[61]

Although migration is usually motivated primarily by economic goals, the outcomes permeate cultural, political, and ideological spheres of rural life, which in turn shape the content of values and lead to the next generation of goals. Values and goals are internalized and develop over time through interactions between social actors and a spatially extended reference group. Therefore, migration strategies are not simply opportunistic and immediate responses to push and pull stimuli; they are also the products of values and life goals inculcated through longer-term socialization and life experiences.[62] This is well illustrated by societies in which particular combinations of environmental factors that generate economic imperatives have intertwined with existing cultural practices to generate a "culture of migration." This means that migration becomes an endorsed and expected means of attaining economic goals and a rite of passage for young people.[63] The culture of migration means that children grow up expecting to spend part of their lives in the cities, and young villagers who do not migrate are derided by their peers for being unadventurous and without ability.[64]

Values operate on two levels. Individuals consciously use certain values at the discursive level as reasons for their actions. At this level, values themselves can be seen as resources that social actors use to give meaning to their actions, legitimate their choices, and cover up inner conflicts generated by the contradictions of the migration process. On the other hand, there exist hidden values and rules that are inherent in the routine everyday practices of social life. People tend not to question this second level of values because they seem natural and part of common sense. However, a researcher can observe everyday life and listen to people talk about matters of importance to them in an effort to identify the culturally embedded values and norms that may contribute to migration decisions.[65] Of course, actions are not determined by a single set of values. When giving content to their goals and legitimating their actions, individuals may choose from a range of potentially competing values.[66] Moreover, migration and return often widen the range of values from which individuals are able to choose,[67] giving "perspective" and thereby enhancing the scope for agency.

Some authors explain values and goals by using the concept of *narrative* – that is, the ways in which people speak about their identities, histories, current situation, and future intentions. These scholars demonstrate that people act in accordance with narratives that fit in with how they understand themselves and that migrants may suspend one narrative while another narrative guides action. So, for example, migrants might explain that they send money home because they are dutiful children or good spouses. At the same time, however, migrants talk in terms of being modern young people and so temporarily suspend "dutiful children" or "good husband or wife" narratives when spending a month's wages on consumer goods for themselves.[68] Some of the competing narratives arise from the fact that – although the aim of migration is to strengthen the household economically and socially – migration entails the prolonged physical separation of family members. As a result, while remaining mindful of the need to fulfill from a distance the obligations associated with their rural identities (e.g., as wives, parents, children, and household members), migrants may develop new goals through the experience of living alone in cities. Manipulating and suspending narratives that embody contradictory values and goals is a way for migrants and other individuals to smooth over their inner conflicts.[69]

Migrants, returnees, nonmigrants, and households deploy resources in order to achieve physical goals, such as warmth and nourishment, as well as goals informed by shared values or collective rationality, such as maintaining self-respect and participating in social activities.[70] This latter type of goal is illustrated by Adam Smith's example of the eighteenth-century English gentleman who wears leather shoes in order to conform to social standards of respectability and to achieve the goal of avoiding shame.[71] Sen points out that the resources required for attaining specific life goals increase with the prosperity of the society. Hence, poverty is viewed not as a result of the deprivation of resources per se but as the incapacity to attain goals.[72] This perspective provides a focus for understanding the strategies and outcomes of resource deployment in sending areas: as societies undergo change, the resource requirements needed to achieve particular goals also change. The social context of migration goals and resource requirements is further suggested by case studies finding (1) that individual and household perceptions of relative deprivation rather than household consumption motivate migration[73] and (2) that the elite migrate to counter tendencies toward social leveling precipitated by the migration of other social groups.[74] As subsequent chapters of this book will demonstrate, return flows of cash and commodities alter the resources required by villagers for maintaining self-respect and for participating in a changing society; this can be seen, for instance, in the rising standards of socially respectable housing or wedding feasts.

The capacity of migrants to obtain further resources depends not only on their control over present resources, such as information and skills, but also on the unobservable components of chance, opportunity, and aptitude. Why some people succeed in obtaining many resources while others barely survive, or why migration alleviates the poverty of some households but forces others into debt by raising standards of social respectability, are just two instances of the many contradictions generated by migration. Such contradictions are not explainable within a neat theoretical framework, in part because it is not possible to separate migration from other social processes[75] or to account for the ways in which contingent factors (many of them unobservable) interact. So instead of trying to present an unsutured reality, subsequent chapters of this book highlight inconsistencies and contradictions – viewing them as integral to an understanding of the ways in which migration changes origin areas.[76]

1.3 PETTY COMMODITY PRODUCERS AND LIVELIHOOD DIVERSIFICATION

In focusing on how return flows of resources and new ideas (either modernizing or, in the view of structuralists, corrosive or conservative) change the countryside, there is the tendency to overlook the resource endowments and the capacity for innovation within the origin areas themselves.[77] These resource endowments and innovations are particularly evident if rural families are viewed as petty commodity producers who pursue migration and return as extensions of their existing strategies for rural livelihood diversification. Following Hill Gates, the term "petty commodity producer" refers to households with small landholdings that produce farm and handicraft goods for their own use and for sale in the marketplace. As a further defining characteristic, the continued reproduction of these households depends on their deployment of labor both inside and outside the marketplace, and this includes "noncapitalist exchanges with kin, friends, and fellow villagers" as well as "the buying and selling of labor power."[78] Petty commodity producers pursue rural livelihood diversification strategies by deploying their labor and other resources in farming and a range of other activities including selling agricultural and handicraft commodities, migrating to faraway places as wage laborers and traders, or outputting for capitalist factories. In combining their economic activities rural households strive to increase their income and minimize their risks.

Petty commodity households are adaptable and resilient in the face of socioeconomic transition because of two mechanisms: flexible labor deployment and familial cultural values. As an example of the former, rural households in prewar Italy and Japan allocated part of their labor to the industrial wage sector. But when unemployed workers returned home during the Great Depression, families adapted through the entrepreneurial "self-exploitation" of their labor, leading to a proliferation of owner–operators involved in sewing, food processing, shoemaking, domestic services, and parts production. In the postwar period these farming family businesses have continued to survive, transform, and prosper within networks of family and local relationships. Although agriculture is of decreasing importance for these Italian and Japanese families, it nonetheless remains significant.[79] Similar examples of flexible labor deployment by petty commodity producers in different historical periods can be found in the Chinese societies of Hong Kong and Taiwan as well as in mainland China, and such family enterprises are now praised by some as the engines of East Asia's economic growth.

As an example of familial cultural values, research in environments as diverse as mainland China, Hong Kong, Taiwan, Thailand, and sub-Saharan Africa reveals that children are raised with the deeply entrenched belief that they owe their parents an irredeemable debt for the gift of life. This means that parents have a lasting and legitimate claim on their children's earnings.[80] In some cultures (e.g., the Philippines), this sense of debt may be cultivated more strongly in females than males with the result that households are more likely to entrust their daughters with the task of migrating to earn wages.[81]

When socioeconomic transition affects patterns of household labor deployment, new opportunities for earning wages may afford subordinate individuals increased leverage, causing patriarchs to intensify ideological measures aimed at preserving the family's authority over its primary resource – labor. This is illustrated in rural Italy, where "Catholic" values of obedience and the unity and cohesion of the family were effective in maintaining family control over women's labor at a time when they were earning independent wages.[82] Similarly, Hill Gates argues that during the Song dynasty, when large numbers of rural Chinese women were earning high wages from silk production, patriarchs sought to strengthen their control over this labor through an intensification of cultural practices that subordinated women, such as foot binding, puritanical morality, and taboos on widow remarriage.[83] However, ideological forces are not always completely successful in asserting family control over labor. This is because the increased leverage of some household members can precipitate the reconstitution of family ties; for example, sojourner sons may accumulate the economic resources for pursuing earlier marriage and separation from parents.[84]

Many debates have centered on the position of rural petty commodity households in a changing world: are they a transitional category or a permanent but changing part of a world in transition? For modernization scholars and many national governments, including the Chinese, rural producers will be transformed into wage laborers and inevitably disappear.[85] Similarly, for some structuralists, circulation is a transitional process, albeit an unstable one, with uncertain outcomes arising from "resistance and reluctant behavioral adaptation" by traditional people to the "pressures of proletarianization."[86] For other structuralists, economically diversified or "rural proletarian" households are a fixed feature of the economy, the products of permanent structural inequalities and endemic rural underdevelopment.[87] These scholars point out that circulation is "deeply rooted in a variety of cultures and found at all stages of socioeconomic change."[88]

More recently, some development scholars have argued that poverty alleviation through rural livelihood diversification is not a transitional economic arrangement preceding the realization of modernization teleology but instead is a satisfactory end in itself. This perspective shifts the policy debate away from whether it is better to try to keep rural dwellers "on the farm" or to encourage their permanent proletarianization in the cities; rather, the policy implications are that government should (1) adopt policies that increase the freedom and range of options for rural households to diversify their livelihoods and (2) enact measures to protect the vulnerable from abuse and destitution.[89] This is not to deny (as comparative studies of China and Mexico reveal) that migration networks are in transition, evolving and maturing, with "daughter migrant communities" and native place associations eventually becoming established in the destination areas.[90] Nonetheless, diversified households pursuing flexible migration strategies are a permanent part of a changing countryside. The concept of rural livelihood diversification is compatible with the insights derived from understanding rural petty commodity households as resilient, adaptable, innovative, and endowed with resources – rather than as transitional, backward, traditional, and devoid of resources.

1.4 TEMPORARY AND PERMANENT RETURN

Shifting combinations of push–pull factors, the evolution of personal goals over time, and changes in individual circumstances mean that return migration embodies a wide range of actions. Some migrants return "temporarily" to the native place, intending to re-migrate after a specified period. Other migrants return home "permanently" and take steps to resettle in the home community. However, those returning for temporary visits may end up remaining in the village for an indefinite period, and those who intend to resettle in the village may re-migrate. Moreover, the convenience of modern transport allows people to act quickly on their migration decisions.[91]

Even migrants who are permanently absent from their villages invoke the "narrative of return" to escape social and moral censure for forgetting home and to avoid confronting their ambivalence toward the native place and the social relationships there.[92] These migrants initially delay permanent resettlement because they lack the funds for achieving their goals in the village. They maintain a homeward orientation, committing increasing portions of their wages to the needs of both family in the village and the requirements of an urban lifestyle, so less money remains for the attainment of their goals. Over time, the migrants form even higher life goals that require more resources or become accustomed to urban life, so they postpone resettlement indefinitely while maintaining links with the native place. The narrative of return means that – throughout their urban-based lives – they remit money, visit home, build a house in the village, and even participate in migrant funeral associations that send the bodies of the dead back to the native place. Thus, despite their absence, migrants exert a continuing influence on their home communities.

Narratives of return migration become institutionalized to the extent that – even when socioeconomic transition, structural factors, or personal circumstances mean that they neither intend to return home nor need to participate in the institution of return – migrants still retain links with their native place. For example, in Latin America, high levels of industrialization in some cities have created a demand for permanent and skilled employees as opposed to the itinerant and unskilled workforce that characterizes labor-intensive production. This increasing demand for a stable workforce has caused employers in some places and sectors to improve wages and living conditions, enabling the migrants to bring their spouses and dependants with them to the cities.[93] Studies the world over suggest that, the more stable the presence of migrants in the cities, the less the remittances.[94] This is because remittances are strongly correlated with the intention to return. Yet despite settling in the cities and despite declining remittances, new settlers maintain an active interest in their native homes and continue to invest in the social networks associated with home. For instance, urban residents in Latin America sponsor construction projects and Saints' festivals in their villages, and overseas Chinese invest heavily in both welfare and entrepreneurial projects in their ancestral homes on the mainland.[95]

Even after the permanent settlement of the third and fourth generation, what appears to be permanent settlement in the host society may not be so permanent. For example, the fallout from structural adjustment in sub-Saharan Africa means that cities are failing to provide sufficient resources to sustain the livelihoods of many urban residents. The continued actions of families and individuals in sustaining the institution of return across generations (through spatially extended reciprocal ties) means that these urbanites are still able to return to their ancestral homes in the countryside and lay claim to resources such as land, food, and social support.[96] A further example, this time from China, is that following the disbanding of the communes, the second- and third-generation descendants of farmers who migrated to live in other villages have been returning to their ancestral homes. The initial migrants were uprooted from their ancestral homes during a variety of periods: fleeing war and famine before 1949, escaping famine in the 1960s, or migrating because of national dam construction projects in the 1960s and 1970s. Many of these migrants and/or their descendants have since returned to their ancestral homes to receive land allocations, partake in a more thriving economy, and return to where they "belong." They are entitled to return because "the native home is the native home and the leaves fall to the root of the tree."[97]

1.5 CONCLUSION

Clearly, in examining the role of migration and return in changing the countryside, it is necessary to consider the ways in which values and resources generated from outside the village interact with social processes, values, and resources internal to rural society. The resulting impact of migration and return on perspectives, resources, and allocative structures has, in turn, implications for the ways in which actors participate in the society and economy. In particular, migration and return strategies of individuals and households precipitate a fundamental reallocation of resources within households, among households, and between rural society and the local state; this is explored in later chapters. In examining the impact of migration on origin areas, it is also important to remember that many changes in rural areas are not precipitated by migration, either directly or indirectly, and that migration interacts with the outcomes of other forces of change – for example, economic liberalization.[98] Viewing rural people as petty commodity producers recognizes their agency in both shaping and being shaped by socioeconomic transition; it also challenges modernization and structuralist classifications of them as backward and traditional. Change through migration and return is not the result of encounters between the modern and the traditional. Rather, through migration and return, individuals and families use, reproduce, and reconstitute values and resources in their efforts to attain goals. This creates a continual feedback mechanism whereby migration and return become institutions internal to the village – institutions in which both migrants and nonmigrants participate, and institutions that interact with the outcomes of other processes of change.

2

China, Jiangxi, and the Fieldwork Counties

THIS chapter introduces the reader to socioeconomic change at three levels: China, Jiangxi province, and the fieldwork counties of Wanzai, Xinfeng, and Yudu. Wanzai is situated in Yichun prefecture in northwest Jiangxi, and Xinfeng and Yudu counties are located in Ganzhou prefecture in the south. The chapter explores the changing position of petty commodity producers in Jiangxi within the context of socioeconomic transition in China as a whole. The analysis is concerned with the historical–structural environment in which rural people struggle to obtain resources for attaining their goals; the ways in which these strategies and struggles shape socioeconomic transition at the national, provincial, and county levels; and the responses of the state to those strategies.

The chapter begins by discussing the pre-liberation (pre-1949) history of migration and petty commodity production in the fieldwork counties and in China more broadly. Next I examine the state's repression of petty commodity production under collectivization and the subsequent efforts of the reformist state to channel the economic dynamism and cheap labor of petty commodity producers toward national modernization. The third section discusses economic conditions in Wanzai, Xinfeng, and Yudu; the migration strategies pursued by petty commodity producers in these counties; and the attempts of the local state to manage migration and claim some of the resources that it generates. The fourth section considers the structural features of the political economy that cause the majority of rural migrants in China to retain links with their households. In the fifth section I argue that state discourses – on the negative consequences of a low-"quality" rural population for modernization – disguise the structural features of the political economy that hinder rural people's access to resources. Finally, I examine current state policies on migration, rural livelihood diversification, and modernization. The chapter demonstrates that through migration and return, petty commodity producers in Jiangxi exploit the opportunities created by the state's modernization agenda while at the same time struggling against structural constraints. In the process the farmers precipitate shifts in national strategies for economic development that assist them in their pursuit of resources and goals.

2.1 HISTORICAL BACKGROUND

Rural producers in Ming and Qing China (1368–1911) operated in a resource environment characterized by high levels of rural and urban integration and interregional mobility. Skinner conceptualizes the relationship between cores and peripheries in China in terms more complex than modernization theory's "urban core" and "rural periphery." In his explanation, China is divided into nine macro-regions, each with its own core and periphery and each comprising interdependent local systems with their own integrated hierarchy of cores and peripheries. According to Skinner, within the countryside of both imperial and contemporary China, the local system consists of villages that surround market towns and towns that surround higher order urban settlements: higher-level places serve a network of lower-level places by providing goods and conveniences that cannot be supplied locally. The market towns typically service between fifteen and twenty villages that are organized in two hexagonal rings around the market town, and these local-level systems are the basic unit of the economic hierarchy. This configuration results from people's consideration of transport costs and economic efficiency when establishing new settlements. In reality, the terrain, drainage systems, natural transport networks (such as rivers), and population density distort the hexagonal arrangement.[1]

Each regional and local system forms a geographically based sphere of human interaction characterized by "flows of goods and services, of money and credit, of messages and symbols, and of persons in their multifarious roles and statuses."[2] According to Skinner, modernization involves the simultaneous diffusion of innovations: vertically, down the "central place hierarchy"; and horizontally, out from the central places to their rural environs. However, the peripheries always lag behind because economic, social, and cultural innovations are continually replaced before saturation occurs.[3]

Although Jiangxi province in pre-liberation times boasted highly integrated networks of market towns, the socioeconomic environment of petty commodity producers was adversely affected from the end of the Ming dynasty (1368–1644) onward by the anticommercial sentiments of an increasingly influential neo-Confucian elite who came to dominate the province. These scholar-officials purposefully emphasized self-sufficiency in agriculture, thereby bringing the Tang and Song periods of thriving industry and commerce to an end.[4] Despite a sociopolitical environment that was contemptuous of commerce, the Jiangxi countryside was nonetheless characterized by substantial in-migration and an economic culture in which families managed resources spanning both town and country. This can be seen in the examples of Wanzai and Yudu, where petty commodity producers continued to secure their livelihoods through migration and handicrafts.

The word Wanzai means "abundance." A mild climate and fertile soil have historically brought high grain yields to the natives, and as a consequence they seldom needed to migrate. In fact, from 1524 onward the county was the site of repeated waves of in-migration. Most of the immigrants were members of a sub-ethnic group known as the Hakka, who came mainly from Fujian and Guangdong provinces.[5] Leong explains the features of Hakka migration by applying the Skinnerian concept of macro-regions. Leong shows, first, that Hakkas typically migrated to the peripheries of macro-regions, often to high-lands close to major commercial cores (e.g., mountain valleys situated within reasonable traveling distance of market centers); second, they were renowned for both their industriousness in inhospitable terrain and their marketing ac-tivities. Leong adapts Skinner's insight that each macro-region has its own economic cycle that results from climate, policies, and politics. He shows that, historically, upturns in the economic cycle of a macro-region corresponded with the timing of mass in-migration whereas downturns corresponded with periods of intensified conflict between Hakkas and natives over resources.[6] In the case of Wanzai, the largest waves of immigration occurred during the late seven-teenth and eighteenth centuries, when upheaval and economic decline pushed the Hakkas out from the Lingnan and southeast coast macro-regions (Guang-dong and Fujian provinces).[7] Furthermore, Wanzai suffered much devastation from the Hakka revolts that occurred during periods of decline in the Gan Yanzi macro-region (Jiangxi province) – for example, in the late 1600s, early 1700s, and mid-1800s.[8]

Although the Hakka–native interactions have historically been characterized by tension, the immigrants contributed substantially to the development of three handicraft industries for which Wanzai was and still is renowned: grass cloth made from ramie, fuse paper, and fireworks. Hakka immigrants stimulated grass linen manufacturing in Wanzai by cultivating ramie on the mountain ter-rain shunned by natives. Their economic impact is revealed by the fact that, during the Ming, 70% of households in the county combined grass linen pro-duction with other activities; these high levels of output continued throughout the Qing.[9] In the early eighteenth century, Hakka immigrants were also closely linked with the introduction of another handicraft to the county: paper making.[10] Rural producers in Wanzai began manufacturing fireworks[11] in the mid-1800s, and the development of this new industry stimulated demand for fuse paper and cylinder card. Petty commodity families in Wanzai rapidly adopted fire-work manufacturing not least because "only splitting the paper requires strong workers. All the other manufacturing steps can be carried out by the old, the weak, the deaf and dumb, by anyone at all."[12] In 1884, the desires of petty commodity producers for prosperity and safe production were expressed cul-turally through the establishment of temples devoted to Li Tian, the legendary inventor of fireworks. By the end of the Qing dynasty, Wanzai boasted thousands of large family workshops producing fireworks and fuse paper. Their products were sold within China and overseas by merchants, some of them Hakkas, who traveled from Guangdong, Fujian, and other provinces.

The Qing dynasty was similarly a period when the predominantly Hakka population of Yudu county enjoyed thriving trade, selling their handicraft skills throughout China and Southeast Asia. Yudu was and still is famous for the "three tools" (the carpenter's chisel, the metal worker's lathe, and the cotton shredder's pounding hammer) and the "three craftsmen" – the bamboo weaver, the builder, and the carpenter, the latter renowned for boat making, house building, and carving. As the economic benefits from sending labor to other cities and countries became evident, household heads and community leaders in Yudu began to cultivate individuals through education and apprenticeships, sponsoring their migration both morally and practically through kinship networks and native place organizations in destination areas.[13] Additionally, following the introduction of the tobacco plant by immigrants from Fujian province in 1627, rural producers within Yudu grew tobacco crops and cut the leaves into pipe tobacco.[14]

Following Cohen's analysis of Chinese family organization, in Jiangxi as elsewhere in China, the resources of conjugal units were subordinate to those of the family (*jia*), with the property being shared out equally among the brothers on "division" (*fenjia*) – a process whereby the brothers, their wives, and their offspring formed smaller family units.[15] The accomplishments of the family were important not only for securing the livelihoods of the current generation but also for honoring duties to ancestors and creating a legacy for descendants. The values of family loyalty and filial piety, and the recognition of an association between one's own progress and that of the extended family and native place, meant that the resources generated through farming, handicrafts, trading, and migration generally remained within the family group.[16]

A picture of innovative petty commodity producers actively pursuing resources and evading bureaucratic obstacles contrasts with the communist state's representation of the "peasantry" as a conservative and shackled population, culturally and economically opposite to urban dwellers. Cohen argues that, in the early decades of the twentieth century, Chinese intellectuals began to apply Marxist categories to the Chinese countryside. They constructed "an image of the old society" that had to be transformed, an image that was elevated to "cultural orthodoxy" after the founding of the People's Republic.[17] During guerrilla resistance against first the Japanese and later the Nationalists, many areas of Jiangxi (including Wanzai, Xinfeng, and Yudu) became the sites of revolutionary bases. These revolutionary bases were home to some of the Party's earliest experiments in social transformation, in which images of the old society were constructed through "speak bitterness" meetings. In these meetings, villagers identified the exploiting classes of feudal society; people were then grouped into good and bad classes, with land being redistributed accordingly. In some places there were rules that each village had to designate at least one "landlord." Although rich and poor peasants existed, social contacts, family clans, personal grievances, and place-specific barometers of rich and poor shaped the class designations. Cohen demonstrates that the cultural construction of China's rural population as simple peasants, rather than as rational and innovative farmers, represents a "reversal of the sequence of events involved in Western perceptions of transition in rural Europe, where modernization was thought to turn peasants into farmers."[18] Indeed, in all of its theories of modernization, the Chinese Communist Party has always assumed responsibility for leading the peasantry through the stages of feudalism, capitalism, and socialism to communism.

2.2 RESTRUCTURING THE COUNTRYSIDE IN COMMUNIST CHINA

Since the early 1950s, the Chinese state has intervened in the political economy in ways that have restricted mobility, reinforced the peripheral status of the rural population, and (more recently) made return flows of migrants and resources to the countryside an integral feature of the labor migration process. Surplus rural labor in China is the product of policies that have divided the countryside and city into separate realms. During the mid-1950s, agricultural production assumed a collective character, and by 1958 the countryside had been arranged into the three-tiered system of production teams, brigades, and communes.[19] At the national level, the state issued directives on production that filtered down to provinces, prefectures, counties, communes, and finally to the production teams at the grass roots.

The household registration system, implemented in rural areas in 1955[20] and enshrined in national regulations in 1958,[21] operated in tandem with broader restructuring in the countryside to keep farmers tied to the land. Under this registration system, each household was allocated an occupational category – either agricultural or nonagricultural – and a place of residence (*hukou*). The *hukou* designation of "peasant" or "urban resident" was inherited through the mother, but in 1998 the policy was changed to allow inheritance from either parent.[22] Through collectivization, the state appropriated control over the family's management of labor, production, and consumption, thereby attempting to reorient rural producers' energies from the needs of their families toward the needs of the collective. The *hukou* was tied to a rationing system, and necessities were distributed through ration coupons.[23] Private markets were virtually eliminated, the collectives replaced the old market towns as the centers of rural activity, and state agencies dominated in the procurement and distribution of

agricultural produce. The absence of alternative markets meant that, if separated from their place of residence, individuals would have no resources to
support their livelihoods.[24]

The aim of these policies was to increase the agricultural surplus that could
be siphoned from the countryside and directed toward the urban centers to
feed the cities, fuel industrialization, and generate export income. In order to
increase the agricultural surplus transferred to the cities and to ensure the con-
tentment of politically articulate urban residents, the grain procurement system
under Mao was characterized by low purchase prices and mandatory delivery
quotas.[25] Rural households were denied the opportunity to manage their resources in the most profitable ways. For their role in industrialization, the city
population received welfare benefits, subsidized accommodation, and access
to social services. A divide was hewn between urban and rural dwellers, and
peasants became second-class citizens tied to the land.

Even though most of China's rural population was tied to agriculture, not
everyone was excluded from industrial work. During the 1950s, prohibitions
on entering the city were interspersed with short periods when the economic
objectives of the state and changes in political climate allowed farmers to enter
the cities. At the end of the 1950s there was a clampdown on migration, with
mass repatriations to the countryside. Then, from 1962 onward, farmers legally
entered cities at the behest of urban authorities to take up temporary work
contracts.[26] The labor of these rural migrants was cheaper and more expend-
able than that of permanent urban workers, and during the Cultural Revolution
it was necessary to import rural labor to compensate for the loss of some 17 million urban youths who were "rusticated." Thus, between 1966 and 1976, over 14
million farmers entered cities with the authorization of urban labor bureaus.[27]
Skilled tradesmen from Yudu were among these migrants.[28] Despite inviting
some farmers to work in factories, urban authorities prevented free rural-to-
urban mobility and regularly deported unwanted persons.

Other farmers participated in industrial work within the countryside. The
Maoist state encouraged rural industrialization as a strategy for promoting rural independence from cities, thereby protecting cities from rural claims on
their resources. Ideally, each rural locality was to become self-sufficient in
daily necessities, fertilizer, machine parts, farm equipment, fuel, and cement
for irrigation and construction projects. This rural industrialization was very
much part of a "cellular" development strategy that kept the countryside isolated from the cities.[29]

Other rural enterprises were created because the state organized petty commodity handicraft producers into cooperatives. In some of the revolutionary
bases where communist power was secure, this occurred during the 1920s. For
instance, tobacco cutters in Yudu were grouped into four large cooperatives.[30]

In other places, the grouping of handicraft producers into cooperatives started after liberation. From 1958 onward, cooperatives throughout China were reorganized into state-owned factories. So, for example, in Xinfeng county between 1952 and 1956, 74.3% of petty commodity producers were grouped into cooperatives; between 1958 and 1972 these cooperatives were gradually converted into the Xinfeng Metal Goods Factory, the Xinfeng Pottery Factory, the Xinfeng Sweets Factory, the Xinfeng County Building Construction Team, and so on.[31] Similarly, the Yudu tobacco cooperatives became the Yudu State Tobacco Factory. As the handicraft sector supplied the goods used in daily life (e.g., basins, buckets, sandals, and cigarettes), the state's actions in separating handicrafts from private commerce adversely affected the rural economy and the well-being of farmers.

Although one of the stated aims of Maoist policies was to mitigate inequalities between town and country, the actual net effect was to widen the gap between rural and urban areas. The general impoverishment of the rural economy hindered the flow of technology from the cities to the countryside, and the distribution of resources through administrative channels led to shortages of raw materials and spare parts. The development of rural enterprises was further hindered by a lack of experienced managers and an environment that favored ideological correctness over economic efficiency. Moreover, Mao believed that only labor deployed in the goods-producing sector could create value, so the service and transport sectors in the countryside were badly neglected, further isolating rural areas.[32] The various structural restrictions on farmers' participation in industrialization and urbanization meant that surplus labor accumulated in the countryside and village economies became like a collection of spinning tops, each rotating around its own axis.[33]

Subsequent events demonstrated the persistence and adaptability of petty commodity producers in the face of an adverse political environment. During the late 1970s, farmers in some parts of rural China – most famously those in Fengyang prefecture, Anhui province – began conducting clandestine experiments with individual and group contracts for agricultural production. When upper levels of the state hierarchy discovered the experiments and the resulting increases in yields, contract farming was cautiously sanctioned. By 1984, the household responsibility system was operational throughout nearly all the countryside, with collective land parceled out to households. Under this system, rural households are assigned land-use rights while ownership remains with the collectives. Farmers sign contracts to deliver grain quotas to their collectives, and they also pay a state grain tax. Any surplus can be consumed or sold on free markets.

Leaders in Jiangxi initially resisted the return to commodity production because, in their eyes, it represented the restoration of capitalism and conflicted with Maoist egalitarianism. During the early 1980s, many local governments suppressed commercial activity through the use of checkpoints on major transport routes to control the flow of goods. These efforts involved mobilizing the public security bureaus, traffic control organs, officials from the bureaus of industry and commerce, and tax officers. Regulations were so strict that persistent rural producers in south Jiangxi had no choice but to smuggle their goods to Guangdong and Fujian by walking through winding mountain trails or sending agricultural produce by river under the cover of darkness.[34] Even today, the peripheral position of the fieldwork counties in the political economy is illustrated by the term "old revolutionary base area,"[35] which goes hand-in-hand with "hill country" (*qiuling didai*) to denote underdevelopment and adherence to Party traditions. Officials often speak of Mao-Deng-Jiang Thought as a unitary ideological framework, and Mao's portrait is displayed in most homes and offices. This revolutionary heritage, together with an earlier history of neo-Confucianism, are blamed for an environment in which petty commodity producers must perpetually struggle against official obstruction in their efforts to obtain and deploy resources.[36]

The reforms restored the household as the basic economic unit of the countryside. In rural China, "household" refers to a set of people who eat together and maintain a common budget. In reality, however, the boundaries between the different households in a family tend to be ambiguous, and after a family has divided into at least two households, the members retain "close economic cooperation and sociopolitical relations."[37] Despite this cooperation, different households in a family usually live in separate houses – or aspire to earn enough money to do so.

As communal welfare provisions under the collectives have disappeared, land is the ultimate security net for rural households. The division of land and the rise of free markets have unveiled a critical problem of rural underemployment. Moreover, China has inherited a "demographic time bomb": under Mao, the government permitted spontaneous population growth; as a result, during the mid-1970s, large numbers of couples reached the age of marriage and parenthood.[38] Nowadays, every time households divide through marriage, household plots become even smaller, making livelihood diversification (through local and migrant off-farm employment) increasingly necessary. Under the household responsibility system, labor can move out of agriculture only if the plot of land assigned to the household continues to be farmed. Unlike the farmers of Europe who were expropriated from the soil, most Chinese migrants have land that provides them with a stake in their villages.

Jiangxi, officially designated as an "interior" or "central" province, is a major exporter of labor: about 20% of the rural labor force is currently working in other provinces, and this figure does not include rural–urban migration within the province itself.[39] Most of the exodus from the rural interior is to provinces described officially as "coastal" or "eastern." This pattern of migration is stimulated by the export-led development strategy and investment patterns of the post-Mao era, the concomitant expansion in the construction and manufacturing sectors of cities and eastern provinces, and the resulting regional and sectoral demands for labor. According to figures for 1995, per-capita gross domestic product (GDP) for the east, center, and west were 6,777, 3,691, and 2,945 yuan, respectively. Jiangxi, with a figure of 2,984 yuan, ranked twenty-fifth out of the twenty-nine provinces. By way of comparison, according to figures for 1997, the per-capita gross domestic product of Wanzai, Xinfeng, and Yudu were 2,438,[40] 2,867,[41] and 1,888[42] yuan, respectively – all below the provincial average of two years before. As a final indication of regional disparities in development, the gross value of industrial output of the eastern regions in 1995 was three times as high as the central and western regions, and the dominance of the east over the center was evident even in light of the bias in population distribution toward the coast.[43] Moreover, Jiangxi continued to be one of the poorest performers.

2.3 MIGRATION FROM WANZAI, XINFENG, AND YUDU

In 1997, the reported populations of Wanzai, Xinfeng, and Yudu were 450,000, 620,000, and 795,000 (respectively), with farmers accounting for approximately 85% of the population in each place.[44] Per-capita allocations of arable land were 0.8 mu for Wanzai, 0.87 mu for Xinfeng, and 0.65 mu for Yudu. These allocations were close to the provincial average of 0.8 mu but below the national average of 1.2 mu,[45] where 1 mu = 0.1647 acres. Although the arable land is generally sufficient to guarantee basic subsistence, the small size of the land allocations limits the potential for risk avoidance through agricultural diversification. Moreover, owing to efforts to distribute the good and bad land equitably, a land allocation of 0.8 mu is often scattered among smaller plots.

Agriculture in all three counties is dominated by double rice cropping. The land is plowed in March and the early rice is planted in April. The first harvest is at the start of August and is immediately followed by the transplanting of the late rice. The second rice harvest occurs in early October. Following this, small areas of rape crop are sown and then harvested before the land is plowed again in March. In Ganzhou prefecture, sugar cane, tobacco, corn, peanuts, and tea are important supplementary crops. In Xinfeng and Yudu, there is a drive to cultivate citrus fruit (and, to a lesser extent, tea) on reclaimed hill slopes. However, citrus trees do not grow well in Wanzai because of cooler temperatures, so the hills are covered with pine and bamboo. The main agricultural products in the county besides grain are lily roots and pork. Each county is endowed

with coal, limestone, clay, minerals, wood, and bamboo. However, these resources are largely unexploited, and rural industries provide off-farm income
for less than one fifth of the rural population. Moreover, many rural enterprise
employees work only part-time, and the payment of wages is unreliable.

In the post-Mao era, migration to factories has become the main strategy for
rural livelihood diversification, although handicrafts also continue to be significant. The mechanized production of knives, axes, locks, and well pumps has
meant that, since the 1960s, Yudu metal workers and pump makers have not
been able to earn income from these trades. Similarly, the increasing popular-
ity of refined tobacco has destroyed the livelihoods of pipe-tobacco cutters.

In Wanzai, much of the market for grass linen has disappeared because of
competition from mass-produced fabrics; even so, several households in my
fieldwork villages still earn money from this activity, with the finished products exported to Japan. Firecracker production brings in a little extra spending
money to most households in Wanzai villages. People of all ages sit around
chatting with neighbors while assembling strings of red firecrackers in their
spare time. The firecrackers are used to celebrate Spring Festival as well as a
variety of life-cycle events such as births, marriages, moving house, or opening a business. However, recent environmental regulations within China that
ban the use of firecrackers in cities have set back sales of this product. Additionally, during the early to mid-1990s, successive heavy winters in Europe
temporarily reduced demand for Christmas and New Year fireworks. But from
1998 onward there has been an increase in the demand for fireworks resulting from millennium celebration events, a larger volume of exports to Europe,
the active marketing of Wanzai fireworks through trade fairs and Internet web-
sites, and government encouragement of private entrepreneurship.[46] I could
see evidence of these changes on returning to my fieldwork village of Qifeng
(Gaocheng township) in December 2000. An entrepreneur from Tanbu township had established a firework factory in the former village office because of
its good roadside location. According to the deputy secretary of the village, the
factory currently employs a hundred women aged in their 40s and 50s. They
assemble fireworks at home or in the factory on a casual basis and can earn up
to 2,000 yuan a year. Although migration to factories generates more income
for families than do handicrafts, the latter nonetheless provides funds for the
initial costs of migration and also enables the spouses left behind, children, the
elderly, and the infirm to bring extra money into the household.

Table 2.1 shows the average wages of workers and the net per-capita disposable incomes[47] for rural households in 1997, the year when most of the fieldwork
was conducted. The figures for the average rural earnings of an administrative
unit include both migrant remittances and income in kind. For the purposes of
this chapter, the data in the table are useful for indicating the roughly middling

Table 2.1. *Economic indicators of the fieldwork counties compared with the national and provincial averages and migrant destination areas, 1997*

	Annual net per-capita income of rural households (yuan)[a]	Annual net per-capita disposable income of urban households (yuan)[b]
Wanzai	2,226	3,500
Xinfeng	2,166	3,700
Yudu	1,851	3,400
Jiangxi[c]	2,107	4,071
Shanghai	5,277	8,439
Guangdong	3,467	8,562
China	2,090	5,160

[a] The figures for annual per-capita rural income presented in the table are from *Jiangxi tongji nianjian* (1999), pp. 322, 323, 376, 377, 442, 443.

[b] The figures for the three counties are estimates from the county heads obtained in 1997.

[c] *Zhongguo tongji nianjian* [China Statistical Yearbook] (1998), pp. 332, 346.

economic standing of the fieldwork counties in rural China. However, it is noteworthy that the GDP rankings for the counties are below the provincial average whereas the per-capita rural incomes of Wanzai and Xinfeng are above it. Moreover, Wanzai ranks higher if income is the barometer whereas Xinfeng ranks higher if GDP is the measure. There are several possible explanations for this. The first is that, in rural China, the reporting of economic figures is an inherently political process and is affected by tremendous pressures on local officials to reach targets, so methods for calculating rural incomes may vary according to the political imperatives specific to each county. Another possibility is that the counties may fail to sell a portion of the goods that they produce and may thus be left with stockpiles. Finally, the contribution of remittances to rural incomes might also explain why the GDP of the fieldwork counties are below the provincial average while the per-capita rural incomes rank higher. In Wanzai and Xinfeng, officials told me that less than 20% of per-capita rural incomes are from remittances, while in Yudu this figure is about 30%.[48] Local taxes are levied at 5% of the stipulated average per-capita income of a village for the previous year,[49] and remittances are included in the calculations of this average. Thus, earnings from urban labor markets help rural governments meet targets for increasing incomes and generating tax revenue.

In 1996–1997, Wanzai inhabitants expressed to me their sense of deprivation in the national political economy by scorning the etymology of the place name – "bountiful." Population increase, relative physical remoteness, and a general failure to develop a strong industrial base are factors explaining why, during the early 1990s, per-capita incomes in the county remained below the provincial average. However, as already mentioned, new demand for fireworks and large-scale labor export have shifted official figures for per-capita rural income to above the provincial and national averages. Yudu is a state-designated poverty county but has nonetheless enjoyed some improvements in recent years. In 1995, the Yudu Long March Bridge was built over the river that divides the county: locals say that previously the only transport was a boat. Additionally, main roads connecting the county seat with highways heading north to the provincial capital of Nanchang and southwest to Ganzhou have been covered with asphalt. Per-capita income in Xinfeng is above the provincial and national averages. The county has benefited from its proximity to the investment zones of Ganzhou city (the capital of the prefecture) and Guangzhou, and since the mid-1990s some investors from Guangzhou have been relocating their factory plants to the county. The 1995 completion of the Jing-Jiu Railway, which cuts through mountain terrain to link Guangzhou and Beijing, is also bringing prosperity to the county seat, now a station along the line.

Approximately one fifth of rural labor from Wanzai has migrated to other provinces, a proportion comparable to the rural average for Jiangxi, and roughly half of the migrants are women. Around 100,000 people from Xinfeng and more than 150,000 from Yudu are working in the cities, accounting for approximately one third of the rural labor force of each county.[50] Both as an absolute number and as a proportion of the total population, there are more migrants from Yudu working in the cities than from any other county in Jiangxi. Xinfeng also falls into the top quarter of labor-exporting counties in the province. In the early 1980s, women accounted for only around 20% of migrants from both counties, but now they make up one third of the outflow.[51]

The higher proportion of women in migration streams from Wanzai as compared with migration streams from predominantly Hakka counties in south Jiangxi (e.g., Yudu) can be explained by the influence of custom on the gendered division of labor. Historically, Hakka men sojourned whereas the women worked in the fields. During the Qing dynasty, when other Chinese women were confined indoors with bound feet, Hakka women moved about freely in the fields and the marketplace on their big feet. It is not clear whether the farming role of Hakka women freed the men to migrate or if, instead, the sojourning tradition of the men pushed the women into farming.[52] Nevertheless, in present-day Yudu, men are trained in off-farm skills; since it is acceptable for women to plow, there have not been practical restrictions on the men migrating. Although there are Hakka populations in Wanzai, they tend to be concentrated in the mountain areas bordering Hunan province. My fieldwork was conducted in the lower-lying hill country of Gaocheng township, where small Hakka populations are interspersed with natives. These Hakkas have assimilated culturally with the native population in many ways, including the gendered division of labor. Among the Wanzai natives it has always been a humiliation for the men of a family if a woman plows the land, and nowadays Wanzai people of Hakka heritage share this view. Many local women explained to me that females in northwest Jiangxi do not plow because the immersion in water that is required for plowing causes gynecological problems. This health problem among farming women has also been observed in other developing countries.[53]

During the early years of migration from the fieldwork counties, most of the mobility was seasonal: migrants performed odd jobs for short periods in the city, returning home for Spring Festival (spring planting) and for the summer and autumn harvests. As elsewhere in rural China, this initial exposure to the cities enabled many village communities to find introductions to longer-term factory jobs, so the length of stay in the cities has been steadily increasing.[54] For the most part, however, migrants in China return to their villages at least once a year.[55] As an example of the gradual transition from seasonal to longer-term migration, in the late 1980s the nephew of a cadre in the Wanzai government forestry office, Mr. Liu, was offered the chance to work for three months each winter growing flowers in nurseries in the factory district of Nanhai. He took several men with him from his home village of Tuanjie in Gaocheng township, and after three or four years some of the men found factory work for both themselves and their female relatives. With the expansion of the urban manufacturing zones, labor agents have been particularly keen to recruit Wanzai women. These women are famous for their ability to assemble firecrackers and weave grass linen, and their "nimble fingers" are seen as especially suitable for work in light manufacturing industries. In Xinfeng and Yudu, longer-term migration has similarly been facilitated by the feedback of information from pioneers who initially migrated on a seasonal basis. A handful of carpenters and cotton shredders left their counties to work in the cities for the winter as early as 1979, and by the 1980s mass migration to factories was already an established feature of the south Jiangxi economy. In Wanzai, longer-term migration did not start until the early 1990s – in part because Wanzai men lacked transportable skills and the county had no pre-collectivization culture of labor migration. In fact, before collectivization, skilled cotton shredders and carpenters came from Zhejiang province to perform these specialized services in Wanzai villages.

Migrants from Wanzai, Xinfeng, and Yudu are concentrated in the coastal factory districts of Nanhai and Dongguan, Guangdong. The migrants from Licun township in Yudu county are an exception in that they work mainly as traders in the prefectural capital of Ganzhou city. Migration from all of the fieldwork counties is largely facilitated through the return flow of information that characterizes "chain migration." As outlined in Chapter 1, social networks are important because trusted family and friends in the city pull villagers to particular destination areas (and often to particular occupations) by providing help with job introductions and accommodation.[56] Chinese sociologists observe that inadequate information is a feature of transition from a planned to a market economy, and although economic rights have been devolved vertically, the legacy of the planned economy hampers the horizontal connections that would mediate supply and demand and interregional resource flows. These researchers report that, with regard to labor migration, the organizational networks of the family and the village fill the information void.[57] When many migrants become concentrated in one destination, the "snowball" divides and the migrants branch out into new localities. More recent destinations for migrants from the fieldwork counties include Shanghai, Wenzhou, and Xiamen.

In Yudu county, the local state is also involved in coordinating labor export – although, as the following tale reveals, there may be conflict between the different levels of the local administration over the resources generated through migration. In 1989, the government of Luoe township in Yudu established contact with the Shanghai Freight Container Company and negotiated a poverty relief arrangement whereby individuals from the poorest households would be given the opportunity to earn money loading cargo at the Pudong docks. To the disgruntlement of Luoe township officials, the Yudu County Labor Bureau hijacked the initiative and in 1992 established direct links with the Shanghai authorities. Now the Yudu Labor Export Company operates on a profit basis and workers are selected according to physical strength.

Shanghai benefits from the arrangement with Yudu through the supply of cheap labor. As explained by Lai Jidong, director of the Yudu Labor Export Company in Shanghai, the Yudu men work three times harder than the Shanghai dock workers for one third of the pay.[58] During 1997, many native Shanghai dock workers were laid off, and in September these unemployed workers marched in protest. Migrants pay fees to the Shanghai Labor Bureau for urban work permits and, as an illustration of the biased flow of resources toward urban centers, this money funds retraining programs for redundant Shanghai workers. The Yudu Labor Export Company has also initiated labor supply programs with other factories in Shanghai. Yudu county cadres stationed in Shanghai are responsible for the discipline of the workers, which involves a "semi-military" style of management,[59] and they also care for the workers' welfare.

In all three counties, private labor exporters operating under the auspices of county government labor bureaus earn money by providing job introductions, organizing transport, and handling administrative procedures for the temporary urban residence permits (these permits are explained fully in the next section). During the early 1980s and 1990s, county labor bureaus were given targets for labor export that were filtered down from the prefecture and the province. Nowadays, migrants have established their own information networks, and some labor agents complain that it is increasingly difficult to recruit workers.[60] The government no longer issues quotas for labor export. Labor bureau authorities in Yudu estimate that only 5% of migration from the county is organized by agencies, and in Wanzai and Xinfeng the proportion is even smaller. Nonetheless, during periods of economic decline, some migrants are willing to go through the export companies, which charge the worker a fee of around 300 yuan.

In all three counties, local state organs are involved to varying degrees in managing and coordinating labor migration, and this affords some officials opportunities for earning money from rural people. If migrants want to enter a legitimate factory then they need an identity card. If they wish to apply for a temporary urban residence permit so that they can sojourn legally in the city, they also need a "permission to migrate" card (*laowu xukezheng*) and a "proof of situation" certificate (*qingkuang zhengming*) that states their marital status and reproductive history. Obtaining these cards and certificates from the relevant township agencies involves the payment of fees, which in some cases total over 200 yuan.

County governments also manage the migrants by establishing urban-based labor export offices. These offices provide assistance for all migrants, including those who have used their own information to find jobs. The assistance includes issuing family planning certificates[†] which must be posted back to the village by female migrants every six months, and providing legal advice for those migrants who encounter problems while in the city. Through these offices, local state cadres are able to maintain contact with their migrant constituents.

2.4 WHY DO INTERNAL MIGRANTS IN CHINA RETAIN LINKS WITH THEIR VILLAGES?

The insecurity experienced by rural dwellers in the destination areas means that return migration becomes structurally embedded and, over time, becomes institutionalized within culture. This cultural institutionalization of return migration is expressed through extensions and adaptations of values endogenous to rural society – such as family loyalty, mutual aid, and love of the native place. The following discussion examines the structural constraints that prevent the integration of rural people into the urban milieu, thereby reinforcing the belief among migrants that, ultimately, the village is home.

The attitude of urbanites toward migrants is one of economic acceptance coupled with social rejection. Rural migrants are described by municipal authorities as *wailai renkou* (meaning "outside population") rather than *yimin*

[†] These certify that a woman is not pregnant and (if she is married) that her IUD coil is in place.

(which means "migrant"), emphasizing that these people are transients. Members of the *wailai renkou* are like migrant workers the world over, confined to arduous, dirty, and dangerous jobs. In China, formal regulations enacted by municipal authorities ban rural migrants from a range of occupations, including those of shop assistant and elevator operator.[61] Migrants encounter hostility in their daily interactions with urban residents,[62] and there are even occasional violent outbursts. In one incident in Guangdong, eleven migrants in conflict with local residents were shot dead by armed troops.[63] Chinese migrants, like their counterparts throughout the developing world, are able to come to terms with their lowly status in the cities because the host society is not the social and spatial reality in which they define themselves.[64] Rather, the city is merely somewhere to earn money for their lives in the village.

The legal right of people with rural household registrations to reside in Chinese cities is tenuous, and although controls on rural–urban migration are steadily relaxing and alternative categories of residence status have been formulated, urban residency is still beyond the reach of most migrants. For example, the "blue permit *hukou*"[65] allows for long-term residency in the city and may be eventually converted to an urban *hukou*. However, in most cities, access to these permits is limited to educated persons with a history of off-farm employment and to those individuals with sufficient savings to purchase commodity housing.[66] There were only two households in my fieldwork villages where the adult children moved to the city for higher education, found work (as medical staff, managers, and teachers), and settled with an urban *hukou*; they all live in the provincial capital of Nanchang. Other migrants become urban residents through marriage, and there were only two such people from my fieldwork villages in Wanzai: one man and one woman. Alternatively, some migrants attain urban residency by "buying green cards" from municipal authorities; this is discussed further in Chapter 7 with respect to returned migrants who settle in rural towns and county seats.

Despite burgeoning unemployment in the cities, people in towns and villages still associate a city *hukou* with better life chances, as illustrated in the following anecdote. I asked a class of 15-year-olds in Wanzai county school to list the qualities of a desirable spouse. Over half of the class of fifty giggling students said that a desirable spouse should have an urban *hukou*. Yet becoming a city resident is only a pipe dream for the vast majority of rural labor migrants and seldom forms part of their goals. This can be seen in the report of a Chinese survey in which many migrants told the interviewer that they wanted to return home. However, further open-ended discussions revealed that what the respondents actually meant was that they felt there was *no choice* but for them to return home.[67] This suggests that migrants maintain the institution of return by adapting their life goals and expectations to those that seem socially possible.

Migrants who successfully obtain urban residence permits are not the main focus of this book. This is because none of the labor migrants in my survey have nonagricultural backgrounds[68] and, aside from the few individuals mentioned previously, none of the household members whom I encountered in my fieldwork have acquired an urban residence permit. Most labor migrants, including the key informants from my fieldwork counties, reside in the city on a temporary basis. These migrants must procure a "labor certificate" that is issued following the inspection of contracts submitted by the employer. Institutions in some cities cannot hire more than a set quota of migrants and must pay a fee to municipal authorities for each rural employee.[69] The migrants must also obtain temporary residence cards[70] and accommodation. The Deputy Director of the Migrant Labor Management Office in the Shanghai Labor Bureau explained to me the following:

> The average length of time spent by a migrant in Shanghai is four years [a two-year temporary residence card with one renewal]. But this is not concrete, and many migrants stay for five or six years if they make contact with another work unit. The aim [of limiting the length of residence in the city] is to make sure that migrants can still adapt to the village on their return.[71]

Migrants who lack the requisite documents are known as "three without" migrants and risk being sent to an urban detention center (*qiansong zhan*). Such a migrant has neither a temporary residence permit from the municipal public security bureau (*zhanzhu zheng*) nor an identity card (*shenfen zheng*) nor a labor certificate. When the numbers of such migrants are sufficient to fill a coach, these migrants are repatriated to their villages at the expense of the state.[72] Chinese scholars describe the peripheral status of the migrants as follows:

> Temporary workers talk most about the fact that, no matter what, the local public security officials come in the middle of the night and inspect the *hukou*, and if there is no temporary residence card, the migrant is fined whatever sum enters the official's head. Those who run are pursued and beaten. There is no human dignity. This makes the workers feel as though they are lost in an alien land, and that the home village is the best after all.[73]

In sum, structural features of the Chinese political economy mean that both planners and migrants internalize the belief that the return of rural workers to their villages is inevitable.

2.5 IMPROVING POPULATION QUALITY: RETURNEES AS EMISSARIES OF MODERNITY

State authorities contend that – since the return of migrants is inevitable or at least desirable – authorities must ensure that the quality of these sojourners is improved through urban exposure.[74] In the Mao era, peasants were praised for their simple "blankness" and ideological purity, and urbanites were even sent to the countryside to learn from them. However, in the post-Mao era, peasants are culturally constructed as ideologically backward subjects who, as a matter of national urgency, must undergo a series of civilizing campaigns.[75] This inversion in the ideological status of the rural population has occurred because economic modernization has replaced class struggle as the means of achieving linear transition from traditional to modern, rural to urban, agricultural to industrial, poor to rich, and backward to civilized. A concomitant feature of these dichotomies is transition from a predominantly low- to high-quality labor force. In a traditional agrarian society where high fertility and high mortality predominate, the economic value of population is determined by quantity. However, in a technologically advanced society, labor needs are based on considerations of quality.

Some Chinese and Western scholars have argued that modernization and the transfer of surplus rural labor out of agriculture both needs and produces "quality" labor.[76] In Chinese policy documents and the popular imagination, "population quality" incorporates three aspects: cultural quality, ideological quality, and eugenics and physical quality. Although migration is seen to advance population quality in all three senses, the cultural and ideological quality components are central to this book. Policy-makers contend that migrants improve their cultural quality through education, skills training, and new experiences, and that therein lies the potential for returnees to enrich the quality of leaders and laborers in the countryside.[77] They further recommend that cash-strapped local governments pursue out-migration and return as development strategies by using migrant work experience as an inexpensive substitute for education.[78]

With regard to ideological quality, migration is said to instill a "commodity consciousness," a good work ethic, and an appreciation of the value of time among rural dwellers.[79] Moreover, the Chinese state envisages a role for returned migrants in diffusing an awareness of civilized manners, hygiene, law, and modern culture into the countryside. To facilitate this end, the Yudu Labor Export Company in Shanghai runs spiritual civilization classes for migrants; activities include praise meetings and occasions such as a visit to sweep the Martyrs Shrine on Qing Ming Festival. These pedagogic projects also warn migrants against urban vices (e.g., gambling and prostitution) and remind them of their moral obligations to the rural household.[80]

The low ideological quality of rural dwellers is also said to be manifest in the revival of such "feudal" practices as elaborate funerals and weddings, ancestor worship, and celebrations of clan and village gods. Jiangxi policy documents portray the extended family and the associated cultural practices as feudal and antithetical to modernization, expressing the hope that exposure to modern values through migration will reduce the influence of lineage ties and the values that they embody.[81] State attacks on these customs have been particularly strong in northwest Jiangxi. On the one hand, the socialist state designates nuclear households rather than families as the basic entities of production, consumption, and accounting, thereby allowing more direct control over social and economic functions within the countryside.[82] On the other hand, the economic reforms have been accompanied by legislation that requires grown-up children – including those who have already divided into separate households – to look after their elderly parents as well as other needy family members.[83] Additionally, state-led household evaluation campaigns praise households that look after the young and the elderly and shame those that do not. Herein lies a paradox. The state is hostile to family-based cultural practices and rituals. Yet these practices are a way for rural producers to invest resources in family and kin networks, and such investments are of growing importance in a transitional economy that is characterized by the absence of safety nets and an increase in spatially distributed economic opportunities.

Finally, commentators state that migration expands the gene pool of particular localities, creating a unique historical opportunity for improving the physical and intellectual quality of the Chinese race.[84] At the Pudong Migrant Floating Population Management Offices in Shanghai, migrants attend obligatory classes on family planning and eugenics.[85] Scholars also express concern that the poor working conditions of some pregnant migrant women might adversely affect the quality of their children.[86] Although this facet of population quality is not pertinent to the state's idea of creating emissaries of modernity, it demonstrates the perception of backwardness as intrinsic to the rural populace. Indeed, staff at the Yudu Dock Workers Company explained to me that, as a former revolutionary base area, Yudu is underdeveloped because those with high intellect were killed during the wars of 1937–1949.[87]

The concepts of modernization and population quality are complementary: although population quality is centered on the notion of poor individuals improving their lot through self-help, a "quality" population requires access to resources for investing in health care and education. However, the poverty of backward areas tends to be explained in terms of a natural reality and the inherent characteristics of the people in such localities. Many people who spoke with me explained either their own poverty or that of their villages in terms of their own low quality or that of the people in their hometowns. Others expressed the view that the only choice for "low quality" farmers is to sell their labor in hard manual work. Stressing migrants' lack of innate ability obscures the *structural* mechanisms that confine villagers to the peripheries of the emerging political economy, limiting their access to resources and circumscribing their scope for forming goals. "Low quality" conveniently explains why rural dwellers are limited to the lowest rungs of the labor market, why they are commonly afflicted with industrial injuries, and why they generally lose out in disputes with their employers.[88] The media gloss over the ban on mobility under Mao and promote the illusion that, prior to their unshackling by Deng, the peasants had always been immobile.[89] Labor mobility is portrayed as a benevolent policy that increases the flow of resources to rural areas and allows the rural populace to prosper, thereby obscuring the vulnerability of migrants in a period of rapid capital accumulation.

2.6 RURAL LIVELIHOOD DIVERSIFICATION

Alarm at the size of the rural exodus has caused policy-makers to advocate a Chinese version of Lewisian modernization – namely, accommodating the *sectoral* transfer of labor while minimizing the *spatial* transfer. During the early 1980s, rural industrialization was guided by the slogan, "enter the factory without entering the city, leave the land without leaving the village." Households were to reallocate labor from farming to industrial sectors while providing the subsistence for unabsorbed labor.[90] Rural enterprises include entities established by various levels of local government or by farmers either as individuals, as family concerns, as partnerships, or in cooperation with their village. In establishing rural enterprises, governments and individuals have used savings accumulated through increased agricultural productivity, thereby capitalizing on differences in returns to different sectors of the economy.

This worked well in the coastal regions, where dense communication networks meant that rural enterprises coalesced around transport hubs. However, in the interior and west, the dispersed development of rural enterprises suggested by this model created difficulties with the supply of raw materials and the provision of services. Each enterprise had to use its own resources to resolve the problems of electricity and water supplies, waste disposal, storage, and transport, which led to inefficiencies. The scattered distribution of the enterprises retarded the development of a rural service sector, because the number of enterprises in any given locality was too few to make the provision of support services and facilities profitable. Frail infrastructure at the grass-roots level exacerbated production costs and weakened the market competitiveness of goods from the rural industrial sector. As economic reforms gained momentum in the cities, many rural enterprises proved unable to compete with the more sophisticated urban industries, forcing even more rural dwellers into the cities. Figures for mid-1994 suggest that, while township and village enterprises had absorbed around 100 million farmers, a further 2 million remained surplus, and three quarters of these were concentrated in the interior and western provinces.[91]

The 1990s approach to rural industrialization is to create rural enterprises that are concentrated in rural towns. This is championed with the slogan: "leave the land and enter the factory, leave the village and enter the town."[92] This principle of developing small towns and cities has been reiterated in the 10th Five-Year Plan (2001–2005); however, some scholars have expressed fears that local leaders will clamber to build small towns regardless of local conditions, resource availability, or the capacity of the population to sustain a town. They state that towns must be established in a planned and rational way; otherwise, the result is a situation of "all towns resembling the countryside and all the countryside resembling towns."[93]

Although national urbanization is a future target, policy documents state that, for a prolonged period, the livelihood of many rural households will nevertheless depend on both agriculture and wages; this is reflected by descriptions of farming households with migrant or local off-farm workers as "rural proletarian" or "amphibious."[94] A principal tenet of the Chinese government's program for poverty eradication by the year 2000 is that every household in poor areas will have one member working in a rural enterprise, in an agricultural sideline such as an orchard, or as a migrant in a developed region.[95] Given these options, rural governments encourage labor mobility because it requires little investment on their part.[96] This idea is illustrated in the Yudu County Yearbook, which lists "labor export" under accomplishments for creating rural enterprises.[97] In rural Jiangxi, low levels of economic diversification, weak industrial bases, and poor town infrastructure mean that remittances are the main source of off-farm income. Cadres in Jiangxi and other agricultural provinces promote migration as a strategy for rural poverty alleviation with the slogans: "the migration of one person frees the entire household from poverty"[98] and "labor flows out, money flows back."[99]

Policy-makers in China see migration not only as a means of rural livelihood diversification but also as a process that generates return flows of higher-quality human resources and capital, which can be used to create employment in the origin areas.[100] Planners seek to integrate the "guided migration" of higher-quality laborers to large cities with the return of migrants to their villages and the retention of people in the countryside.[101] The slogan "using the tide to harness the tide"[102] describes a strategy of using the resources and entrepreneurial acumen of returnees to make the rural towns and industries more effective population retainers.[103] Studies conducted in several developing countries find that (1) migration is a response to the narrow range of occupations that are open to the active population in economically depressed agricultural regions and (2) rates of out-migration are highest in regions where local opportunities for diversifying earning activities are limited.[104] The literature further suggests that rural market towns and rural enterprises are important focal points for increasing the livelihood options of the rural poor.[105]

Towns in China fall into three categories: county seat, town, and township. The county seat is the administrative center of the county (*xian*), and both towns and townships fall under its direct jurisdiction. The towns (*zhen*) are on the same administrative level as the townships and are responsible for the villages within their boundaries. Town settlements are the lowest unit in the urban hierarchy and are generally larger than the townships. The townships (*xiang*) were previously the communes; today they are rural jurisdictions subdivided into administrative villages that correspond roughly with the former production brigades. Before liberation, these towns and townships were mostly the old standard marketing areas described by Skinner. In this book, the settlements where town or township governments are located are referred together as rural market towns.

In Wanzai, Xinfeng, and Yudu, the county seats each have a long-distance bus station, factories, the county government offices, a county court, banks, a government guest house, a New China book shop, a middle school, a hospital, an agricultural market place, and a few streets of small shops and restaurants. The most common form of transport is the trishaw, although in June 1997 Xinfeng began a public bus service with two small vehicles. There is also an abundance of privately operated minibuses rattling between the county seats and the townships and villages. The market towns that I visited had a compound that contained the government office, a rural cooperative, and a family planning center. In addition, there was a single street that had a branch of the Agricultural Bank, a supply and marketing cooperative, a post office, a lower middle school, a clinic, a veterinary depot, an agricultural extension bureau, some small shops, pool tables, and food stalls. Some townships in south Jiangxi even boasted newly built temples – something I never saw during my time in Wanzai, where antifeudal campaigns were common.[106]

As observed in the work of Skinner, goods from the county and surrounding villages are traded in the market towns on market days, lunar calendar dates that have been fixed by custom and observed by locals for centuries. If the towns are near to the county seat, such as Gaocheng in Wanzai, market days are not held and farmers instead visit the agricultural market and shops in the county seat. The various buildings in the towns illustrate the integration between the commercial and administrative functions of these settlements. Skinner's work has stressed the commercial considerations that shaped the spatial arrangement of the Chinese landscape; he has argued that, whereas the rural market towns formed part of an economic system, there was a largely separate administrative system incorporating county seats.[107] This interpretation has been criticized by Gates, who argues that – aside from economic factors – the towns have been positioned with a view toward maintaining the political influence needed for the exaction of payments from petty commodity producers.[108] Gates's position is useful in illuminating the role of county and township officials as both sponsors and beneficiaries of the resources generated by migration, return migrant entrepreneurship, and other petty commodity activities.

As some migration scholars have argued, the creation of jobs that involve daily commuting to nearby towns are more effective in retaining people in the countryside than other rural development strategies – for example, agricultural extension.[109] Working in nearby towns is said to maximize some of the positive benefits from migration while minimizing negative ones, such as protracted family separation.[110] The Chinese state maintains that, by modernizing rural areas through towns and rural enterprises and with reduced disparity in living standards between villages and the cities, the incentives for villagers to migrate will eventually disappear.[111] Some Chinese commentators draw on Maoist eulogies of rural purity and point to wealthy corporate villages in Jiangsu, arguing that the countryside can offer a modern lifestyle that is free from the corruption and impersonal interaction that characterize the cities.

Chinese policy-makers maintain that the spatial and sectoral transfer of capital and high-quality labor that accompanies return migration can also be directed toward agricultural diversification. Since the widespread layoffs from state enterprises starting in the mid-1990s, some urban dwellers have become involved in market gardening, fish cultivation, and orchard businesses. Returning migrants are deemed especially suited to these undertakings because of their familiarity with farming, so they are encouraged to use their capital for opening up barren land and pursuing specialized production.[112] This conforms to another strategy for absorbing surplus rural labor: claiming uncultivated lands for specialized production and creating fish ponds. In Jiangxi, a province blighted with infertile red soil hills covering over 60% of its terrain, the slogan is: "create another Jiangxi in the hills and another Jiangxi in the water." Commentators urge local governments to make such avenues of entrepreneurship more attractive to returnees and migrant investors by improving the security of the contract system and increasing investment in agriculture.[113]

2.7 CONCLUSION

In elevating migration and return to the status of development strategies, the state co-opts a revival of petty commodity production into discourses of modernization, poverty alleviation, and national construction – all of which buttress the state's legitimacy and raison d'être. The attitude of the Chinese state toward petty commodity producers is characterized simultaneously by support and "squeeze." Provincial leaders in Jiangxi have been calling on grass-roots leaders to reduce their squeeze on farmers and to support them in their efforts to prosper. This is because a supportive policy environment is required for rural producers to generate more resources for modernizing and developing the province. In particular, provincial leaders hail migration and returnee entrepreneurship as processes that "liberate the thinking" of local leaders, improve the "quality" of farmers, facilitate a revival of Jiangxi's historical entrepreneurial spirit, and promote economic development.

Subsequent chapters will illustrate that, in leaving their villages and then returning, petty commodity producers exploit niches created by the state's modernization goals and also employ strategies for circumventing structures of the political economy that restrict their capacity to obtain and deploy resources for achieving their own goals. Their success is shown by the fact that rural households are much better off now than under Mao. It is important to note, however, that the living standards of rural people have also improved because of other influences, such as state policies affecting the relative prices of agricultural and industrial goods, the implementation of compulsory education policies, the provision of agricultural extension, health, and welfare services, and state support for infrastructure projects. Even so, migration remains central to any explanation of change in the Chinese countryside. Subsequent chapters will reveal that rural people's mobility and increased control over resources afford them a stronger bargaining position with respect to other members of society (including officials), and many are deploying their resources and achieving goals that are transforming the countryside politically, socially, and economically.

3

Resource Redistribution and Inequality

THIS chapter examines the ways in which migration interacts with village inequalities, the political distributional mechanisms of rural society, and pre-existing tensions over resource allocation. These tensions are present at various levels: within households, between households in a family, within villages, and between the political elite and rural society. The migration strategies of social actors are in part responses to the limited resources and the distributional mechanisms of their households and wider rural society. These migration strategies precipitate a reorganization of resources such as labor, money, and land, as well as a redistribution of burdens; that is, claims by others on these resources. It is important to note that, in an environment that is changing through migration, even those not directly involved in migration change their livelihood strategies. This has carryover implications for resource distribution and rural inequality.

This chapter pursues three main areas of inquiry. The first examines how the demographic composition of households influences their capacity to obtain resources from migration. The boundaries between the different households in a family are ambiguous, with the members maintaining close economic and social relations. But this discussion reveals that there is also considerable conflict between the different households of the same family over the distribution of resources. Such conflict is nothing new; people have pursued competing goals since the beginning of time. The new resources from migration increase the leverage of some family members while others find themselves disadvantaged in the allocation of cash, grain, and labor burdens. Second, migration reduces the influence of local patronage in the allocation of off-farm earning opportunities to households. The political elite tend to control local off-farm earning opportunities, but migration creates an extended social and economic network, thereby allowing villagers to circumvent the political monopoly over off-farm opportunities. The final area is concerned with the ways in which migration affects agriculture; it involves implications for the redistribution of land, agricultural incomes, labor burdens, and taxes. However, before exploring these areas, the reader is introduced to the research methodology and fieldwork sites.

3.1 RESEARCHING THE IMPACT OF MIGRATION
ON RURAL INEQUALITY

3.1.1 *Methodology*

Many studies examine the impact of migration on inequality by assessing the contribution of remittances to household income, but analysis based solely on income fails to produce meaningful results for several reasons. First, it is too simplistic to isolate migration as the cause of changes in patterns of inequality. This is because socioeconomic factors interact in ways that are not always obvious. Moreover, migration is both a cause and an effect of inequality.[1] Second, surveys that investigate the income of a cross-section of households frozen in time do not enjoy the advantage of examining the situation of households before and after migration. Scholars who calculate the total share of income claimed by a percentage of households with remittances – and then compare the same set of households without remittances – assume that labor is a homogenous entity and that the value of an individual's labor contribution prior to migration is zero.[2] Third, the value of income that is both produced and consumed within the subsistence base of the petty commodity household constitutes a significant portion of income that is not amenable to measurement.[3] Fourth, my own research has discovered that it is difficult for interviewees to give accurate retrospective accounts of income sources or to distinguish remittances from other income. Moreover, without detailed records of household budgets, it is impossible to gauge the role of remittances in freeing up alternative sources of household income for productive use, consumption, and savings. Finally, given the reluctance of villagers to discuss money, statements about income and urban earnings are likely to have been distorted. This would be less of a problem if the researcher could be confident that all interviewees adjusted their income estimates to the same extent, but members of wealthier households and individual migrants may have stronger motives than other respondents for understating their income.

The migration literature offers a range of micro- and macro-level studies on the impact of migration and remittances on inequality in rural areas.[4] These studies have been conducted in many different places and vary in terms of their underlying theoretical positions, units of comparison (individuals or households), and research methods. This research has produced a range of contradictory findings.[5] Furthermore, owing to the particular historical and structural context of migration in China, these studies have limited applicability in the present context.

The micro-level study in this chapter captures aspects of social change and resource redistribution that would be omitted from aggregate data, and it also presents original material on the implications of migration for interhousehold inequality in the Wanzai countryside. My research finds that migration broadly correlates with better standards of living for the participating households. Anecdotal evidence suggests that, through migration, poorer households are able to obtain resources for "catching up."[6] It further suggests that remittances enhance the position of wealthier households already enjoying the advantages of many laborers, access to local sources of off-farm employment, and larger land allocations. To determine the extent of the causal relationship between migration and change in the material well-being of households, longitudinal data would be required. However, practical constraints restricted this research to a single moment in time. Despite the absence of a temporal perspective, this chapter is able to draw robust conclusions about the interrelationships between migration and existing sources of inequality such as household composition, off-farm income, and land distribution.

3.1.2 *The Fieldwork Sites*

The research for this chapter was conducted in two villages located in Gaocheng township, Wanzai county. The analysis is based on my survey of 138 households, 102 of which have migrant members. The survey attempted to cover all of the households in one village group (*zu*) in Tuanjie and two village groups in Qifeng.[7] To get to Wanzai county seat from Tuanjie village, it is necessary to walk nearly 5 kilometers to Gaocheng and then cycle the remaining 10 kilometers or take the bus, which runs twice a day. Qifeng is on a surfaced road 10 kilometers from the county seat, and buses frequently pass through the village.

In November 1996, the accountant in Gaocheng township informed me that the annual per-capita income was 1,500 yuan and that the per-capita incomes of the fieldwork villages were also around 1,500 yuan, a middling value for Wanzai. County officials and accountants in Qifeng and Tuanjie corroborated these estimates. The officials were probably referring to the latest available figures, which would have been from the previous year. The average per-capita income for the surveyed households is 1,800 yuan.[8] This higher per-capita income may be indicative of the fact that 45%[9] of the labor force from the surveyed households had migrated, compared with roughly 20%[10] of the rural labor force from Wanzai as a whole. However, the difference may also reflect the different time periods to which the figures refer. In 1996, officials estimated that remittances had increased rural per-capita incomes by at least 150 yuan per year. Between January and October 1996, remittances through the Gaocheng township post office totaled over 5 million yuan, an amount equivalent to just under 9% of the agricultural product value for the same time period.[11] This figure excludes money brought home by migrants in person and funds sent to other post offices in the county, but it includes funds remitted by the natives of other townships to Gaocheng.

3.1.3 *Fieldwork Sources*

My research into the impact of migration on resource distribution and inequality draws on three key sources: census sheets, household evaluation plaques, and household interviews. The census sheets were compiled as part of the First Chinese National Agricultural Census conducted in Wanzai in November and December 1996, which coincided with my fieldwork. These sheets supply basic demographic data on the households as well as information on household land allocations and livestock ownership. Additional information from the interviews, household visits, participant observation, and cadre comments have supplemented the data in these census sheets. For example, the education levels of individuals were recorded in the census by the level of school most recently attended, irrespective of the amount of study completed. Through the interviews I was able to moderate this so that, say, a person who attended middle school for less than one year was classified as having a primary education. As another example, the census interviews were carried out during a period when many villagers had returned for Spring Festival. This led to some households designating the temporary returnees as migrants while others recorded them as present members of the household. As a final example, villagers tended to underreport livestock ownership in order to avoid taxes, and township cadres complained to me that some farmers were hiding their pigs and chickens in the pens of households where married couples had migrated.[12] Village cadres who were aware of this underreporting sometimes pointed out the households with unreported livestock. Similarly, there were instances where the agricultural productivity of poorer households had been overstated because of village targets for increasing livestock production.

At the time of my fieldwork, local cadres were organizing the villagers in conducting household evaluation campaigns, with the performance of each household indicated on a plaque mounted above the door. These plaques provided an indication of the socioeconomic standing of a household, with 9- and 10-"star" households representing the highest stratum of society. Each star denotes a criterion against which the households were assessed. As well as the total number of stars, two particular stars useful for the purposes of my fieldwork were "completion of the agricultural production and tax tasks" and "prospering through hard work." Other categories included good political thought and loving the nation, loving the young and old, adherence to the family planning policy, practicing scientific knowledge and education, environmental hygiene, harmony and

Household evaluation plaque.

willingness to help neighbors, changing social traditions, and being moral and law-abiding. The census sheets and evaluation plaques enabled me to commence each interview with a mental picture of the demographic composition and socioeconomic standing of the household.

The interview questions covered the motivations for migration, the net income of the household, the amount of remittances received during the previous year, remittance usage, other sources of off-farm income, changes in the material standing of the household after migration, and plans for the future. On the whole, respondents were reluctant to disclose the true amount of urban contributions or household income. In the countryside of Jiangxi, faded slogans from the Cultural Revolution are still visible, reminding villagers of a time when the political environment was intolerant of the more wealthy. During one interview, a man informed me that annual remittances from his three sons totaled 10,000 yuan. Later that evening he visited the house of my guide and asked: "What did she write in her notebook? Did I do the wrong thing by answering her question? Did she write that I am a landlord?"[13]

Reservations about revealing the amount of remittances also stem from a desire to avoid taxes, the requests of relatives and neighbors to borrow money, and the jealousy of other villagers. Additionally, secrecy within families over remittances means that not all household members are equally informed about the amount or disposal of income. As a result, the interview responses may have been influenced by the presence of other household members, curious neighbors, and my village cadre guides. However, people were happy to talk about general aspects of daily life, education, house building, and festivals, and this proved to be a fruitful line of inquiry for finding out about the uses of remittances.

Finally, the research was informed very much by immersion in village life. The interviews were conducted in the houses of respondents, so I was able to gain an impression of the quality of their housing and possessions and also view their household evaluation plaques. Living in the villages enabled me to observe day-to-day routines, the return and re-migration of migrants, and social events. I was also privy to villagers' gossip on the livelihoods and life choices of their neighbors.

Following the example of the International Fund for Agricultural Development, I have classified the surveyed households into categories reflecting their material well-being on the basis of income, ownership, and expenditure.[14] Although the income estimates offered by household members are unreliable, they are useful as a guide when considered together with other indicators such as housing quality, livestock ownership,[15] and diet. Moreover, the classification of households in my study is influenced by "insider" views – in particular, comments from my cadre guides and neighbors on the economic standing of a household, and the number and category of stars awarded to a household in the evaluation campaigns. I have divided the households into five categories: poor, lower-middle, middle, upper-middle, and rich; their characteristics are detailed in Table 3.1. In the few borderline cases where a household meets some but not all of the criteria for inclusion in a particular category, I defer to my subjective notes and the comments offered by my guides. Owing to insufficient information, nine of the 138 households were not classified. All of the graphs presented in this chapter refer to these household categories.

3.2 MIGRATION, HOUSEHOLD COMPOSITION, AND INEQUALITY

This section begins by outlining Chayanov's ideas on the relationship between household composition and inequality and then adapts these insights to study how the labor supply and developmental stage of households affect their capacity to obtain resources from migration. It further explores the intrafamily and intrahousehold conflicts that ensue over the distribution of these resources. Finally, the discussion shows that migration interacts with household composition to increase the control that some family members have over resources while others lose out.

According to Chayanov,[16] household composition is the main cause of rural inequality – although this explanation was originally formulated to explain stratification in a purely agricultural economy, without consideration of labor migration or a rural industrial sector. Households are said to have control over

Table 3.1. *Household categories*

Category	Number	Characteristics	
		Households	
Poor	11	Net annual income less than 1,000 yuan, mud house with earth floor, few animals, and no evaluation stars for "completing the agricultural production and tax tasks" and "prospering through hard work."	Gather ferns for fuel. Eat mainly rice at each meal with few supplements of meat, egg, fish, or bean curd.
Lower-middle	36	Annual per-capita income 1,000–1,300 yuan, mud house, fewer than 5 chickens, fewer than 3 pigs, no sow, and no star for "prospering through hard work."	
Middle	50	Annual per-capita income 1,500–2,000 yuan, live in decent housing or in the process of building a new house.	Use both coal and ferns for fuel. Many households raise more than 5 chickens, own sows, or fatten several pigs. Eat a varied diet.
Upper-middle	21	Annual per-capita income 2,300–3,000 yuan[a], have brick houses with cement floors and have a household evaluation rating of at least 7 stars.	
Rich	11	Annual per-capita income more than 3,000 yuan, live in decorated two-story houses, many luxury items (e.g. motorbikes), household rating of at least 8 stars.	

[a] There were no households that gave estimates for income in the ranges of 1,300–1,500 yuan and 2,000–2,300 yuan.

the greatest amount of resources when adult children contribute their labor to the household; in contrast, young couples with children and elderly couples whose children have left the main household face the greatest economic difficulties.[17] The Chinese countryside under Mao was a prime example of a society conforming to this model.[18] For the most part, the Chinese peasants were pure agriculturists with no links to the wider economy.[19] Although rural industries did exist under the communes, their raison d'être was to support the agricultural needs of the villages in which they were located. The authors of *Chen Village* found that most of the households lacking sufficient "work points" to pay for their grain ration (promised under state regulations) were couples with young children and elderly couples with no sons.[20]

In contrast to the egalitarian ideals of the Mao era, the reformist leadership accepts inequality as a necessary consequence of unleashing productive forces in the countryside. The recent emergence of labor and commodity markets is allowing rural households to use their labor, political contacts, and other resources to exploit opportunities for obtaining resources on and off the farm. In localities with low levels of industrialization, as is the case in Gaocheng, remittances tend to be the main source of off-farm income.

Scholars have adapted Chayanovian ideas on labor supply and the developmental cycle of the household to explain the impact of migration on rural inequality. In this approach, household composition is said to influence the capacity of households diversifying their livelihoods through migration and farming to raise their returns to their available labor.[21] These studies show that mobility strategies and the distribution of the resources generated by migration are closely linked with the development cycle of the household.[22] This holds true for Wanzai.

The data presented in Graphs 3.1–3.3 suggest that the amount of resources that a household obtains through migration and other economic activities depends on its demographic composition.[23] In Graph 3.1, households with more laborers aged 15–55 tend to have more migrant members; in Graph 3.2, households with more laborers are generally better off than smaller households. Out of the households with at least five laborers, exactly half belong to the upper-middle and rich categories.[24]

Graph 3.3 shows the relationship between the number of migrants in a household and its economic category. It suggests that there is little difference between the economic standing of households without migrants and those with only one.[25] Households with *at least two* migrant members generally fall into the higher economic categories.[26] But there are also cases where a single migrant from a household advances to a high-paying position and sends home generous remittances.

This survey material indicates that the most prosperous phase of the developmental cycle occurs when adult children have not yet separated from their parents. At this stage, migration contributes resources to the common family property that is ultimately divided among the brothers. In families with an only son, the new couple stays in the same household as the husband's parents. If the sons of a family have not married or if the married sons have not divided, then remittances of all the adult migrant children are commonly pooled to build a big family house. Virilocal marriage customs (whereby the bride marries into the husband's village and family) mean that Wanzai daughters who contribute their remittances toward the building of the family house are net losers because

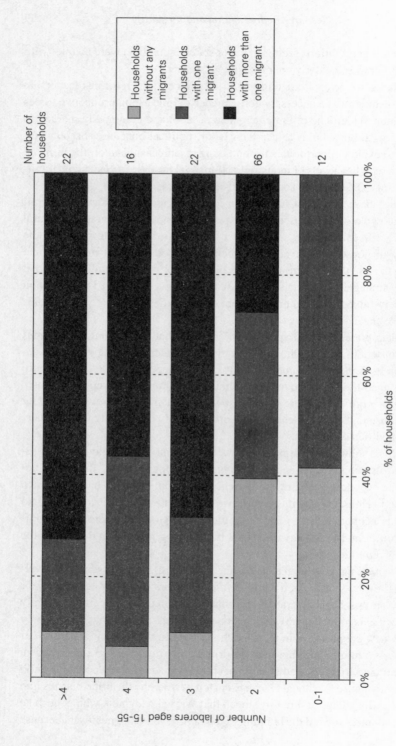

Graph 3.1. Number of migrants in 129 households by number of adult laborers in household. *Source:* Interviews and census sheets.

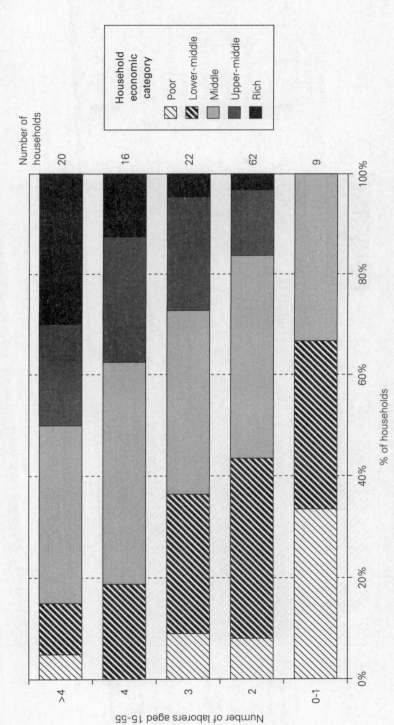

Graph 3.2. Economic categorization of 129 households by number of adult laborers in household. *Source:* Interviews, census sheets, and household evaluation plaques.

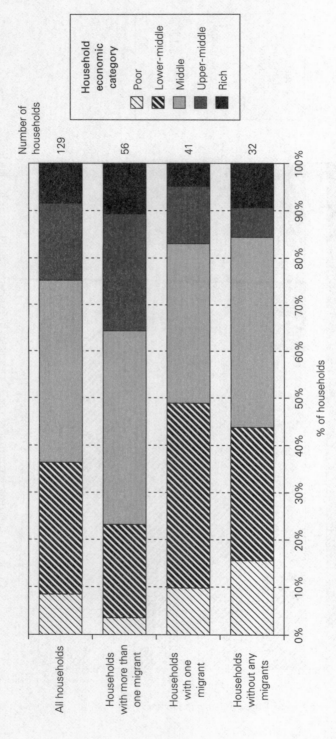

Graph 3.3. Breakdown of economic categories of 129 households by number of migrant members in household.
Source: Interviews, census sheets, and household evaluation plaques.

they do not receive a share of the family property when it is divided. Their goal of a comfortable future and a nice house must be secured by marrying well. This system of family division means that women prefer to marry men with few brothers. Funds remitted by sons may also be individually earmarked for a bride price and wedding ceremony. When asked how the migration of his sons had affected his economic situation, a 61-year-old farmer gave a response that reflected the sentiments of many elderly parents:

> Second and third son going out to Guangdong and earning money is a good thing. Otherwise, my wife and I would have to work ourselves into the ground to get the money for a bride price and wedding. In the countryside, the marriage of a son might be a good thing, but it is also very trouble-some. This way our physical and mental burdens are reduced.[27]

After a few years, the new couple divides from the stem household to form its own household. On division, the new household takes part of its share of the family property. In Wanzai, migration provides the means for young couples to accumulate the material resources necessary for establishing their own house-holds, enabling them to achieve the goals of family division and independence earlier. The brothers share the resources embodied in the family house: one keeps the house, and he pays money to his brothers for their share of the build-ing. In some Gaocheng villages (including Tuanjie), the first brother to father a son receives an extra allocation of the family property. In dividing the fam-ily property, brothers often record their informal agreements in writing. If a brother has migrated, a written agreement may note that a particular brother is entitled to his equal share of the family property because – despite his physical absence – he continued to contribute to the family through remittances.

Division into smaller households occurs differently in rich and poor fami-lies. In rich families, each new household tends to move into its own separate house. However, poorer families are unable to accumulate the resources to build a house and so must postpone this goal indefinitely. As a result, the new nuclear families live in their allocated rooms of the same house but function as separate households, managing their funds and eating independently.

At this stage of the development cycle, the economic pressure of raising chil-dren propels the longer-term migration of one or both young parents, who remit money to support their families.[28] In this survey, about half of the households with migrants consisted of married couples with children. In 23 of these house-holds, a couple has migrated, in 19 only the husband has migrated, and in 12 only the wife has migrated.[†]

[†] These figures include one stem household that has been counted twice because a married couple and a husband have migrated.

However, some parents with young children feel unable to migrate for long periods because they do not want to leave their children in the village, so they participate in seasonal migration. There are eight households in my survey, all with young children, where the parents migrate for three to six months following the autumn harvest and then return in time for spring planting. The seasonal migration of only one family member does not seem to be sufficient to lift these households into the middle economic category. Middling households usually have two seasonal migrants. Alternatively, they combine the seasonal migration of one member with either local off-farm employment (such as working part-time in the village brick factory) or the contracting of extra farmland.

Some households with young children are able to reach the middle economic category through the migration of adult children. For example, in three households, widows with school-age children rely on the remittances of a teen-age migrant child to provide for school fees and basic necessities. In another three households, which also fall into the middle economic category, a parent and a 15-year-old child have migrated together, leaving one parent with school-age children in the village.

However, in some households the adult laborers feel too burdened with caring for children or infirm parents to migrate. When asked why no one has migrated, the members of these households replied: "above there are the old, below there are the young, there is no way to go" (*shang you lao, xia you xiao, zou bu liao*). Households that have neither sufficient labor to participate in migration nor the resources needed for working off the farm at home tend to be relatively poor. In some instances, disabled or ill members also restrict the capacity of these households to participate in migration, and they often shoulder heavy debts for medical care.

Household units that consist of only elderly parents tend to be net losers from migration through decreased resources and increased burdens. After division, resources obtained by the family are generally diverted away from the older generation as the new nuclear household struggles to establish itself by building a house and meeting the expenses associated with pregnancies and early child care. The elderly become dependent on their sons, who take turns supporting their parents: the parents eat at the house of one son for a couple of months and then move on to the next son.

Elderly parents commonly spend their twilight years laboring to support the migration of their children. In households where young parents have migrated, the burden of housework, children, and farming is transferred to the elderly. Many women breast-feed their babies for about six months and then return to the city, leaving the child with the husband's parents. The illness or death of elderly parents often prompts the return of migrants. When there are no grandparents, migrants entrust their children to in-laws in the village or even hire nannies to care for their children. Elderly villagers complained to me that in recent years values of filial piety have been forgotten and even reversed, as it is now parents who are expected to perform a lifetime of "filial duties" for their children.

In Tuanjie village, some grandparents have revolted against the failure of their adult migrant children to honor traditional values of filial piety and collective welfare. Discontent with paltry remittances and being expected to labor on the land and in child care, they have used their good health, strong personalities, and knowledge of urban labor markets to head for the cities and earn some savings for their old age. One feisty widow summoned her daughter-in-law home to look after the grandchildren and then headed for Guangzhou the following day. She told neighbors:

> They go to the city and earn money for themselves and leave me with three grandchildren, the problem of building the house, and the village cadres chasing me for a family planning fine .... I may as well go and earn some money for myself while I am still able.[29]

Although adapting Chayanovian ideas to the study of migration suggests that households with younger adults are wealthier because they are better able to take advantage of migration opportunities, this does not hold true for all households. Despite participating in migration, 32% of households in my survey fall into the poor and lower-middle categories, compared with 37% for non-migrant households. This is because the economic standing of a household is influenced not only by the number of migrants but also by the quantity of resources contributed to the household: not surprisingly, households suffer when migrants fail to remit.

Factors explaining the success or failure of migrants include their prior control over resources, chance, and unobservable aspects of individual aptitude. Many migrants return home disillusioned, cheated of their wages by labor contractors only to try their luck again after the busy farming season. Some migrants are deceived by labor introduction agencies that either take money for arranging jobs that pay only a fraction of the promised rate or send migrants to the cities to find factories that do not exist. In 1997, the operators of several labor introduction agencies in Wanzai county were prosecuted, and new operating guidelines for these businesses were introduced.[30] Other migrants find only low-paying jobs and spend their time "factory jumping" in search of good fortune, losing their entrance deposit with each move. Still others return home with illnesses and injuries, burdening their families with medical expenses.

The economic well-being of the constituent households in a family is affected not only by the amount of resources obtained through migration but also by the ways in which resources and burdens are distributed. Conflicts within families over the allocation of resources occur throughout the developmental cycle and in all socioeconomic settings, irrespective of whether or not there is migration.[31] However, in families where migration becomes an increasingly important source of income, conflicts over resources sometimes intensify. As an example, young migrant males may find themselves torn between cultural values (underpinning filial obligations to the parental household) and other values, frequently invoked by brides, by which able men (*you benshi*) should accumulate sufficient resources to build a separate house and buy consumer goods.

Those who lose out in the distribution of migration resources sometimes pursue strategies that run counter to family ideals and so, for example, sons may be disloyal and mothers may be unreliable. Interviews with both migrants and people remaining in the village reveal that entrusting money to the care of family members at home has pitfalls. Consequently, it is common for migrants to send remittances to trusted friends or relatives who are unlikely to lay claim to the money. As an example, values of filial piety and family loyalty underpin an implicit understanding that the parents have some right to the earnings of their sons even if the sons have married and divided from the stem household. Many male migrants circumvent the obligations associated with this implicit intergenerational contract by sending their wages to their mothers-in-law. A daughter may also prefer to remit to her mother, who is seen as more committed to defending the daughter's interests than are her husband's parents.

However, as the following case illustrates, even mothers are not totally reliable. A woman in Tuanjie village explained to me that her eldest daughter and her husband, who live in a neighboring village, both work in Guangdong. Originally, the couple entrusted their savings to the mother with the intention of using the funds to build a house. However, the mother borrowed from these savings to build her own house. She betrayed the trust of her daughter because she wanted to be a good mother to her son. She needed to ensure his eligibility in the marriage market, maintain the social respectability of her family, and indirectly ensure that her son would provide care for her in old age. The woman explained:

> I had no choice but to use 6,000 yuan for building a house. What could I do? You can see that our house is falling down around us. My youngest son is 19 and he will want to marry. Where will he find a wife who would be willing to live in this house? They don't send their money to me any more. Instead they are entrusting their savings to a neighbor .... I must return the 6,000 yuan because my daughter is already in a separate household.[32]

The confidential transfer of money to a private account is the preferred arrangement of many migrants, but only some have the necessary connections with a rural credit cooperative or a branch of the Agricultural Bank. Such contacts are a valuable resource: they enable migrants to keep more material resources for themselves, and earn interest on their savings, while avoiding censure from the family for actions contravening values of selflessness and collective welfare.

In summary, migration strategies are shaped by the demographic composition of the household, which changes over its developmental cycle. In interacting with the developmental stage of the household, migration strengthens the economic position of some within a family while weakening the position of others. Households with more adult laborers are better able to obtain resources through migration, so they tend to be wealthier. However, households that include elderly members lose out in the reallocation of income and burdens resulting from the migration of other family members. Although in theory all households with enough labor can benefit from involvement in migration, in practice some households lose out because the migrants either fail in the cities or choose not to remit. Furthermore, migration feeds into existing inequalities and conflicts over the allocation of income and burdens within families, with people devising a variety of strategies to gain or retain control over remittances.

3.3 THE ROLE OF MIGRATION IN INCREASING OPPORTUNITIES FOR OFF-FARM EMPLOYMENT

Scholars writing about rural society in China and other developing countries identify off-farm income – either local wages or migrant remittances – as the key determinant of inequality.[33] My research findings concur with this position: Households that diversify their income portfolios to include off-farm earnings tend to be more prosperous than their purely agriculturist neighbors.[34] In places with low levels of industrialization and commercial development, such as Gaocheng township, there are limited local off-farm earning opportunities, and political contacts[35] and family history tend to determine which households have access to the more lucrative ones. By enabling households to operate outside the local social and political distributional mechanisms, migration expands the range of off-farm earning opportunities.

This section begins by describing what local sources of off-farm employment are available in Gaocheng township and how these opportunities are distributed. Then the discussion shows that households without local political contacts or traditional skills are nonetheless able to earn off-farm income through migration. This is because barriers to entry into urban labor markets are fewer than for local off-farm employment. The only prerequisites for household participation in migration are sufficient household labor and money to cover the initial costs of moving to the city, whereas access to local off-farm employment tends to require a certain social or political background. Finally, the economic standing of households with migrant members is compared with the economic standing of those households that have local off-farm workers. This comparison suggests that migration increases the opportunities for poorer households to better their situation while also enabling some of the richer and better-connected households to move even further ahead.

In Wanzai, 30% of the rural population participate in local off-farm employment. Roughly 55% of these assemble firecrackers and fireworks at home, while 35% engage in fireworks production in collectives.[36] The remaining 10% work in institutions such as the local government administration office, post office, electricity depot, reservoir, school, and petrol station; others work as doctors, electricians, or hairdressers. In Gaocheng, additional avenues for off-farm employment include casual work in township and village enterprises (ceramics and brick factories), part-time work in the local gold mine, handicraft production such as bamboo and ramie weaving, and local trading. A boom in local construction is also creating work for laborers, builders, plasterers, and carpenters. Off-farm jobs other than manufacturing fireworks tend to be better paid but more difficult to secure; an exception is gunpowder makers, who receive over 10,000 yuan a year to compensate for the danger in their work.

Households participating in the better local off-farm jobs generally have either local political contacts or a traditional skill passed down through generations. Political contacts are useful for obtaining the special permits needed for profitable activities such as trading in seeds, feed, and fertilizer or acting as a firecracker agent. Many villagers complained to me that the political elite has an unfair monopoly over these opportunities, and some wryly commented that in the household evaluation campaigns, the landlords came first and their cronies second. The tendency for Party households to be awarded 10 stars suggests that they have more of the political, economic, and human resources needed for progressing within the locality. Similarly, an article in *Nongyou ribao* (praising the progressive nature of the Party) states that there are Party members in 94% of the most prosperous households in Xinfeng county.[37] Studies in other parts of China document the division of collective assets and communal businesses during the decollectivization process and note the prominence of local officials and their friends and relatives in assuming control over these resources.[38] In Gaocheng township, cadre-dominated businesses include oil presses, grain processing depots, and shops selling farming supplies. Political contacts facilitate access not only to resources but also to jobs in local administration and enterprises. However, other households are able to participate in local off-farm employment not because of political contacts but because of traditional family skills such as carpentry, Chinese medicine, and ramie weaving.

Unlike households receiving income from local off-farm employment, households benefiting from remittances and urban savings do not require political connections or inherited skills. Migrants tend to work in easy-entry occupations, and neither their socioeconomic standing in the village nor their level of education affect their capacity to find work of some sort.[39] In China (as elsewhere), pioneer migrants establish chain migration connections; as migration from a village takes off, these networks become available to households throughout the village.[40] Once in the city, regardless of whether a village cadre or beggar, the migrant is regarded as an outsider and a bumpkin whose employment options are generally restricted to unskilled tasks.[41] Indeed, a leading cadre from one of the fieldwork villages told me that he returned after a few months in the city convinced that life is better at home. Of course, this is two-edged in that better-connected people may have a better life to which they can return.

The low barriers to migration mean that both poorer and richer households are able to operate outside the limited resource base and distributional mechanisms of their home communities. Households can participate in migration provided they have both sufficient labor and enough money to meet the initial costs of moving. The importance of labor supply is suggested by a study (conducted by the Chinese Ministry of Agriculture) finding that household size and composition directly influence the amount of earnings from migration, but these factors do not affect the amount of income from local sources of off-farm employment.[42] The entry costs of migration include transport fares, permit fees, and the initial expenses of living in the city. Wanzai farmers raise these funds from their land, by assembling firecrackers, or by borrowing money from friends and relatives. Some labor brokers also cover the initial costs of migration in exchange for the first month's wages of the migrant.

Graph 3.4 shows a breakdown of the economic categories of households by their participation in both migration and local off-farm work. Overall, the data suggest that households with more migrants or a local source of off-farm employment are generally better off. When the households without migrants are divided into those *without* local off-farm workers (bar A) and those *with* local off-farm workers (bar B), the households with local off-farm workers appear to be better off than their purely agriculturist counterparts.[43] Households without migrant members but with *local* off-farm workers (bar B) tend to fall into higher economic categories than households with one migrant member and no local off-farm employment (bar C).[44] Households with both one migrant member and involvement in local off-farm work (bar D) appear to be slightly better off than households with only one migrant member and no local off-farm employment (bar C).[45] Households with at least two migrant members fall into

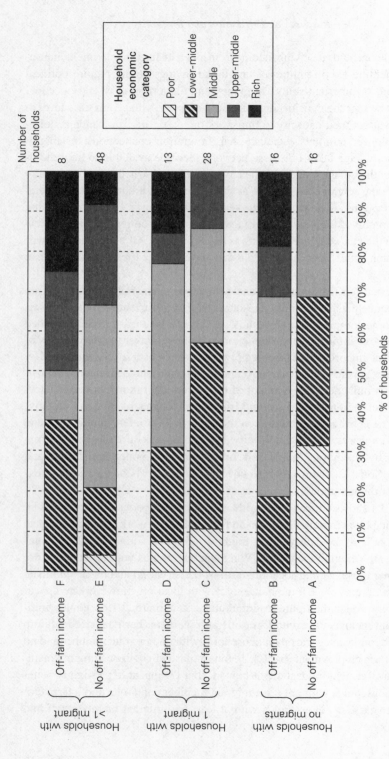

Graph 3.4. Breakdown of economic categories of 129 households by household involvement in migration and local off-farm employment.
Source: Interviews, census sheets, and household evaluation plaques.

the wealthiest economic categories (bar E), and households with the strongest economic position generally have at least two migrant members *and* involvement in local off-farm work (bar F).[46]

Migratory labor creates a view among villagers that everyone is able to pursue material goals through their own efforts. However, as just observed, those households combining migration and off-farm work are best off. Villagers likewise note that, although all households may participate in migration, those that also have political contacts maintain the strongest economic position in the village. An example of this from my fieldwork is the household of a high-ranking village cadre whose two sons were working in Guangdong; the eldest had recently returned to open a shop selling pig feed and fertilizer, goods that require permits. The family has built a grand house, the sons are praised as filial, and the daughter-in-law is regarded as virtuous. Villagers cite the leather shoes that she sent her in-laws from Guangzhou as evidence of her goodness.

Some returned migrants use funds or skills obtained through migration to gain access to off-farm employment locally. There are 38 individuals in the survey who have returned permanently to the village. Ten male permanent returnees found off-farm employment in institutions and businesses in the county seat or township. A further three returnees used their accumulated resources to establish private entrepreneurial sidelines: the agricultural supply shop established by the son of a village cadre, a taxi service based on a small three-wheeled vehicle, and a barber shop set up by a returnee woman who used her urban savings to pay for hairdressing classes in the county seat. The households of these returnees are generally wealthier than those of migrants who return and rely on farming. Nonetheless, some households use savings accumulated from two to four years in the city to invest in agriculture, thereby achieving a middling livelihood. One married couple returned because of the death of grandparents and, unable to migrate because of children, have taken over the farming of a large area of land. Two other households with returnees have also contracted additional land, each farming over 7 mu.

Not all returnees have urban savings that they can use to gain access to local off-farm employment. As might be expected, households with migrants who return owing to ill fortune in the cities tend to be relatively poor. Two men and two women in the survey returned because of illness and have vowed never to go back to the city. Three men and five women returned because "life in the cities is too harsh." The remaining eight permanent returnees are women who have returned owing to pregnancy, the demands of parents or spouses, or the death of an elderly parent who was caring for their children. The economic standing of their households is influenced by the amount of off-farm income generated by other household members via remittances or locally earned money.

In sum, households with off-farm income – either local wages or migrant re-mittances – tend to be better off. Migration reduces the importance of local patronage and family history in allocating off-farm earning opportunities to rural households. This is because barriers to entry into urban labor markets are lower than for entry into local off-farm jobs that generate comparable amounts of cash income.

3.4 MIGRATION, LAND, AND INEQUALITY

The impact of migration on land transfers and on the distribution of income and burdens associated with farming receive in-depth discussion in this chapter be-cause most migrants in China have land at home. This section begins with a brief review of findings from the broader migration literature on the relation-ship between migration, land, and inequality. Following this, I introduce the reader to the land allocation system in Wanzai and demonstrate that land-use rights underpin the economic well-being of migrant households. I also illustrate that, although land is important for the household economy, the migration of Chinese villagers is seldom precipitated by land inequalities and is never moti-vated by the goal of earning money to acquire farmland at home. In this respect, Chinese migrants differ from their counterparts in many other countries. The remainder of this section explores the role of migration in precipitating the reor-ganization of agricultural production through the informal transfer of land-use rights and the implications of migration and land transfers for the redistribution of agricultural incomes, taxes, and labor burdens.

3.4.1 *Review of the Literature on Migration and Land*

Literature concerning the impact of migration on land inequalities is unde-cided. The findings depend on context-specific factors such as the extent of commercialization in agricultural production, indigenous inheritance customs, and local tenure systems. Some studies report that farmers who have little land earn sufficient funds through migration to buy small plots, thereby improv-ing their socioeconomic standing in the village.[47] Other research finds that the richer families, which already have larger landholdings, are best able to use their remittances for acquiring fertile and well-irrigated land, thereby consol-idating their economic strength.[48] Finally, case studies in Mexico reveal that property acquisition by migrants exacerbates inflationary trends in local land markets, undermining the well-being of poorer nonmigrants;[49] in some cases, the increasing consolidation of landholdings (fueled in part by migrant remit-tances) forces even more tenant farmers off the land.

Land acquisition is commonly identified in the literature as a goal of labor mi-gration. This goal is widespread despite differing patterns of land distribution in the villages of origin. Comparative studies of villages in India indicate that in-equalities in land distribution *within* villages are positively correlated with high rates of out-migration among all economic classes, although it tends to be the rich who use their remittances to buy both land and labor-saving equipment.[50] Furthermore, within these villages, shame about landlessness in younger sons prompts the children of the *landed* to migrate.[51] In contrast, research on south-ern Italy in the early 1900s finds that rates of migration were highest in regions where property was most widely distributed, because the availability of land for purchase created incentives for people to emigrate and remit money for ac-quiring land. Return migration to these areas was particularly high, sometimes equivalent to two thirds of the original outflow.[52] As a final example, research in Egypt indicates that – owing to the self-sustaining momentum of migration and the widespread availability of migration opportunities – the distribution of land does not determine the propensity to migrate, but purchasing land none-theless remains a priority goal for poorer farming households.[53]

Migration precipitates a redistribution not only of land but also of the inputs and outputs associated with the land. Inputs include resources such as labor, fertilizer, pesticides, and equipment; outputs include grain and crops. Migra-tion removes labor from households but mitigates this by providing cash that can be used to purchase labor, machines, and inputs. The well-being of those who rely solely on the land for their livelihoods is determined by the reorgani-zation of agricultural production triggered by migration. Changes observed in various parts of the developing world include increased mechanization, switch-ing to less labor-intensive crops, and hiring labor.[54]

The literature presents contradictory evidence about the capacity of migrant and returnee households to progress beyond their neighbors by investing their remittances in farming innovations. Some studies find that neither remittances nor returnees play a significant role in modernizing agriculture.[55] Others docu-ment the positive impact of migrant money and innovation on the mechanization of farming, the adoption of high-yielding grain varieties, and the introduction of new crops.[56] Finally, as mentioned in Chapter 1, some scholars contend that remittances provide insurance that enables farming households to experiment with new crops and agricultural techniques.[57]

3.4.2 *Migration and Land Distribution in Wanzai*

In China, most migrants have access to land in their villages, and the manda-tory purchase quotas of grain (under the household responsibility system) mean that it is difficult for rural households to completely abandon agriculture.[58] Moreover, although generally dissatisfied with low prices for agricultural pro-duce and the rising costs of farm inputs, most households wish to retain their land-use rights because they provide a basis for diversifying their livelihoods and insurance in the event of migrant failure.[59]

The average land allocations for the surveyed *zu* are typical for the province, where the average is 0.8 mu, but are below the national average of 1.2 mu.[60] The average per-capita allocations of arable land in the three *zu* are 1.12 mu, 0.9 mu, and 0.7 mu. These land allocations include around 0.2 mu of dry land, which is vital for generating cash income. Farmed mainly by the women, this land produces the bok choy and sweet potatoes needed for pig fodder: a household can earn 500 yuan a year by fattening two pigs. The dry land also provides vegetables for household consumption. The remainder of the land is paddy – used for growing grain for both subsistence and sale at market and for cultivating some rape in winter. According to farmers, as the land is well irrigated, the contribution of the paddy to the economic standing of a household is determined mainly by the input of fertilizer and pesticide.

Although land is fundamental to the economic security of rural households in Qifeng and Tuanjie, there is no statistical evidence to suggest that smaller allocations of land cause out-migration at the *village* level: regression of the data in Graph 3.5 finds that there is no significant relationship between the size of the landholdings and the proportion of labor that has migrated from a village group. This may be because migration relies on the feedback of information from previous migrants, which over time becomes more influential than land distribution in propelling migration.

Anecdotal evidence, however, shows that in certain circumstances members of households are forced to migrate because of a land shortage. Within a *zu,* land is allocated to a household according to its size, yet two factors undermine the equality of distribution. First, some households have their land requisitioned. For example, a few Qifeng households reported losing over a mu of paddy with the building of a new school in 1991. In some parts of China, households on the outskirts of towns have their land requisitioned for construction, making them "farmers without land." For instance, when an official accompanied me to his village near Yudu county seat, farmers asked him about compensation for land requisitioned the year before. They said that, with only 0.3–0.4 mu remaining, there was no choice but for household members to migrate. In some Jiangxi villages, households from weaker families may have their land taken over by stronger family groups. Alternatively, migrants from weaker families may return to find that stronger families have claimed their land, so they are forced to re-migrate to the cities or move to another village that has fellow group members who will allocate land to them.

Second, to encourage farmers to have faith in the security of their tenure and to invest in agriculture, village committees have minimized the frequency of readjustments in land allocations: death does not immediately reduce the area of land

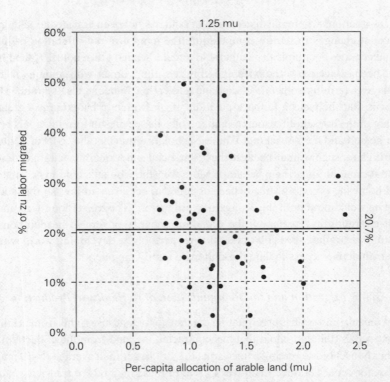

Graph 3.5. Per-capita allocation of land within the *zu* in Qifeng and Tuanjie villages, and percentage of labor that has migrated from the *zu*.

contracted by a household, nor does marriage or the birth of a child increase it. The group leader decides when to adjust land distribution: in one *zu*, adjustments were carried out three years ago; in another *zu*, ten years ago.[61] In my Wanzai survey there are eight instances in which the new members of a household (wives and/or children) have not been allocated land. In one case, a widow who remarried moved to her husband's village and brought two children with her, adding a burden of three landless people to the household. They have lived in hardship for many years, though two household members migrated as soon as they could.

Unlike rural households in other parts of the world, households in Jiangxi with little land do not try to change their situation by using remittances to buy land. This is because, under the present contract system, land-use rights cannot be bought or sold. Nor are land leases completely secure. Two Jiangxi migrants told me that they had considered leasing large areas of hill land from the local government for specialized agricultural production but feared that the contract might be terminated prematurely once they had invested in the seedlings and prepared the soil.

In situations where the distribution of land has not been adjusted to take into account changes in family composition, the long-term out-migration of husbands creates economically vulnerable female-headed households. If land has not been allocated to the wife and children, the woman who remains in the village is farming someone else's land and eating someone else's grain. This means that she lacks a fallback position[62] from which to bargain for a greater share of the household resources and to voice her desires in forming goals both for herself and her household. Chinese scholars argue that the costs of divorce are high for such women because they face social and economic marginalization in the event of a marriage breakup. Moreover, the woman's land in her maternal home has probably already been assigned to her sister-in-law, so she would not be welcome should she decide to return there.[63] The role of long-term male out-migration in threatening the economic security of female-headed households has similarly been observed in other parts of the developing world where women derive access to land through male family members.[64]

3.4.3 *Migration and the Reorganization of Agricultural Production*

In Wanzai, migration is precipitating the transfer of land-use rights from original contractors (the household that has contracted the land from the collective) to other households, creating some farms that are larger than average (5–10 mu).[‡] Transfer occurs in three main ways. Two of these methods of transfer, *zhuanbao* and *zhuanrang,* are noteworthy in that they do not involve the payment of rent, and the latter method sometimes even involves the payment of negative rent. *Zhuanbao* occurs when land-use rights are transferred from the original contractor to a person who undertakes all the tax burdens associated with farming the land as well as completing the grain production quota. *Zhuanrang* is a situation in which the original contractor gives land-use rights to friends or relatives. Sometimes this involves payment to the original contractor. In Wanzai, where opportunities for local off-farm employment are limited, villagers are generally willing to pay for better-quality land. If the land is middling, migrants pay others to relieve them of the land and meet the production quotas, because they will be fined if the land is left barren. Responsibility for taxes varies. The final way, *chuzu,* involves the original contractor renting out land-use rights to the tenant. The original contractor pays the taxes and completes the grain production quota. The tenant pays rent in kind, 150–200 kilograms

---

[‡] The average amount of land farmed by a household in this survey is 3.98 mu. This approaches the national average allocation of arable land to a household, which is 4 mu. See Xing Ying, "The joy and worry of peasant income," p. 51.

of grain or 200 yuan cash per mu: nearly two thirds of the sixteen tenant households in my survey pay their rent in grain.

Graph 3.6 shows the economic categories of households according to the amount of land that they actually farm, taking into account transfers: this may differ from the amount of land initially contracted by the household from the collective. Regression analysis on the raw data presented in the graph finds that there is no significant relationship between the area of land that a household farms and the economic category of the household.[65] However, eyeballing the graph indicates that, within the 5–7-mu bracket, there are fewer households in the poor and lower-middle economic categories.[66] It is difficult to gauge the impact that the amount of land cultivated by a household has on its economic standing, because the amount of land initially contracted by a household is based on the number of people in that household. So, unless land has been transferred, the amount of land farmed is just a proxy for household composition: of the 50 households with at least 5 mu of land, 66% have at least three laborers, 42% have at least four laborers, and 28% have at least five laborers. Almost half (48%) have at least two migrant members. However, 30% of the households farming at least 5 mu cultivate larger areas by taking over the farming of the plots of absentees. Moreover, nine of the ten households farming over 7 mu work the land of absentees.

Both poor and rich households transfer their land-use rights to other households, leaving themselves with only small plots to farm. In my survey, the majority of the 29 households that have transferred their land-use rights to others have deployed either part or all of their adult labor in the cities. The poorer households tend to be those where only the infirm or elderly remain at home and where remittances are insufficient to hire labor or purchase farm inputs. The richer households in this group are those that are able to relinquish the land because they earn enough income from other sources. Here, I echo the view of McKinley that, in China, landlessness does not necessarily "reflect restricted opportunities or forced decline into poverty as it does in so many other developing countries."[67]

In 1997 farmers informed me that, once agricultural expenses had been deducted, they could earn a net income of around 2,000 yuan for double cropping an extra 3–4 mu of land. At the time of fieldwork, this sum approached the annual average amount of remittances from one migrant. However, two to three years later, in 2000, the central government removed subsidies for purchasing early rice in preparation for China's entry into the Word Trade Organization. On my return visit to Qifeng in December 2000, the deputy secretary told me that, because the price for the early rice had plummeted by half, some farmers had headed for the cities without even sowing a winter crop. Out of a total of

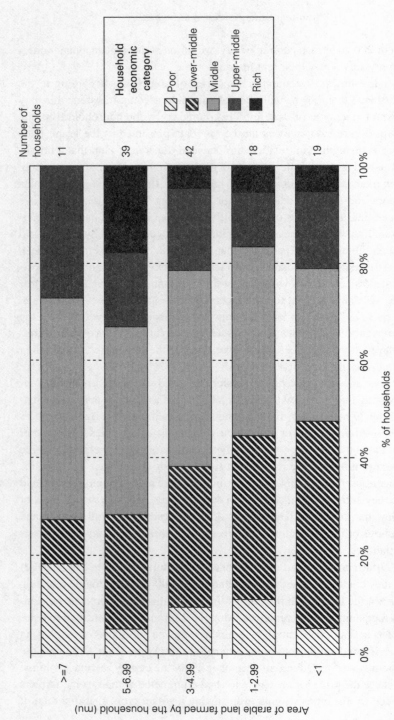

Graph 3.6. Breakdown of economic categories of 129 households by area of arable land farmed by household. *Source:* Interviews.

3,724 mu of arable land, 20 mu's worth had been left barren, which was the first time that farmland in the village had ever been abandoned. The fall in grain prices in the year 2000 is likely to reduce the incentives for villagers to farm transferred land.

Migration reduces the person-to-land ratio within families, and at the time of my fieldwork this often enabled family members who remained at home to generate extra income from the absentees' land. So, for example, some households rented out the absentees' land. Other households used remittances to buy farm inputs and cultivate the extra land themselves. In 1997, a household with two migrant members was able to earn a gross income of 800 yuan by farming the absentees' land and selling their food allocations. For example, Mr. Wu received a pension from the township pottery factory, and his wife earned a wage as a primary school teacher. Their four sons were married and had all migrated with their spouses, leaving their father to manage their land. Mr. Wu used his off-farm income and remittances to hire labor and purchase inputs for farming 3 mu of land. He transferred the remaining 4 mu to other households, which paid him 150 kilograms of unhusked grain per mu.[68] The rent payments provided for the subsistence of the elderly couple, and any surplus grain generated cash.

However, not all elderly parents are as fortunate as Mr. Wu. In some instances, the migrants do not permit their kin to control either the land or any income it generates. Rather, they act as absentee landlords and claim the rent payments for themselves. These adult migrants may give some or all of the rental income to support elderly parents who are caring for their children. This enables the migrants to fulfill their obligation to ensure the material well-being of kin in the village while drawing less on their urban earnings.

Chinese policy documents state optimistically that land transfers allow land to become concentrated in the hands of the most capable farmers.[69] In practice, demographic composition rather than aptitude determines who farms. Those who farm extra land tend to be either couples with school-age children who feel that they cannot migrate or the elderly with migrant children. These people vary considerably in terms of their energy and aptitude for farming and in their capacity to invest material resources in the land. Furthermore, as noted by policy-makers, informal land transfers compound the problem of scattered farm plots, limiting the profitability of farming for those who remain at home.[70]

In a bid to improve the efficiency of the land transfer system and encourage professional farmers to cultivate larger areas of land, local governments in certain Jiangxi counties experiencing high levels of out-migration have experimented with the introduction of the "two land system" (*liang tian zhi*).[71] Each person is allocated subsistence land (*kouliang tian*), 0.4–0.5 mu, and the remaining plots are grouped together and contracted out to individuals, households, or cooperatives. Officials in some areas have forcibly introduced the system and instituted land contract fees in excess of 50 yuan per mu, aggravating the burden on farmers. The two-land system has been criticized by the central government because introducing a new system undermines the credibility of the state promise that the household contract responsibility system is to remain stable for thirty years.[72] Other publications have praised the system for modernizing farming and encouraging returnee farmers to invest in agriculture.[73] In Jiangxi, the two-land system has been banned except in circumstances where farmers pursue this system through their own initiative.

3.4.4 *Migration, Land, and the Distribution of Burdens*

Households concentrating their productive resources in farming tend to bear a heavier tax burden than those deriving income from migration or local off-farm employment. Many taxes and fees are levied on the basis of land area, where the per-mu rate is set according to the village's average per-capita income (including remittances) for the previous year. This disadvantages those households that rely solely on agriculture, because migration causes an increase in their tax rate yet they do not benefit from remittances. A central government decree stipulates that the average tax burden of villagers must not exceed 5% of the per-capita income of the village for the previous year.[74] Despite this attempt to protect farmers from becoming overburdened, migration increases the amount of tax that can be legally levied.

Regardless of whether land is transferred between households within the same family or between unrelated households, there is often tension because it is not clear who is responsible for the taxes and levies. Parents often farm the land of their married adult children who are working in the cities, and brothers farm the land of their migrant siblings. Some of these farmers feel displeased at migrants who earn money for themselves in the city but refuse to pay the land taxes. As an example, an elderly widow whose three sons are migrants has sublet her 3 mu of land to three different households. She explained: "After they have been given such good land, two of them ... ask[ed] me to pay the 20 yuan per mu levy for the education fund. My kids finished middle school years ago."[75]

When collecting the village tax and other levies, cadres might well be informed by the householder that "[t]his is not for me to pay. It is the responsibility of my [migrant] son. I am so poor. He never sends any money. Go and see if *you* can get money from him."[76]

Another burden that falls disproportionately on the shoulders of those who remain on the land is the twenty days of labor requisitioned from households on an annual basis for projects such as repairing irrigation channels. Migrant households escape this obligation by paying 6 yuan per day as a substitute for their labor. One father, complaining about his undutiful son, told me: "The state tax, the village tax, the fertilizer, he leaves it all to me. And the labor contribution, well there is only me to do it ...."[77]

In the seven villages that I visited in different parts of Jiangxi, cadres commonly identified the collection of fees and the mobilization of labor for public works as the tasks that, together with family planning, have become increasingly difficult since the onset of large-scale out-migration.[78] In some villages, the high level of out-migration means that a per-mu system of appropriating levies is increasingly perceived as unfair and unworkable. This has prompted some local governments to start exacting levies on a per-capita basis,[79] a system that could well produce its own inequities.

3.4.5 *Remittances and Farming*

Most remittances are directed toward "nonproductive" goals such as building a house or buying commodities, but in some cases remittances also enhance the capacity of a household to generate income from the land. Chinese policymakers recommend that measures be taken to encourage the investment of remittances in agricultural production. At a national summit on migration, local leaders were advised to guide the use of remittances toward agricultural development.[80] Other articles optimistically proclaim that migrants no longer spend their money on consumer durables and instead bring home books on agricultural techniques.[81] They also advocate that migrant worker associations be established in the destination areas to coordinate the accumulation of relief funds and money for investment in agricultural production in the home villages.[82] In particular, local governments hope that the money that migrants bring back with them or send to their families over the Spring Festival holiday period will be used to purchase fertilizer and seed for planting the land in early March.[83] According to Wanzai farmers, an optimal yield requires an annual expenditure of 130 yuan per mu for fertilizer and a further 20 yuan for pesticide. Prices for farm inputs are rising rapidly, increasing the need for cash within the farming economy.

In order to study the impact of migration and remittances on the agricultural productivity of households, I asked village accountants in Qifeng and Tuanjie to provide information on the grain yields and the value of pigs for fifteen households. The accountant in Qifeng contributed data on twenty households,

Table 3.2. *Value of per-mu grain yields and pig production for 31 households*

Type of household	Number of households	Average yields per mu (kg) [Rank]	Average value of pigs (yuan) [Rank]
Returnee	2	590 [1]	2,750 [1]
Local off-farm, no migrants	5	560 [2]	1,680 [2]
More than 1 migrant	11	540 [3]	1,660 [3]
Seasonal[a]	1	510 [4]	1,300 [6]
1 migrant	6	500 [5]	1,320 [5]
Agriculture only	6	450 [6]	1,420 [4]

Note: Per-mu grain yields for 1996 should normally have reached at least 650 kg. The low crop yields are the result of crop disease in 1996. There is also the possibility of underreporting. This does not affect the conclusion, because I am comparing households within the same place and the same year using the same reporting method.
[a] Works in the city for three months every winter.

and the accountant in Tuanjie provided information on eleven. In gathering this material, I requested that the accountants select both migrant and nonmigrant households with varying standards of living.[84] Table 3.2 shows the ranking of different household types according to the average per-mu grain yields for two harvests in 1996 and the value of the pigs raised in that year.

Only tentative interpretations about the impact of migration on agricultural production can be made on the basis of this small sample. Nonetheless, in Table 3.2 at least, the strongest agricultural performers are returnee households, followed by households that are involved in local off-farm activities. In the two returnee households in Table 3.2, married couples have spent over two years in the city and have accumulated substantial funds prior to their return. One of these households has contracted an additional 3 mu of land, farming a total of 7.5 mu.[85] Households in the table that are involved in local off-farm employment have higher per-mu grain yields and greater values for pig production than households currently receiving remittances. An explanation for the strength of returnee and "local off-farm worker" households over migrant households might be that the former have more money to invest in production, and family members may be more aware of the full extent of locally earned income than of urban wages. Nonetheless, the higher values for agricultural production in households with at least two migrant members suggest that remittances are still an important source of investment for farming.

Even among households with low grain yields, remittances play an important role in financing production. The main survey of 102 migrant households shows that, prior to their participation in migration, fourteen of these households borrowed fertilizer from neighbors and made repayments in grain after the harvest – but did not need to do this after migration. This suggests that migration enables poorer households to generate cash, which substitutes for the limited availability of micro-credit and so provides funds for fertilizer and pesticide. My material on land transfers also suggests that remittances provide the cash inputs needed for farming absentees' plots. Out of the 27 households cultivating extra land, over three quarters have either an adult child migrant with school-age siblings or returnee members; these households have access to either remittances or the savings brought home by the returnees.

Another reason for the economic advantage seen in Table 3.2 of the households with returnee members or local off-farm workers might be that they have more labor present in the village. In the households with at least two migrants, the migrated members tend to be adult children and so the labor of a parent couple remains in the village. However, in three of the six households in Table 3.2 that have only one migrant, a husband (rather than an adult child) works in the city. In each of these three cases, the value of pig production is less than 1,100 yuan. This is because raising pigs is a labor-intensive task, and the wives who remain in the village are too overworked to devote their labor to sideline activities.

Few of the 102 migrant households in my main survey use their remittances to hire labor in response to a labor shortage. The 22 households that did report hiring labor generally employed cheaper labor from nearby villages. In Tuanjie, for example, labor is hired from the poorer neighboring mountain village of Guyuan. The reluctance to hire fellow villagers and the predominance of land transfers as a way of coping with labor shortages mean that only four people in my survey earn money by hiring out their labor.

The gender of the spouse who remains in the village has important implications for a household's use of remittances for hiring labor. Some rural households see it as a more profitable deployment of household labor and income if the wife migrates and the husband farms. Cultural values designate plowing as a male task; hence, in the absence of a man, money must be used to hire farm labor. Conversely, some households justify the husband migrating because staying at home and looking after the children is considered a female task. I suggested to a woman's cadre that – just as the women who are left behind can hire men to plow – the men left behind could hire women to cook, clean, and take care of the children. Her retort was: "But that would be the same as taking a concubine!"[86] Usually, the men struggle with the extra burden or female relatives help out with child care.

3.4.6 *Migration and Agricultural Innovation*

My fieldwork in Wanzai found no evidence of returnee or migrant households advancing themselves ahead of other households through farming innovations. Owing to the hilly terrain, the small size of plots, and the scattered distribution of the land farmed by a single household, no one in my fieldwork villages has invested in a tractor, and all but the very poorest of the farming households own a draught animal for plowing. In discussions with interviewees about the use of remittances for agricultural investment, respondents never mentioned tube wells or irrigation pumps, though the potential for remittances to improve irrigation is a question that demands further research. It is possible that insecurity surrounding the contract system underpins a general reluctance among farmers to invest substantially in the land.

In contrast, in Songpu township (Fengxin county), the investment of remittances in farming technology and services has been coordinated by the local state. The migrants from Songpu are traders who tend to leave their villages as entire households, which means that – unlike places where most migrants work in factories – few family members remain on the land. In response to the shortfall in labor and the new availability of capital for investment in mechanization, the Songpu township government has established a mechanized farming service collective. The migrant households pay the collective to plow and even harvest their land, with wives shuttling back from Shanghai at periodic intervals to carry out supplementary farming tasks at home. Providing mechanized farming services in Songpu is made easy by the fact that the township is situated on a flat plain.

Although not investing directly in agriculture, some better-off households in Qifeng and Tuanjie have invested in subsidiary enterprises such as village oil presses and threshing machines that are available to all villagers for a small fee. But these small processing businesses existed in the villages during the collective era and are not recent innovations.

However, by December 2000 many farming households in Wanzai had invested in a *choushuiji*: a small diesel-powered machine that can be attached to a threshing machine to substitute for footpower when harvesting in the fields and that can also be used to pump water. Village cadres said that people had begun buying these machines the previous year. Additionally, some households had bought plows with metal frames rather than the wooden plows that I watched the village carpenter fashioning in his client's house only three years earlier. This pace of technological change in quite rapid, and it is likely that investment in such innovations will reduce the labor intensity of farming, releasing more labor from the land.

The potential for migrant households to progress beyond their neighbors through cropping innovation is constrained by the local government's control over most facets of agricultural production and its highly effective and accessible extension services. Crops or animals falling outside the local state's agricultural plan are banned. Farmers who contravene these rules face steep fines and have the offending crop or animal removed by township inspection teams. In Tuanjie in 1997, township cadres descended to kill chickens (*caoji* – wild grass chicken) that were not of the approved breed (*huangshanji* – golden mountain chicken), so that villagers would not be wasting resources by raising an inferior type of poultry. The capacity of returnees to outpace their neighbors in agricultural terms is also limited by the role of the government extension service in ensuring that the more advanced technologies and inputs are available to most households. Thus, all seeds are distributed through state-approved outlets in order to guarantee their quality. In Wanzai, high-yielding varieties were introduced in the early 1980s. In April 1997, the local state introduced a less labor-intensive variety of rice: the seedlings are broadcast rather than transplanted in rows. Every evening the county television station shows programs publicizing new farming techniques and instructing farmers in the tasks appropriate for the season. Moreover, at crucial farming periods, cadres from the township and county levels supervise farm work in the villages.

The scope for returnees and migrants in Wanzai to innovate in agriculture may have expanded since the time of my fieldwork. This is because there have been growing calls from the central state since the late 1990s for local cadres to move away from "administrative measures" (*xingzheng cuoshi*) whereby rural producers are told what they must do. Instead, cadres are urged to use "demonstration measures" (*shifan cuoshi*). This involves supporting a handful of progressive households in their efforts to cultivate new crops or raise new varieties of livestock, then giving technical and material support to other households that choose to emulate these torchbearers. In autumn 2000, some farmers in Wanzai and other counties told me that township cadres were increasingly working in this manner.

3.5 CONCLUSION

Research in rural Wanzai suggests that migration influences resource distribution and inequality in three main ways. First, migration represents an extension of households' existing strategies for obtaining resources, and it feeds into existing intrafamily struggles over the distribution of resources and burdens. Second, migration enables rural households to operate outside the social and political distributional mechanisms of the home area. Finally, migration precipitates land transfers and a redistribution of the resources and burdens that are associated with cultivating the land. The cumulative impact of migration is therefore a redistribution of resources within households, among households, and between rural society and the local political elite.

Migration strategies are influenced by the developmental cycle of the household, and the capacity of households to obtain resources through migration depends very much on their labor supply. Although remittances alleviate the hardship of many of the poorest households and facilitate the improvement of rural livelihoods in general, households may nevertheless be net losers from migration for two reasons. First, not all households benefit from their involvement in migration because various factors (including chance, unobservable aptitude, and control over resources prior to migration) mean that some migrants fail to earn money in the cities. Second, households may lose out because of inequalities in the redistribution of resources and burdens precipitated by the migration strategies of their families. For example, households consisting of elderly couples or a spouse left at home with children sometimes incur an increased work burden but do not necessarily benefit from the resources generated by migration. This has led to several instances of villagers – the elderly in particular – migrating themselves in revolt against family members who neglect the traditional values of filial piety and collective welfare.

The distribution of resources within households and between the households of the same family is characterized by tension and conflict, and these conflicts become acute as migration generates new resources and new burdens. Individuals employ strategies to enhance their control over family resources and avoid the claims of other family members on these resources. Such strategies involve subterfuge and placing money in safe locations. For these people, migration is a way of operating outside the distributional mechanisms of the family or household to obtain sufficient resources for achieving the goal of personal economic security.

The extent of a household's involvement in migration is constrained only by household composition, whereas local off-farm employment generally requires local political contacts or inherited family skills. By enabling people to operate outside the political networks of village society, migration enables more households to obtain more resources.

Finally, migration precipitates land transfers and a redistribution of the incomes and burdens associated with agriculture. Large households enjoy a double advantage: a larger land allocation and more potential migrants. Migration also enhances the profits derived from the land because the subsistence grain of the absentees can be sold or the land of migrants can be rented out to other households. In Wanzai, households are responding to the out-migration of labor by arranging informal transfers of land with other households. By cultivating absentees' land, some rural producers increase their income by an amount approximately equivalent to the average annual sum of remittances from one migrant. However, existing methods of taxation mean that, compared with migrant households, farming households bear a disproportionate amount of the burden of levies and labor requisitions. Also, the fall in grain prices in 2000 may make farmers see land as more of a burden than a resource, discouraging future land transfers.

4

Migration, Remittances, and Goals

THIS chapter examines the ways in which villagers in Wanzai use the resources generated by migration to achieve goals such as improving their
material well-being and participating more fully in the social life of both the
village and the city. The analysis focuses on the spending patterns of rural
producers in terms of the most common uses of remittances in the developing world: education, life-cycle goals (such as house building and marriage),
and consumer goods.[1] Scholars have widely observed the tendency for villagers to allocate a large portion of remittances and urban savings toward these
three "nonproductive" goals while directing a comparatively small proportion
of urban funds toward "productive" investment in agriculture and business.[2] As
discussed in Chapter 1, there is much scholarly debate about the implications
of this aspect of remittance usage for development in the origin areas.[3]

Structuralist and modernization approaches evaluate the impact of remittance
usage on rural development in different ways, and here I offer crude simplifica-
tions of these two perspectives. For structuralists, rural dwellers are malleable
subjects whose values, life goals, and spending activities are manipulated by
powerful images of urban lifestyles displayed on billboards and in shop windows. "Taste transfer" is said to increase the dependency of traditional populations on imported items, undermining the market for indigenously produced
goods.[4] According to structuralists, the inculcation of urban tastes molds migrants into disciplined workers who are dependent on wages for satisfying their
new consumer desires. Despite a proletarianization in outlook, these migrants
retain their links with the countryside – undermining their potential to organize
in protest against low pay – so circulation is maintained.[5] New values of selfish
individualism fostered through urban exposure are said to erode traditional rural
values of collective welfare, adversely affecting the well-being of other household members who rely on remittances for meeting basic needs and purchasing
agricultural inputs.[6] Even education, which could be considered as an investment in socially productive capital, is viewed by some scholars as often consti-
tuting a private form of investment. This is because, in obtaining paper qualifications, the prospects and material gains of the qualifiers increase by the same
amount that the prospects and material gains of the nonqualifiers decrease.[7]

On the other hand, modernization theorists equate the diffusion of cash and modern commodities into the backward rural milieu with progress, enlightenment, and urbanism.[8] Various studies evaluate positively the demonstration effect of migrants who return for visits to their natal villages wearing stylish urban clothes and sporting fashionable commodities.[9] Exposure to modern urban values is said to motivate villagers to break through their accommodation to poverty.[10] Moreover, some scholars suggest that the expenditure of remittances on such consumption items as food, housing, and education might enhance rural productivity by improving the quality of household labor.[11]

Unlike the perspectives just outlined, this chapter neither laments nor celebrates the role of migration in diffusing cash and commodities among a passive rural populace. Nor does it see rural spending patterns as being determined by macro-level processes. Rather, this chapter focuses on the active role of social actors in acquiring the material and cultural resources required for attaining goals.[12] As discussed in Chapter 1, these goals include meeting basic physical needs (such as warmth and nourishment) as well as socially oriented goals that are similarly experienced by all social actors as basic needs – for example, maintaining self-respect and participating in community activities.[13]

In rural Wanzai, migration is changing the amount of resources required by villagers to attain their goals. This is because rural spending patterns are shaped through interactions between (a) values and social practices that are internal to the village and (b) resources that are generated from outside of it. As an example, rural households in Wanzai that build new houses and display modern commodities are able to obtain better access to other resources that are distributed through the political networks of village society. Moreover, by meeting obligations to family members in the village and attaining life-cycle goals, migrants gain a respect for their material achievements that is denied them in the cities. The experience of migration also shapes the new life goals formed by rural people – in particular, those of becoming educated or being able to visit people in far-off localities.

Although migration is important for introducing new commodities and shaping new consumer goals among villagers, modern urban commodities do not automatically bring modern values that transform village society. Rather, social actors adapt these commodities within the village to attain livelihood goals specific to their socioeconomic environment.[14] Some poor households in Wanzai pin plastic sheets at their windows to stop drafts and mosquitoes, achieving a more comfortable place to live. They are able to do so because of modernization, but this does not make them "modern." Indeed, Hugo points out that – although some returned migrants may be more educated and hold more modern values than other villagers – urban earnings may actually hinder change by financing forms of expenditure that reinforce traditional values, traditional

Young migrants dressed in their city clothes returning for Spring Festival, Qifeng village.

power structures, and customary means of status attainment.[15] My research in Wanzai shows that migration and remittances are linked with change, though not necessarily through the diffusion of modernity. Rather, the values internal to rural society that inform rural spending practices are continually reinvented to suit emerging social and economic contingencies,[16] and many of these contingencies are precipitated by migration.

I conducted a survey into priority areas of remittance spending among 102 migrant households. The answers were unguided and all responses offered by each informant were recorded. Out of a total of 190 responses, 24% identified house building as the priority area of remittance usage, followed by education and raising children, accounting for 13% of responses. The breakdown of responses for other areas of remittance usage are as follows: daily livelihood goods (food, clothes, provisions, coal), 14%; farm inputs, 12%; repaying debts, 10%; savings, 8%; marriage, 8%; hiring labor, 7%; investment in business, 2%; paying fines, 1%. In two categories of responses, "repaying debts" and "savings," interviewees generally identified marriage and house building as the main end uses of this money. Moreover, the "marriage" and "daily livelihood goods" categories of remittance usage include consumer durables such as clothes and appliances. I have no way of confirming how people actually spend their money in practice. Nonetheless, the anecdotes of villagers and the visual evidence of house building and new commodities in the village are consistent with the statements of migrant households identifying these two areas as spending priorities.

Some scholars have argued that, by directing resources toward goals such as education, building a house, and marriage, the family benefits collectively and this mitigates the intrahousehold tensions engendered by expenditure on goals of a more individual nature.[17] In reality there is a fine balance, and migrants are caught among their obligations to family in the village, their need to prepare for setting up their own households, and their personal desires to purchase modern commodities. This suggests a tension between the individual purchase of modern consumer goods, on the one hand, and more traditional forms of expenditure (involving obligations to the rural family and life-cycle goals) on the other. Tensions over claims on resources are a persistent feature of family dynamics throughout the world,[18] and these tensions become more acute when new resources, new household earners, new values, and new life goals are generated through the migration process.

With regard to the spending practices of rural migrant households in China, there is nothing that limits the individual to purchasing only new commodities or that restricts the rural family to expenditure on traditional goals. Instead there is a synthesis of both modern and traditional goals as well as considerable overlap between individual and family-based expenditure. As an example of this synthesis, modern consumer durables are coveted by brides as part of their personal dowries and also by villagers as part of their betrothal gifts and house decorations. As another example, although migrants may devote urban savings toward their personal education, their end goal may be to find a better job so that they can contribute more to the future welfare of the rural household. The following discussion examines the extent to which migration enables villagers to attain goals in a social world where the village and the city are increasingly intertwined.

4.1 EDUCATION

Migration increases the resources available to pay for education but has contradictory effects on the demand for education. Other socioeconomic influences are also important in shaping the education goals of villagers and their capacity to attain these goals. One such influence is the state, which has expended considerable effort in ensuring that children receive an education and that future generations feature high-quality laborers who are able to contribute to national modernization and live contented lives. For instance, during the household evaluation campaigns in Wanzai, cadres arranged for Operation Hope funds to sponsor the schooling of poor children, with cadres themselves donating money to the charity. Other influences that may generate either positive or negative attitudes toward education include existing cultural values, the economic prosperity and increased labor demands resulting from economic liberalization, and new values inculcated via television. Migration interacts with these and other socioeconomic influences in ways that are not always observable, giving rise to contradictory forces that simultaneously depress and stimulate spending on education. This section explores the contradictory impact of migration on education.

Beginning with the negative impact of migration on education, decades of political intervention both during and after the Maoist period have served to restrict the life expectations of farmers to unskilled work. The two sons of a woman in Tuanjie, now aged 26 and 30, were the first from Gaocheng township ever to attend university. Both sons won scholarships to study at the county middle school – rather than at the township middle school, from where their chances for university entrance were negligible. During the years that the family was scrimping for the living expenses and books for their sons, their neighbors would ridicule them: "How do they expect to plow the land with fountain pens?" Nowadays, owing to the ease of entry into unskilled city jobs, many rural parents continue to hold the view that education is a futile goal; they believe that, as farmers, their children are born to earn their living through the sweat of their labor. Parents see even less value in investing in the education of daughters, because girls marry into another family. One girl informed me that her father had withdrawn her from school when she was 14 and instructed her to assemble firecrackers at home until the following year, when she would be old enough to go to Guangzhou. Farmers tend to resent school fees, considering them as part of government-imposed burdens rather than as an item of spending.[19] In Tuanjie village, annual costs for tuition and school meals amount to 500 yuan for a primary-school student and 1,200 yuan for a lower middle–school student, which is a significant burden considering that average per-capita income for the villagers in the study is approximately 1,800 yuan.

Aware of their peripheral status in urban labor markets, many middle-school students, like their parents, conclude that an additional one or two years of schooling makes little difference to their job prospects and so head for the cities without graduating. A journalist at the *Jiangxi Daily* visited ten primary schools in Ganzhou prefecture and surveyed over 1,000 students. He discovered that more than 30% of the students had migrant parents. The article refers to a 15-year-old boy whose parents have been working in Guangdong for four years. The boy does not wish to attend school because he plans to follow in the footsteps of his father, who has never studied but nonetheless earns lots of money. The journalist laments that "this kind of situation is by no means an exception."[20]

The informal employment introductions that characterize chain migration mean that even the youngest and oldest villagers can obtain factory employment. Rural workers are employed precisely because they perform unskilled tasks. Chinese industry is characterized more by intensive labor than by sophisticated technology and therefore requires large numbers of itinerant wage laborers. This is because, as discussed in Chapter 1, industries that use primitive technology do not require a stable and skilled labor force. Moreover, case studies in other developing countries suggest that Todaro's assertion – that rural migrants can move from menial work into higher-skilled and better-paid jobs – does not correspond with the experience of most migrants, who must contend with labor markets segmented into different jobs for natives and outsiders.[21]

Several studies on migration in China suggest that, contrary to findings in other parts of the world, educational attainment is not a characteristic of those who are able to find some form of nonagricultural employment outside the village.[22] These scholars suggest that the Cultural Revolution cut off educational opportunities for a decade, so that the selectivity of migration may be as much an effect of generation as of education.[23] Graph 4.1 (see page 98) shows the education levels of individuals aged 15 years and over from the 138 households in my survey. Although it supports the orthodox position in the broader migration literature that migrants tend to be more educated than their nonmigrant counterparts,[24] the difference in levels of education between the migrants and nonmigrants is not huge: over 85% of individuals in both the migrant and

Attempt of local cadres in Tuanjie to discourage truancy, (i): "It is forbidden to
recruit child laborers, protect the right of minors to be educated!"

nonmigrant groups are educated to at least the primary level, and over 35%
of individuals in both the migrant and nonmigrant groups are educated to the
lower middle–school level.

The local state in Wanzai has instigated measures to try to counter the outflow
of ungraduated middle-school students to the urban factories. Poor families are
permitted to pay school fees in installments and schools are urged to waive the
fees of impoverished households. Teachers must notify village leaders of truancy, and cadres visit families to carry out "persuasion" work. Schools are also
required to send telegrams in order to track down students who have migrated
to work in the city.[25] However, village cadres told me that when they go to persuade a student to stay in school, the parents and the student nod politely and
yet – on the following day – the student is on the bus to Guangdong. A newspaper letter from a township official in Wanzai county states the following:

> The Spring Festival has just passed and all areas have again witnessed the
> exodus to the cities. Lingdong township has a population of only 11,000
> and by 15 February over 20% of the total population had left. But how
> many children are going to work in the cities? On the morning of 15 Feb-
> ruary I found that there were six boys aged between 13 and 15 on board
> a minibus hired by male migrants. All levels of government should take
> measures to prevent child labor migration.[26]

Attempt of local cadres in Tuanjie to discourage truancy, (ii): "Prevent children dropping out of school, family heads will be fined!"

A breakdown of the age, education levels, and migration status of the males and females in my survey suggests that the onset of migration from the villages may coincide with a fall in the level of education among females. Data presented in Graph 4.2 (see Section 4.5, Education Appendix) show that, among the individuals in the 138 households covered in the survey and across all of the age groupings, females generally have a lower level of education than males. Moreover, the level of education among girls in the 15–19 age group appears to fall as compared with the level of education among females in the 20–24 age group. Out of the 60 individuals (33 men and 27 women) represented in the 15–19 age cohort, 43 (71.6%) individuals are currently working in the cities, five men and six women (18%) are still in school, and the remainder are either working or farming locally. People in the 15–19 cohort would have been of age 9–13 years at the time when out-migration from the villages was becoming prevalent. Owing to the small size of the sample, it is difficult to know whether or not the fall in levels of education for girls in the 15–19 age group (as compared with the 20–24 age group) reflects a general social pattern. If Graph 4.2 shows a real social trend in the area, then more robust investigation and a wider survey is needed to determine whether or not migration is a causal factor. In order to study this question, a researcher would need longitudinal data on levels of enrollments, repeat students, and drop-outs for each level of schooling, figures on the age and gender breakdown of the total Gaocheng population, and annual data on the numbers of out-migrants.

Graph 4.3 (also in Section 4.5) shows that the gap in the ratio of girl to boy students at Gaocheng Middle School widens between 1986–1987 and 1997–1998. These data alone are not sufficient for ascertaining a relationship between migration and male and female enrollments. In particular, gender differences in enrollments might be due to other factors, such as the birth patterns of previous decades. Nonetheless, it is certainly the case that the proportion of girl students in Gaocheng Middle School has decreased between the late 1980s and the mid-1990s, and that this is also the period when interactions between socioeconomic transition and existing cultural values were leading to changes in household patterns of labor and resource allocation. The most dramatic aspect of socioeconomic transition has been the decollectivization process, which began in 1980 and by 1984 resulted in the completed implementation of the household responsibility system throughout the county. Then in 1986–1987, there were state campaigns to ensure that children who had not completed eight years of education were enrolled.[27] During the late 1980s, de facto school fees (*zafei*) became increasingly expensive, forcing some households to withdraw their children from school. Also in the late 1980s, Gaocheng men started migrating on a seasonal basis, coinciding with the time when the proportion of girl students in Gaocheng Middle School begins to fall. Evidence from other parts of the world reveals that the migration of household members exerts an adverse impact on the education of the young (and of girls in particular) by drawing them into agricultural and domestic work.[28] The same is true in Wanzai, where the rigidity of the gendered division of labor – together with the fact that domestic help cannot be hired – means that older daughters often take over the running of the household to the detriment of their studies. Finally, the enthusiasm of factory bosses for hiring young female laborers interacts with other factors, such as expensive school fees and existing attitudes about the value of educating daughters relative to sons, which further inhibits Gaocheng girls from completing their middle-school studies.

A final negative impact of migration on education is the common practice of grandparents fostering their grandchildren. This problem has received much media attention,[29] and there are concerns that the "quality" of the next generation may be adversely affected: do the children receive a proper upbringing and sufficient help with study?[30] These concerns are also frequently raised in Gaocheng. For example, teachers from Tuanjie village primary school expressed anxiety to me that grandparents, who are often illiterate and overworked, are unable to properly supervise the homework of their grandchildren.

Although migration works in many ways to depress investment in rural education, this is only a partial representation of a contradictory picture in which migration is also starting to stimulate investment in education. The emerging tendency toward increased investment in education is produced through interactions among the internal processes of the village, the resources generated from return flows, and gradual shifts in the recruitment conditions in urban labor markets. Migration stimulates spending on rural education in three specific ways. First, remittances are an important source of funds for education. The wages of adult children are commonly used to pay for the school fees of their siblings and, in some cases, finance more advanced education. In three of the surveyed households, girls were sending money home to pay for the vocational college fees of their elder brothers; in another instance, remittances from four brothers were paying for their sister's college education.

Second, the financial contribution of migrants to the welfare of the parental household encourages parents to invest in the education of their children. Girls in particular may benefit from this because, owing to virilocal patterns of marriage, rural parents have always regarded investing in the education of a daughter as "fattening a pig for someone else." Anecdotal evidence suggests that, as a result of receiving remittances from daughters, some parents now see that investing in the education of daughters is worthwhile in that they can eventually contribute as much money to the parental home as sons.[31] This parental strategy may be not so much because education yields higher wages as because investing in the education of daughters is also a way for parents to invest in a reciprocal intergenerational contract with their daughters. Such a strategy strengthens daughters' sense of obligation to care for their parents in old age. Graph 4.3 suggests that, from 1997–1998 onward, there has been a narrowing in the imbalance between male and female enrollments in Gaocheng Middle School. However, it is difficult to assess the extent to which this trend can be attributed to migration on the basis of these figures alone. Another possible influence is that, since the late 1990s, counties in Yichun prefecture have been issued with strict targets for improving school completion rates and the local state has been active in ensuring that girls are enrolled.

Third, the experiences of migrants in the urban labor markets are creating awareness among rural producers that education is valuable when living in a modern society, so villagers seek to avoid shame and challenge their peripheral status as "bumpkins" and "coolies." While in the cities, migrants encounter difficulties with filling in application forms for temporary jobs or reading simple instructions. A rudimentary education is also required before skills can be learned at a city night school. The importance of education for being able to function in the city is illustrated in the following anecdote, related by a former labor recruiter for the Wanzai Labor Export Company:

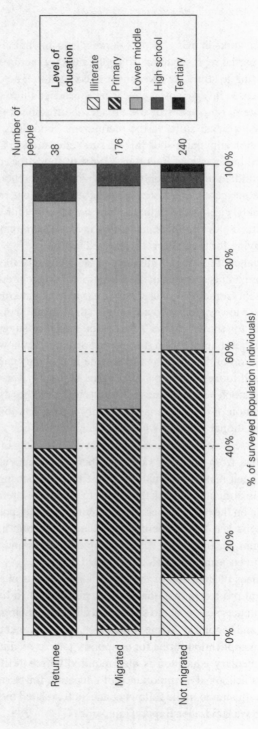

Graph 4.1. Breakdown of individual education levels from 138 households, by migration status. *Source:* Census survey sheets (1996) and my household survey (1997). Based on data for 454 of the 456 individuals aged 15+ years in my survey of 138 households (for two of the individuals, I do not have an indication of education).

In 1993 I dispatched a group of girls to a factory in Dongguan. When some of the girls returned home for Spring Festival, they told the parents of one girl that their daughter was missing. The father and brothers ... accused me of trafficking in women and beat me .... I spent six months standing outside factory gates [trying to find her] .... Eventually I returned to Wanzai .... One day the girl's father came, knelt on the floor and apologized profusely. It turned out that the girl had switched factories. She had written a letter home but, as she only had three years of schooling, she didn't know how to address an envelope or mail a letter. She had not written the name of the province on the envelope and paid only two mao in postage. Organizing labor export for factories is too much trouble when you are dealing with low-quality people .... I will change to the export of girls for service work. They are better educated, better looking, and fetch more money.[32]

Material presented in Graph 4.1 suggests that the migrants from Qifeng and Tuanjie are more educated than the nonmigrants; if the education levels of the returned migrants are also considered, then the difference in the education levels of the "ever migrated" and the "never migrated" people is even greater. Qualitative data suggest that, as the urban labor markets become increasingly meritocratic, education may feature even more prominently as a factor of migrant selection. Large-scale layoffs from state enterprises and the swelling ranks of rural migrants allow the enterprises with higher wages and better working conditions to tighten their recruitment criteria. At one labor introduction agency, I witnessed young women express disappointment because they were not able to go to the same factory as others from the village. The factory had a reputation as a good employer but was now demanding upper middle–school graduates for assembly-line work and had just recruited a group of women from Sichuan who met this requirement. Although false middle-school certificates can be purchased for 30 yuan from schools and labor introduction agencies, it is not possible to buy upper middle–school graduation certificates. Moreover, when it comes to competition for good jobs, a fake certificate does not substitute for genuine schooling to this level.

Joint venture companies commonly use exams as a selection tool. Candidates are required to write out the English alphabet, translate English words (such as "on," "off," "up," and "down"), calculate fractions, and answer a reading comprehension test about the company. Applicants are also interviewed so that the employer can assess the overall quality of the worker, including the dexterity of their hands and their ability to speak Mandarin. Labor agencies covertly obtain these exam papers in order to tutor their clients, but only a small proportion of migrants go through the agencies – deterred by a fee of about 300 yuan.[33]

Major cities in China are currently introducing a national certificate system that grades the skills of workers (*dengji gong*) and influences both their job prospects and the level of remuneration they receive. In the *dengji gong* system, there are eight levels of skill, with level 8 as the highest. In the Pudong factory district of Shanghai, most migrant workers are ranked between 1 and 3. At the end of 1996, 45% of Pudong migrants were graded under the *dengji gong* system, and municipal authorities aim to increase this figure to 60% by the year 2000. Officials hope that this accreditation system will improve the quality of production,[34] though it may also be that a lower grading is habitually used to legitimize using rural migrants as cheap labor.

Migrants' impressions of a competitive and increasingly meritocratic labor market are filtering back to the countryside, with the result that some villagers are reassessing the value of investing in education. Migrants write home exhorting their siblings to stay at school. For example, at Spring Festival, a 19-year-old migrant from Qifeng village told me the following:

> My parents ... wanted me to study upper middle school. But I wanted to go out, so I headed for Guangdong as soon as I had finished middle school. Now when I write to my parents I tell them: "make sure that my younger sister studies hard at school and don't let her work carrying heavy bricks in the village kiln. Life outside is difficult if your level of education is low. If you have no learning, all you can be is a coolie."[35]

As a further example, I listened to one young returnee woman talking to a group of friends in Tuanjie village about her reasons for leaving a private shoe factory and about her regret at failing a recruitment exam for a better job. After three years of working in the factory and performing a repetitive task for thirteen hours a day, seven days a week, at a low rate of pay, she felt too tired to continue. Both she and her sister had taken the recruitment exam of a joint venture company that was offering six-day weeks and eight-hour days at a good wage, but only her sister had passed.[36] Hearing such stories about recruitment exams creates an impression among villagers that literacy and numeracy skills have a real impact on a person's life chances. Moreover, as shown in the next photograph, recruitment notices pasted in the countryside alert villagers to the importance of education, because the advertisements generally stipulate that applicants must be educated to a least lower middle–school level.

An awareness of the competitiveness of urban labor markets is shaping new goals for more education among both intending and returning migrants. Some migrants use part of their Spring Festival vacation and city savings to attend vocational training classes in the county seat in a bid to improve their job prospects on their return to the city. Popular subjects include welding, tailoring, accounting, driving, typing, computing, hairdressing, and cooking. In addition, there

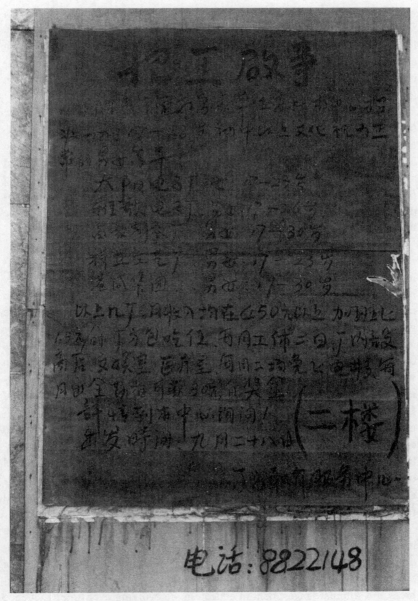

A recruitment poster from a Wanzai labor agency details factory jobs available in Guangzhou. It stipulates that applicants must be aged 17–28 and be educated to at least middle-school level.

are life-skills classes that give instruction in filling out forms and posting letters as well as in arithmetic, basic legal knowledge, and first aid. Courses range in length from one week to a couple of years. Such classes are often run through county labor introduction agencies or government labor bureaus. Enterprising individuals also set up training classes in the villages, most commonly in tailoring.

Through working in the cities, some migrants find the motivation and the financial resources to return to the village and finish their schooling. Newspapers feature stories of migrants who return home to complete their education because of the contempt that they faced in the cities, where they were perceived as ignorant.[37] While teaching in the local schools I encountered several young people who had been pushed out of the classroom through poverty and boredom, only to return home because life in the cities is full of drudgery for the uneducated.

Evidence from Wanzai reveals a contradiction: on the one hand, migration reinforces existing prejudices against education, but on the other hand it is starting to stimulate spending on education. Qualitative data suggest that easy entry into unskilled employment may act as a barrier to raising school completion rates. Moreover, a fall in the level of education among women in the 15–19 age group was observed, which might reflect the reallocation of household labor and resources in response to economic liberalization, of which migration is one part. The contradictory impact of migration on education might explain why, from the late 1980s onward, there are sharp rises and falls in the percentage of Gaocheng Middle School students not progressing to the next class (see Graph 4.4 in Section 4.5). The zigzag line possibly reflects the role of chain migration introductions in suctioning groups of students out of the school system at periodic intervals. On the other hand, Graph 4.2 suggests that each generation of individuals in the survey of 138 households has achieved a higher level of education than the previous generation. Moreover, Graph 4.5 shows a leveling off in the percentage of students at the county level who fail to re-enroll for the following year.

By alerting the rural populace to the qualifications required for obtaining resources in a modern society, migration reinforces existing trends toward increased investment in education. Longer-term migration from Wanzai did not commence until the early 1990s, and the relative balance of forces that depress and stimulate investment in education are evolving over time. Evidence from countries with long migration histories suggests that the increasing exposure of villagers to urban labor markets encourages investment in education.[38] However, the use of urban savings to fund education may ultimately work to the detriment of the home community, because educated people are more likely to form newer and higher life goals that can only be attained by migrating.

4.2 THE LIFE-CYCLE GOALS OF HOUSE BUILDING AND MARRIAGE

The first year that someone has migrated, the family eats their fill, after the second the family wears new clothes, after the third the family builds a new house, and after the fourth year, a bride is taken.[39]

Since time immemorial, the Chinese farmer has had three life goals: to eat so that the stomach is full, to build a house, and to marry. You ask how do they spend their remittances, well that's how. – A former farmer and my guide in Yudu, Guo Guopeng

Building a house and marrying are interlinked life-cycle goals that are fundamental to social reproduction, the transmission of resources from present to future generations, and the long-term viability of the family. Marriage and house building are traditional areas of expenditure that reveal the importance of migration in increasing the opportunities for social actors to attain other related goals, which include improving their material livelihoods, avoiding shame, and participating more fully in the social life of the village. Through building a house and marrying, migrants achieve a sense of belonging that counterbalances their precarious existence in the cities: this is described by migrant poets as the quest for *guisu,* "a home to return to" or a place at which to rest.[40]

This section demonstrates that migration and remittances promote change not only by infusing cash and modern goods into the countryside but also, and more significantly, by transforming the shared values and social practices that are associated with spending on life-cycle goals. The discussion first examines the role of the house in enabling villagers to maintain self-respect and participate in village society; it then illustrates this by demonstrating that a house is both a goal and a resource that assists social actors in achieving marriage. Next I argue that migration shapes new life goals and also increases the resources required for attaining existing goals. This is illustrated through the changing composition of wedding gifts and by observing the inflation in costs associated with marriage and house building. Finally, I demonstrate that – although remittances provide funds for conserving social arrangements that are endogenous to rural society – migration generates forces that actually change the values and social relationships expressed through marriage and house building.

4.2.1 *House Building and Marriage*

House building is the means by which individuals who have prospered in the cities enhance their public face in the village by demonstrating their increased control over economic and social resources; in this sense, the front of the house corresponds with the face of the family.[41] Building a house is a social and economic goal that is attained through the use of both money and mutual aid.

Migrants who want to build a house return home and, in the months following Spring Festival, withdraw their savings from the bank and mobilize their social contacts in the village to help with dredging sand and laying bricks. Those who cannot participate in reciprocal labor exchanges (often because they are in the cities) donate money instead. The role of the house in enabling villagers to achieve the goal of self-respect is evident in the account of Chinese researchers studying migration from a village in Hunan:

> Only those few who had built a house ... urged us to take photographs with them outside their new houses .... And those who had not built new houses ... said that they were "disgraced" and told us to wait until they have built their new houses, then come again and take photographs.[42]

Villagers in Wanzai similarly associate their houses with their self-respect. Poorer people described to me both their shame at living in a decrepit house and their aspirations for a *xiaokang lou* – literally, "comfortable living building." *Xiaokang lou* demonstrates the role of migration in raising the standard for a respectable house and in promoting wage labor as a means of obtaining the resources to achieve this standard. *Xiaokang* is an overtly political term: Deng Xiaoping prescribed three stages for improving living standards – subsistence, living comfortably (*xiaokang*), and prosperity – each defined by indicators for income and the provision of social and cultural facilities. Cadres are urged to adopt *xiaokang* as a local development goal, and *xiaokang* houses are visible representations of progress within a locality. In describing their ideal house as a *xiaokang lou,* petty commodity producers adapt the state's discourse of development and modernization targets to make sense of their own goals for securing the material and social advancement of both their families and native place in the reform era.

The new houses in Gaocheng township range from single-story brick shells (with mud floors and large cracks in the walls) to double-story *xiaokang lou* with cement floors. A single-story shell costs 10,000 yuan, a double-story shell costs 30,000 yuan, and a decorated two-story house costs around 60,000 yuan. All houses in Qifeng and Tuanjie have electricity, though none has running water. A number of the richer households decorate the outside of their houses with white tiles and paint. A few houses have even replaced traditional wooden lattices with glass windows. Yet, as several anthropologists of house building argue, the use of building materials imported from cities does not necessarily represent the diffusion of modern values into the countryside.[43] Villagers use these materials to build better-quality housing, thereby achieving goals such as improving their level of physical comfort and gaining a sense of self-respect. Some owners of two-story houses proudly explained to me that their homes are more spacious than the cramped apartments of many urban dwellers.

Regardless of their quality, new houses are distinguished from the yellow mud buildings of the poorest households.

In Wanzai, building a house is an important goal for men because a house indicates the value of the groom in the material exchanges associated with marriage and thus his capacity to offer a good material life to a future wife. For those without lucrative local off-farm employment or political capital, migration is the key means for obtaining the resources needed to build a house. Moreover, in geographically and economically peripheral societies such as Wanzai, most inhabitants have few opportunities for using capital in other ways, so the house is a particularly important form of investment.[44] In the event of competing claims over the resources generated through migration, building a house may avoid the tensions that arise with more individual forms of expenditure, because all the household members can enjoy the benefits: a roof that does not leak and walls that block the wind.

The importance of a well-constructed house for attaining social goals becomes evident when examining betrothal customs in Wanzai. The betrothal process begins when an intermediary brings a young man to a woman's home. If he regards her as a likely marriage partner, he leaves her some money. In Gaocheng township this is called "hot water money" (*kaishui qian*) because on leaving, the male suitor places money in the cup from which he has drunk his tea. The role of the house in demonstrating the eligibility of the suitor is illustrated by the second stage of the betrothal process, known as *cha fang* – literally, "inspecting the house."[45] This involves the woman's family visiting the man's house, primarily to assess his socioeconomic standing. The man's family hosts a meal for the girl's relatives and gives red envelopes containing money to each guest. If both sides agree to the union, they discuss the bride price through intermediaries, and the agreement is recorded on a piece of red paper (*hongdan*) that is signed by both fathers. The significance of the house for the marriage prospects of the young man is further illustrated at a metaphorical level by the maxim *men dang hu dui,* which means that "the gates to the houses are even," that is, both parties have equal socioeconomic standing. In practice, when finding a spouse, individuals interpret *men dang hu dui* to mean that they must find someone who is *at least* equal to themselves. Another village saying is that "the fortunes of a man are determined by the gate of his mother's womb and the fortunes of a woman are determined by the door to her in-laws' house."

By investing in good-quality housing, migrants are able to marry spouses from better-connected families. Within the villages, people speak in terms of families, rather than individuals, being rich or poor. Although there is a trend toward early household division and nuclearization, the extended family is still important because nobody wants the embarrassment or burden of poor in-laws.

Migrant and nonmigrant neighbors, Tuanjie village, Wanzai.

This is especially true now that recent improvements in transport facilitate regular visiting among family, and market reforms have enhanced the economic opportunities that may be gained through well-connected affines.[†] Migrant children feel pressure to contribute money in order to lift the socioeconomic standing of their immediate family and to improve their own eligibility in the marriage market. In one family, the second son found a fiancée in the city, also a Wanzai native, and his choice drew fierce objection from his parents because her family is poor. In contrast, the eldest son made a wise choice in that his wife is from a wealthy family with relatives in Taiwan.

Although the burden of demonstrating financial eligibility falls heavily on all households with unmarried children, the burden is heaviest for households with sons. The parents of three single migrant daughters explained to me that they do not plan to emulate their neighbors in building a new house because they do not have a son. In contrast, the parents with a son explained to me that they are choosing to build a large house mainly for his benefit. Contrary to studies in other countries suggesting that daughters remit more,[46] Chinese social scientists have argued that single sons tend to remit more money because of the pressure on them to demonstrate their financial eligibility for marriage.[47] In my sample of unmarried migrants who have been in the city for at least half a year, 88% (38 out of 43) of daughters remitted money as compared with only 76% (41 out of 54) of sons. Even so, comparing parental estimates of the annual amount of remittances from sons and from daughters suggests that a larger proportion of remittances from sons exceed 2,000 yuan. The unreliability of information on remittances and the small size of the survey mean that the material from Wanzai is inconclusive in showing whether sons or daughters remit more.

Proving eligibility for marriage involves not only building a house but also purchasing modern consumer goods for the bride price and dowry. The bride price is presented by the groom's family to the parents of the bride, though most (if not all) is returned to the bride and groom through indirect dowry. *Indirect dowry* refers to the portion of the bride price that is transferred to the bride by her parents, and *direct dowry* refers to the items that are either given to the bride directly or purchased by the bride herself in preparation for her married life. In Gaocheng, a local saying on the ratio of the bride price returned as a dowry by the bride's parents is as follows: "good people give more than they receive, middle people neither gain nor lose, and poor people gain."

The few individuals who have secured their socioeconomic status in the cities and see their futures there spend very little on the bride price and dowries. As mentioned in Chapter 2, there are two households in my fieldwork villages

---

[†] "Affines" are people related by marriage or by ties other than blood (e.g., adoption).

where the adult children moved to Nanchang for the purpose of higher education and – after obtaining employment as doctors, nurses, teachers, and
managers – acquired a Nanchang *hukou*. The father of three daughters who
are now settled in Nanchang said that he had not asked his sons-in-law, two of
them city residents, for a bride price because he saw it as unnecessary. The
mother of two sons who have settled in Nanchang explained that her sons had
not given any bride price when they married city women. However, she added
that her younger son who had failed to get into university is now working in
Guangdong to earn money for a bride price. Money from all three sons has
contributed toward building a *xiaokang lou,* which will "go to younger brother
because he has to marry and live in the countryside."

Giving modern commodities as wedding gifts helps the couple to prepare for
a better material life in the countryside, and this attracts the esteem of other
villagers. One woman who married in 1995 explained to me that for her marriage the hot-water money was 360 yuan and the bride price consisted of 6,000
yuan, 180 kilograms of fish and pork, a bicycle, and a watch. In her case, the
meat and fish contribution went toward hosting guests in the bride's house on
the first day after the marriage was registered; the remainder of the bride price
went toward the dowry. The direct and indirect dowry items included an elec-
tric fan, a sewing machine, an edging machine, a black-and-white television,
a mattress bed (which replaces the traditional engraved canopy bed), two bed-
spreads, a cabinet, a dressing table, a table, two trunks, a leather case, a flask,
a kettle, and a straw mat for sleeping on in the summer.

In Wanzai, a locality with few off-farm earning opportunities, modern goods
have become a common component of marriage gifts only since the onset of
migration. This differs from the situation described in the ethnographic account of *Chen Village* in Guangdong province, where viable rural industries
and substantial remittances from Hong Kong émigrés have meant that some
households had sufficient income to start incorporating modern commodities
into their bride prices and dowries as early as the 1970s.[48]

Studies of marriage in China show that shifts in the political economy that
increase the value of women's labor also propel a rise in the bride price.[49] In particular, male out-migration and labor shortages on the land increase the value
of a woman's labor in farming, as she assumes more of the burden of agricultural work.[50] Applying the same principle, it is also possible that factory
employment for women pushes up the bride price. Yet this explanation accords a passive role to the woman who is transferred between families with the
payment of compensation. According to Yan and Siu, values stressing individualism and increasing nuclearization mean that the significance of the bride
price and dowry items as gift exchanges between affines is declining. At the
same time, marriage gifts are becoming more important as the means through

which couples obtain control over resources for establishing their own house-holds. As a result, the property that is transferred to the new conjugal unit through both indirect and direct dowry is increasing. Yan reveals that a bride commonly lobbies on behalf of the new couple for more contributions from the groom's parents and that much of her lobbying is at the instigation of the groom, who is unable to directly challenge his parents for more property.[51]

In Wanzai, migration fuels existing trends toward inflation in the cost of the bride price and dowry by informing young rural couples about urban house-hold commodities and by generating the remittances to purchase them. Villagers struggle to meet these costs – not as indulgent consumption, but as a means of achieving the goals of social reproduction and securing the respectability of the family. These goals are not luxuries or optional extras but are fundamental human needs. In Gaocheng, in the days before liberation, hot-water money was given only to widows who were remarrying. The migration of villagers coin-cides with a revival of hot-water money, which is now given by all male suitors to their desired partners. My interview material suggests that with each year the respectable amount of hot-water money increases, so that in 1990 a woman received about 50 yuan and only six years later she could expect to receive, in the more lavish instances, about 500 yuan. Moreover, young women who re-ceive betrothal gifts of gold jewelry are the envy of their peers.

The political environment of fieldwork in Wanzai hindered my investigation into bride-price costs. Household evaluation campaigns were in full swing, and feudal ceremonies were a target of this movement. One of the criteria against which households were assessed was for their role in "transforming so-cial traditions" (*yifeng yisu*). Each village group also established a "red and white" committee (red is the color for marriage celebration and white is the color of mourning) to dissuade families from holding lavish wedding or funeral ceremonies.[52] Interviewees were therefore generally cautious in discussing the bride price. However, private conversations reveal that bride prices average several thousand yuan, and one family told me that they had given 20,000 yuan. Villagers explained to me that if the amount is too high then the woman loses face, because everyone will say that she has been bought; if the amount is too low, she loses face because everyone will say that the man does not value her. Young women use the hot-water money and bride price gifts as a barometer for assessing their self-worth, and this has received explicit criticism in local gazettes.[53]

The inflationary impact of migration on bride-price costs has been observed in many rural areas of the developing world[54] and is a serious problem in poor areas of China, where the eligibility of young men in the marriage market is con-strained by the village of their household registration (*hukou*). This is because the *hukou* system, combined with virilocal and village exogamous marriage patterns, means that the permanent settlement of the bride in her husband's im-poverished village is almost inevitable. Farmers in richer villages seem to give a smaller bride price than those in the poorer villages. Residents in middling vil-lages such as Qifeng and Tuanjie spend less on the bride price than those in the poor mountain village of Guyuan, which shares a border with Tuanjie. One ex-planation for men in poorer villages giving expensive wedding gifts is that such gifts encourage the bride's family to agree to an arranged marriage. Another reason is that the groom uses expensive wedding gifts as a way of demonstrating to a bride and her parents that, despite the poverty of his village, he has suffi-cient resources to offer an adequate material life to the woman. However, there are also differences in bride-price costs within villages. Villagers in Guyuan told me that households on the west side of the village have land irrigated by the Guyuan Brook, so the bride price they have to pay seldom exceeds 10,000 yuan. However, land in places on the east side is drier and of poorer quality, so these households must pay bride prices of nearly 20,000 yuan in order to gain a bride. Migration is giving women wider opportunities to meet potential spouses, and their unwillingness to marry in that part of Guyuan has earned it the nickname of "bachelors' corner."

Migration inflates the real costs of resources required to attain life goals, so that people are forced to incur debt in order to attain the goals of maintain-ing self-respect, participating in community activities, and marrying. Here it is worth noting that, before 1949, weddings and funerals – rather than the costs of agricultural production – were the main causes of household indebtedness.[55] Migration therefore interacts with pre-existing social trends, and the inflation is not all due to migration.

In Wanzai, the influx of cash into the rural economy is making *xiaokang lou* the new standard for a "respectable" house. As for marriage, remittances are increasing the number of guests and quantity of food required for a respectable wedding feast. Much of this expenditure is financed with borrowed money, and 10% of migrant households in the survey report using remittances for re-paying debts from house building and marriage. In seventeen instances, the migration of an individual has been motivated by the intention of repaying in-formal loans. Local officials say that these villagers "make themselves appear fat [prosperous] by beating their faces."

Migration is also inflating the expenses for the social gift exchanges associ-ated with marriage and house building. Relatives and close friends attend ban-quets arranged by the host family and give cash in red envelopes to help finance the attainment of a particular life-cycle goal. Once given, each contribution begets another, resulting in a continuing cycle of exchange and obligation that both reinforces and is reinforced by affective ties and familial and mutual aid values. Villagers establish these gift relationships before marriage, anticipating the need for capital to finance marriage, house building, the birth of a child, and the funerals of parents. As people must save face and be respectable by repaying gifts with either an equivalent or greater amount, the value of each person's gift is recorded in a red paper booklet. This social custom provides resources in a manner similar to informal loan associations. The inflow of migrant remittances, combined with this customary need to give gifts that exceed the value of those received, produces an inflationary gift economy.

On his return to the village for Spring Festival, a migrant from Qifeng expressed to me his view on the practice of incurring debt in order to pursue customary forms of expenditure:

> Working outside is like a drug, the more you go out the more you spend, and then you have to go out again. It is just like opium. I still haven't cleared the debt from house building and people never clear their debts with me. A triangular debt is prevalent in the countryside. Everyone is spending money that they don't have. Everyone is trying to run ahead of others for a face that is not really theirs. You build a house so I build a house. You give a 20-yuan wedding present, so I give a 30-yuan wedding present. But if face is gained through debt then there is no face at all. People still haven't paid me for the use of my truck in the days when I did transport. They say that they have no money. Doing business here is so difficult because no one pays up. They are all friends and relatives or else someone else's friends and relatives and they use my money to build their houses. We build houses because this land has raised us. But when you think about it, it is dead money.[56]

Once migrants have returned home and spent all of their savings, new sources of money are needed for attaining further goals, so migration becomes a way of life unless alternative sources of income become available within the home area. The local government in Wanzai is concerned that, in setting new standards for property acquisition and new expectations for gift exchanges, migration causes disruption and dissatisfaction. This is seen as a threat to the legitimacy of the state in the countryside, which is grounded in the Party's historical promise to improve rural livelihoods and alleviate rural poverty. Policy documents use the term *fanpin* – "the return to poverty" – to describe the consequence for rural households that spend beyond their means in order to chase the moving goal of keeping up with social standards.[57]

4.2.2 *Migration and Change*

Remittances provide funds needed for maintaining the social customs associated with house building and marriage, while migration changes the values and relationships that social actors reproduce through these customs. These changes result not only from modernization or diffusion but also from more fundamental transformations occurring within rural society. I discuss this in relation to house building and to marriage. To begin with house building, banquets are traditionally held at the laying of the foundation (*qi gong*), the raising of the central roof beam (*shangliang*), and the finishing off of the house with plastering and roofing (*yuangong*). These banquets raise funds to finance each stage of the building process. The banquet to celebrate raising the central beam is traditionally the most important. Until recently, all houses had a central wooden beam. According to custom, a villager who is deemed to enjoy good fortune (or else the oldest or most educated person within the family group) is invited to write auspicious characters on the beam, paint the symbol of the *bagua,* and write the date on which the beam is installed. This is not unique to Wanzai, and studies of house building throughout the world identify the roof beam as important for reinforcing the familial values and affective ties that are centered on the house.[58] Nowadays, the capacity to purchase new construction materials means that the structure of some houses is changing. In recent years, a few of the richer households in Wanzai have been opting for flat reinforced cement roofs so that there is no place for rats and mice to scurry and there is a surface on which grain can be dried in the sun. The new structure of these houses renders the central wooden beam obsolete. Moreover, the fact that many migrants are absent from the village means that, in some instances, the ceremonial aspects of constructing a house are abbreviated – so that just one meal is held to commemorate the completion of the house.

Migration puts new constraints and demands on the labor-exchange aspects of house building. Households must juggle migration with various obligations in the village, one of which is labor-exchange commitments for house building. Production in some factories declines periodically if demand for the product is seasonal. Migrants use this time to return home and help with both house construction and farming. Spring Festival is another opportunity for migrants to deal with matters in the village such as marriages, settling debts, and helping to build houses. Many migrant households are unable to meet their reciprocal labor obligations for house building and so compensate with large cash donations. Absentee laborers sending remittances means that hired labor for house building is starting to replace labor exchange. Construction teams are appearing in the townships to perform tasks associated with house building. Wives who remain in the village assume responsibility for coordinating the volunteer labor of their relatives and neighbors, purchasing the bricks and cement from factories, and hiring construction teams. Previously, such dealings with people from outside of the family were the responsibility of the husband.

The social practices associated with marriage are also being transformed through mobility and migrant expenditure on urban goods and services. For instance, as a result of migration, the "modern" photograph is increasingly adapted to playing a part in the customary function of marriage introductions. In a situation where adult children are absent from the village for long periods, photographs have become integrated into the traditional system of arranging marriages. Moreover, they allow rural youths to package themselves as eligible mates by posing in modern city clothes and sunglasses against the props and sophisticated backdrops of the photo salons. Through the photograph, the migrants prematurely achieve the traditionally cherished goal of the Chinese sojourner, to "return home in gilded garments." In March 1997, a woman in Tuanjie village was delighted with her son's fortune in finding a pretty girlfriend from the same factory, and her picture was displayed in the house even though the woman had never met the young lady. Later, word filtered back to the village that the girl was of loose morals. The woman immediately wrote to her son informing him of the girl's shameful background. In September 1997, when I returned to the village, the woman informed me that her son had broken up with his girlfriend. A number of intermediaries, all armed with photographs, wasted little time in approaching the woman with recommendations of suitable daughters-in-law.

Migration is also changing values that inform the criteria for judging an eligible mate. One Chinese case study reports that, although migrant women prefer to find spouses from their hometowns, they favor men who have had migration experience so that they have "more in their heads than soil."[59] Migration is precipitating a restratification of the rural marriage market in that migrant men who prosper in the cities are better able to marry the daughters from well-connected households. Several male migrants explained to me that, although originally despised by their in-laws for their poverty, they have since earned money in the city and achieved recognition as good sons-in-law. Because the urban labor markets are open to anyone, young men do not have to rely on the power-based distributional mechanisms of the natal community in order to obtain the resources and social experience needed to attain the goal of becoming a "worthy" husband or son-in-law.

Migration gives young people in Wanzai the means to accumulate the savings and material goods for marriage, affording them a greater say in other aspects of their marriages. As an example, sons in Wanzai are no longer reliant on their parents for providing resources to enable their marriage, so they are now deciding when and whom they marry. With regard to young women, in the one instance where gifts from a suitor's family had placed the girl's family in a "goodwill" debt, the migrant daughter earned the money to repay the value of the gifts, thereby undoing the obligation to marry. Migration is also enabling young women to earn money to augment their dowries. As scholars of marriage in China have observed, a large dowry gives the woman the dignity of her own property and accords her the status of a wife rather than a purchased woman,[60] and this control over resources also affords her greater equality in her interdependence with her husband.

In summary, expenditures for attaining the life-cycle goals of house building and marrying illustrate that migration is important for expanding the opportunities for villagers to obtain more resources for attaining the related goals of improving material comfort, maintaining self-respect, and participating more fully in the social life of the village. However, migration also increases the value of resources needed to attain the goals that social actors experience as basic needs, thereby forcing some households into poverty. In supporting customary forms of expenditure, migration and remittances help to finance and preserve values, customs, and relationships that are endogenous to the origin village. More importantly, migration is a dynamic force in changing the social values that underpin these traditions.

4.3 MIGRATION AND CONSUMER GOODS

Mo Wuer had unexpectedly made quite a name for himself. Skinny Dog Cliff was a village without a single forked tree, but still a phoenix had landed. On returning from Guangdong he hadn't sat down long enough for his bench to get warm before he was carting back a large color television set from the county seat. News that he'd prospered blew through the village like a mad wind and blew so that the faces of those mud-treading pole carriers were full of admiration and surprise.... Even the most well-to-do Xinghua family had only a 14-inch black-and-white television ....[61]

Migration enhances the capacity of rural people to attain consumer goals because remittances increase per-capita incomes in the countryside. In 1992, the increase in remittances accounted for half of the increase in rural incomes in Jiangxi province for the year.[62] An article in a 1996 edition of the *China Daily* estimates the total contribution of remittances to the annual income of rural dwellers in four interior provinces, including Jiangxi, at 30%.[63] In 1996, postal remittances to Gaocheng accounted for more than 10% of per-capita income for the year. Although the figures vary, the fact that is pertinent for this discussion is that remittances increase rural incomes.

Remittances also enable rural people to more readily achieve their consumer goals because this income arrives in the form of regular installments of cash. Unlike factory wages, the material rewards from farming are not immediately tangible: approximately one third of remuneration from farm labor is in kind, and the cash income from grain sales can only be obtained at the end of each harvest. In contrast, urban wages are paid on a monthly basis, facilitating the more immediate satisfaction of consumption desires. This is particularly the case in townships where migrants can arrange a 24-hour transfer of cash from an urban bank to a branch of the Agricultural Bank in the rural township. Migrants described to me the satisfaction of receiving a regular pay slip, and the occasion is often celebrated with the purchase of refreshments to be shared among workmates.

Migration enables villagers to obtain more of the cultural and economic resources required for improving the quality of their lives and for participating more fully and equally in an expanding social and economic world that incorporates both the city and the countryside. This is demonstrated by the increasing importance of expenditure on four types of commodities: livelihood goods, household appliances, popular cultural products, and transport.

Despite the high level of self-sufficiency in the Wanzai countryside, villagers prefer manufactured goods because they are generally more durable, efficacious, and convenient than home-made equivalents. Petty commodity farmers produce for most of their own consumption needs: private plots and mountain terrain provide vegetables, tea leaves, tea-seed oil, fuel, and wild herbs; items such as slippers, woolen clothing, and bamboo furniture are made by hand. Nonetheless, remittances enable villagers to meet more of their basic needs by purchasing goods such as fuel, food, medicine, soap, toothpaste, tobacco, matches, utensils, cloth, wool, and blankets. One young mother (whose husband works in Guangdong) informed me that she spends 100 yuan a month of the remittances on powdered milk because she cannot lactate. Before the days of migration she would have paid a wet nurse or fed the child with soup left over from boiling rice. Another migrant, acting in accordance with the values of filial piety, brought Brand's Chicken stock for his convalescent mother as an alternative to home-brewed tonics. As a final example, an increase in disposable income allows villagers to replace clothes more frequently instead of wearing "patches on patches."

The role of migration in enabling Wanzai farmers to acquire modern appliances and share in the material benefits of the national commodity economy is particularly evident among the richer households. In the villages that I visited, there were generally one or two households that had achieved an exceptionally high standard of living through migration. For example, a woman from Qifeng married another Wanzai native who had become the deputy manager of an electrical goods factory in Guangdong. To celebrate the wedding, the general manager of the company sent gifts to the girl's family in the form of a large color television and a refrigerator. According to the villagers, it is an enviable achievement for a country girl to find a husband who is so adept at earning money. The girl is also envied because she travels from Guangdong to Yichun (a city near Wanzai) by plane rather than train or bus. In one village, a high-ranking cadre's three sons are migrants. His household boasts a new house, a large color television with a frequency antenna, a refrigerator (still encased in cardboard), and an upstairs room decorated with modern furniture. The capacity to purchase the refrigerator indicates to other villagers that the cities offer the resources needed to improve material well-being, especially as the cost of a refrigerator approaches the annual per-capita income for the village.

The purchase of some modern appliances, especially those associated with telecommunications, results from interactions between labor migration and other dimensions of socioeconomic transition that integrate farmers into a national economy. For instance, on a return visit to Qifeng village in December 2000, I learned that over a hundred households had installed telephones. Moreover, China Telecom advertisements painted on walls throughout the Jiangxi countryside advise rural people to "keep in touch with migrant workers by phone." This differed from the situation during my fieldwork, when there were no phones in either Qifeng or Tuanjie – although in December 1997 one communal phone was finally installed in front of a village shop in Qifeng. The expansion in telephones is partly the result of a drive by China Telecom to make cheap services widely available. In this way, China Telecom can establish itself with domestic consumers before foreign telecommunication companies are allowed to compete in the Chinese market following China's entry into the World Trade Organization. Thus, broader socioeconomic changes make telephone connections more widely available; at the same time, migration is one of the factors both generating a need for telephones and providing funds for purchasing them.

Popular cultural products are especially coveted by young migrants who buy brand-name goods, pop tapes, clothes, cosmetics, and youth magazines in order to participate in a youth culture that transcends the boundaries of the village. A plethora of cultural products has emerged that offer migrants a sense of the shared life experiences and goals that straddle both rural and urban worlds as well as a feeling of belonging to a distinct migrant worker generation referred to colloquially as *dagong zu*. These products include literary magazines that publish the contributions of migrant writers and pop music tapes with songs about migrant life. The chorus of a song called "Dear Lover Goes South" is as follows:

> *The train is leaving*
> *The south is vibrant, the south has neon lights*
> *But don't forget the sweet fragrance of home*
> *I don't want your gold, I don't want your silver*
> *I just want your heart*
> *Tell me all is well, come home.*

Transport is another new area of migrant expenditure that reflects the increasing opportunities for petty commodity households to obtain resources from ever wider spatial realms and to realize their goals of participating in ever wider social networks. As one official in Yudu county explained:

You look at the sign on the front of all the buses that run between Yudu and Dongguan (Guangdong) and see an arrow connecting the two place names. Well, actually we can say that such a sign means that Yudu equals Dongguan, Dongguan is Yudu. Now they are one and the same place.

Perhaps after several more years, officials in Wanzai will make similar observations about the social significance of buses running between their county and the coast. Improvements in the means of transport are propelled by the needs of temporary returnees, and these improvements are enabling the further participation of villagers in urban labor markets.[64] Migrant earnings fund the costs of travel between the destination area and home. Bus ticket sales, especially over the Spring Festival period, inject large amounts of cash into the local economy. Spring Festival ticket sales for 1996 totaled around 16 million yuan (over $1.9 million) in Wanzai and over 80 million yuan (over $9.6 million) in Yudu. In both counties there are daily buses running between county seats, rural townships, and major migrant destination areas on the coast. Transport operators also offer the on-board services of security guards to protect migrants from extortion or road bandits.[65] Long-distance transport between various townships and migrant destination areas with sleeper buses is an industry that has attracted the investment of many returnees. In some Jiangxi counties these businesses involve accommodations with local authorities and the establishment of "black" (illegal) bus stations (*heizhan*) in the destination areas. Because long-distance transport is lucrative, there have been fights between different lineage groups in the townships over control of bus routes.

Local transport has also received a boost from migrant money in that returnees pool savings and invest in some of the minibuses that rattle between the villages and townships of the Jiangxi hill country. Moreover, remittances are used to purchase "modern" motorbikes, thereby facilitating the more "traditional" goal of maintaining contact with kin and affines. The impetus to maintain contact with distant kin has been strengthened by the economic opportunities that can be enjoyed in the reform era by those who "cast their net wide."[66] Motorbikes have prompted an expansion in the number of retail outlets located in the county seats and repair stalls located in townships. These advances in transport change the perception of distance among the rural populace. Guangzhou is only a day and a half away, and visiting in-laws in more remote townships takes only a short trip by minibus or motorbike.

4.4 CONCLUSION

The impact of migration on the countryside is generally positive in that return flows of resources increase the number of people who can achieve life goals. For an individual, the attainment of a goal is experienced as the satisfaction of an absolute need, and the capacity to meet such needs constitutes poverty alleviation.[67] However, not all villagers are equally empowered to attain goals; as discussed in Chapter 3, migration decreases the claims of some of the young and elderly people on resources while increasing their burdens. Moreover, migration works in ways that inflate the real value of resources required to fulfill goals (e.g., those associated with house building and marriage), so that some households are forced into debt. These outcomes are of concern to the state, which bases its legitimacy on a promise to improve rural livelihoods and alleviate rural poverty. Migration also generates new life goals and becomes the means for obtaining the resources required for attaining these goals. In this sense, migration functions as a valve for relieving the dissatisfaction that accumulates among the rural populace because of an inability to achieve goals.

Although it does not refute the importance of exposure to a new environment in molding aspirations for urban commodities, my fieldwork does suggest (a) that modern and urban values are not simply diffused into the countryside and (b) that there is no neat dichotomy between traditional and modern forms of expenditure. The impact of migration on rural spending patterns is complex in that the money and commodities generated from outside of the village interact with values, social processes, and resources internal to it. This is demonstrated, for instance, by adult children who remit money to pay for the vocational training of their siblings, by single men who migrate in order to afford a *xiaokang lou* decorated with shiny tiles, and by women migrants who augment their dowries with new consumer goods. This incorporation of external processes into the internal values, practices, and distributional mechanisms of rural society gives rise to contradictory forces that are illustrated, for example, by the role of migration in both depressing and stimulating investment in education. As a further example, remittances alleviate the poverty of some households while indirectly precipitating the return to poverty of others.

The combined evidence from Chapters 3 and 4 suggests that, by participating in migration, villagers obtain more cultural and economic resources and then use these resources to achieve a higher level of physical comfort, to maintain self-respect, and to engage with a changing social world. The view of villagers as active agents who obtain and deploy resources to attain their goals moves beyond both the structuralist tendency to see them as passive victims of political economy as well as the modernization perception of villagers as objects that are "washed" by modernity and urbanism.

4.5 EDUCATION APPENDIX

Graph 4.2 shows the education levels of 452 out of a total of 456 individuals aged 15+ years in the 138 surveyed households; information for four individuals is incomplete. The data gathered on the education levels of the individuals

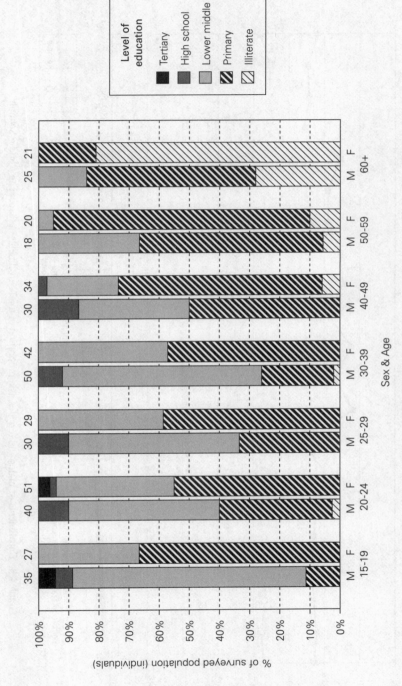

Graph 4.2. Breakdown of individual education levels from 138 households, by age and sex.

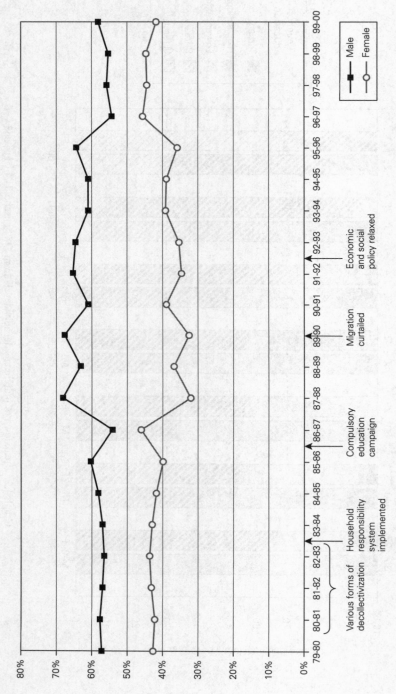

Graph 4.3. Enrollments of males and females as a proportion of total enrollments at Gaocheng Middle School.

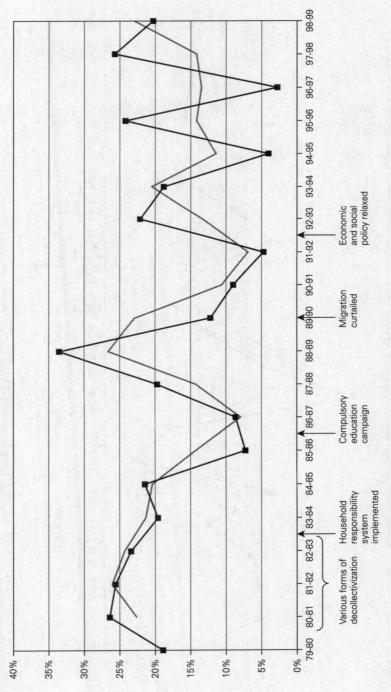

Graph 4.4. Percentage of students not re-enrolling for the following year at Gaocheng Middle School.

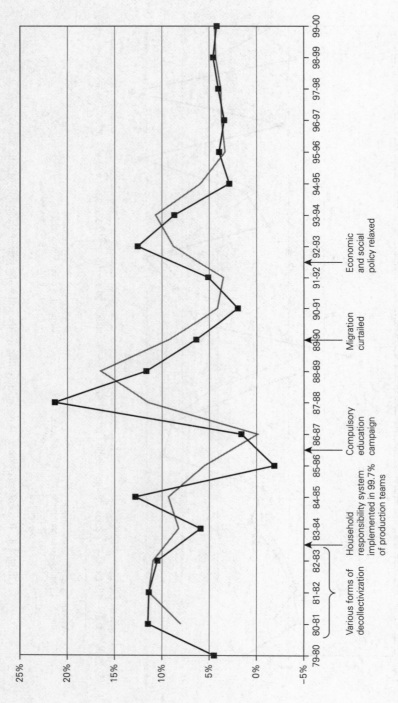

Graph 4.5. Percentage of students in Wanzai county not re-enrolling for the following year.

in these 138 households differ from the entries in the census sheets because my interviews reveal that those who have attended only a few months of middle school have been marked down in the census as having completed middle school. I have adjusted this so that individuals who have attended less than one year of middle school are classified as having a primary level of education, and individuals with one or more years of middle school are classified as having a middle-school education.

The figures for Gaocheng and Wanzai county in Graphs 4.4 and 4.5 include students from the town and the villages. The population is relatively stable, with less than 0.25% of the rural population transferring their place of household registration in any year. The similar pattern of the two-year moving-average trend lines (gray line in the two graphs) suggests that the numbers of students dropping out of school is due to the set of socioeconomic factors operating at the township and county level.

5

Recruiting Returnees to Build Enterprises and Towns

In the end, peasants must return home. This is the law of time immemorial. If all our peasants leave the villages, shoulder their wells on their backs and go to build prosperity in the cities, then that silent sacrificial lamb, the countryside, when will it call out? When will it become civilized?[1]

LOCAL state cadres struggle with other social actors for control over the resources generated by labor migration, and this can be seen particularly in their efforts to encourage return migrant entrepreneurship. The "local state" refers to the government and Party bodies that run the townships and their constituent administrative villages. The County Rural Work Office evaluates local state cadres according to their ability to improve economic conditions within their jurisdictions, and such improvements are particularly tangible and powerful when in the form of newly created enterprises, upgraded town infrastructure, and increased tax revenue. In some parts of the Chinese countryside, the local state encourages successful migrants to return home and create businesses as a way of obtaining more resources for attaining their political and economic goals. In appealing to migrants to invest at home, local cadres invoke values such as loyalty to the family and love of the native place, and they offer incentives such as improved access to local resources and opportunities for deploying resources profitably. At the same time, local states also encourage those migrants who have been "pushed" back home (and who are not necessarily successful) to support themselves and contribute to the local economy through self-employment. This chapter explores how the local state in Xinfeng and Yudu influences conditions in the origin areas in ways that both encourage the return of some successful migrants and make the local environment more conducive to the entrepreneurial deployment of skills, knowledge, and capital.

5.1 RETURN AND ENTREPRENEURSHIP AT THE NATIONAL LEVEL

Since 1995, return migration and entrepreneurship have become major issues across China as a whole. There has been an increase in return migration to various parts of the Chinese countryside, with the level of return to different regions affected by trends in regional economic development. The ratio of returnees to migrants is highest in the coastal provinces, where the reforms have yielded the greatest benefits.[2] For example, the volume of return to north Jiangsu is now 25% greater than the volume of out-migration from the region, and many of the returnees have set up businesses.[3] However, because most migrants have come from the interior, in terms of absolute numbers there are far more migrants returning to these key labor-exporting provinces.[4] According to the China Rural Development Research Center, 36% of rural migrants from the interior provinces of Jiangxi, Anhui, Hubei, and Sichuan are already returning home, and a portion are using their skills, capital, and contacts to establish undertakings that range from small service stalls to large manufacturing entities.[5] For instance, an article in a 2000 issue of the *China Daily* states that, in Sichuan province, 4% of some 10 million surplus rural laborers have used their earnings to establish businesses back in their home towns.[6] A multitude of Chinese-language reports on return migrant entrepreneurship in various counties and provinces suggest that counties enjoying the benefits of return migrant entrepreneurship tend to have long migration histories and extensive local government support for the returnee entrepreneurs.[7] Most of these counties also tend to have average or above-average levels of per-capita income. Chinese commentators predict that return migrant entrepreneurship will continue into the twenty-first century as those pioneers who went out in the 1980s and 1990s return home.[8]

The central state in China has instructed administrators at all levels to support returnee entrepreneurship because farmers are said, through the experience of migration and return, to "both earn a ticket and exchange a brain."[9] At the Fifteenth National People's Conference, then-premier Li Peng called upon local officials to encourage migrant farmers who have learned skills to return home and assist poverty alleviation by starting businesses. Since 1993, the Research Committee for the Development of China's Rural Labor Resources and the China Poverty Relief Foundation have been holding "stars of entrepreneurship" forums on a biannual basis. These forums praise former migrants who return home to help organize the poor in creating rural industries that exploit new resources and contribute to local tax coffers.[10]

Although Chinese policy-makers are enthusiastic about the entrepreneurial potential of returnees, the English-language migration literature is (as discussed in Chapter 1) generally more skeptical. The only empirical study of return migrant entrepreneurship in China is by Yuen-Fong Woon and is based on a survey of 180 migrants in the destination area. In her study, highly educated factory employees and suburban farm contractors sharing the same cultural and linguistic background as the host society were successful in obtaining permanent urban residence permits. In contrast, the 28% of respondents who intended to return home were the least educated migrants, and the author observes that they had not learned any skills that would help them in business.[11] Though the majority of rural migrants in China are undoubtedly confined to unskilled tasks in the cities and though the perception that they have few learning opportunities is a fair one, I would argue that it is difficult to assess accurately the extent to which a migrant has obtained skills, knowledge, or other resources. Studies in other developing countries find that returnees have in fact obtained valuable resources but that officials tend to ignore their simple pieces of equipment, ideas, or skills, denying them the micro-credit and administrative support needed for some small undertaking.[12]

Giving priority to building rural towns and enterprises is one dimension of state policy in China that is particularly important in increasing the opportunities for migrants to deploy their resources in entrepreneurial ways when they return home. The market towns act as urban pockets for absorbing resources and innovations from the cities, thereby helping to overcome the incompatibility between urban work skills and the rural setting, which is blamed in the literature for hindering returnee innovation. Moreover, in much of China the gap between the level of production technology in the labor-intensive factories of cities and the level of technology that can be absorbed by the natal communities is small enough to allow for the spatial transfer of skills and production techniques.[13] Not only do towns absorb returnee skills and material resources, but returned migrants also direct their resources toward the building of these towns. According to scholars and policy advisors at the Development Research Office of China's State Council, returned migrants tend to locate their houses and businesses in towns and county seats rather than in villages, and this promotes the 1990s policy of integrating rural enterprise creation with town construction.[14] Additionally, Chinese policy-makers see a role for returnee entrepreneurs of filling in "holes" in the rural economy left by decades of economic planning – for example, a lack of services and an underdeveloped industrial sector.

Local state policies to build towns and encourage return migrant entrepreneurship help to explain why, in finding that returnees make a positive contribution to development in the origin areas, the research presented in this and the following two chapters differs from the dominant view in the migration literature. These chapters draw largely on fieldwork conducted in the towns. Gmelch has observed that scholars are generally skeptical about returnee entrepreneurship, yet they tend to carry out their field research in the villages even though a "majority of returned migrants in many countries have resettled in towns and cities."[15] Also, whereas returnee innovators in other parts of the world tend to be ignored or even discriminated against by local officials, the local states in Xinfeng and Yudu have been particularly proactive in incorporating return migration into their local development strategies.

The Chinese policy of using return migrant entrepreneurship as a development initiative warrants particular attention in light of a World Bank investigation into rural enterprises. That investigation finds that, owing to previous restrictions on internal mobility, counties in China have relied upon their own stock of entrepreneurs in the development of businesses. According to the study, grass-roots entrepreneurs have generally included government cadres and former cadres, supply and marketing personnel in township collectives, skilled workers in government enterprises, former state enterprise employees, and also farmers.[16] These entrepreneurs typically have strong local contacts, and this further compresses the geographical and social scope of market linkages and information exchange. The authors explain that the counties poorly endowed with entrepreneurs and experienced managers have failed to develop viable enterprises. If the explanation for a weak industrial and commercial base lies in a "human resources" deficiency, then a handful of returned migrants with managerial experience and contacts with coastal business people has the potential to make a significant impact on the origin economies. I suggest that the actions of the local state in encouraging return migrant entrepreneurship have helped to bring about such an outcome in Xinfeng and Yudu.

5.2 RETURNEES TO XINFENG AND YUDU

5.2.1 *Concentration in Time and Numbers*

Returnees in Xinfeng and Yudu have been targeted by the local state for special treatment because their returns are concentrated in time and their numbers are significant. Returnee entrepreneurship came into prominence from 1995 onward. During the early to mid-1990s, some migrants began to feel that – after a decade of laboring alone in the city – the migrant lifestyle could not continue indefinitely. Also around this time, local officials started to realize the advantages of creating a policy environment congenial to private entrepreneurs. If only a few migrants had returned, then the attributes that distinguish them from local inhabitants may not have been expressed in any tangible way. Moreover, if the return of migrants had been dispersed over time then it is unlikely that their potential would have become the focus of local policy initiatives.

Although the enterprises established by returnees do not represent a large number in either Xinfeng or Yudu, the incidence is sufficient for local officials to identify the returned migrants as a new and important group of rural entrepreneurs. The contributions of returnees to business creation are summarized in Table 5.1.

However, migrant enterprises are more important than their numbers alone would indicate, because they tend to be much larger than the average: of the

Table 5.1. *Returnee business creation in Xinfeng and Yudu*

	Xinfeng	Yudu
Getihu Service and Manufacturing (1997)		
Total number of *getihu*	15,000 (approx.)	13,836[a]
Approximate proportion of returnee *getihu*	one fifth[b]	one third
% of total commercial tax from returnee *getihu*	not available	14%[c]
Getihu and siying qiye manufacturing (end of 1995)		
Number of returnee enterprises	153[d]	1,450[e]
Returnees working in these enterprises	1,349	4,000
Industrial product value of returnee enterprises as a proportion of 1995 total (nearest whole %)	13%[f]	>46%[g]

Note: In the early 1980s, "individual operators" (*getihu*) were forbidden to hire more than two employees and five apprentices, because hiring more would constitute exploitation. Most *getihu* were traders or repairers. In 1987 a new term came into being, "private enterprise" or *siying qiye,* meaning those who employ over eight people. As the private sector has evolved, private businesses have differed from individual enterprises not only in terms of size but also in terms of their tendency to engage in industry and manufacturing.

[a] Total number of private and individual enterprises registered with the Bureau of Industry and Commerce.

[b] Interview, Ou Yangfeng, County Head of Xinfeng, 18 June 1997.

[c] Interview, Deputy Director of the Yudu County Labor Export Bureau, 30 October 1997; Chen Puhua (1996), pp. 35–6.

[d] Xinfeng xian geti qiye xiehui (1995). The smallest business in the table has one employee and the largest business has 48 employees; the average number of employees is nine.

[e] Ji Enze, "Phoenixes returning to the nest," p. 31; *Guanghua shibao* [Guanghua Times], 11 April 1997, p. 3; *Jiangxi qingnianbao,* 18 February 1997, p. 2; Chen Ru (1996), p. 26.

[f] Xinfeng xian geti qiye xiehui (1995). Total product value of these enterprises is 135,224,000 yuan. According to the 1996 *Jiangxi Statistical Yearbook,* the total industrial product value for enterprises registered at the village level or above in Xinfeng county is 1,042,710,000 yuan. See *Jiangxi tongji nianjian* (1996), table 18-3, p. 566.

[g] Ibid., p. 567. The total industrial product value of industries at the level of village and above is 797,060,000 yuan. Compare this against the total product value of the three enterprises with an annual product value of 100 million yuan plus the 69 enterprises with an annual product value of 1 million yuan.

1,450 returnee manufacturing entities in Yudu, the three largest businesses have an annual product value of 100 million yuan. And in 1996, out of 109 new projects with annual product values of around 1 million yuan, 69 of these (63%) were either created or initiated by former migrants.[17] The product value of returnee enterprises as a proportion of the total industrial product value for the county is higher in Yudu than in Xinfeng, partly because Yudu returnees have been successful in encouraging Hong Kong merchants to establish large clothing factories. Moreover, the manufacturing base of Yudu is weak, so the several large factories established by returnees make a substantial contribution to the total industrial product value of businesses in the county. In Xinfeng, small furniture workshops are the most common form of enterprise among returnees.

The figures just cited on the contribution of returned migrants to the economies of Xinfeng and Yudu cannot be taken at face value. To begin with, industrial product value is by no means the most reliable indicator of the economic standing of a business, but these are the only figures that I have. Moreover, the data for industrial product value shown in Table 5.1 are drawn from different published sources that may have categorized industrial product value in different ways. Caution is also required because local governments tend to "add moisture" (*jia shuifen*) to their production figures and newspapers may overstate economic successes. Additionally, officials in both counties stress that the numbers of returned migrant entrepreneurs are in constant flux – many set up for a few months, fail, and are forced back out to the cities. Neither do these figures account for cases where a migrant introduces an urban contact to local officials who establish a project and invite others to contract the management of the business. Despite difficulties in obtaining accurate data, the available figures are at least consistent with the empirical evidence that the contribution of returnee entrepreneurs to the economies of Xinfeng and Yudu is "significant."

5.2.2 *The Local State's Imperative to Encourage Enterprise Creation*

The situation of returnee innovation in Xinfeng and Yudu contradicts the conventional wisdom on return migrant innovation partly because China is different. Sinologists have long been criticized for adopting the attitude that all developments in China have uniquely "Chinese characteristics." Yet China *is* unique in its inheritance of a Party–state apparatus that penetrates right down to the grass-roots level. The counties devise and direct economic plans for subordinate townships and towns. Local cadres are representatives of the central state, the Party endorses their appointments, and their work is assessed regularly by cadres from upper echelons. Township cadres are entrusted by the state to levy taxes and oversee the quota purchases of agricultural produce. Additionally, they are responsible for education, family planning, land use, public security, and social stability. The nature of the local state is significant because, as several migration scholars have suggested, if returnees are to promote development then coordination and support from all levels of the leadership are required.[18]

The Party–state has tremendous power in terms of both its vertical command and its horizontal reach. As described in Chapter 3, county and township officials periodically lead village cadres and village group leaders (*zuzhang*) in conducting household evaluation campaigns. Households assess themselves and their neighbors in terms of adherence to state policies: conformity with family planning regulations, completion of production quotas, moral behavior, providing for the welfare needs of household members, and politically correct thought. Of course, in daily life people do not really judge themselves or others by these criteria, but evaluation plaques fixed outside the door of a house reflect on the "face" of the household, and people care about how they are evaluated. These evaluation campaigns are coordinated at national, provincial, and prefectural levels, and they demonstrate the capacity of the state to penetrate every household. The county almanac for Yudu 1986–1992 shows that such activities were in force for successive years right up until 1992,[19] and my conversations with residents in Jiaocun village (Yudu) reveal that they were conducted also in 1996. As for Xinfeng, my guide there (Mr. Lu) has worked in such campaigns at the village level since 1994. In both counties, the visitor sees plaques above doorways that are relics of previous social education campaigns. The Chinese state has the administrative apparatus to implement policies, and the lower-level cadres have so much influence that their support for any individual initiative is essential to its ultimate success. This is not to suggest that the Chinese state is monolithic. Certainly there is struggle between the various levels of the hierarchy, particularly with regard to revenue, as well as considerable regional variation in the way that policies are interpreted and implemented.

Before looking at *how* the local states in Xinfeng and Yudu encourage return migrant entrepreneurship, I will briefly discuss *why* they have an interest in initiating linkages with migrants and urging their return. First, the motivation for different levels of government to encourage return migrant entrepreneurship is intertwined with broader incentives to support rural enterprise creation. In particular, financial reforms have pressured all levels of government to generate additional revenue. Second, the local state has a vested interest in enhancing its own legitimacy by improving rural livelihoods and promoting social stability through the absorption of surplus rural labor. Finally, there is the influence of directives from higher levels in the state apparatus. Each of these is discussed in turn.

On the first point, by creating enterprises, returnees help the local government to attain revenue goals. Fiscal reforms in the early 1980s have meant that counties, townships, and villages have assumed increased autonomy over the revenues they generate. Previously, all revenue was surrendered to the center and expenditure was allocated from above. Now each administrative level signs a contract with the one above to fulfill negotiated goals for revenue and expenditure. There are two kinds of revenue: budgetary and extrabudgetary. The budgetary revenue is levied at the township level and channeled up to the counties, prefectures, and provinces and finally up to the central government. The main sources of this revenue are the taxes levied by the Bureau of

Industry and Commerce on county enterprises and rural industries, as well as agricultural taxes.[20] The pressure on lower levels of government to contribute to budgetary revenue is intensified by the link between economic achievement and the political careers of leaders. In order to minimize opportunities for nepotism, government leaders at county and township levels are rotated to new locations every three years, and Party leaders are reassigned posts every five years – or at least this was the case in the counties I visited in Jiangxi province. Their appointments at the end of their terms are often dependent upon surpassing state revenue targets. Moreover, at the time of my fieldwork, local state cadres were being threatened with redundancy as the reform-minded central state discussed ways to reduce the farmers' tax burden. On my return visit to Jiangxi (in September–December 2000), the trimming of local state bureaucracy was underway. Some 20%–30% of cadres were dismissed, and many of them marched to the county and prefectural government offices in protest. Increasingly, cadres feel under pressure to attain targets in order to retain their posts. Thus, different levels of the state commit themselves to targets that they cannot hope to honor, placing pressure on those below them to deliver the results. There is competition between the townships within a county to reach targets, and some local states meet their quotas by taking out loans.[21]

Since the tax reforms of 1994, counties have claimed an even greater advantage in the struggle with the townships over the allocation of budgetary funds, because counties stipulate the portion of tax revenue that is to be redirected to the subordinate level for expenditure. The exact portion redistributed to the lower level depends on the economic conditions of the counties and townships, the special political or economic significance attached to a particular locality, the interpersonal connections between the leaders at various levels, and complex political negotiations. In some cases, the lower level receives generous subsidies so that the budgetary allocation exceeds the initial tax contribution. In other cases, the amounts of the budgetary allocation and the tax contribution are comparable, while in still other cases the budgetary allocation is far smaller than the amount of the original tax contribution, resulting in a net loss for the lower level. Townships and counties are not able to rely on budgetary allocations to meet all of their expenditure needs. Consequently, they have become responsible for raising additional funds needed for investment in capital construction, social expenditure, and welfare in the form of extrabudgetary revenue.[22]

The local state's need for extrabudgetary funds at the grass roots is exacerbated by two factors. First, there is political pressure to build up town infrastructure, and this is a contributing cause of debt in many counties.[23] In Xinfeng, for instance, there is an ambitious push to achieve the standard that allows for conversion to a county-level city, thereby providing access to generous state subsidies and greater autonomy in fiscal management – and it is the farmers who are required to contribute. Second, the economic autonomy afforded by the reforms has increased opportunities for local corruption, with such "benefits" perceived by officials as just returns for a poorly remunerated job. In recent years, some township governments have been using extrabudgetary funds to build commodity housing in the county seat for administrative personnel, with township leaders commuting weekly between the county seat and the township rather than living in their place of work as stipulated in cadre guidelines.[24]

The county-level government receives some funding from the state budget for local expenditure, but it is also heavily dependent on extrabudgetary income from its own state enterprises. In Xinfeng and Yudu, these industries include breweries, printing presses, fertilizer factories, cement factories, machine parts factories, foodstuff factories, bamboo furniture factories, firecracker factories, and some mines. However, since 1994, there have been widespread retrenchments from such enterprises, and state enterprise employees are a new social group now availing themselves of introductions from labor agencies for city jobs.[25] The county also receives income from the townships and villages, collected through various fees and taxes.

Township and village governments receive some funding from the county for the wages of personnel, but they are essentially reliant on their extrabudgetary funds. In underdeveloped regions with weak industrial bases, most of the extrabudgetary funds are exacted from the agrarian sector, and the pressure to generate income often results in "the three indiscriminates": exorbitant taxes, fees, and fines levied on an overburdened peasantry. Petty commodity producers can only be squeezed so much, and in August 1997 there were riots in Yudu that were appeased only when national authorities intervened and instructed township governments to curb exactions, freezing the tax burden for three years.[26]

The fieldwork paints an ambiguous picture in which the local cadres not only facilitate returnee entrepreneurship but also seek to control the resources that are generated through return migration. This conforms to a broader historical interpretation of state–entrepreneur relations in Chinese society which says that the position of the state is characterized by the contradictory but not necessarily exclusive positions of repression and stimulation.[27] Gates argues that, owing to the structural features of the political economy in Chinese societies both past and present, the economic activities of petty capitalists are embedded in a dominant tributary mode that is managed by state officials who put their own requirements for revenues and continued hegemony above the perceived need for economic expansion.[28]

The enthusiasm of local leaders who encourage returnees to set up businesses or contract out any project must be understood in terms of the economic imperatives that give them an interest in anyone setting up anything. In the words of a township leader in Yudu: "We send out labor, but if the labor works at home then we get the tax income."[29] The returnee campaign operates alongside other (albeit less successful) strategies for encouraging investment. Investment invitations are issued to people who were rusticated in Xinfeng and Yudu during the Cultural Revolution and have since returned to cities such as Shanghai and Guangzhou. Yet most of these people have such painful memories of their rustication experiences they are loath to return.[30] Nonetheless, many "returned youths" from Shanghai and Guangdong sponsor the education of children in rural Jiangxi through the quasi-governmental organization known as Operation Hope. The local states have also formulated preferential policies to cover a whole typology of potential investors, ranging from overseas Chinese to anyone from outside the county. As any hapless researcher in the field will know, the volume of investment proposals presented to a foreigner can be quite overwhelming. Yet for locals, establishing contact with outsiders and convincing them of the advantages of Xinfeng and Yudu is a difficult feat. By the end of 1995, enterprises with foreign or overseas Chinese investment numbered only five in Yudu and six in Xinfeng.[31]

Through encouraging returnee entrepreneurship, local states expand their horizontal linkages into urban centers to reach the business contacts of the returnees and, by extension, the resources of these contacts. Some migrants have connections with bosses in coastal cities, including overseas Chinese. This idea is expressed in the following extract from an open letter to Yudu migrants:

> We welcome each migrant worker to return to the county and engage in commerce or set up a business. We hope you can use all the skills and capital you acquired outside to return to the townships and take the lead in setting up businesses. In order to inject new vitality into the economy, please use all channels and contacts to introduce Hong Kong, Macao, and Taiwan members of the business community to invest and set up factories and develop tertiary industries in your home towns. Let us cooperate closely and join hands in order to accelerate poverty relief, and make the contribution you ought for the early glory of the economy at home! – Yudu County Party Committee, Yudu County People's Government, 18 January 1995

Outreach programs to migrants have extended the networks of the township and county governments to include other groups of potential investors. The original impetus for establishing representative offices in key coastal cities was to coordinate labor export from the counties and to provide services for migrants. These offices have since expanded their functions to include advertising local products and promoting business opportunities. Both Xinfeng and Yudu have offices in Dongguan city (Guangdong province), and there is a Yudu office in Shanghai.

Support for return migrant entrepreneurship must also be seen in terms of (a) the social welfare commitment of the national and local governments and (b) the moral values and sense of obligation that cause officials to channel resources into local economic construction. An illustration of the welfare concerns of leaders is the situation in Xinbei township, Yudu, whereby township and village cadres donated their labor to help build houses for those families whose homes were destroyed in the floods of spring 1997. Villagers in Jiaocun village told me about this as they pointed out some of the newly built red brick houses.

Cadres not only feel the need to improve the livelihoods of people in the countryside, they also feel the need to be *seen* to be making a positive difference to people's well-being. Supporting returnee entrepreneurship in the creation of any sizeable business enhances the legitimacy of local power holders. In poor townships with weak industrial bases, the establishment of a factory indicates that cadres are doing something more substantial than the huff and puff of slogans. When the household evaluation meetings were being carried out in the countryside of Wanzai, the villagers would say to me: "Every time they come down, they just increase our mental burden. Why don't they do something to ease our worries like set up a factory, give us food to eat?"[32] My guide Mr. Lu, who spent three years carrying out ideological work in the Xinfeng countryside, expressed a similar sentiment: "If you are not doing something real, showing ways to make money, the country cousins will turn their faces from you."[33] In creating businesses, returnees help the local state cadres achieve the goals of improving their status in the eyes of both upper-level authorities and the local populace.

All levels of the state hierarchy support returnee participation in business creation because in doing so they help to ensure their own political survival. Burgeoning surplus labor in the cities and the countryside threatens social stability and undermines the legitimacy of the state, which rests in part on its capacity to improve the well-being of the rural populace without compromising urban living standards. High levels of surplus labor in the cities restrict the opportunities for rural people to pursue their material goals through migration. This is because some of the urban poor are now competing with rural migrants for jobs: whereas unemployed workers previously would have been too embarrassed to attend the labor recruitment markets frequented by migrants, necessity is now conquering their pride.[34] Moreover, municipal authorities have instituted regulations banning migrants from a whole range of occupations because they are anxious to reserve jobs for unemployed natives.[35] During periods of economic downturn, millions of workers trudge back to the countryside and threaten social order, as was the case during 1989–1990. Again in 1996, the first year of the 9th Five-Year Plan, money supply was contracted and many state enterprise workers were laid off.[36] Campaigns at national, provincial, and local levels urging county and township cadres to welcome returnees are designed, in part, to diffuse the frustrations of young migrants by redirecting their aspirations for improved livelihoods from the cities toward home soil.

While alleviating stress in the cities, the return of "unemployed" migrants often causes disruption in the countryside, and Chinese observers express concern that some returned migrants engage in kidnapping, the selling of women and children, prostitution, and criminal gang activities.[37] Although never encountering anything as serious as this, my fieldwork confirms the perception that return migration can undermine social stability. Many parents in the villages complained that when economic decline sends the migrants home, the youths gamble with cards and mah-jongg and the young men drink and fight.[38] Chinese commentators urge that rural towns and industries be developed as a way of resettling the returnees, thereby avoiding social upheaval.[39]

According to an article in the Jiangxi Women's Federation newspaper, returned migrant entrepreneurs contribute to social stability, albeit indirectly, by creating local job opportunities that enable rural households to diversify their livelihoods while staying together. This is because local off-farm workers are able to commute on a daily basis between the town and home rather than enduring the family separations that are inevitable with long spells in distant cities.[40] Commuting to towns also allows for a more flexible deployment of labor in agriculture because workers can contribute toward household farming tasks during busy seasons. Moreover, returnee entrepreneurs and employees can participate in their social roles as community leaders, parents, and spouses, thereby easing the physical and emotional stress on household members who are left behind.

Finally, the campaign to encourage returnee entrepreneurship in Xinfeng and Yudu functions within the context of nationwide initiatives. Youth magazines, newspapers, government circulars, and television programs are used by the central state to mobilize a variety of audiences in support of returnee entrepreneurship. Commentators proclaim the return of phoenixes to their nests, herald the historical transition of the tide of migrant workers into a tide of returning entrepreneurs, and chronicle success stories. Like the rural reforms and decollectivization campaigns discussed in Chapter 2, the campaign to encourage return migrant entrepreneurship operates vertically even though much of the impetus originated spontaneously from the ranks of petty commodity producers, only later being recognized and supported by higher levels. Ganzhou prefecture has followed provincial recommendations and urged counties under its jurisdiction to encourage return migrant entrepreneurship.[41] Government publications instruct cadres by detailing the measures and successes of counties where the government has been supportive of returnees.[42] At the end of the chain, government documents and newspaper articles in Xinfeng and Yudu identify returnee enterprises (*dagong qiye*) as a new point for growth in the rural economy and recommend supportive government action.[43] The local government claims that: "The tide of returnee entrepreneurship is no coincidence but is the combined result of preferential policies from the county government and the love of migrants for home soil."[44]

5.3 COAXING THE PHOENIX TO LAY EGGS IN THE NEST

5.3.1 *The State Campaign to Encourage Returnee Entrepreneurship*

The local state attracts returnee entrepreneurs through a set of measures that are based on policy and publicity. These policies include temporary tax reductions as well as assistance with access to land, factory space, credit, raw materials, water, and electricity. The county and township bureaus of rural industry also provide information on viable projects. In Xinfeng, administrative procedures for business permits have been simplified, and returnees are allowed a six-month grace period before registering: "first get on the bus, then buy a ticket."[45] In Yudu, there has been a crackdown on unregistered private enterprises, but officials are instructed to ensure that procedures for returnees are handled promptly.[46] Finally, cadres help returnees resolve reintegration problems such as arranging schooling for their children.

Publicity campaigns in Xinfeng and Yudu have been assisted by national and prefectural praise meetings that reflect the capacity of the state to confer "face" on model returnees – that is, to recognize their increased control over social and economic resources and reward this with visible political endorsement. Model returnees exemplify values such as home-town loyalty, persistence in the face of adversity, and the pursuit of progress. They appeal to the aspirations of migrant youths by demonstrating that goals for social mobility can be achieved within the home town. Although readers familiar with the role that models have played in the Chinese political process may be skeptical that such publicity measures can yield results, it is important to remember that – like out-migration – return migration is inspired by the "demonstration effect" of others. Renowned returnee entrepreneurs are persuasive because they are intimately linked to the target communities: people witness their home-town fellows' progress from farmer to worker to boss and seek to emulate this pathway in attaining their own goals.

Although the following "models" received their awards for entrepreneurial success rather than for returning home, their past migrant work experience is featured in local and provincial publicity reports and their returnee status is well known among locals. In 1994, Ouyang Xiaofang of Yudu, director of the Jinda

Shiye Group Company, was named "All-China Outstanding Entrepreneur of the Private Economy" by the All-China Federation of Industry and Commerce; he was also awarded the title of "All-China Rural Entrepreneur" by the Ministry of Agriculture. The Yudu County Government rewarded him with a Santana car in 1993 and an imported Jeep worth 280,000 yuan ($33,000) in 1994.[47] The Ouyang Complex, the tallest building in Yudu, incorporates a restaurant, shops, a hotel, and offices. It stands in the middle of the county town and metaphorically proclaims the rise of a lowly farmer: he earned money as a labor contractor in Guangzhou and Xiamen, then invested in mines and factories at home. However, this tale has a twist in that, according to rumor, Ouyang is now heavily in debt. As a further example, Zou Jinsheng, founder and manager of the Shenta Snake Development Industrial Company in Xinfeng, was winner of a 1997 "Ganzhou Prefecture Private Entrepreneur" award. In addition to a plaque and certificate, he was presented with a large, remote-control television.[48]

Other returned migrants enjoy a de facto model status that is similarly created through the local leaders' public recognition of their control over social and economic resources. In the local media these returnees expound such values as love of the home town and advertise the advantages of entrepreneurship at home, including abundant natural resources, cheap labor, improved infrastructure, and government policies. Officials participate in the televised opening ceremonies of larger businesses, and gestures of support include congratulatory speeches and donations, such as clocks bearing the name of a government department. Lai Tianyang, proprietor of the Jinlong Furniture Factory, proudly invited me to take a photograph of him in front of a symbol of political endorsement: calligraphy scribed by the Xinfeng County Head and carved into the company sign.[49]

Spring Festival is an occasion for local officials (a) to remind those migrants who have prospered not to forget the home soil that has nourished them and (b) to inform them of preferential policies for returned migrants who set up businesses. From January to March, newspapers carry stories of migrants who have donated money to development projects or who have prospered through entrepreneurship at home.[50] Returnees are greeted by banners at bus stations proclaiming: "Welcome Migrants to Come Home and Set Up Businesses." In gazettes and on the county television news, migrants are offered festive tidings. Flyers are distributed to village households detailing recent advances in the county economy and urging migrants to establish businesses. Those who return for Spring Festival are invited to participate in county and township conferences, which have a dual function: one is to inform the migrants of changes in the county and recommend avenues for investment; the other is to solicit suggestions from returnees on the implications of urban business practices for local reforms.

The rural–urban information network created through migration is used by cadres for initiating contact with migrants in cities and for attracting projects and investment. Remittance slips and hearsay from villagers enable cadres to identify high-earning migrants or those who have reached white-collar positions within a factory and are likely to have influence with bosses. Each year, delegations of cadres from villages, townships, and the county visit locations in coastal cities where home-town migrants are concentrated.[51] Apart from bringing good wishes and distributing information on family planning, the delegates try to persuade successful migrants to launch projects at home. Some returnees have been recruited in this way to serve as village cadres and to contract the running of government enterprises.[52] Township labor management offices also contact rural households for the mail addresses and phone numbers of successful migrants.[53]

Local state organizations in both Xinfeng and Yudu run pilot projects that integrate labor export with training so that migrants promote poverty alleviation on their return home. These initiatives are underpinned by population quality and modernization discourses that locate the cure for rural docility in the benevolent government sponsorship of urban exposure. The Shanghai Dock Workers' branch of the Yudu Labor Export Company runs night-school classes. The courses range from numeracy and literacy classes to training in car repairs and electronics. Known as the "Cradle Culture Project," the Yudu initiative has been widely commended in the Shanghai media.[54] The following comments on the cultural projects initiated by the Yudu Labor Export Company appear in *Jiangxi Daily*:

> Using labor export as a means to relieve poverty cannot be based solely on earning money; even more importantly, it must use the radiation effect of the city to improve the *quality* of the peasants. This relates not just to the future of the company, but also to the role of return migrants in leading peasants to prosperity.[55]

In 1996, cadres in Daa town (Xinfeng county) established a Migrant Youth Society, which has received praise from a representative of the Communist Youth League. According to *Jiangxi Daily,* township officials became concerned at the blind outflow of youths who had spent their lives "behind closed doors keeping watch over the fields." The society was formed to give purpose to the migrant experience, so that the youths "earn money, learn skills, and grasp management experience which can serve development at home." The society aims "to diligently improve the *quality* of migrant youth workers, and to build bridges for migrant youths to return and set up businesses."[56] Society activities include labor export, vocational training, and initiatives to encourage the return of successful migrants.

5.3.2 *Building Rural Market Towns*

With the sponsorship of the local state, returnee entrepreneurs participate in the creation of rural market towns. One initiative that township cadres partially attribute to the suggestions of returned migrants is "special economic zones." According to a 1997 article in *Xinfeng News,*

> the townships of Jiudu, Xiaohe, and Daa have established "returnee migrant enterprise and industry mini-zones," which have attracted over one hundred returnee enterprises ... one Xiaohe returnee who has benefited greatly, Wang Wensheng, sighed with much feeling, saying, "The preferential and supportive policies of the Party and government can be likened to a vast body of water in which fish are free to swim; entrepreneurs are even more able to raise a great sail among one hundred ships."

The special zones reflect a commitment on the part of local leaders (a) to assist entrepreneurs with access to land close to the town center and (b) to concentrate the geographic distribution of fledgling rural enterprises.

As in rural areas in other developing countries,[57] the contribution of migrants to the construction of rural market towns in Xinfeng and Yudu can be seen in the wave of building that has swept through the countryside in recent years. When traveling through the countryside, the visitor sees a proliferation of brick kilns. Having had occasion to visit numerous villages in Jiangxi, either as a guest at the homes of friends or in an attempt to arrange fieldwork access, I have also had the opportunity to inquire about the ownership of local brick factories. Thus I have informally conducted a survey of ten brick factories, all of which turn out to be founded, funded, or contracted by returnees.[58] Most are established as village collectives, though some of the larger ones are registered at the township level. In regions with low per-capita allocations of land and a weak industrial sector, brick factories are an attractive avenue for investment, especially now that remittances are fueling a demand for bricks. Because the bricks can only be made in good weather, the factories operate for only about half the year, and workers earn between 300 and 400 yuan a month. Kiln operators earn around 800 yuan a month for their hot and dangerous work. The construction industry also creates local employment for builders, carpenters, and electricians. Thus, the overall implications of the building boom for diversifying rural livelihoods and increasing incomes are significant.

The movement of some returnees from the villages to the towns is indicative of their social advancement and illustrates the strong correlation between the social and spatial hierarchies of China. Entrepreneurial returnees prefer to build their houses in the township because of the commercial advantages of location, with the ground floor reserved for some business such as a shop, restaurant, or repair booth. At either side of township roads, the visitor sees two- and three-story red brick constructions in various stages of completion. These new buildings contrast with older, yellow, mud brick buildings. The designs are simple, with one large room at ground level and a few rooms above with no internal connections; the entry to each room is via an outside balcony. The buildings have electricity, though water is fetched from a well outside. According to officials from the land management bureaus of various townships, migrant money is behind well over half of the construction activity.[59] As my guide explained: "One thing is obvious, these houses are built by people who have money, and most of those who have money do not earn it in the countryside of Yudu."[60]

Migrants use their money to negotiate with the local state to obtain strategic sites. Under Mao, both land ownership and land-use rights belonged to the collectives. Since the implementation of the household responsibility system, land ownership and land-use rights have been divided: ownership rights belong to the collective; and usage rights are contracted to households for designated purposes, usually agriculture. As opportunities for market participation in rural areas have increased, land-use values have soared. The state has been critical of people who use the land as if it were private property to trade commercially, accusing them of selfishly neglecting the interests of the collective.[61] The central state is particularly alarmed at the amount of farmland being used for construction purposes. Even in the less developed hill country of Jiangxi, increasing integration into the cash economy is leading to the appropriation of farmland for construction purposes.

Returned migrants are using the emergence of an "invisible" (*yinxing*) land market in the areas surrounding towns and transport routes to gain collateral for their business activities. A house situated along a transport route in the township or on the outskirts of the county seat can be used as security for obtaining loans from rural credit cooperatives. In Xinfeng and Yudu, applications for a loan are dependent upon a "house property certificate." These certificates state the value of the house and are issued after an official from the Township Land Bureau has evaluated the property. In practice, the geographical location of the land is incorporated into the value of the building, so that buildings are assessed at a value much higher than the bricks and mortar. An official in Xinbei township, Yudu, explained that the houses built by migrants in their village hamlets cannot be used as security for obtaining a loan.[62] Prime sites for house building are obtained through political contacts, or else migrants pay "land administration fees" and per-mu land-use fees, providing revenue for the local state. Thus, the resources earned in the cities provide a means for those deficient in political capital to acquire a desirable property location and, by extension, to gain access to local credit.

Although offering land-use rights as security for loans is criticized as one of the anomalies of the invisible land market,[63] the trend is pervasive and unavoidable in a situation where the market economy intersects with imperfectly defined land policies. A legitimate means of obtaining property that can be used as security for a loan is to purchase a commodity apartment in the county seat: two interviewees reported purchasing such homes for this purpose. A basic apartment in the Yudu county seat involves an outlay of about 300,000 yuan. Building a house in or near the township costs about 100,000 yuan, and building a house in the village costs about 30,000 yuan. A house in the county seat is beyond the reach of most returnees, so the township is an attractive option for rural dwellers who have substantial savings.

A contrast to the situation in Xinfeng and Yudu is the experience of Rongtang township in a different part of Jiangxi (Fengcheng county), where the local state has also been keen to direct migrant and returnee resources toward commercial development. The state has sponsored the construction of the Bright Star Development Zone as a site for returnee business creation. In the Bright Star Zone, land is sold at 500 yuan per square meter, and this money is used to lay roads and power lines. This official project consists of 124 three-story buildings: the ground floor functions as a stall or workshop and the upper stories are for residential purposes. The road surfaces and buildings in the development zone are superior to those in the rest of the town, or indeed any other town that I have visited. Since 1992, a total of 1 billion yuan has been invested, and 90% of this money is from migrants.[64]

Although the local state may undertake initiatives to direct migrant resources toward entrepreneurship in the native place, migration has afforded rural people considerable latitude in exactly how and where they pursue their goals. Most Rongtang migrants are clothes traders on Hainan Island; their energies are expended primarily in developing their Hainan businesses, so they tend not to return home. One migrant who had returned for his mother's birthday explained: "This is our home and we must come back eventually. Even if it is a dump, it is still home. So some people buy a place here. But in Hainan, the weather is beautiful, the economy is developed, and life is better."[65] Even though the migrants do not create businesses at home, the state initiative has been successful in harnessing migrant funds for town construction. Furthermore, the shop buildings, electricity connections, and roads have improved the physical environment in which local nonmigrants earn their living as petty entrepreneurs.

5.3.3 *A Weakness in the State Campaign*

Although the local state in Xinfeng and Yudu has been inventive in devising measures that improve the local business environment and encourage return migrant entrepreneurship, there is a lack of sound business guidance for would-be entrepreneurs. Officials tend to focus on the short-term goal of attracting projects and money rather than providing support for the longer-term survival of the returnee businesses. State measures to encourage returnee entrepreneurship have assumed many of the features of the "campaigns" common to the Chinese political process: publicity posters, praise meetings, political meetings, models, banners, and directives. As a consequence, some individuals have been caught up in this campaign – seduced by official courtship and the idea of becoming a boss – without much attention to the viability of the project.

This is illustrated by the story of Mr. Chen, a former worker and production supervisor in a steel rolling mill. On returning to Xinfeng for Spring Festival, Mr. Chen saw that migrant remittances were fueling a housing boom, and he perceived a potential market for steel rods used in the reinforcement of cement floors. In 1994, at the suggestion of local leaders, Mr. Chen set up the Xiniu Township Steel Factory. He purchased machinery from a rural industry in Guangzhou for 600,000 yuan. Half of this money took the form of a loan from the Xinfeng County Finance Investment Company, which charges higher interest on loans than do banks or local credit cooperatives.[66] Unfortunately, Mr. Chen's product turned out to be of inferior quality to the steel rods imported from Guangzhou, so he failed to attract customers. Moreover, most of Mr. Chen's capital was tied up in machinery, so he had no money left over for the purchase of scrap metal or the payment of electricity bills or workers' wages. Mr. Chen explained his predicament as follows:

> I was spurred on by the enthusiasm of the local government. At the time there was a lot of talk. But now that I need help, the government is not so interested. They just want to know when I will pay back the money. Now that things have gone wrong I am totally on my own. I can see that that my cultural quality is too low. Otherwise, I would not have sunk all of my money into the fixed capital. Before there were over twenty employees. But production has stopped for the past two months. I can't back out now or I will lose too much. I am trying to scrape together more money to resume production in a couple of months' time.[67]

My guide's opinion of Mr. Chen's predicament is that he had failed because of his "little peasant mentality" – pursuing short-term gain to the detriment of long-term interests:

> You see the rods he makes. They are so thin; they are the sort used in shoddy construction projects that end up falling down and killing people. That's the thing about China's peasants – they only see today. Today he wants to set up a factory, but after you have the physical fact of the factory, what do you do next?

Whereas failed entrepreneurs are said to be handicapped by their "peasant mentality," successful entrepreneurs are said to have had their minds opened by urban exposure. By invoking discourses about the lower quality of peasants, the local state absolves itself of responsibility.

5.4 CONCLUSION

The local state has enacted a range of publicity and policy initiatives designed to encourage return migrant entrepreneurship. In terms of publicity, the local state invokes values of loyalty to the family and the native place, and it gives visible political endorsement to those who return home to "get rich." Policy measures involve cadre promises to provide access to local resources (such as credit and land) and to assist returnees in the entrepreneurial deployment of their savings, skills, and information. In harnessing the resources generated by return migration, the local state is pursuing policy goals as well as goals pertaining to its own strength and survival. Policy goals include building rural towns and creating rural enterprises, diversifying rural livelihoods, absorbing surplus rural labor, maintaining social stability, and improving "population quality." Directing returnee resources toward these projects helps local cadres attain the related goals of increasing tax revenue, enhancing their legitimacy in the eyes of the rural populace, and gaining the approval of upper levels in the state hierarchy.

The enthusiasm of the local state for business creation means that returnees can use their money and contacts to lobby for concessions, preferential access to resources, and land situated near the rural towns and county seats. The commercial advantages of the rural towns and the 1990s policy of integrating town construction with rural enterprise creation mean that the towns serve as urban pockets that absorb returnee innovations, thereby accelerating the slow core–periphery diffusion process envisioned by Skinner and other modernization theorists. Through supporting returned migrants in setting up their businesses in the towns, cadres ensure that local town infrastructure is visibly improved under their leadership and guidance, thereby enhancing their legitimacy. The local cadres are inventive in devising measures to encourage returnee entrepreneurship, but their failure to evaluate the longer-term viability of business projects and provide sound advice aggravates the financial problems of some returnees. Nonetheless, the local state campaign to encourage returnee entrepreneurship is attracting projects that contribute to the local economy.

6

The Enterprises and the Entrepreneurs

THIS chapter examines the characteristics of returnee enterprises and of the entrepreneurs themselves. The returnee enterprises are discussed in terms of their scale, type of business activity, and form of ownership. The smaller-scale businesses arrange their operational structure according to the familial petty commodity mode of production, whereas the larger-scale businesses adopt more of the formalized management and production features of urban factories. Returnee business activities are concentrated in the manufacturing and service sectors, with only a few businesses engaged in specialized agricultural production. The ownership structure of these enterprises varies: returnees establish private-sector entities and they also purchase or contract the running of collective and state enterprises.

Analyzing the characteristics of the entrepreneurs facilitates an understanding of the migrants' capacity to obtain resources both in the cities and at home, with implications for the scale and strength of the businesses that they create on their return. These characteristics include the duration of their absence in the cities, age on return, level of educational attainment, and reasons for return. Although most of the returned migrant entrepreneurs are men, women returnees receive separate in-depth discussion because gender-specific considerations affect their decisions to return as well as the scale and type of businesses that they create. The chapter shows that, while the returnees in south Jiangxi differ from each other in terms of their characteristics and hence in the kinds of businesses they create, they share a goal in common with returned migrants all over the world: that of becoming their own bosses, free from both agricultural work and the control of an employer.

6.1 THE ENTERPRISES: SCALE, TYPE, AND OWNERSHIP

6.1.1 *Scale and Type of Returnee Enterprises*

Through interviewing the returned migrant entrepreneurs at their operating premises, I have classified the businesses into several overlapping categories based on the scale and type of their activities. For classification according to scale, scholars stress that the relative terms of "small" and "large" should denote not only *size* – for example, the number of workers and amount of capital – but also *complexity,* as revealed by assets and the depth and breadth of social and market interactions.[1] Since there is no absolute criterion for scale, I designate the returnee enterprises encountered in this study as "small" and "large" according to the size of their workforce, their amount of start-up capital, their management structure, and the radius of their marketing activities, without claiming broader applicability.[2] Table 6.1 summarizes the characteristics of the 81 enterprises in the survey according to their size and type. In four of these enterprises, two entrepreneurs were interviewed, so the total number of entrepreneurs in the survey is 85.

The small returnee enterprises in my study include both small-scale manufacturing businesses and services. These enterprises generally do not employ more than ten people, although one business has thirteen employees and another has fifteen. The businesses are run by families or friends who describe themselves in terms of fictive kin – for example, workmates who return together and call themselves "brothers." Most of the investment for these enterprises comes from personal savings and informal borrowings, and all of the small returnee enterprises in my survey have start-up capital of less than 150,000 yuan. The small manufacturing enterprises sell their goods locally, usually at stalls in front of their workshops, though some also sell to shops in the county seat.

Some structuralist scholars observe that the defining characteristics of off-farm micro-enterprises – such as labor intensity and an emphasis on local materials and markets – may, over time, hinder expansion.[3] They further argue that, in common with subsistence agriculture and migration, petty commodity production ensures the survival of a labor reserve that can be mobilized according to the demands of capital; as a result, these small-scale producers are confined to a niche that prevents them from competing with city firms.[4] While not refuting the above, I maintain that informal small-scale producers, particularly returnees, provide important goods and services in economies with low levels of diversification.

The 27 large enterprises in this study are engaged in manufacturing and include individual, private, collective, and state enterprises. These larger businesses generally have at least twenty employees, although one business has eighteen employees and another only sixteen. The average number of employees for the large enterprises is 45.[5] Over 80% of the larger businesses receive financial support from outside investors or formal loans; in my survey, the larger businesses have at least 150,000 yuan in start-up capital. Entrepreneurs who pioneer the large manufacturing entities in Xinfeng and Yudu have accumulated not only skills but also management experience and contacts within the white-collar stratum of urban labor markets. Their enterprises are located

Table 6.1. *Number of enterprises surveyed, by type and scale*

Type and scale of enterprise	No. in survey	Typical start-up investment	Number of employees	Other characteristics
Manufacturing				
Large scale	27	>150,000 yuan[a] Survey range: 100,000 to 5m, median 375,000	>15 Survey range: 16 to 860, median 40	Hierarchical management Specialized production workshops Goods sold nationally and overseas Some have formal loans Ownership: 2 registered as collectives, 2 contracted state enterprises, 4 contracted township collectives, 4 overseas Chinese invested, 15 private
Small scale	25	<150,000 yuan Survey range: 2,000 to 200,000, median 30,000	<16 Survey range: 1 to 15, median 4	Informal management Operated by family and friends Complete product made in one workshop Goods/services sold locally
Service sector				
Small scale	22	<120,000 yuan Survey range: 2,000 to 120,000,[b] median 7,000	<14 Survey range: 1 to 13, median 4	Personal savings and informal loans Private ownership, though 2 are registered as township collectives
Agriculture				
Not ranked by scale	7	2,000 yuan to 500,000 yuan	Hire help at busy times	Family run

[a] This figure does not include four enterprises that are township collectives contracted by returnees. These returnees did not invest more than 10,000 yuan in these enterprises, although they pay between 10,000 and 60,000 yuan in contract fees.

[b] Two returnees have set up building materials shops with loans guaranteed (by local entrepreneurs) for at least 100,000 yuan. Two other returned migrants have invested 80,000 yuan and 50,000 yuan in their restaurants – but this also includes investments for their houses, which are part of the restaurant building. The remainder of the returnee service businesses have start-up investment of no more than 20,000 yuan.

toward the capitalist end of the petty commodity–capitalist spectrum and they adopt the management methods of city factories: managerial agents control the labor through hierarchical supervision, clock-in cards, piece-rate wages, strict discipline, and dismissals for poor performance. The production process is divided among several workshops, whereas in smaller manufacturing enterprises the craftspeople make complete products. The large businesses also differ from their smaller manufacturing counterparts with regard to the geographical radius of trading. Over half of the large factories have formalized subcontracting or supply and distribution linkages with businesses outside of the county, and over three quarters of the large enterprises sell at least some of their products to domestic markets outside the county or to export markets.

Type refers to the kinds of goods and services that the enterprise provides. Over 90% of the entrepreneurs in my survey set up businesses that replicate the urban ventures in which they had previously worked. The manufacturing ventures, accounting for 52 of the enterprises in this study, include workshops producing furniture, garments, shoes, leather goods, and toys. Among the large manufacturing enterprises in the interview sample, furniture and garment factories account for over half; other manufactured products include handicrafts and toys, steel rods, plastic wire coating, and bricks. In both counties, the most common items produced by small workshops are clothes, furniture, and shoes. Overall, furniture workshops tend to dominate in Xinfeng, whereas clothes factories are more numerous in Yudu.

In examining the type of manufacturing enterprises established by the returnees, it is useful to apply the concept of "incubator organization," that is, "the entrepreneur's place of employment immediately prior to the founding of the new venture."[6] As documented in research on business creation among other social groups in China (e.g., former cadres and state enterprise employees), new entrepreneurs often use the skills, contacts, knowledge, and even equipment from their former places of employment to set up imitation businesses.[7] To give a recent example from Jiangxi: since 1998, laid-off workers from Wanzai beverage factories have formed several cooperatives and set up beverage factories of their own in various parts of Yichun prefecture. The incubator organization similarly influences the range of resources and social connections available to returned migrants as they pursue their business goals. For example, through migration many young people have participated in apprenticeships or obtained work skills. They have also gained information from their former workplace about where to purchase raw materials (e.g., shoe canvas) and where to package their products. Many return with their work tools from their urban jobs – for example, a welding torch or box of tools. Moreover, some bring their former workmates home with them to work in the new workshop.

Because the returnee enterprises are established in relatively isolated counties, the linkages established via migration are crucial in providing material
resources and information. The types of manufacturing industries established
by the returned migrants did not exist in those localities that I visited over
the course of 1997, where the occurrence of returnee entrepreneurship was
minimal – for example, Rongtang town in Fengcheng county and Wanzai and
Fengxin counties. An exception in Wanzai is that, at the time of my fieldwork,
three sisters had returned to set up a factory manufacturing fake jewelry stones.
Also a postscript must be added here: On my return to Wanzai three years later
in December 2000, there were a dozen returnee shoe manufacturing workshops
in the county seat, one large shoe factory employing over fifty people, and a
returnee workshop in Qifeng village making school furniture and employing
twenty other returned migrants. Returnees are not the only agents of enterprise
creation, but in less-developed regions they are important actors in information
transfer and entrepreneurship.

The type of returnee business activity is affected not only by the resources
obtained from the incubator organization but also by the natural resources in the
native place. Plentiful timber in Xinfeng has made the furniture business a popular choice: of 99 returnee enterprises surveyed by the Xinfeng Association of
Individual Entrepreneurs, 54 produce furniture.[8] Returnees are a dynamic force
in the furniture industry throughout Ganzhou prefecture. A celebrated symbol
of the return initiative is "furniture city": some 700 workshops established by
former Pearl Delta migrants concentrated in 500 square kilometers along the
new railway line at Nankang.[9] "Furniture city" acts as a central supply and
distribution point for materials and final products within Jiangxi and Guangdong. According to the Xinfeng Bureau of Township and Village Enterprises,
returnees have advanced the local furniture industry by twenty years. The bureau head envisages the Xinfeng furniture industry emulating the success, scale,
and specialized organization of the Nankang example, especially now that the
railway line runs through the county seat.[10] Although there are furniture workshops established by returnees in Yudu, they are not as numerous as in Xinfeng.

Apart from furniture, there is a range of returnee businesses in Xinfeng that
do not exist in Yudu; this is because there is a more vigorous consumer market
in the former and there has been a recent construction boom in the county seat.
Small manufacturing endeavors in Xinfeng include the production of items such
as foodstuffs, curtains, and security doors. An official led me to a street where
several household security door workshops are located and explained that the
operators are all young migrants who have returned home after learning how
to weld in the cities. Informal conversations confirmed that this was the case.

The service and retail operators in both counties include restaurant owners,
mechanics, electrical repairmen, shop owners, and "beauticians." The beauty

parlors (*meirong ting*) are more stylish than the humble barber's shop, and one such business in Xinbei township, Yudu, is called "OK *meirong ting*" – a name which my guide joked is "neither fish nor fowl." Returnee service businesses in Yudu tend to be limited to replicating existing service sector entities such as restaurants, shops, and repairs, whereas in Xinfeng the undertakings are more varied. In Jiading township, a new street merges into Xinfeng county seat and is lined on both sides with about two hundred small businesses that include shops, restaurants, repair stalls, hairdressers, tea rooms that screen videos, and karaoke parlors. This Famous, Excellent, and Special (*ming you te*) street is renowned to be the place where returnee businesses are concentrated, and random conversations with stall owners confirm this. Additionally, on the single street that *is* Daa town, returnees have introduced chic urban facilities such as a photography studio (where rural dwellers can be photographed against scenic backdrops while adorned in costume), a miniature roller-skating rink where children congregate after school, and three dance halls.

The interview sample of returned migrants who have established specialized agricultural ventures (seven in total) is smaller than I desired. The paucity of agricultural examples in the study may reflect an aversion to farming on the part of returnees. It may also reflect practical difficulties in identifying entrepreneurs with previous migration experience.[11] In Xinfeng and Yudu I relied on officials for introductions, and they were possibly more aware of returnees who were engaged in nonagricultural undertakings and those whose projects were located in the towns, as opposed to the villages. Also, in Xinfeng, officials were keen to portray the county as a booming investment prospectus; some leaders seemed to feel that paddy fields and oxen may taint this image. County officials were also unwilling to let me near a village, as my research coincided with a crackdown on those evading family planning restrictions. Officials in Yudu were more relaxed and permitted long rural sojourns.

Products from the specialized agricultural businesses in my survey include American bullfrogs, eels and bait, pigeons, oranges, pears, tea (Yudu), chickens, and watermelons (Xinfeng). The frog farmer and the eel and bait farmer have formal contractual linkages with coastal companies. Both commenced their ventures in early 1997 and plan to subcontract production quotas to households within their villages. Owing to anticipated multiplier effects for the villages, the farmers have received substantial poverty alleviation loans administered through the township government. The other farmers' undertakings are financed primarily through domestic savings, though some have received modest loans from rural cooperatives. These farming ventures rely on household labor, though the orchards hire local women and children at harvest time. The products are sold to local consumers and are also marketed to other counties and provinces through government agencies. Although most of the farming

Qingshi Township Furniture Factory, Yudu county.

projects are localized in scope, the bullfrog and eel businesses exemplify rural–urban migration linkages that provide the information, materials, and markets for initiating specialized agricultural projects.

6.1.2 *Return and Categories of Enterprise Ownership*

Returnees are enlisted by rural cadres to use their resources for salvaging state-owned and collective enterprises and for invigorating the private sector. Before examining the activities of the returnees in Xinfeng and Yudu, I briefly describe the different ownership categories of enterprises. Broadly, enterprise ownership falls into the categories of state, collective, and private. At the county level, state enterprises are under the jurisdiction of the county government. Many of these enterprises were established during the collective era and produce items such as fertilizer, building materials, animal feed, machine parts, textiles, and foodstuffs. The local state appoints managers, intervenes in the daily running of these factories, assists with supplying raw materials, and claims a large portion of the revenue. Another category of ownership is the rural collectives, which belong to either the township or village. The collectives are controlled largely by officials at the corresponding level of the administrative hierarchy.

Precious Pearl Toy and Clothes Factory, Xinfeng county. These two photographs of large-scale businesses show their "modern" production layouts: workshops manufacture for specialized stages of the overall production process.

In 1984 it became legal for individuals or partners to pay an annual contract fee to the local government and take charge of enterprise management and profit distribution. Some contractors also invest substantially in the businesses. In poorer areas, managerial decisions tend to be determined by imperatives other than economic efficiency – for example, providing employment for a maximum number of people or diverting enterprise funds to community projects instead of reinvesting in the enterprise. A feature of initial capital formation in rural collectives is dependence on loans, with access to credit facilitated by local government ownership of the enterprise. In poorer areas there is a high reliance on debt among both state-owned enterprises and rural collectives, because few enterprises are able to accumulate capital through reinvestment.

Many collectives are "false" in that they are private enterprises that have attached themselves to a government entity, a practice known as *guahu*. In exchange for the payment of management fees, *guahu* provides preferential access to credit and protection from extortion by government agencies. Yet private enterprises have been coming out of the closet in recent years. Following the endorsement for all forms of ownership at the 15th Party Congress in 1997, Xinfeng and Yudu have started auctioning off county-level enterprises and collective orchards, tea plantations, and factories to their former contractors and other individuals. Nonetheless, the collective sector remains full of ambiguities: it is not always clear who owns the enterprise or who is responsible for profits, losses, and debts.

Part of the local state corporatism thesis advanced by Oi and Nee states that rural cadres use the collective enterprises to maintain their power.[12] However, in localities with weak industrial bases, selling collectives does not necessarily diminish the power of the local state – although it invites new players, including returnees, to bid for resources. If, as in Xinfeng and Yudu, many collective entities are operating at a loss and if bailing them out is a drain on local fiscal resources, then the sale or contracting out of these enterprises are ways to generate revenue. People buy these businesses because they believe that the premises, equipment, and other established dimensions of the factories provide the basis for them to build up strong businesses using their own initiative and managerial skill. If the new operators are successful then the collectives survive as revenue-generating entities. Moreover, the new operators inevitably run their businesses in some form of alliance with community leaders.

6.1.3 *Returnees, Government Enterprises, and New Businesses*

Local cadres hope that, as emissaries of modern urban management, returnees will improve the fortunes of ailing collectives and state enterprises and contribute to local coffers by paying contract fees. The position of returnees as potential saviors of the enterprises affords them greater influence with officials in terms of managing the enterprise. However, the introduction of coastal factory management practices is also to the detriment of the traditional welfare considerations of these enterprises, which have been reflected, for instance, in a reluctance to lay off workers and a relaxed working environment.

To illustrate the role of returnees as instruments of a national modernization and efficiency agenda, I introduce the reader to Mr. Yang, who worked for ten years as a manager in a coastal factory. He was contacted by local leaders and offered a position as a village leader as well as the opportunity to contract the running of one of the large workshops in the Xinfeng Textile Factory, a state-owned enterprise situated on the edge of the county seat. Mr. Yang recalls:

> The place was running at a loss before I took over. Two fifths of the workers weren't skilled enough so I fired them. It is much better to hire the

migrant girls who have come back from Guangdong, so I sent out word and got twenty returnee workers as replacements. If you are running a business you have to use modern management methods, otherwise you will always be walking behind somebody else .... Since I came, the factory has started using clock-in cards and the workers know that if they are late then they pay a fine.

Mr. Yang has also instituted a working day of ten hours. He has substituted the fabric used by the factory with a cheaper variety and he has negotiated a series of subcontracting arrangements with Pearl Delta factories.[13] Of his future plans he says: "Now that Hong Kong is coming back to the motherland, I want to find ways of dealing directly with Hong Kong." Mr. Yang has transformed the workshop into a viable economic entity, and he has been offered the opportunity to contract out the remaining factory workshops.

Local officials enlist former migrants as managers and technical consultants as a way of harnessing badly needed skills and managerial experience for the state and collective sectors. According to the head of the Xinfeng Bureau of Township and Village Enterprises:

One way to compensate for our lack of quality workers is by sending people on courses, but this requires both money and time for them to learn the skill, and even then they don't necessarily have sufficient experience. Our bureau sometimes writes letters to particular workers in the city and asks them to return to be managers or to solve technical problems. In one of our crockery factories the glazing wasn't sticking to the pots, so we recalled some workers from Guangzhou who were working in this area to fix the problem. Likewise, in a textile factory there was a problem with one of the machines that held up production for around six months, and we employed migrant workers from Guangzhou to solve it.[14]

The practice of enlisting former migrants for their skills and managerial competence may help to diversify the leadership base of local state enterprises to include people without official backgrounds. However, another side of the story is that recruiting returnees enables cadres to unload their white elephants. As an example, the contractors of a township brick factory have found themselves burdened by a site of useless clay.[15]

Cadres use their control over permits and local resources to try to incorporate returnee businesses and their resources into the local state fold; for their part, the returnees use their capital and contacts to enlist the cooperation of the local state in establishing their businesses. Six of the large manufacturing enterprises and two of the small manufacturing enterprises visited by this author have formed partnerships with local state agencies or have registered as collectives. These enterprises have gained protection, tax exemptions, and access to credit. However, some returnees are so fixed on the goal of becoming their own bosses that they reject overtures from local cadres. The founder of the Yudu Garment Factory was initially approached by the Duanwu township government about registering as a collective. Fearful that the local state might assume a dominant presence in running his business, he declined. His rejection of township government overtures was partially facilitated by the physical move of his premises to the county seat. The desire for independence among returnees is a common trait, and fifteen of the large manufacturing enterprises newly created (rather than contracted) by the returnees in my survey are privately owned and registered.

Chinese scholars have suggested that returnees promote new forms of private enterprise ownership in the countryside.[16] Certainly, returnees to Xinfeng and Yudu have participated in the establishment of transregional partnerships and, in Yudu, migrants have set up joint stock companies with Hong Kong clothing merchants. The potential for returnees to innovate with new forms of business organization is sometimes limited by their cursory understanding of concepts encountered while in the cities. For instance, two of the large manufacturing entities visited by the author tried to raise funds by floating shares.[17] The businesses subsequently converted to single-person investment because the entrepreneurs did not understand the nature of shares. Owing to a reduction in capital, the scale of production in these businesses has declined. Returnees have also established many of the smaller workshops and individual businesses that are attractive to governments in agricultural regions because they are financed primarily through domestic savings. Especially in poorer areas, these businesses offer an inexpensive way to create employment and to provide goods and services.

6.2 WHAT KIND OF PHOENIX LAYS AN EGG?

This section considers the characteristics of returned migrants in terms of the duration of their absence, age upon return, urban work experience, urban wages, level of education, and vocational skills. The characteristics of the migrants influence the range of resources that are available to them and hence the size and scale of the businesses that they create on return. The larger business operators tend to have spent more time in the cities; they tend to be older at the time of return; most have held white-collar positions in urban factories and earned higher urban wages prior to their return; and most boast higher levels of education and skills attainment. Yet the fortunes of individuals in the cities are also influenced by their access to resources prior to initial migration, and there are interrelationships among the different characteristics of the more entrepreneurial of the returnees. As examples, education may influence duration of absence, as the better-educated migrants are more likely to experience socioeconomic advancement in the host society. Duration of absence influences the age of the migrants on their return and thus also their social position and access to resources within the natal community. Level of education may also reflect socioeconomic background and therefore preferential access to resources that are beneficial for entrepreneurship at home. Gender may affect level of education: males are more likely to complete or exceed the obligatory eight years[18] of schooling; whereas virilocal patterns of marriage mean that some parents view investing in the education of a girl as "sprinkling water on someone else's garden." Daughters are also expected to help more with farming and household chores than are sons. Finally, both gender and age may influence the nature of family obligations and generate different pressures for return. Although the returnee entrepreneurs differ in the respects outlined here, they are similar in that – prior to initial out-migration – their occupational designation was agricultural.

6.2.1 *Duration of Absence and Age*

There is a general hypothesis in the migration studies literature that those who have spent longer periods in the city are more innovative than other returnees.[19] My survey material, presented in Graph 6.1, confirms this hypothesis.[20] Longer urban sojourns enable migrants not only to accumulate funds and gain management experience but also to forge business contacts in cities. Longer stays also permit greater socioeconomic advancement in the host society, which is convertible to increased status at home and therefore to improved access to resources in the counties. Of all the large-scale manufacturers in this study, over 80% have spent a minimum of six years in the city and over 60% have spent at least eight years in the city. Moreover, the average duration of absence among those who fall into the "8+ years" category depicted in Graph 6.1 is ten and a half years. In contrast, over 80% of the small-scale enterprises in both counties have been established by people with fewer than six years of migration experience. There is no statistically significant difference in the duration of absence between returnees establishing small manufacturing workshops and those setting up service-sector undertakings.[21] Yet as shown in Table 6.1, small manufacturing enterprises tend to have more start-up capital than service entities. It is possible that the production skills of small manufacturers have enabled them to accumulate more money and equipment than the service-sector operators even though the length of urban sojourns for the two groups are comparable.

Within each category, the longer the absence, the greater the likelihood of success. Among the large-scale manufacturers, five struggling entrepreneurs

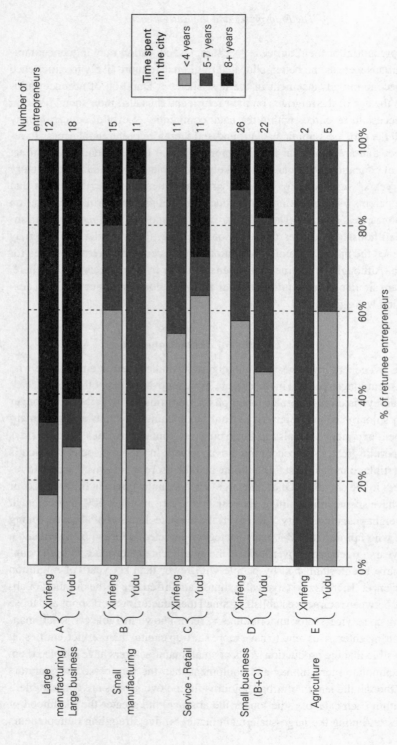

Graph 6.1. Duration of returnee absence, and scale and type of returnee businesses.

report stays in the city ranging from two and a half to four years, and they told me that insufficient work experience is contributing to their current woes. Returnees who have established the more successful small-scale workshops that employ several people have generally spent longer in the cities than individuals who return to set up craft stalls as single owner–operators.

In Xinfeng, about 65% of large manufacturers returned home at the age of 30 or above, whereas the figure for small business operators is just under 20% (see Graph 6.2). In Yudu, over 85% of those returnees engaged in large-scale manufacturing returned after turning 30, compared with just over one third for small business operators.[22] A Chinese saying, *sanshi er li,* means that family and career should be established by the age of 30. Age corresponds with longer periods of work experience, maturity, and social knowledge. Older people may have a greater say in the deployment of family resources and they may also attract more respect from rural community leaders and urban business contacts.

6.2.2 *Education, Skills, and Work Experience*

Education is associated with greater levels of skills acquisition, better access to information, and higher personal aspirations. By extension, educated people should be better placed to obtain resources from urban labor markets, and they should be better able to engage with the local state in manipulating their resources in pursuit of entrepreneurial goals on their return. This contention is supported by scholarship – on both migration and entrepreneurship – that identifies education as a factor that positively influences both the propensity to migrate and the chances for long-term success in business.[23] However, as mentioned in previous chapters, the evidence for China is not conclusive: slightly higher levels of education among migrants as compared with the rest of the rural labor force may be mainly a generational effect because most migrants are drawn from a young age pool, which is likely to have received education.[24] Some research in China has found that, although the level of education does not greatly affect the propensity of villagers to migrate, it does influence the duration of absence: the more educated migrants tend to be absent for longer periods.[25]

Levels of educational attainment among the returnee entrepreneurs in this study, illustrated in Graph 6.3, are higher than for other migrants and for the rural labor force as a whole: at least 50% of returnees in both Xinfeng and Yudu have finished lower middle school, and about 30% have completed upper middle school. Education levels are highest among those who return to establish large factories, with over 40% of Yudu entrepreneurs and 50% of Xinfeng entrepreneurs having finished upper high school.[26] By comparison, the breakdown

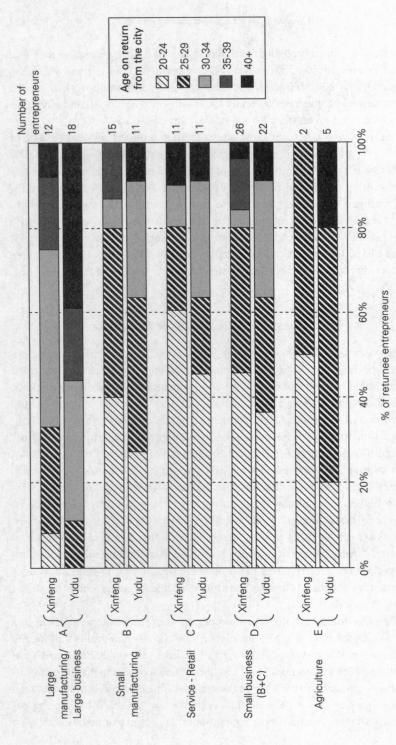

Graph 6.2. Age of entrepreneurs on return, and scale and type of returnee businesses.

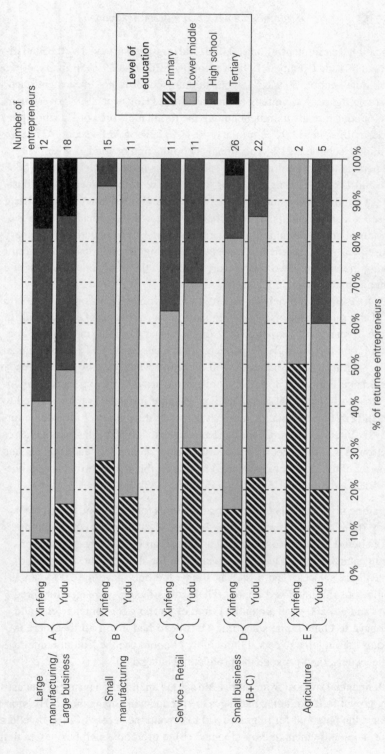

Graph 6.3. Level of education of returnees, and scale and type of their businesses.

for educational attainment among 60,000 rural migrants surveyed by the Statistical Bureau of Yudu County in 1992 is as follows: illiterate, 2.1%; primary, 47%; lower middle school, 50.9%.[27] Upper middle school is not even mentioned. Comparable figures for Xinfeng are not available. However, 1995 government figures for educational attainment among the rural labor force of Ganzhou prefecture are: illiterate, 12.92%; primary, 40.41%; lower middle school, 37.49%; upper middle school, 8.21%; vocational schooling and beyond, 0.96%.[28]

The percentages of returnees with special skills prior to migration are 53% in Yudu and 47% in Xinfeng.[29] Among those who returned to set up larger businesses, two thirds of the entrepreneurs in Yudu and three quarters in Xinfeng possessed vocational skills. Among poorly educated individuals, skills function as a form of compensation. Of the fourteen interviewees with only primary education, ten were qualified in carpentry, tailoring, or electrical repairs prior to leaving the village. Two others were trained in the army, one as a chef and the other as a mechanic.

Over 70% of the interviewees reported some form of gain from migration in terms of the refinement of an existing skill, the acquisition of a new skill, or exposure to managerial experience. Similarly, in a Chinese survey of 737 returned migrants, most of the respondents (a staggering 95.1%) reported a gain in skills.[30] Although approximately half of the interviewees in my study already possessed nonfarm skills prior to out-migration, urban work experience has enabled most to improve these skills. For example, carpenters have learned to design and craft pieces that are more stylish and refined than crude village furniture. Six interviewees used their urban wages to attend night-school classes in electronics, Chinese medicine, beauty therapy, accounting, and English, and one quarter of the interviewees learned new skills through informal apprenticeships. As an example, Hu Zhensheng explains the following:

> On failing my university entrance examinations for the second time, I went to my room and slept for a month. In the end my parents convinced me that I should go south to try to find another road in life. I was an apprentice in a small private factory in Guangzhou for about a year. The factory makes jelly sweets. The boss was stingy and only gave me 200 yuan a month, but that included board. Then I was factory manager for three years and got 500 yuan a month. I tired of working for someone else and you have to come home sometime. Besides I had learnt all that there is to know about jelly sweets. I thought that I could use the fruit at home to make sweets, then package the product in Guangzhou.

With financial support from cadres, Hu started an imitation business that uses locally grown fruits and then packages the products in Guangzhou.[31] His story illustrates the potential for migration (a) to expand the access of rural dwellers to informal employment and training and (b) to promote small businesses that meet the needs of the rural poor who cannot afford goods produced with so-phisticated technology.

It is not only returnee bosses who have gained skills through migration, but also returnee workers. The bosses of larger garment and furniture factories express the opinion that return migration has enabled them to create businesses and has also provided them with a technically competent workforce accustomed to the discipline of modern industry. Most employees in the returnee manufacturing enterprises are former migrants, and the majority of bosses identify previous migration experience as a condition of recruitment. Moreover, "reverse chain migration" means that a portion of employees in all of the returnee enterprises were previously subordinates or workmates of their returnee bosses during their time in the urban factory.

In addition to skills and a skilled workforce, migration also enables returnee bosses to obtain experience in urban management practices. Within the large manufacturing sector, 83% (10) of the Yudu returnees and 89% (16) of the Xinfeng returnees had advanced from manual factory workers to become white-collar administrators, labor contractors, or small business operators. Moreover, about one third of interviewees who returned to establish small-scale manufacturing and service entities had gained experience as labor contractors or lower-level supervisors.

Among the agricultural returnees, one served a two-year apprenticeship raising American bullfrogs and then returned to raise frogs at home. The dove farmer worked for one year as a floor manager and the chicken farmer learned tailoring skills while in the city. All learned something of the market economy. Even if the skills acquired via urban migration are not directly employed in the rural setting, the experience provided these returnees with access to general market information that has assisted their farming ventures. For example, the dove farmer found the information about raising doves in an advertisement printed in a Guangdong newspaper.

The link between urban occupation and the resources available for pursuing entrepreneurial goals on return is further suggested by the fact that entrepreneurs in the large manufacturing sector tended to have higher wages prior to their return than the creators of smaller enterprises. Moreover, those engaged in manufacturing generally had higher urban wages than their service-sector counterparts. This is summarized in Table 6.2.

6.3 REASONS FOR RETURN

6.3.1 *Push and Pull*

Those who return more for "pull" reasons are generally more successful as entrepreneurs than those who are pushed home, in part because the relative

Table 6.2. *Average monthly wage (in yuan) of interviewees
prior to their return*

	Large manufacturing	Small workshop	Service sector
Xinfeng	2,391.67	1,066.67	800.00[a]
Yudu	1,950.00	890.00	790.90

[a] In the Xinfeng service sector, one highly educated returnee who set up a business service company in the county seat was earning much more than other service-sector entries prior to his return. He initially returned to set up a plastics factory but encountered so many bureaucratic restrictions that he changed his plans. Once his wage is subtracted (as here) from the figures, the average wage for the service-sector operators in Xinfeng is comparable to that in Yudu.

balance of push and pull factors reflects the range and quality of the returnee's bundle of resources. Migrants choose to return because they see the home town as the place where they can best achieve economic independence and realize the related goal of escaping subordination in urban society and labor markets. As discussed in Chapter 1, much of the migration literature explains mobility decisions by listing an inventory of push–pull factors. These lists invariably stress social connections and economic opportunity, but they are reducible to one obvious assertion: people move to places of "higher utility."[32] With regard to return migration, *push factors* describe the urban conditions that tend to drive migrants away from the cities, such as limited job opportunities, poor working conditions, abuse, and discrimination; *pull factors* refer to the attractions of home such as resources, improvements in the natal economies, preferential policies, and the support of kin. In reality, mobility decisions are shaped by personal goals formed over the longer term, the personal characteristics of returned migrants (discussed in the previous section), and a multiplicity of mutually conditioning factors that are both push and pull.

Over 80% of the entrepreneurs who returned to set up large-scale manufacturing entities stress the attractions of the native place, whereas only around half of the small-scale entrepreneurs (both manufacturing and service) mention pull factors. This is because people who are better able to harness resources in the city are also more likely to be informed of opportunities in the origin community. These people are therefore more likely to receive support in deploying their resources for entrepreneurial gain at home and are more likely to be successful entrepreneurs.

In my survey, 10% of the returned migrants have not directly transferred their skills from the city to the countryside. These people returned home after a couple of years as migrant workers and mention only push factors when explaining their decision to return. Owing to a lack of success in finding suitable work, they try to use the resources of kin groups to achieve a nonfarming livelihood at home, usually as shopkeepers or owner–operator tailors. With the exception of the eel and frog farmers who have established household contracting programs, the farmers who run small specialized households also explain their return home solely in terms of push. Furthermore, among the small business operators in the study, four are atypical in that they spent long periods – between ten and sixteen years – in the city and were already in their late 30s and 40s at the time of return. They have created businesses that do not relate to their urban occupations. These interviewees represent migrants who toil for many years in lowly occupations, never achieving financial security and eventually returning home in search of an adequate off-farm livelihood.

6.3.2 *Push Factors*

The push factors prompting returnee entrepreneurship in Xinfeng and Yudu can be explained by the subordinate position of migrant workers in urban labor relations and their low social status in the cities. Urban manufacturing zones offer capitalists a disciplined labor force whose maintenance the state assists by repressing nongovernment trade unions or organized labor protest. For factory employees, the day begins with a morning line-up and roll call, followed by regimented morning exercise before filing into the workshops by 7:30 A.M. Talking or tardiness results in fines. The working day commonly exceeds ten hours, with breaks on alternate Sundays. Withholding wages is a strategy used by many bosses to retain workers while at the same time earning interest on the money withheld. Some migrants also report verbal and even physical abuse by bosses. Dormitories are generally cramped, and unappetizing food must be consumed with haste. Many returnees told me that they set up a business at home to escape their lives as somebody's "ox or horse." Freedom and independence are attributes universally valued by migrants, and authors writing about returnees in various parts of the world note their preference for self-employment, their distaste for both agriculture and wage labor, and their aspirations to become shopkeepers, tailors, and carpenters.[33] Many Jiangxi migrants similarly express the intention to become an independent boss. The following was recounted to me by a 30-year-old male returnee who opened an electronics repair shop in Xinfeng county seat:

In 1991 I [took] an exam and entered a Taiwan–mainland joint venture electronics company and worked there for three and a half years. Life out there is tough because you are cursed and controlled by your employer. I worked until 2:00 A.M., so that my eyes were always strained and I was perpetually exhausted. When there is a toilet break the bell rings and you have five minutes to pee. If you are a minute late you lose 1 yuan. Your heart is always on edge and you hate the sound of the bell. Now if a boss asked me just to sit at a desk for 30 yuan a day and do nothing I would refuse. I don't want to be controlled. I want to be free.[34]

Some of the migrants who advance to management positions while in the city also find themselves subjected to random outbursts of temper from bosses. Even in cases where there is a rapport between boss and employee, in setting up a business at home the entrepreneurs are creating something of their own. A common feeling among returnees is that selling one's labor to the boss cannot be an indefinite arrangement.

A contrast between wage laborers and trading migrants provides further evidence that subordination within the urban workplace underpins returnee entrepreneurship in Xinfeng and Yudu. I interviewed officials and household members in Rongtang *zhen* (Fengxin county[35]) and Songpu township (Fengxin county[36]) and discovered that return migration to these two locations is rare. Rongtang migrants have established clothes shops on Hainan island and Fengxin migrants are predominant among decorators in the Putuo district of Shanghai. Migrants who had returned home briefly for family reasons – and migrants whom I interviewed in Shanghai – explained that their energies are to be directed toward their urban businesses for as long as this strategy is profitable. Although trading migrants are subject to various exactions as well as discrimination in the cities, at least they are working for themselves and investing in their own businesses. Thus, whereas traders consider their distant future in terms of home, factory workers are subject to different imperatives and thus see their immediate future in the natal community.

In recent years, attaining the status of "boss" (*laoban*) has become a legitimate social goal.[37] The word *laoban* has evolved in colloquial language to denote anyone who has standing in an economic or even an administrative sense. When I addressed interviewees as *laoban,* they would reply, "I am only a little *laoban*," to which my guide would say, "But a little *laoban* is still a *laoban*." This sentiment is expressed by the founder of the Xuehao Shoe Factory in Datangbu town, Xinfeng: "I returned home because I wanted to be a boss, and less investment is needed at home for setting up a business. I earn less money here than in Dongguan [Guangdong] but for better or worse I am a small *laoban*."[38]

A handful of more ambitious migrants, five in this study, left for the cities after unsuccessful attempts at becoming a boss at home. Qiao Songsheng is one such person. Following two unsuccessful efforts to establish a business in Xinfeng county, he migrated south with the intention of recouping his losses, learning about the market economy, and returning home to set up a viable enterprise. Well educated by local standards and with a vocational certificate in electronics, he commenced work in a Guangzhou household appliance factory. Within six months he was promoted to deputy manager and later transferred to management positions in three different furniture factories. Although not a carpenter by trade, he learned how to operate a business; after his fifth year in Guangzhou, he went home and urged some of his former subordinates (also from Xinfeng) to return home and work for him. Together with another returnee, he is now joint owner of the highly successful Huadi Furniture Factory. Mr. Qiao rejected a lucrative job offer – complete with Guangzhou residence permits for himself and his family – in favor of becoming an independent boss at home.[39]

The goal of becoming a boss marks a departure from the 1980s, when most entrepreneurs were social and political undesirables who were excluded from the state fold and had little to lose in terms of status or wealth. Until the recent layoffs from state enterprises, one of the most desirable positions in the People's Republic was the "worker," because state employees have traditionally benefited from accommodation, basic income, and welfare provisions as well as relative political security – derived from their historical role as vanguards of the revolution. Now there is an apparent inversion. In advocating returnee entrepreneurship, the Chinese media advocate set stages of social evolution: peasant to worker and then, for the more progressive, worker to entrepreneur.[40] However, the "worker" in this formulation differs from the "worker" of state institutions. The state-sector worker works (*gongzuo*) in a factory or another institution. But the neologism for selling labor to a boss is *dagong*. When I asked a man in Jiaocun village why he chose to *gongzuo* in the city, his facial muscles contorted with scorn. He replied, "I don't *gongzuo*, I sell my sweat and blood to the boss for a pittance, I *dagong*." Then he crouched down to the ground gesturing with his hand an inch above the soil and said: "Without money a person is only this small. So I must *dagong*."[41]

In confronting their peripheral status in urban labor markets and imagining themselves as a *laoban*, the salient attractions are independence, status, and comparative wealth. Many migrants report thinking, "if he can be a *laoban* then so can I!" Migrants who later participate in a business relationship with their former bosses proudly note their change in status. One man explained: "Before I was just a *dagong zai* but now I am a customer and he treats me like an equal."[42] Evolution to the status of a boss is sanctioned by political rhetoric, and policy research documents praise returnees for achieving their transition to a nonfarm status through their own efforts.[43] Returnee entrepreneurs gain face through being courted by local officials, and even the little bosses – the tailors and carpenters – enhance their status through their economic independence, off-farm occupation, and higher income.

6.3.3 *Pull Factors*

Return is motivated by pull factors that persuade migrants it is easier to become a boss on home soil than in the cities. Pull factors include active government recruitment and support, access to social and material resources at home, the presence of family, and values of loyalty to the family and the native place. Each factor is discussed in turn. On the first point, local state initiatives that entice migrants to return have enjoyed relative success. In this study, half of the large-scale manufacturing enterprises and two of the small-scale manufacturing entities in Xinfeng were founded in response to direct representation by local officials. In Yudu, 40% of the large-scale businesses, two small-scale workshops, and one farming venture were established as a result of overtures from cadres. Additionally, policies and publicity measures that target returnees have yielded results. Given the official presence in the interviews, it is possible that some interviewees may have overstated the "concern of the Party for the people" as one of their reasons for return. Nonetheless, grass-roots cadres are eager to form alliances with successful returnees, and entrepreneurs are willing to establish ties with them.

In terms of social resources, the advantages of home include networks of kin, friends, and former classmates who use their connections with local authorities to clear the bureaucratic road relatively free of obstacles. Such contacts help in obtaining permits, gaining access to operating premises, and negotiating tax concessions. The proprietor of the Xinbei Township Furniture Factory in Yudu explains:

> I would rather be a poor boss than a rich worker. But there is too much competition in Guangzhou for setting up a business. Land and electricity are cheaper at home, plus there is the convenience that my brother is the deputy head of the township.[44]

Many township governments turn a blind eye to unregistered businesses, enabling the entrepreneurs to circumvent the taxes and fees of upper-level tax bureaus. As the proprietor of a shoe workshop explained: "We have decided to start the business in the *xiang* because we are familiar with the people so we won't be disadvantaged. If we had set up outside or in the county, the Bureau of Industry and Commerce would have been stretching out its hands." In return for protection, the businesses pay a more generous tax contribution to the local coffers.

The complicity of the local state and the remoteness of townships provide a protected space for activities that would meet with the disapproval of higher levels. Returnees use their urban connections to arrange for the packaging of various imitation products, such as Chinese brand-name cigarettes. Additionally, some workshops make imitations of famous Chinese designer shoes. The parts are later assembled with poor-quality glue, zips, and soles. Coincidentally, on one day of interviewing, my shoes fell apart just as we reached the door of a returnee shoemaker. For 50 yuan I purchased a pair of replacements – soft leather boots that turned out to have a life-span of two weeks.

Material attractions of the natal community include cheap labor, natural resources, and improvements in infrastructure. Labor in Jiangxi province is among the cheapest in China, with employees earning an average per-capita wage of 3,450 yuan per annum, 25% less than the national standard.[45] The average annual salary for employees in six cities located along the Jing-Jiu Railway is 3,641.8 yuan, 20% lower than the national average and equivalent to two thirds of the average annual salary in Guangdong.[46] Subcontracting clothes manufacturers seek to exploit this advantage, and virtually all of the returnee bosses of clothes factories say that they emphasized the cheap labor of their hometowns in enticing coastal bosses to invest in their ventures. Government leaflets distributed to returnees stress cheap labor but also advertise other inexpensive resources, such as land, electricity, water, and timber. Indeed, much of the wood used in the Guangdong furniture factories comes from Ganzhou prefecture in Jiangxi. Wang Qisheng, co-proprietor of the Huadi Furniture Factory, is quoted in *Xinfeng bao* as follows:

> Xinfeng has Xinfeng's timber resources and an abundant supply of labor. What it lacks is new skills and new ideas. If it is possible to integrate skills learned from the coastal regions with the natural resource advantages of home, then it forms an unstoppable economic force.[47]

Xinfeng and Yudu have recently begun to experience changes such as a relaxation of controls on the private sector and an increase in the consumer capacity of rural households; these changes have created niches in the newly emerging "socialist market economy." At the same time, the urban markets in coastal areas that benefited first from reform policies are now becoming saturated. Several Jiangxi carpenters told me that there is too much competition for them to set up a workshop in Guangdong. They explained their decision to return home by pointing out that there are two different migration streams in China. The first involves the movement of relatively low-skilled migrants from poorer areas to richer areas. The second stream entails movement from affluent areas with a high geographic concentration of skilled labor to underdeveloped localities that offer many market niches for goods and services. The most renowned example of this latter stream is migration from rural areas in Zhejiang to the market towns in the poor western provinces. According to the returnees themselves, their movement is comparable to that of the Zhejiang migrants because they move from developed areas to use their skills in less developed areas. Speaking in this way, the returnees identified themselves with a superior and innovative category of migrant, placing themselves above migrants in general.

Correspondence with family and friends, as well as impressions obtained when returning for brief sojourns, inform the Jiangxi migrants of potential opportunities for entrepreneurship at home. For example, Tan Shaohua worked for three years in a Guangzhou plastic helmet factory, first as a spray painter and then as production manager. On returning home for Spring Festival, he noticed that many households had purchased a motorbike and saw an opportunity for selling helmets. So Tan returned to Xiniu township (Xinfeng) to set up a workshop that assembles and paints helmets with the parts and materials supplied by his former employer. Around half of the goods are assembled for the Cantonese company, and the remainder are sold in the county.[48]

For migrants who decide to return home and set up businesses, the disadvantages of location are lessened considerably by recent improvements in transport and telecommunications. In the past five years, mobile phone and fax lines have opened up in both counties. These developments reduce the "distance" between Xinfeng, Yudu, and the coastal cities, facilitating various forms of rural–urban cooperation that include contract manufacturing arrangements for the production of clothes and toys. The improvements in transport described in Chapter 2 are, of course, also relevant here.

The decision of intending entrepreneurs to return to their native place also stems from values associating home with ancestors, immediate family, and future descendants. Furthermore, migrants feel that they are obliged to return home and contribute to the material well-being and prestige of their families. Ellen Judd conceptualizes the Chinese entrepreneurial ethic as incorporating two temporal goals, both of which are informed by family values. The first may be conceived as the long-term advancement of one's descendants, patrilineal or uterine. Although building an estate is important, there is also the project of establishing a social network that will benefit one's descendants. Second, ever mindful of policy fluctuations, Chinese entrepreneurs are deft in their pursuit of short-term strategies that exploit a favorable environment yet are cautious to minimize risks to their long-term goals. The short-term advantages may include generating a quick profit to build a house or converting a child's registration to a nonagricultural status.[49]

Returnee entrepreneurs who are involved in larger undertakings and more ambitious agricultural projects are pursuing the goal of creating something tangible for themselves and their grandchildren. In the words of the Yudu eel farmer: "If I continued to sell my labor to a boss and my sweat to another place while my home is so poor, then I would be unworthy of my home. This is for my children."[50] Another returnee explained:

We Chinese all want our sons to become dragons, but first the son must be nurtured by a dragon. I had a furniture workshop in Guangzhou, but what is the use of the years of toil alone if the next generation goes to waste?... I came back and set up a factory here in Yudu county, and bought a house in the county seat so that my son can go to the key school ... if he doesn't get into university, then I have created something for his future.[51]

In returning and setting up a business, family members can be reunited. Here, it is again instructive to compare the trading migrants of Rongtang and Fengxin with the wage laborers of Xinfeng and Yudu. Whereas traders tend to move as nuclear or joint families, migrants to factories are usually separated from their loved ones and feel guilty for neglecting their roles as parents and spouses. The income from local off-farm employment provides a way for returned migrants to maintain the higher levels of remuneration experienced through migration without enduring protracted separation from family members.

It is important to observe that, if deployed in the city, the savings and skills of most migrants would not change their peripheral social status; when transferred to the natal community, however, these resources enable entrepreneurial returnees to demonstrate their socioeconomic progress in tangible ways – for example, a new house and small business. This facilitates the long-term life goal of establishing social contacts and family prestige. There are also short-term goals – for example, elevated status is an asset in local marriage markets, especially those characterized by gender imbalance.

6.4 WOMEN RETURNEE ENTREPRENEURS

Women account for seven of the interviewees in Xinfeng and six in Yudu, or 15% of the total. The smaller proportion of women entrepreneurs reflects (1) the low female-to-male ratio in initial out-migration from these two counties and (2) the dominance of patriarchal values in the "home community." According to the 1993 survey of out-migration from Yudu county, women comprised only 22.2% of the migrants.[52] Comparable figures for Xinfeng are not available, but in the four townships that I visited in Xinfeng, leaders' estimates for the proportion of female migrants range from one quarter to one third of the out-flow.[53] The patriarchal values that produce the concept of "home community" further explain the small proportion of women returnee entrepreneurs. Marriage patterns are virilocal and village exogamous, and women migrate in part because they are expected to earn money to support their parents and male siblings before marrying into somebody else's home.[54] Yet, as discussed in Chapter 4, women prefer to marry near to their natal village. In recent years, many migrant women have demonstrated continuing loyalty to their parents by returning to

Returned migrants in Jiading town, Xinfeng.

marry near to their villages, thereby keeping their new wealth close to home.[55] As more women participate in migration, the numbers of women returnee entrepreneurs may increase proportionately.

Most of the businesses established by the women I interviewed are small-scale. These include five tailor's shops, two hairdressing salons, one photographer's salon, and one tea shop. In addition, one woman runs a bakery in partnership with her husband. Smallness of scale, lower profits, and the provision of personal services are noted characteristics of women's businesses in many countries. Scholars explain these characteristics in terms of women's tendency to rely on domestic social resources instead of on more formal contacts from wider social spheres; the attitudes of financial institutions that favor men with lending arrangements; and culturally ascribed gender roles that determine business choice.[56] Although access to independent income through urban employment enables some rural women in Xinfeng and Yudu to pursue their own ventures, gender socialization and differential access to social resources intersect with limited opportunities for acquiring independent property to produce patterns of female entrepreneurship that are similar to those in other societies.

The women (three in this survey) who have assumed the management of large manufacturing enterprises have done so in varying degrees of cooperation with their husbands. One of the female returnees has contracted a township brick factory in partnership with her husband. She claims that her husband is too soft, so she is responsible for chasing up outstanding debts.[57] Fei Ying manages the

Fei Yangcheng Garment Factory that was originally contracted by her returnee husband. Her husband later became preoccupied with an alternative venture, so he transferred the running of the factory to his wife. She says that being a woman is neither an advantage nor a disadvantage in her career, though she explains that her courage now matches that of a man. The final female interviewee is a native of Guangxi who met and married her Yudu husband while working in Guangzhou; she then returned with him to Duanwu *xiang* because he was contacted by cadres to contribute his expertise to the establishment of a pottery factory. She has contracted the township toy factory, a business riddled with debt and operating problems, and has given herself one year to turn around the fortunes of the enterprise.[58] These women are forceful partners in the running of the businesses. They have experience as workshop supervisors or labor contractors and feel that this has given them the boldness to pursue their current careers.

Marriage and family both influence the return of the women to Xinfeng and Yudu and support their business activities at home. Seven women returned either because of pregnancy or because they were following their husbands, and four returned with their boyfriends. The remaining two women are single and in their early 20s. One girl was recalled from Guangzhou by her parents because of reports from her sister, a nurse in the Xinfeng county hospital, about returned migrants afflicted with illness. The other girl returned home because of poor working conditions. Investment for these small businesses takes the form of informal loans from their families and, to a lesser extent, personal savings. None of the women has financed her business by using a house as security for a loan, which may reflect a lack of say in the deployment of household property or simply that the undertakings require little capital. The three women who manage the larger businesses have access to loans, political contacts, and other resources through their husbands.

Officials explain the small proportion of women among both out-migrants and entrepreneurial returnees – and their minimal presence in the large manufacturing sector – in terms of the "quality" of their labor. The assumption that women are innately less able than men is not peculiar to China. As several development scholars observe, women and men are segregated in labor markets throughout the world, and the tasks performed by women workers are generally designated by employers as "less skilled" than comparable tasks performed by men. Ideological values that present women as inferior are bound up with the objective consequences of these values. For example, lower levels of education among women both produce and confirm a belief in society that women are less worthy of educational investment because they are not able to earn as much as men. Hence, women remain a cheap and compliant source of labor.[59] In the urban labor markets of Chinese cities, migrant women are less well positioned than men to obtain resources that can be fruitfully deployed on return. In many developing countries, rural women who work in factories may experience a double devaluation of their labor and abilities: first on account of their rural origins and second because of their gender. They are the least skilled of the low-skilled workers.[60]

This is only a partial perspective, and my analysis suggests that many women have the same exposure to urban production processes as male migrants. Both male and female migrants work in factories that manufacture shoes, clothes, or toys, but most of the returnee businesses producing these items are set up by men. Women respond to social expectations about their own capabilities, and in their own minds they exclude the possibility of establishing a venture. Most of the village women whom I interviewed in the counties of Wanzai and Yudu returned to marry or look after family. They regarded migration as a transitional phase between leaving school and returning home to be wives and mothers. The women generally scorned the suggestion that they could learn skills in the coastal factories that could create opportunities for themselves at home. They explained that they only performed one part of the production process and never learned how to make a complete product.

In both the city and the countryside, rural women have poorer access to resources that can be obtained via social networks – for example, investment from urban business people, loans from rural credit cooperatives, or political backing. Women are generally excluded from upper-level management positions, so their opportunities to forge business linkages with city factory bosses are limited.[61] Within the townships and villages, men dominate positions of authority except for those concerned with family planning and women's affairs.[62] Women are often paid less than men for attending village meetings. At official–entrepreneur dinners in townships, the majority of my co-diners were male. Exchanging cigarettes and playing drinking games at these dinners are essential for demonstrating human feeling and recognizing the status of other participants. Both male and female informants explained that women are no good at business because they are unable to drink or smoke.[63] Women who network within the male-dominated world of gift giving and banquets are regarded as having questionable sexual morals. Rather, the gift giving and visiting activities of women are concentrated among affines, relatives, and female neighbors and are less strategic and more affective than those of the male domain.[64] For example, women in many Jiangxi villages give eggs to their female neighbors on the birth of a child as well as when a woman is sterilized,[65] and the women visit their natal homes on a regular basis with gifts such as hand-stitched slippers or a chicken. Nonetheless, this second example of gift giving also produces tangible economic benefits in that the wife's family is often an important source of loans.

Kellee S. Tsai demonstrates that female arenas of economic organization have become increasingly influential in parts of Fujian and Zhejiang provinces with high levels of male out-migration and a thriving private sector. In these places, socioeconomic transition and changes in the gendered division of labor have led women to assume control over many facets of the local economy, including the operation of credit rotation societies dealing with large sums of money.[66] Tsai explains that the female domination of credit rotation societies has resulted from three interacting factors. One factor is that structural constraints limit the access of women to formal credit. The second is that, owing to the relative immobility of the women and their close personal relationships with others in the credit rotation societies, the women perceive each other as reliable debtors. Finally, the running of a credit rotation society is perceived as an extension of household budget management, which is a female domain, and so cultural stigmas discourage men from participating. In Xinfeng and Yudu, village women have formed *banggongdui,* work teams coordinating reciprocal help during the busy farming periods, but I did not encounter parallel examples of women coordinating reciprocal financial aid. Moreover, none of the women returnee entrepreneurs in my study cited credit rotation societies as a source of investment, although some of the men did.

Even though structural and cultural factors limit the capacity of returned migrant women in south Jiangxi to form and pursue entrepreneurial goals, these women still use their resources and new perspectives on life to increase their independence and status vis-à-vis their families. Through migrating to the cities, they have proved themselves worthy of support from kin for their business ventures at home. The women's pursuit of entrepreneurial goals and activities in the wider economy is also facilitated by their independent control over urban savings. Over half the women have used their savings to contribute either substantially or totally to the start-up capital of their businesses: three women have used their savings to receive training and purchase equipment needed for beauty therapy, photography, and tailoring.

Nicole Constable argues that, on returning home, women migrants must create another space to fit into and that this enables them to rework traditional relationships with menfolk and family members.[67] Interviews in south Jiangxi suggest that returnee women set up businesses in the towns partly as a way of creating such a space. For example, young women who set up businesses in the town or county seat evade the scrutiny and demands of the rural household while escaping alienation in the cities, and this advantage is especially valued by those returning with their boyfriends. By relocating themselves from the rural household to the town for most of their working day, women entrepreneurs participate in the civil society and mark out a space of relative independence for themselves. This differs from the general situation, in which the entrepreneurial activities of rural women are confined within the "court-yard" economy.[68] In Xinfeng and Yudu, courtyard industries include raising chickens and pigs as well as the production of handicrafts for sale at market. In these industries, both the labor of the women and the income they generate are subsumed within the household.

Some writers argue that, although women may earn a wage that gives them more influence in family matters, their status does not improve. This is because women gain power only when they are able to transcend the domestic sphere and form ties in the public domain, enabling them to deploy resources independently of the household.[69] My analysis partially endorses this view, but it also contends that the liberation of women is more than simply striving for the independent control of resources. As various scholars point out, the worth of family members in rural China is assessed according to their capacity to contribute material resources, and this has an almost contractual character.[70] Women do not pursue complete independence; rather, they seek increased equality in their interdependence with other members of their households. Chinese women in the countryside gain status by fulfilling obligations associated with being daughters or wives: as daughters there is the filial debt to the parents, and as a wife there is the pressure to earn approval as an industrious daughter-in-law.

Returnee women use resources and new perspectives from the cities as well as the space provided by the towns to fulfill customary duties (e.g., being industrious wives and daughters) and also to challenge social expectations about life for rural women. Characteristics commonly ascribed to typical peasant women are simplicity, diligence, virtue, thrift, and obedience – qualities that are applied in farming, raising children, and mediating family relationships. The returnee entrepreneurs talk in terms of being unlike typical peasant women and evaluate this as personal progress. Fei Ying, who manages the Fei Yangcheng Garment Factory, shares the following thoughts:

> I can do all the mundane work of the countryside, but now I have learned lots and would not be the me I am today without having worked in Guang-dong. My parents-in-law treated me badly after I gave birth to a girl, so I entrusted the care of the child to my mother and left the village. My husband went out two years before me, so I went to work in the same factory as him. I worked for four years at a sewing machine, then I was a production manager for two years. My husband was contacted by the township government to return and become the village head, so I came back home as well and farmed for a year. But interacting with the soil every day is a waste of my life, and somebody was needed to manage the factory. These days I am much bolder. I am no longer a typical peasant woman.[71]

Of course, some farming women are renowned for being *lihai* – "fierce and able" – so there is also an element of stereotyping in how successful women entrepreneurs such as Fei perceive themselves.[72] Fei supervises forty employees and confers with bosses in five Pearl Delta factories. To her satisfaction, the land contracted under the responsibility system has been sublet to another household in the village. Thus, women use the spatial and temporal distance from the village to reflect on their lives in the countryside and, on return, they resolve to deploy whatever resources are at their disposal to pursue an alternative life.

Returnee wives who follow their husbands home after several years of working in the city constitute an invisible source of capital and labor in returnee endeavors. The urban savings of the women form part of the couple's funds that are invested in the business. As an extension of their domestic roles, the women prepare meals for the workers and clean the workshop. They assume duties such as looking after the shop front, and some of the women also farm during the busy seasons. Of the 56 married male interviewees, just over half have carried out their business activities with both capital and labor contributions from their returnee wives. Yet returnee women are able to escape agricultural duties: farm labor is hired on a seasonal basis or the land is sublet. In enabling rural women to make an initial break from farming, earn money, and improve their status vis-à-vis the family, migration strengthens their agency in forming and pursuing personal goals. This agency derives from broadened "perspectives," improved knowledge of livelihood alternatives (e.g., how to obtain urban employment), and increased control over resources. In contrast, most of the nonmigrant wives of returnee male entrepreneurs in this study remain tied to the farm, and their lives consist of looking after in-laws, raising animals, and cultivating land. Even one of the most successful entrepreneurs claims that his wife must stay on the farm in case his business fails. The men acknowledge that their wives are farm-bound against their will and that this is a source of conflict in the marriage. When I asked one man how he intends to resolve the problem, he replied, "I explain to her patiently that someone must stay on the farm because we need the economic advantages of both the business and the farm."[73]

6.5 CONCLUSION

Returnees to Xinfeng and Yudu pursue their goals of becoming independent bosses by combining skills, capital, information, and social contacts from their "incubator" organizations with resources and opportunities in the origin areas. The importance of the incubator organization is revealed by the fact that returned migrants set up businesses that largely replicate the urban ventures in which they had worked. The entrepreneurs in my study innovate mainly in the manufacturing and service sectors but only to a small degree in agriculture. The tendency of returnee entrepreneurs to duplicate the business in which they previously worked explains why there are no shoe workshops or larger work-shops producing toys and refined furniture in the places that I visited, where the incidence of returnee entrepreneurship is minimal.

For most migrants, returning home and participating in commercial innova-tion is a way of achieving other related goals, such as making money, reuniting with loved ones, escaping subordination in the urban labor markets, and re-dressing the peripheral position of the native place within the broader political economy. For women in particular, migrating and then returning home to es-tablish a business – usually a small service-sector entity – is a way of reworking relationships with family members and actively forming and pursuing life goals. This holds true despite the fact that many of the women return because they are following their boyfriends or spouses or responding to the call of parents.

Although migration and return enable people to pursue goals, describing urban labor markets as the "big school of society"[74] and implying that urban exposure is sufficient to inspire individuals with ways to extricate themselves from poverty actually disguise the structural mechanisms that disadvantage peripheral areas in terms of their access to resources. Such a position endorses migration as a substitute for other development initiatives that make claims upon the resources of the state. In order to function as effective agents of information transfer and entrepreneurship, migrants need improved access to education, training, and material resources. However, various structural mech-anisms supported by the central state confine migrants to the least-skilled and lowest-paying jobs.

Although rural dwellers are able to improve their access to skills and money through migration, they are nonetheless differentially positioned in terms of their opportunities for both acquiring these resources and deploying them in entrepreneurial ways at home. Those with higher levels of education tend to spend longer in the cities, experience greater economic advancement in the urban labor markets, have better contacts at home, return at an older age, and be male. Furthermore, entrepreneurs who are relatively successful and estab-lish or contract the larger manufacturing ventures tend to have returned more in response to "pull" factors, whereas those who experience considerable dif-ficulties with their businesses or else establish small service stalls tend to have returned home more in response to "push" factors. The relative balance of push and pull factors combines with individual characteristics to shape a social ac-tor's control over resources and thus his or her capacity to form and pursue entrepreneurial goals. Although there are considerable differences among the returnees, they all share the goal of escaping wage labor and prospering through independent means.

Entrepreneurs, Socioeconomic Change, and Interactions with the State

THIS chapter focuses on (1) the role of returned migrant entrepreneurs in promoting social and economic change in their home communities and (2) their contributions to the modernization goals of the central and local state. Local states in Xinfeng and Yudu try to harness the resources generated through return migration and direct them toward wider development strategies sanctioned by the central state – for example, the construction of rural industries and towns, the absorption of surplus rural labor, and the expansion of commodity markets. Returnees use their urban experiences and resources to engage with the local state in ways that improve the local policy environment and the local infrastructure, thereby making the native community more conducive to the pursuit of entrepreneurial goals. In this way, returned migrants struggle against local-level obstacles that prevent them from prospering through self-employment while contributing to broader development objectives.

The following discussion contributes a rural perspective to a growing body of literature on internal mobility as the new element in state and society relations in post-Mao China.[1] It examines the dynamic role of returned entrepreneurs in injecting investment into the local economy; broadening the political criterion determining eligibility for loans; lobbying for changes to local tax policies and contesting the official "squeeze" on businesses; increasing local opportunities for rural livelihood diversification; integrating poorer rural areas into the national market economy; reforming business management practices; and building rural towns. Each of these contributions is examined in turn.

7.1 INVESTMENT

Returnees to Xinfeng and Yudu inject money into the home economy, either their own savings or the funds of external business contacts, and for this reason they have been targeted by the local state. Data on investment in returnee enterprises are based on estimates offered by respondents and may be vulnerable to inaccuracies of exaggeration or understatement. Where possible, the figures given by the owners of the manufacturing enterprises were checked with township leaders and, in the case of prominent factories based in the county seats, double-checked with government officials. The information on sources of investment is only partial, as entrepreneurs were not always willing to reveal complete details of their business alliances. The main findings are laid out in Table 7.1.

In the large-scale manufacturing sector of Yudu, the percentage of investment funds from urban labor markets is higher than for Xinfeng; this is because, in Yudu, Hong Kong bosses have invested in subcontracting clothing factories. Additionally, much of the investment takes the form of equipment and tools from the cities, another important contribution to the rural industrial sector. The amount of investment in the service sector is larger in Yudu than in Xinfeng because several of the Yudu restaurant owners built the physical premises of the businesses as part of their houses, so the value of the business includes that of the house.

Although the urban savings of the returnees make a significant contribution to their start-up capital, 90% of the entrepreneurs who are engaged in manufacturing cite insufficient funds as a major obstacle to expansion. Three of the clothing manufacturers say that they have been forced to contract out part of their production quotas to factories in other counties because they do not have the money to purchase more machinery and employ more workers. The capital deficiency is exacerbated by three key factors. First, as already discussed, the high taxes and fees levied by grass-roots cadres limit the amounts of funds available for reinvestment in the businesses. Second, because the returnees are operating in their home environment, they must act in accordance with "human feeling" and collective welfare values by not pressuring certain customers (such as relatives, neighbors, and political patrons) to settle their debts. However, they are forced to obtain high-interest loans from informal credit rotation societies to meet the day-to-day running expenses of their businesses. Third, although migration and return have gone some way toward countering regional protectionism by enabling entrepreneurs to tap markets in other localities, some returnees report that the resolve of leaders in other regions to defend their own local enterprises means that, if a customer in another place fails to settle a debt, there is no viable recourse for obtaining the money.

An important part of the local state publicity campaign to attract returnees is the promise of help with obtaining credit. The linkage between deposits and loans, together with the virtual impossibility of obtaining loans from financial institutions in other townships or localities, means that in poor areas the amount of credit available is highly restricted. In allocating whatever funds are available, preference goes to those projects and persons supported by the local state. Returnees who can demonstrate reliable access to a coastal market, substantial funds of their own, or the backing of a partner in the special economic zones

Table 7.1. *Investment in returnee firms, and percentage of investment brought from the city*

Enterprise	Total investment (thousand yuan)	Percentage of investment from outside	Average investment per enterprise from outside (yuan)	Number of enterprises with at least 15% of investment from sources other than savings and informal loans
Xinfeng large manufacturing	5,600 (4,100[a])	27.68 (35.36[a])	125,000	Gov. loans – 4 Mortgages – 2 External investors – 2 External & gov. loan – 1
Yudu large manufacturing	4,675[b]	52.26[b]	143,705	Gov. loans – 3 Mortgage – 1 External investors – 3 External loans & mortgage – 1 External & gov. loan – 1
Xinfeng small manufacturing	729	62.26	30,466	Gov. loan – 1 Gov. investment – 1
Yudu small manufacturing	675	67.41	45,500	Gov. loan – 1 Mortgages – 2
Xinfeng service	76	57.89	4,000	None
Yudu service	389	52.18	20,000	Loans guaranteed by local traders – 2[c]
Xinfeng agriculture	7	100.00	Two enterprises with total investment of 5,000 and 2,000, respectively	None
Yudu agriculture	715	6.99	Five enterprises with total investment (in thousands) of 500, 120, 60, 20, and 15, respectively	Poverty alleviation loans – 2 Gov. loan – 1

[a] Excluding Shenta Snake Company.
[b] Excluding the Yudu Woolen Sweater Company. The total amount of outside investment for this single venture (5 million yuan) is more than that for all other Yudu returnee ventures combined.
[c] Both loans are to building materials shops.

are able to more effectively lobby for the backing of community leaders. This is of course entirely reasonable, given that any bank would make loan decisions like this. The larger-scale businesses in particular have benefited from loans that use houses for security, loans guaranteed by local governments, loans from financial investment companies set up by tax departments and county governments, and high-interest loans from credit rotation societies – some of which operate under the auspices of government institutions (e.g., Party schools).

Funds for investment in rural enterprises have also increased as a result of the inventive measures of the local state in harnessing migrant remittances. Migrant remittance deposits mean that more credit is becoming available in the countryside. As more returnees lobby community leaders for funding and as more policy documents recommend channeling increments in deposits toward the support of returnee businesses, some of the political criteria determining eligibility for loans may become more fluid. State agents and financial institutions use various measures to harness the remittances. County and township financial institutions send representatives to destination areas where migrants are concentrated and encourage them to entrust their remittances to these urban-based agents. As another development, in the latter half of 1997, electronic linkages (*dianzi jikuan*) were established between branches of the Agricultural Bank, located in destination areas where migrants are more concentrated, and branches in the townships of Yudu. These electronic linkages allow for the transfer of cash within 24 hours, and parents and spouses in the villages can withdraw the money with their shiny new bankcards. Furthermore, post offices, branches of the Agricultural Bank, and credit cooperatives are starting to use customer services and interest on deposits to compete with each other for the business of migrants. The potential for a massive injection of migrant remittance deposits to be channeled into financial support for returnee business creation has not been lost on Chinese planners, but as yet the idea has not been transferred from policy documents to practice.[2]

7.2 IMPROVING THE POLITICAL ENVIRONMENT FOR BUSINESS

Returnees improve the local economic environment by actively complaining about the reluctance of local officials to curb their interference in the private sector and by contesting the dominant presence of the local state in distributing opportunities and resources and making its claims on rural incomes. Both returnees and nonmigrants express the opinion that, although the policies of the central government are good, their benefits are sometimes lost or distorted because of how they are implemented at the local level. They say: "above there is a policy; below, a counterpolicy" (*shang you zhengce, xia you duice*). In particular, returnees tend to compare the developed economies of the coastal cities with their rural home towns, explaining the differences in terms of local-level policies and government behavior. The words of one migrant reflect a common sentiment:

My boss asked me why all the Jiangxi country cousins (*laobiao*) come to work in Guangzhou. I told him that it is all to do with the policies. Your policies are open and ours are backward. At home they tell us to run but tie our legs. If your policies were like ours and ours were like yours then Guangzhou people would be coming to work in Jiangxi.[3]

The potential for such sentiments to promote change is dependent upon the individual's control over resources and his or her capacity to generate more resources. Returnees who do not have useful contacts prior to migration must use their resources to acquire such contacts on return. Only the more successful entrepreneurs – or those who return with useful information or a valuable contact – gain a substantive voice in their consultations with the local state.

Although entrepreneurs lobby for reduced government interference in their enterprises, their capacity to contest the "squeeze" and meddling of local officials is limited by the fact that the returned migrants are able to pursue their entrepreneurial goals only with the consent of the local state. This means that the returned migrants must use their urban resources to negotiate with officials for access to the local resources essential for entrepreneurship. These include permits to run a business, permission to use an operating site, access to raw materials, and (in some instances) loans. In turn, the local government siphons off income generated by entrepreneurs though a plethora of taxes, fees, and fines. Entrepreneurs must also donate to politically important projects such as funds for building village schools or carrying out grass-roots ideological education campaigns. Moreover, giving gifts and hosting banquets are important for maintaining patron–client ties and for facilitating the entrepreneur's negotiations with the local state over such issues as obtaining a town *hukou,* acquiring an operating venue, and negotiating tax levels.

During the course of the interviews, returnees often directly complained about exactions – or else they euphemistically alluded to the problem. Almost half of the entrepreneurs running privately registered manufacturing entities stated that, after one year of operating their businesses, pre-return promises of tax concessions had failed to materialize. Two of the interviewees, who operated businesses in the city prior to their return, claimed that the total sum of exactions by local cadres is much greater than the burden imposed by city officials. "Because social morality is not good, investing at home is like pouring water into the sand," sighed one entrepreneur. The operator of a township brick factory complained that the cost per unit of electricity in the township (Yudu) is three times the cost of power in Xiamen.[4] Only one fifth of the interviewees reported that they considered the level of taxes and fees to be reasonable. This is all despite the fact that, in many cases, these interviewees had kin ties with cadres or had established their business in partnership with local state institutions.

The predicament facing returnee entrepreneurs in Xinfeng and Yudu mirrors a nationwide situation whereby officials stake claims on the resources generated by entrepreneurs. Studies of returnee business creation conducted by Chinese social scientists in rural Shandong and Anhui similarly report that local state exactions are one of the main problems faced by the entrepreneurs.[5] The central state fears that such actions by grass-roots cadres may dampen the inclination of returnees to direct their higher-quality human capital and money toward economic diversification at home. For instance, according to an article in *Guangdong Labor News,* government authorities in the administrative region of Tianmen city (Hunan province) are mounting signs outside large-scale returnee enterprises in order to protect these businesses against the random appropriation of fees, fines, and levies by cadres. The purpose of the "sign protection system for key returnee enterprises" is to allow the entrepreneurs to feel at ease while operating their businesses in order to encourage the "flourishing development of the return project."[6] Moreover, the official publication *Jiangxi zhengbao* urges local-level cadres to curb their extortion of returnee businesses and to refrain from becoming a "mother-in-law" to these enterprises, so that migrants have the confidence to return.[7]

For many migrants, the perceived certainty of cadre exactions acts as a deterrent to both return and entrepreneurship. Hence, continued absence from the natal community might be a way of expressing dissatisfaction toward local-level politics. In 1997 this was certainly the case in Wanzai county, where – unlike Xinfeng and Yudu – the incidence of return migrant entrepreneurship was minimal. A migrant from Wanzai related the following:

> At home I wasn't doing too badly compared with everyone else. I had a tractor, a small shop in the village, and 2 mu of land. In another place that would be enough. But we were still poor and there was always some official or the tax bureau holding out a hand. In 1995, over the course of eight months, I paid over 4,000 yuan in taxes and expenses like road fees. They don't care if you are earning or not and they just walk away when it all falls down. I went out to escape poverty and those parasites, but it seems there is no escape. What good to me is a receipt from the Bureau of Industry and Commerce when they don't give me help or service in return? On Women's Day they wanted my wife to give money and the Grain Bureau comes and exacts a levy from the shop even though I don't sell anything

to do with grain. People would love to come home and set up, but the policies aren't right.[8]

Some Yudu dock workers whom I interviewed in Shanghai expressed similar sentiments claiming that "little people" without contacts in either urban or rural locations would be unable to withstand the onslaught of financial demands if they tried to establish a small business. Another objection to the idea of setting up an enterprise is that "most township and village enterprises are going broke these days, so if the government can't keep its businesses afloat with its power and money, what hope is there for someone like me?"[9] In Wanzai, although there are isolated examples of returnees who create businesses, migrants have not been targeted as a group of potential entrepreneurs. One Wanzai official even expressed doubt that persons of such low "quality" could reasonably be expected to innovate.[10] The small number of returnee entrepreneurs to Wanzai as compared with Xinfeng and Yudu is also a reflection of the fact that, whereas migration from the southern counties started in the early 1980s, migration from Wanzai only really commenced in the early 1990s, so migration from Wanzai has not yet produced a substantial return flow. Hence government policy is an influential factor but not the only one.

In Xinfeng and Yudu, the operators of larger entities in the county seat and the outlying *xiang* voice complaints and draw the attention of cadres to the more liberal policies in the special economic zones. For instance, at one dinner that I attended, an official asked a prominent returnee businessman: "Why don't you use spare space on the factory site to build another workshop, lay another egg?" The businessman replied, "As it is there are fewer eggs for you to break." He then expounded on how the cadres in Guangdong have the right attitude in encouraging the creative potential of people, whereas leaders in the interior tie up innovation with bureaucracy and exactions.[11] The returnee entrepreneur runs one of the largest businesses in Yudu and has introduced much investment from a Hong Kong boss. He has also employed a "high-priced oldie" (*gaojia laotou*), a retired cadre from the Yudu County Bureau of Foreign Trade, who provides access to contacts within the local state. Thus the businessman is well positioned in his exchanges with local-level power holders. By entering into these kinds of cooperation with the local state, returned migrants are in a better position to express dissatisfaction with the behavior of officials and to appeal for changes in their attitudes toward business.

Returnee entrepreneurs face the challenge of promoting reform in an environment where poor remuneration for administrative personnel and changes to the taxation system cause cadres to act as revenue maximizers. The efforts of returnees to protect their business interests are, however, assisted by the fact that the county and township governments have a vested interest in allowing

Table 7.2. *Job creation by returnee enterprises visited by the author*

Business category	Number of enterprises	Number of employees	Employees per enterprise[a]
Xinfeng large manufacturing	12	364	30
Yudu large manufacturing	14	808[b]	58[b]
Xinfeng small manufacturing	15	76	5
Yudu small manufacturing	10	48	5
Xinfeng service sector	11	44	4
Yudu service sector	11	30	3

[a] Average, to the nearest whole number.
[b] This figure excludes the Yudu Woolen Sweater Company, which employs 860 people.

returnee enterprises to survive as revenue-generating entities. Moreover, officials recognize that adjustments to local policies are necessary in order to attract the phoenixes and their resources. Hence, a Yudu Party Committee publicity brochure advises migrants that "we are going to further liberate our thought, become more open, formulate preferential policies,"[12] the clear subtext being, "we are changing things so that you can make money at home!"

7.3 ABSORBING SURPLUS LABOR

In both national and local-level development policies, returnee entrepreneurship is hailed as a mechanism for absorbing surplus rural labor. To what extent are the hopes of policy-makers and officials realized in Xinfeng and Yudu? Figures in Table 7.2 suggest that returnee enterprises help to provide jobs for people in the native place, though in the survey overall, 58% of returnee enterprises employ fewer than ten people and 43% employ fewer than five. These figures for employment are respectable in light of limited empirical evidence from other developing countries, which finds that the majority of rural industries employ fewer than ten people. For example, in both Sierra Leone and Honduras, over 95% of rural enterprises employ fewer than five workers.[13] Yet these figures for the number of employees in returnee enterprises do not tell the whole story. Rather than absorbing the nonmigrants, most of the factories and workshops that produce furniture, clothes, shoes, and metal doors tend to employ former migrants. In these factories, the skill requirements are relatively high and the wages reflect this. By contrast, in the few factories in which most of the laborers have never migrated, tasks are simple and the wages are low; the outflow of labor to the cities means that only young teen-agers and very old workers remain in the countryside to perform these tasks. The managers of these factories complain that it is difficult for them to operate a viable enterprise because the young work slowly and are difficult to train.[14] As a result, production often falls short of the quotas set by the parent company, so payment for the goods barely covers wages and operating expenses. Some service-sector operators (e.g., mechanics located in the townships) also report that it is difficult for them to find apprentices, since most of the young men prefer to head for the cities. However, returnee businesses offering apprenticeships in more lucrative trades – for example, carpentry and welding – provide nonmigrant youths with the skills to earn an above-average livelihood.

Although policy-makers and local cadres are keen for rural industries to absorb surplus rural labor, the unfavorable employment conditions in poor rural areas mean that the laborers most needed for the development of rural industries – that is, younger and more educated workers – are most likely to reside long-term in the cities. The issue is not as simple as returnee enterprises addressing the problem of *surplus* labor. Returnee enterprises remedy the problem of a *shortage* of skilled labor in the countryside by attracting, retaining, and training some of the labor resources needed to develop a fledgling manufacturing sector. Returnee enterprises have not played a major role in providing livelihood opportunities for the local population. Rather, by expanding the occupational structure of the home economy, returnee entrepreneurs have made it possible for other migrants with various kinds of urban work experience to earn a living at home. This helps to alleviate a shortage of skilled workers in economically peripheral areas and, over time, may enhance the capacity of the industrial and tertiary sectors of the countryside to provide income-generating opportunities for the nonmigrant population.

Although returnee enterprises do not employ local nonmigrant labor, there are instances of individual returnees providing opportunities for several households in a village to supplement their farming incomes through specialized agricultural production or off-farm processing activities. Owing to the anticipated multiplier effects of these returnee ventures, the bulk of the investment comes from poverty alleviation loans arranged by the township government. A key example is that of an agribusiness in eels and bait set up by two Yudu returnees. One of the returnees had worked in Fujian province cultivating bait and, during that time, had made the acquaintance of a Shanghai merchant. They signed a contract with the merchant for the initial supply of bait and eel eggs and the later purchasing of eels. While in Shantou city (Guangdong), the other returnee established contact with some restauranteurs and other potential customers. The plan is for each household in Yiwu, a very poor village in Xinbei, to use 0.2 mu of land for cultivating bait to feed the eels. The average per-capita income of the villagers is 900 yuan per annum, and they are to receive an additional 300 yuan a year by selling their bait to the eel farmers. A long-term aim is to involve the entire village in raising eels. Similarly, a young man from Duanwu *xiang* in Yudu worked for two years raising American bullfrogs in the suburbs of Guangzhou. In 1997 he returned home to set up a frog farm on 40 mu of land contracted from the village. His former boss provides the feed and has agreed to purchase the frogs. Next year, other households in the village will also begin raising frogs. The government-administered loans to these two businesses are for 500,000 yuan and 120,000 yuan, respectively.

The story of Mr. Long of Qifeng village in Wanzai illustrates the potential for an individual returnee to provide off-farm employment for several village households as well as the enthusiastic (albeit not entirely successful) efforts of village cadres to support entrepreneurship. In 1987, far earlier than any of his contemporaries, Mr. Long left the village to work in a sofa factory in Guangzhou. In 1990 he returned to Qifeng and decided that, with more people building new homes, there was a local market for sofas. In 1992 the village acted as guarantor for a loan of 60,000 yuan to support him in setting up a sofa springs factory. The village committee also provided a roadside site and a two-year tax exemption. Mr. Long posted a notice calling for workers; out of the 200 people who arrived on his doorstep, he chose 40. In spite of the enthusiastic support of local cadres, the factory closed down in the latter half of 1994 because of the unreliable electricity supply. Mr. Long placed his factory equipment in storage and has been trying to accumulate sufficient funds to relocate the venture to the county seat. Despite this initial setback, Mr. Long has persisted with the sofa-making side of his business, this time buying the sofa springs from Guangdong. As the bulkiness of sofa foam makes it too expensive to transport from Guangzhou, Mr. Long devised a way of making sofa filling. This involves shredding bamboo scraps from local cane factories into a straw-like texture and then drying them in the sun. Mr. Long and his father designed the shredder, and all of the rural households that supply him with sofa filling have such a shredder – made by a local carpenter for around 100 yuan. A total of fifteen rural households supply Mr. Long with sofa filling, which he resells to household furniture industries throughout the Wanzai countryside. In 1990, he paid 0.05 yuan per jin of filling and sold it for 0.45 yuan per jin (a jin is approximately 0.5 kg). By 1996, he was paying 0.2 yuan per jin and selling at 1.2 yuan per jin. I was informed that each rural household earns approximately 4,000 yuan a year for processing the bamboo, although this does not include their electricity or transport costs. Mr. Long also acts as a wholesaler for soft leather, cloth, and springs from Guangzhou that he purchases from his former employer and supplies to some 300 manufacturing households distributed throughout the county. Mr. Long's story has been featured in the state-run *Jiangxi ribao* and *Yichun ribao,* causing him to receive

Returned migrants providing a livelihood for other villagers: shredding
bamboo scraps to make sofa filling, Qifeng village, Wanzai county.

several letters a month from people asking advice about setting up a sofa-filling
business.[15] These articles praise him for his persistent efforts to create a business and because his eventual success was achieved without making claims on
state resources.

7.4 "MODERN" MANAGERS

As discussed in Chapter 6, returnees are introducing changes to the managerial practices of rural enterprises. This occurs with the blessing and encouragement of the local state, which is anxious to reform, modernize, and salvage ailing state and collective enterprises. In poor townships such as Duanwu (Yudu), which has almost no industrial base, the local state hopes that the expertise and managerial experience of returnees will contribute to the initial founding of a rural industrial sector.[16] Exposure to the management practices of the cities is causing cadres to begin valuing managerial efficiency over state control and also productivity over the traditional "human feeling" considerations of rural enterprises. However, it must be noted that economic pressures within the rural areas are also precipitating these changes in management practices independently of the returnee influence.

The strong association between "modern" and "development" in the political context of the reform era enables cadres and entrepreneurs to overlook the exploitative aspects of management practices imported from urban factories. These management practices are designed to extract maximum surplus from the work force and usually involve long working days. Moreover, one of the main reasons that returnee bosses prefer to hire former migrants is because they are accustomed to the rigorous labor discipline of the urban manufacturing zones. However, some employers explain that, as a result of their own experience of the hardships of *dagong,* they are more understanding of their employees. Modern management methods are used most commonly in larger-scale ventures and in ventures that are located in the county seat. In contrast, the petty commodity mode of production that characterizes smaller-scale workshops is widely perceived by rural residents to emphasize "human feeling." Yet this mode of production also extracts maximum surplus from the workers, through long hours and low rates of pay, and from the owner–operators through self-exploitation.

In larger returnee enterprises there is a tension between (a) the desire of the employer to maintain efficiency through modern management and (b) cultural values that lead workers to expect they'll be treated with leniency and generosity. As the founder of the Red Star Shoe Company said to me: "We import the management style of the city and add some human feeling." The "human feeling" makes allowances for the fact that rural workers are burdened with the responsibilities of home and land and that all of the workers live in the immediate locality. The owner of the Xinbei Furniture Factory explained:

> When I managed a factory in Guangzhou I had to delay the payment of wages by two months, otherwise the workers would disappear after payday. But here I know the house where everyone lives and I know that they

are not going anywhere. And when they ask me to advance them a little money because they need to buy fertilizer or food, I know that they will come to work the next day.[17]

In the larger enterprises, considerations of human feeling do not extend to employing relatives; they are avoided because they are perceived as difficult to manage. This differs from the situation in many collective enterprises run by the local state, which are virtual "kinship" corporations.

Modern managers are also valued by the local state because they help to integrate the home market into a more national economy by creating supply and marketing linkages with coastal cities. These linkages are forged across institutional and geographic boundaries with the blessing of local officials, and they also create opportunities for rural residents to respond to market signals and deploy resources with a degree of independence from the local state. So, for example, entrepreneurs can sell their products directly to their customers rather than going through intermediary government sales companies that cream off a little of the profit. Successful migrants enrich the local supply of managers because they have information networks, personnel experience, and an insight into production layouts and marketing. A core group of returnees who have experienced socioeconomic advancement in the coastal cities perceive themselves in terms of the values and social stratification system of the cities. These entrepreneurs are generally in their 30s and have spent at least eight years as migrant workers. Some returnees (four encountered in this study) are so integrated into the host societies that they commute regularly between the parent factory in the Pearl Delta, where they hold managerial positions, and the factory at home, where they are bosses. Two other returnee bosses in the study are members of the Guangdong Furniture Association.

According to the head of the Township and Village Enterprise Bureau in Xinfeng, returnee enterprises are more successful than other businesses because

they import the advanced management systems from the *sanzi qiye*[18] and coastal enterprises and they have a preference for not employing relatives. Also the operators of these enterprises have been in Guangdong and have seen the rules of the market, so they know that if an enterprise fails it is natural for it to go bankrupt. They have the ability to be self-reliant and don't expect the government to bail them out when there are problems.[19]

A Chinese survey of returnee entrepreneurs in Fengyang prefecture, Anhui province, likewise finds that their enterprises tend to perform better than other rural businesses because of superior management practices and better market contacts.[20] Additionally, the observed strengths of returnee enterprises are causing some managers of collectives and state-owned enterprises to begin revising their own management practices.

7.5 INTEGRATING NATAL COMMUNITIES INTO A NATIONAL MARKET ECONOMY

Returnee entrepreneurs help to integrate rural areas into the national market-place through the direct introduction of new fashions, goods, and services from the coastal cities to the market towns of the hinterland. The products from small returnee workshops have special features. They do not compete with urban manufactured goods but rather cater to a rural market, and they are more fashionable than locally produced alternatives. As an example, cheap returnee replicas of urban footwear, handbags, and belts offer stylish alternatives to the ubiquitous black cloth shoes and canvas bags. There is a stark contrast between the crude benches crafted by the village carpenter and the varnished chairs produced in the township workshops. And rather than choosing the traditional option of ornate wooden canopy beds, affluent households now prefer to purchase a bed with a mattress – colloquially referred to as *ximensi* (a transliteration of the brand name Simmons!).

Towns function as spaces for receiving new consumer values that social actors can use in negotiating greater personal freedom, and returnee entrepreneurs are instrumental in introducing these values.[21] Although many of the service-sector entities established by the returnees duplicate existing ventures, there are certain services that draw their inspiration from the cities – for example, the roller-skating rink and the dance halls. The introduction of the dance halls to Daa town is not viewed as a positive development by all rural residents, especially local women, who (fearing the influence on their husbands) disapprove of places where unmarried couples are allowed to hold hands.[22] Although the dance halls are beyond the consumption capacity or social aspirations of most of the rural population, their presence symbolizes the challenge of facets of an urban lifestyle to rural moral values. As a further example, a young returnee photographer expressed delight that she was bringing something new and urbane to local women. For a small outlay of money and an hour of time, she could give them a permanent souvenir of their temporary transformation from a farm worker in faded clothes to a film star in a sparkling dress.[23] Structuralist scholars may well argue that this kind of commodification promotes the reliance of rural people on the modern cash economy and that, through diffusing a taste for fashion and beauty care, the women themselves appropriate some of the qualities of commodities.[24] Yet personal possessions such as new clothes and cosmetics can also be viewed as cultural and economic resources that women use to challenge their marginal status within the broader political economy and to contest those values within the immediate village society that they find oppressive. In this way they define their life goals as different from those of their "clay-treading" counterparts.

However, the contribution that returnee entrepreneurs make to rural commodity markets sometimes occurs in an environment in which most households have little disposable income. I recorded that the primary items of expenditure in Jiaocun village (Xinbei township, Yudu) are salt, cigarettes, soap, fertilizer, medicine, school fees, house building, marriages, funerals, and social gifts. Indeed, for many households, guaranteeing even basic survival is a problem. As an illustration of frugality, villagers unweave fertilizer bags in order to make string. Moreover, in some households laundry powder serves as an all-purpose soap for washing dishes, clothes, the body, and the hair. It is not surprising that many shopkeepers complained to me that it is difficult to do business.

In one sense, the contribution of returnees to a rural commodity market legitimates the local state by suggesting economic progress, often rightly so, and by providing a focus for the attentions of the rural populace. Conversely, the introduction of new goods and services is a source of cultural disruption in that the endogenous values of frugality and modesty are challenged, and frustration swells in the hearts of those who can only look but not acquire. A diversified commodity market is imbued with values such as economic advancement and personal freedom. Moreover, the emergence of a realm in which rural dwellers can choose commodities brings with it the political implication that individuals and families can have private property and, by extension, private interests.

7.6 BUILDING TOWNS IN THE COUNTRYSIDE

In Xinfeng and Yudu, the state-sponsored revival of rural industries and towns in the 1980s and 1990s creates spaces in both geographic and market terms to which migrants can transfer their urban-acquired skills and money. In poor areas, where town construction is hindered by a lack of resources, the local states designate a special role for towns in helping to erode the sharp divide between urban and rural (*er yuanzhi*) by becoming the central link in a three-tier system (*san yuanzhi*): the rural market town is a center from which fledgling rural industries can develop as well as a place where villagers can be exposed to urban culture.[25]

Although the towns form an important basis for rural livelihood diversification, poor infrastructure and physical isolation create difficulties for returnee entrepreneurs with production and marketing. Production is often inconvenienced by an irregular supply of electricity and poor roads, so workshops can manufacture for only a few days a week or for a few hours per day. Furthermore, many township roads turn to sludge with the onset of spring rains. These obstacles are especially serious when the factory is contract manufacturing for an urban partner who must meet export deadlines.

Problems in marketing stem from the fact that the urban work experience or incubator organization – rather than the needs of the rural market – is the key factor in determining the type of business that returnees create in the natal community. For instance, a returned migrant to Yudu set up a factory producing shop display mannequins; but there was no local demand for mannequins and he had no way of finding customers elsewhere, so he went broke. Some entrepreneurs resolve the problem by modifying their products to suit the low-income rural markets and the needs of local consumers. As previously mentioned, shoe workshops produce cheap vinyl replicas of the stylish leather fashions of the city. If there are solid subcontracting arrangements with a coastal factory, then the entrepreneur does not face the dilemma of marketing the product. Yet the reliance of returnee subcontractors on specific coastal companies leaves them vulnerable to market fluctuations in the special economic zones and susceptible to exploitation in their negotiation of prices and contracts. "They eat the meat, we chew on the bones," explained the boss of the Huaguang Leather Company.[26]

In comparison with other players in the national economy, returnee entrepreneurs located in isolated towns are disadvantaged with regard to information and competitive access to national markets, so it is difficult for them to find alternative customers when coastal factories cancel agreements. As an example, the Yudu Wig and Eyelash Factory initially manufactured wigs in a subcontracting capacity for a Taiwanese firm located in the coastal city of Xiamen. But then mannequin manufacturers began to make dummies with plastic hair, so the Yudu wig factory converted to the production of false eyelashes. However, in recent years, many laid-off workers in the coastal cities have also begun making eyelashes because the production costs are low. Between 1995 and 1997, the number of employees in the Yudu factory has decreased from one hundred to twenty.[27]

In drawing unfavorable comparisons between home and the cities, returnees in effect lobby for improvements to infrastructure. Following North and Oi, "infrastructure" here refers not only to such physical aspects as roads, electricity, and telecommunications but also to less tangible facilities such as market linkages and information.[28] To address the problems of poor infrastructure and relative isolation, township and county governments in Xinfeng have cooperated to facilitate the physical relocation of larger enterprises from the townships to the county seat. Township governments are generally unwilling for their enterprises to move farther afield, as this would compromise their control over the resources they generate. Consequently, the county government has allowed the *xiang* or *zhen* to receive the tax revenues of these firms despite the change in location. A total of seven of the large manufacturing enterprises that I visited in Xinfeng had relocated from towns to the county seat. This involved some negotiation between both levels of government and conforms with the recommendation of Chinese policy-makers that measures be taken to selectively relocate a portion of rural enterprises to the counties.[29] The overall policy is still one of developing rural market towns, but having said this, primacy is given to developing those towns higher up in the settlement hierarchy.

The central state hopes that – as an extension of the current role of returnee entrepreneurship in absorbing surplus rural labor and diffusing urban culture into the countryside – returnees will eventually promote a more permanent and complete urbanization of the countryside. Policy-makers see returnees as agents for promoting the *permanent transfer* of rural labor out of the villages and agriculture and into rural towns and industries. A current view is that migration allows for only a partial evolution from the status of peasant to worker. Hence, migrants are described as "amphibious people" (*liangqiren*). According to economist Chen Hao, returnees who set up businesses or lead in the establishment of village enterprises not only consolidate the transformation of their own social roles, they also help even more peasants realize a transition in status from farmer to worker. He suggests that they do this by enabling more of the rural labor force to enter the industrial sector and by allowing professional farmers to cultivate larger areas.[30] Several independent surveys of Chinese workers in destination areas find that a large proportion of migrants intend to return home, and many express a desire to either establish a business or find employment in rural enterprises.[31] These studies demonstrate that, although some migrants may feel that they must eventually return in the geographic sense of the word, they are not content to return to their former lives as farmers and see the nonagricultural sectors as spaces for upward mobility at home. The state's modernization and urbanization goals are an important part of its sponsorship of return migrant entrepreneurship.

Even so, the situation in Xinfeng and Yudu suggests that, in poorer localities, return migrant entrepreneurship does not necessarily lead to a severing of ties with the land. Although many entrepreneurs have located their enterprises (and often their houses) in the towns and the county seat, 86% of respondents are unwilling to transfer their household registration to the towns, since this would mean relinquishing their hold on farmland. In 1997, transferring the *hukou* out of agriculture also involved a substantial outlay of money: about 5,000 yuan per person. At the time of the fieldwork, many returnees explained that, with the rise of the market economy, money can buy all of the advantages offered by a town *hukou*. As a further development, in June 2000 national policy-makers called on local governments to lift residence restrictions in towns and small cities and to eliminate administrative decrees deterring farmers from living in these settlements.[32] Moreover, following falling grain prices in the latter half of 2000, some local states have been encouraging farmers who still have land in the village to build houses and businesses in the towns as a way of facilitating livelihood diversification.[33]

Returnees have been able to create enterprises at home precisely because they are able to combine their savings from the urban labor markets with their land in the village. In order to be able to compete with the goods produced in the special economic zones and in order to entice external bosses into establishing businesses in the hinterland, labor and subsistence costs must be lower than in urban areas. Agriculture provides enough portion of subsistence for the returnee entrepreneurs and their workforce to allow a competitive basis for these industries by depressing labor costs. For some, the land is farmed by family members; for others, the land is rented for grain. Most of the interviewees state that, although the total sum of their earnings is less at home than in the cities, their economic situation in both locations is more or less the same because in the natal community there is no rent to pay and grain does not have to be purchased. Also, the land functions as a security net should the enterprises fail. Thus, as both land tillers (or land leasers) and petty capitalists, many of the returnees are better off than both rural residents with nonfarm status and villagers who are largely reliant on agriculture for their income.

Nonetheless, a limited amount of transfer to a nonagricultural household status is taking place. Of the 85 returnees, twelve have either converted their residency and occupational status or have expressed an intention to do so. But half of the men who have converted to a nonagricultural status have maintained their spouses' agricultural registration so that the household retains access to some land. This strategy also assists couples in pursuing their reproductive goals vis-à-vis state policy. For instance, one respondent explained that, because his wife is a farmer and their first child is a daughter, the couple is allowed to try again for a son.[34] Many returned migrant entrepreneurs see advantages in having a county seat *hukou* but believe that it is too late for them to benefit because they are already too old. They convert the *hukou* status of their children so that the next generation can avoid the occupational designation of agricultural laborer. These returnees also want their children to attend the county school so that they will have an improved chance of entering university. Although it is certainly the case that returnees in Xinfeng and Yudu promote the integrated construction of rural towns and industries, and that some *hukou* conversions are occurring, it is premature for returnees to fulfill the state-designated role of helping to permanently transfer rural labor into towns and factories.

7.7 CONCLUSION

Returned migrants negotiate with the local state to promote reforms in local business policy and improvements in town infrastructure. They do so because the actions of rapacious cadres and the underdevelopment of market towns inhibit their capacity to realize their entrepreneurial goals on home soil. Immediate contributions of the returnees to their home economies include injecting in-vestment into the local economy, broadening the political criteria determining access to loans, contesting the illegitimate claims of officials on the resources of businesses, introducing "modern" management practices, expanding market linkages beyond the confines of the local state, and cooperating with the local state to improve the infrastructure of rural towns.

The contribution of returnees to modernization, rural livelihood diversifi-cation, and the establishment of enterprises in towns is supported by various levels of the state hierarchy that have in mind the longer-term project of shift-ing a large proportion of farmers permanently out of agriculture. But returnee entrepreneurs have made only a limited contribution to the national modern-ization goal of permanently transferring labor out of agriculture and villages. Explanations include the early history of return to Xinfeng and Yudu, the under-developed economic conditions of these counties, and the fact that most rural dwellers are reluctant to lose their links with the land because farming forms a crucial basis for rural livelihood diversification.

Although returnee enterprises create employment, their contribution to pro-viding off-farm jobs for local nonmigrant labor is limited. Rather, by expanding the occupational structure of the native place, returnee entrepreneurs have made it possible for other migrants with various kinds of urban work experience to earn a living at home. This helps to alleviate a shortage of skilled workers in economically depressed areas and, over time, may enhance the capacity of the industrial and tertiary sectors of the countryside to provide income-generating opportunities for the local population.

Returning Home with Heavy Hearts and Empty Pockets

T HE previous chapters concerned the successful returnees, the entrepreneurs; however, there is another side to the story. Many migrants are compelled to return to their villages because of ill fortune in the cities or family obligations at home. Through migration, these returnees have been exposed to new values and alternative ways of living, causing some of them to form goals that are incompatible with village life. At the same time, migrants who are forced to return home often lack the resources required to attain their goals and so feel frustrated. But not all of the disruption is detrimental to village society, because the experience of living in the cities gives some returned migrants the impetus to challenge the values and social arrangements of home that they find oppressive.

Migrants who are compelled to return home often increase the complexity of the local state's work tasks, particularly in the areas of welfare, social stability, and family planning.[1] The contract responsibility system has been accompanied by legislation making the household legally responsible for the welfare of its members. Yet as illustrated in the following discussion, this does not negate the obligation of the local state to respond when the well-being of its constituents are at stake or if the activities of the returnees threaten the integrity of national policies. Such responses include providing welfare, appealing to urban employers on behalf of injured migrants when compensation is owed to them, using publicity to urge migrants not to commit crimes in the city, and monitoring the fertility of migrant women.

This chapter examines the adaptation and welfare hardships faced by the returnees and their households and the responses of the local state to the situation of migrants who return home for one of the four major reasons – unemployment, illness or injury, pregnancy, and family obligations.

8.1 UNEMPLOYED RETURNEES

Few urban employees and municipal authorities feel remorse at sacking migrant workers because "they can always go back and farm the land." This dismissive attitude overlooks the goals of the migrants themselves, especially their desire to escape an existence of "face to soil, back to sky." Unemployed returnees negatively affect the welfare of their households in two main ways. First, the rural household may have partly financed the initial move from the village and so loses its investment. Second, returned migrants may intensify pressure on household resources unless they find local off-farm employment or a specialized agricultural sideline. Initially, migration can relieve the problem of underemployment within the household and lead to greater productivity per head.[2] Even when migrants fail to remit, the household may be better off because there are fewer people eating from the common rice pot.[3] But households can lose these advantages when migrants return.

Owing to the information feedback mechanism of chain migration, most intending migrants have an accurate perception of the vagaries of urban labor markets and therefore many leave the villages with enough money for a return fare. This means that most individuals head for the city with at least some sort of security in the event of unemployment.[4] Friends in Wanzai county seat explained to me that, with the large-scale layoffs of workers from collectives and state enterprises, the country cousins are now in a better position than town residents because "at least they have some land." Though it is certainly the case that land provides important security for migrants and the rural household, in many villages this land allocation barely covers the subsistence of household members. Moreover, in times of economic downturn, the access of rural migrants to land gives employers an excuse for dismissing these employees first.

Although all temporary rural laborers are vulnerable in the cities, richer families are not as badly hit by the ill fortune of a migrant member as are poorer households. This can be seen in the experience of a young man from a village in Duanwu township, Yudu, whom I will call Mr. Li. Mr. Li is the son of a village teacher; he has finished high school and so is well educated by local standards. He is married and has a baby son. Above the door of his house a plaque states "three excellent household." Before migrating, Mr. Li had successfully contracted the running of a village orange orchard, so he was initially better off than most of his rice-farming neighbors. However, he heard of fellow villagers earning money in Guangdong and decided to try his own luck while still young enough to earn money for the future of his family. He found himself locked in a plastics factory with bars at the windows, forced to work long hours. He eventually escaped with several months' wages unpaid, convinced that his orchard in the village offered better prospects for a good life. I encountered many people with good political or socioeconomic standing in their villages who had similarly endured misfortune in the cities and decided to return home. Of course, this is double-edged in that migrants from families of higher socioeconomic standing in the village may return rather than try to find another job in the city, because they have more waiting for them at home than do migrants from poorer families.

Chain migration and the resulting concentration of fellow villagers in certain destination areas mean that dismissals from particular factories often result in migrants returning *en masse*. As an example, while I was in Tuanjie village in September 1997, over 250 workers from a Xiamen factory returned after a vicious fight with Sichuanese migrants over access to a meager trickle of water in the dormitory showers. The Wanzai workers were dismissed with two months' wages unpaid. Because of the bad reputation of Wanzai migrants in Xiamen, they were unable to find work in any other factory. Penniless, they were forced to more or less hijack buses heading to Wanzai and were detained in the county police station until family members came to pay their bus fares.[5] Although migrants generally leave their villages with enough in their pockets for a return fare, these migrants may not have had enough money for the fare because they had jobs and were anticipating the payment of wages owed to them.

Concern regarding the negative impact of unemployed returnees on rural livelihoods and social stability has prompted local governments to take measures aimed at preventing mass returns. In order to ensure the good reputation of Wanzai natives in the cities and hence their continuing access to factory jobs, the local state has followed the example of other counties in Jiangxi by adopting measures that monitor the behavior of their migrant constituents.[6] The next photograph, a poster in the activity room of the Tuanjie village office, lays down guidelines for migrating cadres to monitor their fellow migrants. According to the poster, village cadres and Party members who migrate must register in a County Labor Bureau booklet. They are also urged to maintain regular contact with their home-town fellows in the destination area, providing moral support and dissuading them from engaging in disruptive or violent activities. Another measure aimed at preserving the goodwill of municipal authorities toward Wanzai migrants is the establishment of public security linkages between Wanzai police and police in Dongguan and Nanhai. In some parts of China, the police responsible for working among migrants go so far as to videotape messages of contrite migrant criminals apologizing to their parents; these messages are then screened in the home village.[7] Furthermore, in accordance with Jiangxi province policy documents,[8] the activities of Wanzai migrants in the destination areas are explicitly included in the evaluations of rural households within the villages. So, for example, one household was not awarded any stars for the categories of "changing social traditions" or "law-abiding conduct" because two migrant members were serving prison sentences in Guangdong for bicycle theft. Finally, local states in Jiangxi enlist rural families to help keep migrants law-abiding. In Xinfeng this has involved local officials broadcasting television appeals to rural parents, urging them to write and warn their migrant children about the dangers of drugs. Here, with Xinfeng's proximity to Guangdong and the presence of the railway, part of the concern is to prevent social problems being brought back to the county by disaffected youths.[9]

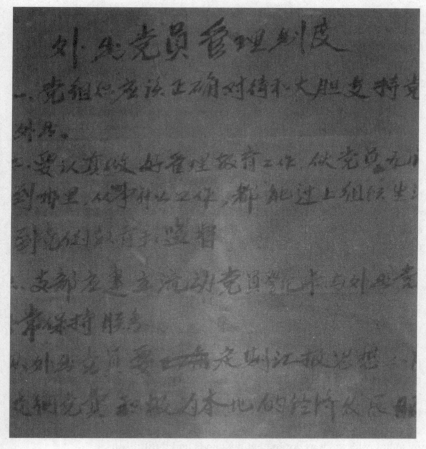

Guidelines for migrating Party members.

By migrating, many young villagers mentally remove themselves from the lifestyle and work that accompanies their farmer status, and they consider themselves "unemployed" on their return. Local officials express alarm at the trend of "agricultural de-skilling" (*nongmang*), whereby rural youths return home with neither the inclination nor the knowledge to farm.[10] De-skilling occurs partly because migration creates a view of a labor market hierarchy: traditional forms of employment become degraded to the point where they are uniformly shunned.[11] Young girls who return home with painted nails, delicate clothes, and high-heeled shoes are, in effect, announcing that farm work is no longer for them. The reluctance of young returnees to farm is further illustrated by some male youths who borrow money from friends and relatives to buy a motorbike for about 3,000 yuan. They congregate on the corners of the county seat and township, waiting to transport paying passengers between villages, townships, and the county seat. Since the motorcycle fare is significantly higher than the cost of a bus ticket and since the spending capacity of the local population is limited, many spend their days sitting on their stationary bikes, smoking and talking. In informal conversations many concede that they may be forced "to go south" again.[12]

Villagers who are forced to return to their former lives in the village because of failure in the cities often feel a sense of shame at their lack of progress. When asked if they had ever worked in the city, a few women laughed with embarrassment and said "no," but then their husbands interrupted to say something like: "Don't lie. You were out for only a month then wanted to come home." Return under such circumstances reinforces patriarchal ideas that women cannot be independent outside of the home. However, women return to the domestic realm, which is seen as their rightful place, so failure in the city seems to produce a lesser sense of self-denigration than among men. As an example, one married woman explains her return as follows:

> I returned because one of my children became ill, and they are both studying. If the parents are away, the children do not do so well at school. The month that I was out I worked over ten hours a day. My place is at home and I won't go out again.[13]

In contrast, culturally ascribed gender roles make it difficult for men to explain their return to the village in terms of children or family. Unless the men return home to a lucrative form of local off-farm employment, they are forced to admit that failure in the city has pushed them back to the land. Failed returnee men suffer from a sense of inferiority, and this may be because their capacity to earn money is linked with village assessments of their performance in social roles such as competent husbands and dutiful sons.

8.2 ILLNESS AND INJURY

Illness and injury push many migrants back to their villages. Within the circulation pattern of migration, the rural household provides for the welfare needs of the migrant. As structuralist authors point out, this arrangement is exploitative because the wage sector escapes the burden of providing for the welfare needs of migrants.[14] The disbanding of the collectives has resulted in the disintegration of subsidized medical care in the Chinese countryside. Consequently, the health-care burden on households is particularly heavy at a time when increasing numbers of rural dwellers are exposed to a hazardous working environment. The social welfare implications are serious because – as several development scholars point out – health is the most important asset of the poor.[15]

A multitude of Chinese surveys confirms the detrimental impact of factory conditions on the health of the migrants. A Chinese academic article identifies a lack of sleep as one of the main pressures faced by migrant workers, the other two being marital problems and the inability to adjust to life in their new environment.[16] The Chinese magazine *Migrant Worker* conducted a survey of 160 migrants in the Pearl Delta and found that over 80% regularly spend money on visits to the doctor. The authors state:

> the working hours in many factories are too long and occupational safety standards are too poor. The excessive work burden of migrants leads to a negative impact on their health and because many of these illnesses are not the direct result of industrial accidents, the migrants have no choice but to pay for the medical treatment themselves. Therefore, at the same time as improving their own physical quality, migrants must fight for reasonable working hours and working conditions.[17]

In Jiaocun village (Yudu), I met a former dock worker who had returned after two years because his body could no longer stand the physical strain of the work. He had previously served as an accountant and returned to his position on the village committee. The accountant also farms the land, and this provides the main part of his household's income. According to the village head, originally around thirty men from the village worked at the Shanghai docks, but in the past two years over half have returned because they can no longer endure the physical demands of loading cargo. Labor export to the Shanghai docks is coordinated through the county labor export company, so a basic welfare net is provided and injured workers are entitled to compensation. Each worker also accumulates a "retirement and resettlement fund" (*yanglao anzhi zijin*), which is payable on leaving the company; the amount increases according to the number of years in service. After five years of service the worker is entitled to 4,500 yuan, and after fifteen years of service the sum is 30,000 yuan – enough to build a house.[18] The resettlement fund stabilizes the work force in an arduous and low-paying industry. It also provides a basic security net for migrants upon their return.

The vast majority of migrants who work in the factories of the Pearl Delta enjoy little in the way of protection. A recent survey of foreign investment, joint venture, township, and private enterprises by the Guangdong Province Workers' Union finds widespread abuse of migrant workers' rights – in particular, no compensation or medical coverage for industrial accidents. The authors complain that the response of government departments is always "much thunder but little rain."[19] In the course of conversation, a police officer in Duanwu township, Yudu, related to me that there are large numbers of serious accidents among migrant workers. Like public security personnel in other townships of Yudu, he sometimes represents the migrants and their dependants in compensation claims. He said that cases are very difficult to win because Jiangxi country cousins have low standing in the cities. He explained that, in instances of death, 30,000 yuan is owed to the family, but that in most cases they are lucky to receive one third of this amount.[20] The burden of medical care for an injured migrant generally falls on the rural household. In poor households in Wanzai and Yudu, the illness of one member is enough to plunge a family into poverty.

8.3 PREGNANCY AND CHILD CARE

Another common circumstance of return is pregnancy and child care. Migration has increased the incidence of premarital pregnancies in the countryside, which is making village attitudes more accepting of such situations. This does not actually represent a radical change in village values, because much of the acceptance stems from the fact that transgressions can be absolved through marriage. The event of a young man returning to the village with his pregnant girlfriend is received as good news by his parents: it is generally felt that the introduction of a grandchild into the household is an inevitable part of life, even if this occurs before the wedding wine is drunk. There are also isolated examples of single pregnant women who have returned to give birth in the natal home. In one case in a Wanzai village, the boyfriend was still working in the coastal city; in another, the man's hometown was in a far-away province. This differs from the traditional practice whereby women marry and bear children in the home of the husband's family. The response of the families is to accept that "the rice is already cooked" and regard the boyfriend as the husband. Some elderly people expressed the view that it is wiser for such girls to live with the in-laws during their pregnancies, seeing as they must eventually become part of the husband's family. Others felt that young people should be left to manage their own lives and recalled those hard days when parents-in-law controlled all the daily affairs of young couples.

Although village society has become more accommodating of single mothers who return to their natal homes, the local state is less lenient, and offenders incur steep fines – more than the annual per-capita income of the county. A regional newspaper praises the work of family planning officials in one Wanzai township for their efficient work in targeting migrant women who returned to the village during the Spring Festival period. The investigation into family planning involved both incognito and regular official inspections. Particular attention was paid to the content of couplets pasted on either side of the door at Spring Festival, and households announcing a marriage or pregnancy were inspected. The article states that both married and single pregnant women were investigated on arrival home and that this seasonal work of the cadres resulted in 84 abortions.[21] The words of a 22-year-old villager illustrate the predicament of a household that is burdened with family planning fines:

My elder brother also went out for a couple of months but he couldn't find work with decent pay. Instead of money, he brought home a pregnant girl-friend and a big family planning fine. They have to buy special food for her and she has to go and see the midwife, so my maternal home is just as poor as ever.[22]

Apart from fines, the local state attempts to prevent migrants from returning home with illegally born babies by integrating fertility control with other administrative procedures for monitoring migrants. Intending migrants must obtain three kinds of certificate. First, they need an identity card. Second, single people must obtain a certificate that proves their unmarried status (*weihun zheng*). Married people must obtain a "proof of status" certificate (*qingkuang zhengming*) testifying to their reproductive history. Every three months, women with a "proof of status" certificate are required to undergo an IUD inspection and a pregnancy test, either at home or in the city, and every six months they must return to their hometowns for check-ups. The proof of status and the single certificate bear the stamp of the township family planning clinic, a photograph, and the identity card number of the migrant. These certificates are essential for obtaining a work permit card[23] (*laowu xukezheng*) from the township labor office.

Another measure to prevent women returning home with out-of-quota births involves the couple paying a family planning guarantee of 2,000 yuan to the township government.[24] In some townships, the government even requires the payment of a second guarantee by someone related to the migrant; so, for example, the parent of an adult migrant may be required to pay a deposit – which becomes a fine if the migrant family member has an illegal birth. These measures are not uniform throughout the Jiangxi countryside, but in some locations the official fear of unpermitted births by migrants has certainly inflicted a heavy financial burden on both migrants and their families. The rationale for such measures is the family planning responsibility system: village cadres and township family planning officials lose their wages if even just one person under their jurisdiction has an out-of-quota birth, and migrants are seen as the most likely culprits. Throughout Jiangxi, this policy is publicized with the slogan *yi piao foujue* ("one strike and you are out").

8.4 MARRIAGE AND FAMILY

Many migrants return home in response to the expectations and demands of family members in the village. Although in some instances the individual may aspire to abandon the household, broader structural constraints precluding security in the cities mean that the majority of migrants demonstrate continuing membership in their households through remittances as well as varying degrees of compliance with the wishes of family members in the countryside.

In Sen's model of "cooperative conflict," household members who contribute more resources to the common pot enjoy a stronger bargaining position when competing for a share of household resources, and those who have no means of supporting themselves outside of the family tend to lack a fallback position and so fare worst in the competition over resources.[25] In this model, the *visibility* of a person's contribution is also important. For example, women who work in factories enjoy more leverage within the household than those who engage in out-putting from the home. Here I extend Sen's analysis to suggest that (1) through migration, many returnees have visibly demonstrated that they have a fallback position in the form of knowledge of urban labor markets, and (2) the temporary absence of women from the rural household increases the visibility of their domestic work. In these ways migration increases the leverage of all returned migrants but in particular that of married women, enabling them to pursue some goals relatively independently of other household members.

So even though the eventual return of migrants to the village is seldom a negotiable issue, the terms and conditions under which migrants return to their families are increasingly subject to negotiation. Negotiations are evident in the following typical instances of "family-oriented" return: young people who return home to marry, women who return at the behest of their husbands, and children who return in response to parental pleas. Each is discussed in turn.

Although migration enables young people to temporarily escape oppressive patriarchal values and family control, Chinese scholars argue that the household registration system means that the vast majority of migrants must eventually return to the village and the confines of a traditional marriage.[26] Young people in Wanzai generally regard migration as a stop-gap event between leaving school and marriage, and (as illustrated in Chapters 3 and 4) initial migration is often precipitated by the need to accumulate resources for a bride price, dowry, and house. Many migrants are in their early 20s, so "finding a friend" is the topic on everyone's lips. Those who fail to find a mate through their own efforts feel under pressure to return to the village and find someone before they are considered too old to marry. Chinese social scientists have observed that, owing to the strong gender segregation in urban labor markets, finding a suitable spouse is not always easy, so returning to the village is a common course of action.[27] Yudu dock workers were definitely unhappy about the lack of opportunities for meeting young women in Shanghai, and they explained to me that their families in the village were helping them find a bride.

Wanzai and Yudu parents play an important role in marriage arrangements. In the past, young people spent most of their time in the village, and puritan moral values – together with the sharp surveillance of other villagers – meant that they had little opportunity to interact freely with members of the opposite sex. Even into the mid-1980s, the majority of engagements were organized through friends and family members. Female relatives would investigate the families of possible in-laws and play an important role in facilitating the union. Many marriages are still organized in this way, and young people returning home for Spring Festival are introduced to prospective spouses. Families advise young people of an auspicious date, and if both sides agree, the migrants return to the village in order to marry at the specified time.

Although marriage generally involves returning to the village, migration is creating the social distance and economic leverage for migrants to assume greater autonomy in marriage decisions. This in turn is enabling more young people to find their own partners. In the villages visited by this writer, it was common for girls to persist in the choice of a spouse against the wishes of their parents. Parental objections were usually on the grounds that the family had someone else in mind, the prospective boyfriend lived too far away, or the young man concerned was of questionable moral character. One mother explained to me that her daughter's engagement to a man from Guangxi had been broken on account of parental protests that his hometown was too far away, though it remains to be seen if this injunction will continue to be effective.

Despite geographical mobility, the majority of migrant men find brides whose natal homes are within the township or neighboring locality, so migrant women generally return to settle in a village near to their natal homes. This is because migrants from particular counties are concentrated in the same destination area, and social interaction is mainly with each other. There is also a traditional preference for marrying near the natal home. In particular, young women in Wanzai told me that they were reluctant to marry into provinces where the dialect and customs are different and where chili is not added to the food. Nonetheless, the geographical realm for finding a spouse is expanding. Now young people have the opportunity to meet spouses from townships farther away, and the recent proliferation of minibuses within the county makes it easier to visit in-laws. The event of young people going to work in the coastal cities has also seen the advent of interprovincial marriages, though the occurrence is rare. Gaining permanent urban residency by marrying a partner with an urban *hukou* is a dream for many migrant youths, but only a small proportion achieve it. One young man from one of my fieldwork villages married the daughter of his Hangzhou boss, though villagers explained the unequal rural–urban match in terms of the slight physical disability of his bride.

The fact that marriage generally involves a return to the village is a source of anguish for many rural youths who have re-formed their life goals to include staying on in the cities. Following an in-depth study of attitudes toward marriage among migrant women in Guangdong, Chen Yingtao concludes:

Migrant women must improve their own quality and create conditions [for a better life]. They must also recognize that regardless of whether migrant laboring is for developing a career or establishing a family, the vast majority of people must ultimately return to the countryside and adjust their marriage expectations to the reality of their situation. Otherwise they find themselves between the devil and the deep blue sea and as they reach an ever older age, greater vexation results.[28]

Returning to the village and re-adapting to village society within the context of marriage is a challenge confronting not only single but also married migrant women. A regional newspaper reports that almost 10,000 married rural women from Wanzai county are working in the coastal cities, and their net annual remittances are at least 50 million yuan. The article praises these women (*dagong sao*) as being a great production army that contributes to the home society and economy with its sweat.[29] Factors that commonly precipitate the return of these women are the demands of their husbands in the village and the need to look after children or the elderly.

Wives are often recalled from the cities by husbands who feel uncomfortable with the double burden of farming and housework. Mr. Li of Qifeng village explained to me that "I no longer care about earning money, all I want is warm clothes, a full stomach, and my wife to come home and ease my work load."[30]

As a result of migration, some husbands are taking on the culturally unfamiliar roles of child care and cooking; this makes the value of the women's domestic labor more visible, increasing her leverage within the household. This is suggested by a number of dialogues that I heard in which women used the threat of returning to Guangzhou as a bargaining chip with their husbands. In my survey, sixteen married women returned to their villages after working in Guangzhou. Although some returned with their husbands after long stays in the city, others returned after only a few months because they found that urban life was grueling and the opportunities to earn money limited. Still others returned home under ultimatum from their husbands and, when asked if they would consider going out again, replied that they were not allowed.

Migration is providing the economic means for some women to refuse forthrightly to return to the village on a permanent basis. Chen is a recently married woman who decided to go back to her factory job on the coast even though her husband wished her to stay at home. She explained to me:

I have been working out for two years, and came home in 1996 to get married. I want to go out again. My husband does not agree. But if I stay here then I must rely on his family for my livelihood. I want to be independent so I will return to Xiamen after Spring Festival.[31]

In some extreme cases, migrant women use the economic independence and social privacy afforded by migration to refuse to return to their husbands in the village. One woman from Tuanjie village (who had initiated a divorce) went to work in a Zhejiang shoe factory and then found employment as an assistant to a leather jacket trader. Two years later she returned to the county and is now operating a successful leather jacket shop. This year she plans on transferring her household registration from the village to the county seat. She explained that her failed marriage has been a blessing:

> I was forced out into the world and now have my own career and money. I am not like other peasant women who work for a few years in the city then go back to the village, look after the baby, and raise the pigs. My life is much better.[32]

Although there are instances in which women refuse to return to their husbands, the threat of divorce is usually sufficient to recall recalcitrant wives from Guangzhou. This is because, even though they have the economic basis for autonomy, they still experience a social need for acceptance within the village. As suggested by the words of Chen, social pressure in the village prevents the separation of couples:

> Some women want to have money of their own and they want to see something different. Last time when I came home for Spring Festival, two of my neighbors asked me to take them to the city and introduce them to my factory. But I refused and said that there were no jobs. If I had taken them to Nanhai, their husbands and in-laws would curse me and make trouble at my house.[33]

The thought of permanent return to the village may generate greater emotional hardship for women than for men. This is because out-migration no longer exists as an outlet for the frustrated life goals of these particular women after they have returned to the village, and the opportunities for women to achieve personal advancement at home may be more limited than for men. Of the 38 permanent returnees in the Wanzai survey, 12 out of 19 men participated in local off-farm activities after returning home; these activities involved commuting between the village and the township or the county seat. In contrast, the returnee women identified marriage, pregnancy, or family demands as the main reasons for coming back to the village, so they generally returned to the confines of the village and family. Some authors describe out-migration as an alternative to more extreme forms of action such as suicide or revolution.[34] Although beyond the scope of what I was able to investigate in the villages, some Chinese academics hinted to me that in the countryside there is a high suicide rate among returnee women.

A recent study in rural China finds that the suicide rate among women is five times higher than the world average. Moreover, the victims tend to have above-average levels of education and some degree of exposure to the outside world.[35]

Women who have had migration experience but who return by themselves to the countryside while their husbands remain in the city encounter much emotional hardship in re-adapting to village life. A woman whom I call Lin worked in Guangdong with her husband, but she returned to the village alone following her pregnancy. She proudly shows visitors a photograph of herself and her husband taken in a city salon. She told me that her son often wants to know why his father is present in the photo but seldom at home. Secretary Wu helps Lin by telling her which agricultural tasks she needs to carry out at a particular time, because previously her husband organized the farming of the paddy. Although women in Wanzai do not plow, if their husbands are in the city then they are forced to assume responsibility for every other aspect of rice cultivation. On his return to Qifeng village for Spring Festival 1997, Lin's husband organized for nearly 2 mu of land to be transferred to the care of another family in the village, leaving her with 1.5 mu to farm. This reduced her work burden somewhat but did not increase her enthusiasm for life in the village. He also brought a pair of sneakers rimmed with flashing lights for his son as well as a fashionable coat and pair of shoes for his wife. A week after her husband had returned to Guangdong, Lin sighed to me:

> What is the point of the coat and the shoes? When am I ever going to wear them? I am an old farming woman walking around in mud all day. I have no energy. Life is meaningless.[36]

As another example, on his return for Spring Festival, a Wanzai migrant related to me the hardship faced by his wife:

> My wife and I went to Guangdong together and found jobs in a hat factory. Then she became pregnant with our son, so went back to the village to stay with my parents. She stayed in the village with our son, and wrote letters to me saying that she cries herself to sleep every night. She was better off than other women in the village because she ran a small hairdressing shop along the roadside so only did a little farming. In the end I felt so bad that I told her to come to Guangdong. She works as a hairdresser in Nanhai now, and I am a deputy manager. We both work hard, though wonder what it is all for. When I come back to the village, my 7-year-old son doesn't recognize me as his father.[37]

Women who return to the land after some migration experience may have marginally more leverage for control over remittance money than their nonmigrant counterparts. This is because, if remittances fail to arrive, former migrants have sufficient knowledge of the urban labor markets to threaten their husbands with abandoning the fort at home and heading off to the cities themselves. In some instances, the husband remits all of his money to the rural household and leaves the wife to use these funds as she needs. In other cases, the husband retains control of the funds and remits according to his anticipation of her needs – for instance, when it is time to buy fertilizer or pay school fees. For an outsider, investigating who controls the household income is virtually impossible, and villagers tended to treat this line of questioning with much humor. Men and women often joked that: "The woman controls the mah-jongg money, the fives and tens, and the man controls the hundreds." Unlike farming women who have never left the land, returnee women, migrant women, and women who participate in local off-farm employment tended to compare their own situation favorably with that of their mothers. They explained to me that, whereas their mothers had to ask their husbands or mothers-in-law for money, they have a say in the deployment of household income.[38] By gaining knowledge of urban labor markets, a resource in itself, and by demonstrating their capacity to earn cash and/or survive in the cities, women generally improve their bargaining position within the rural household.

Nevertheless, migration and return can be a source of instability for rural marriages. Through an urban sojourn villagers are exposed to city values of romance and ideal marriage; on their return to the village, they may feel dissatisfied with their spouses. Migrant men from Wanzai described to me their preference for city girls who know how to dress and carry themselves well (*qizhi hao*). Young women who returned for Spring Festival explained that they prefer well-groomed and educated men rather than men covered in soil. Migrants internalize the value systems of modern cities and use this criteria to assess those who are subject to the same forces of marginalization as themselves. As the two cartoons (see page 210) suggest, on return, one spouse may decide that the other is no longer an equal match and too "bumpkin."[39] Long periods of separation may mean that, while one partner has been stuck on a small plot of land, the other has been exposed to new experiences.[40] This was the case in two out of the four divorces that occurred in Tuanjie village between 1994 and 1997: migrant men met new spouses while in the cities. Dissatisfaction with rural partners may be particularly intense in cases where the marriage has been arranged by parents.[41] This problem has been observed in many countries where labor migration divides couples for protracted periods.[42]

In the townships of Jiangxi I saw a multitude of posters advertising cures for syphilis and other sexually transmitted diseases, and it is generally observed by local officials, villagers, and health workers that the majority of patients are returned migrants or their spouses.[43] This is because migration creates a level of freedom that would not be tolerated in the village. Within the village,

"She and I have no common language," says the returned migrant. *Source: Wailai gong* [Workers] 11 (1997), pp. 44–5. In the first cartoon, the girl's mother explains that there is fish for the wedding. The girl's father chastises, "You rotter, after a few days in the city you forget about her." However, the migrant (in his smart city clothes) feels that the cultural gap between himself and his fiancée is too large. In the second cartoon, the returned migrant asks, "How have you changed to look so stupid?"; his girlfriend replies, "This is how I looked three years ago."

adultery is regarded as a serious offense, and beating perpetrators is seen as a valid course of action. While working in the cities, however, migrants are afforded greater separation from the control and the emotional support of primary social groups. This creates emotional pressures but at the same time allows migrants the freedom to deal with stress in ways that contravene traditional moral values. As a result, spouse substitutes occasionally develop in the cities.

The local state is concerned about the negative implications of migration and family destabilization for rural society as a whole, and it seeks to create an environment to which migrants willingly return. Aside from improving everyone's ideological quality, policy-makers suggest that measures be taken to increase opportunities for rural livelihood diversification within the countryside. By creating rural towns with improved cultural and economic facilities and opportunities for returnees to participate in local off-farm employment, it is hoped that migrants can meet their social and economic needs within the countryside. In this way, the long-term separation of couples is avoided.[44]

Another instance of return is that of an adult child who goes back to the village in response to parental pleas, often because of a shortage of labor at home. The labor shortage may result from the death or illness of an elderly parent who is fostering grandchildren or from the out-migration of other household members. As an example, 19-year-old Xing Muxin explained to me:

I returned home because my brother and sister-in-law went out. My parents are old and need my help. If I have a chance I might go out again. It's okay at home, but sometimes I think that I like the idea of going out.[45]

Migrants who return to the village are unlikely to slip back into the same relationship with their parents as before they left. It is difficult to assess the extent to which exposure to new values and experiences in the cities leads young people to pursue independence in their relationships with their parents. On the one hand, as described in Chapter 6, the experience of many migrants in urban factories is of total obedience. On the other hand, some migrants have encountered experiences that have taught them to be assertive. For example, several have participated in strikes in response to the delayed payment of wages. Others have advanced to positions such as floor managers and workshop supervisors, which require the capacity to make decisions independently. A much clearer facilitator of social independence is economic independence. Children are less dependent on family income or land. Indeed, family members often become reliant on migrant contributions to the household economy. However, narratives of return strongly influence the actions and choices of the migrants, and most are reluctant to burn the bridge home.

8.5 PROBLEMS OF READJUSTMENT

Many migrants are not accepted by urban society yet find that they can no longer accept life in the village. This leads the migrants to move periodically between the village and the city, their sense of alienation intensifying and changing with each move. This pattern of repeated returns shapes the goals and consciousness of an entire generation that is referred to in Chinese as the *dagong zu* (literally, "the working stratum"; see Chapter 4), with the socialization process continuing throughout the time spent in each location. A physical return to the village often heightens the migrants' feeling that they are deprived people from deprived areas. Mud houses, buffaloes, and pigsty toilets[46] remind them of the backwardness that precipitated their initial move. At the same time, the exposure to shopping malls and neon lights afforded by migration creates an awareness of the dynamic and prospering community from which they are excluded. This is illustrated by one young man who returned to Qifeng for Spring Festival and wore a pager wherever he went. As we walked along a muddy path, the beeper sounded and he cursed the fact that his underdeveloped village did not have a telephone.[47] Nonetheless, on every subsequent day that I saw the young man, his prized pager was always prominently displayed on his hip. To return home with pockets empty after exposure to a world of commodities and wealth leaves the migrants with an acute sense of their own failure and a feeling that the city has failed them.

Returnees explain the backwardness of home in terms of inefficiencies in the management of the home economy. In particular, returnees express dissatisfaction at the perceived corruption of cadres, the prevalence of petty jealousies among households, and troublesome obligations within the village. They scorn the failure of their neighbors to value time and lament the absence of a strong work ethic in the village. This is reflected in the words of one young factory production manager who returned for Spring Festival: "There are plenty of natural resources here, so why does everybody just sit around playing cards and mah-jongg? No wonder this place never prospers."[48]

Another source of returnee dissatisfaction is the dull social atmosphere in the countryside. Returnees find life at home boring, because most of their peers are in the cities and there are few recreational activities in the village. Even the television offers little in the way of entertainment. The program content of the Wanzai Television Station is highly localized, and it broadcasts for only a few hours in the evening (however, this station is an invaluable source of information for agricultural producers).[49] The reception of prefectural and provincial stations is not always clear, and (because of problems with electricity supply) it is sometimes not possible to watch television.[50] It is certainly not correct to say that all of rural China is hooked up to cable and satellite television. At the time of my fieldwork in Wanzai, Yudu, Fengcheng, and Fengxin, I encountered only one household with a satellite dish, and none of the villages that I visited had cable television. On my return visit to Qifeng in December 2000, no households had cable or satellite. In my fieldwork in another part of Jiangxi during September–November 2000, officials told me that 20% of townships had recently been hooked up to cable television, but later in the conversation they also explained that only one "natural" village (a subdivision of the larger administrative village based on historically resident hamlets) in each of these townships was connected. Indeed, in 2000 the central state responded to the fact that over 300 million rural residents lack clear television reception by launching a project to ensure that all rural households can receive a national, provincial, and county station by the year 2004 (*cun cun tong dian*).

The lack of entertainment in the countryside contrasts with the situation in the cities, where young people can watch many television channels, play cards, socialize with workmates in the dormitories, and – on their days off – go to the small karaoke bars located in the factory districts to sing Cantonese songs. During the Spring Festival period, I visited a karaoke bar in Wanzai county seat with some local teachers. Much to the irritation of the politics teacher, the songs booking sheet was dominated by the requests of a group of returned migrants for Cantonese songs. Young people also changed the words of a well-known karaoke song from "I want to go to Guilin" (a popular scenic spot) to "I want to go to Shenzhen" (the most prosperous of China's special economic zones). The politics teacher disapproved because he saw Cantonese as a Trojan horse for the infiltration of superficial lifestyle values into the minds of the migrants. The migrants told me that they planned to return to Guangdong straight after Spring Festival because they were unable to tolerate the monotony of village life or the attitudes of nonmigrants.

The use of Cantonese or Mandarin rather than the local Gan dialect in the home village is a further illustration of the cultural distance between returnees and nonmigrants. Cantonese is associated with a fashionable, carefree, and wealthy lifestyle, and young migrants sometimes show off to their peers by tossing a few words of Cantonese into conversation. The Mandarin language is associated with education and refinement. Those returning from the city distinguish themselves from other villagers by their ability to speak standard Mandarin, and those who speak only the local dialect feel a sense of shame. During interviews, villagers would often apologize for their heavily accented Mandarin and explain: "In these parts we never need to speak Mandarin so we are not accustomed to it. It's only the young ones who go out that need to use it."[51] Some young returnees also confuse their parents by using borrowed English words such as "bye-bye."

Villagers are often unimpressed with the changed attitudes of their returnee children. For example, one young man in Qifeng boasted high and low of his exploits as a film actor and as proof produced laminated photographs and a video (even though there are no VCRs in the village) of his glorious career. Returning co-workers burst his bubble and made him the laughingstock of the village by revealing that he paid 80 yuan each time to be an extra on film sets and a further 20 yuan for each photograph. His poor parents scolded him for forgetting about the needs of his family and for adopting the superficial and selfish values of the city. The elderly often complain that "in the first year migrant children are of the soil, but by the third year they don't recognize their parents anymore." The response of the young to the tensions between their own goals and the conservative values and limited resources of home is generally to re-migrate until marriage and family force them to return to the village again on a more permanent basis.

8.6 CONCLUSION

Migrants are not accepted by urban society, but on their return home they are unable to accept village society. Ill fortune in the cities and binding obligations at home mean that they no longer perceive migration as a viable outlet for pursuing goals and dealing with the frustrations of rural life. At the same time, migration may intensify the frustrations of returned migrants by generating higher life goals while failing to provide the resources required to satisfy these raised expectations. Consequently, return migration produces a discontented and restless group of people within the villages, and a large portion of them are reluctant to farm in order to earn a living. Those who cannot find local off-farm employment become an economic burden on their households and threaten rural stability.

In my Wanzai survey, most of the permanent returnee men have used their skills and savings to find off-farm employment in the township or county seat. In this way their migration experiences have assisted their resettlement into the natal community. In contrast, women generally explained their return home in terms of marriage, pregnancy, and family obligations. The possibility of higher levels of discontentment and even suicide among returnee women than among men may be associated with women's limited opportunities for escaping the drudgery of farming, domestic work, and family duties.

The circumstances of return discussed in this chapter support the structuralist view that urban centers exploit cheap migrant labor while leaving the rural sector to shoulder the burden of social reproduction and welfare. Rural cadres attempt to alleviate this burden on rural areas by appealing to city institutions on behalf of their migrant constituents. As examples, they contact factory bosses in order to protect the job security of home-town natives; in cases of industrial accidents, they lobby for workers' compensation.

Although the local state represents the interests of those returned migrants who face welfare difficulties, it also indirectly helps to maintain the working conditions under which their migrant constituents suffer. This is because, in trying to guarantee the migrants' continuing access to urban jobs and prevent them from returning home *en masse,* the local state helps to ensure that migrants remain a disciplined source of labor for the city factories. Examples of local state efforts in this respect include the incorporation of migrant behavior into rural household evaluation campaigns as well as televised entreaties for intending migrants to be orderly and law-abiding in the cities. The local state also enacts measures designed to ensure that returnees conform to the central state's family planning regulations. Furthermore, the local state's response to returnees is very much centered on the national modernization goal of orchestrating the absorption of surplus rural labor.

Not all of the disruption caused by return migration is to the detriment of rural society. Although return is often unavoidable, the experience and knowledge of living and working in the cities has exposed the migrants to alternative values and life goals, broadening their perspective on life. As illustrated in the example of the negotiations that occur within marriage, the experience of migration is a resource that gives returnees a stronger fallback position for bargaining with other family members over the conditions of their return.

9

Conclusion

THIS book has focused on the effects of rural–urban labor migration on China's countryside. This is a massive phenomenon affecting hundreds of millions of people. But people are not simply swept along by social and economic forces, they also actively create and manipulate them. Macro-level descriptions and figures, of necessity, omit the individual human detail. I believe that this detail is central to the explanation of migration and the changes it precipitates. My in-depth qualitative data has permitted an understanding of the human strategies and experiences that lie behind macro-processes.

I have shown that many people directly benefit from migration while others suffer increased hardships. Nevertheless, overall, migration improves the lives of the rural population by broadening perspectives, improving the availability of resources, and increasing the opportunities for attaining goals.

In much of the Western literature and in Chinese policy discussions, migration tends to be seen as a process that is external to origin areas. However, I have argued that migration and return are extensions of existing diversification strategies and are facilitated through values and resources that are internal to the village. Migration is underpinned by pre-existing values such as family loyalty and love of the native place. These values are adapted to the migration process because migrants are socially, economically, and legally vulnerable in the cities and so need the safety net of the rural household. On the other hand, rural households invoke these values to try to retain control over the migrants and the resources that they generate. Of course, some migrants try to reduce the burden of family obligations through secrecy about earnings, simultaneously keeping both face and the family safety net. Existing resources such as land and social networks underpin migration. Land provides security for the migrants and money to fund the initial costs of migration, and social networks supply information for intending migrants and support for new arrivals in the city. Over time, migration and return become culturally entrenched pathways to the time-honored goals of marrying, building a house, creating a legacy for descendants, and honoring ancestors.

Migration and return also incorporate new values and resources into rural society. Goals are continuously formed and re-formed through social interaction, and migration contributes to this by exposing people to a wider set of values and possibilities. Migration is not simply a response to short-term fluctuations in rural and urban economies; rather, it results from such longer-term processes as the internalization of values, the evolution of goals, and the institutionalization of acceptable pathways to them. In addition to migration, other changes in the sociopolitical climate are important in informing the aspirations of social actors because they make new goals "respectable." In the post-Mao era, such goals include becoming competent in technical skills, desiring to prosper, coveting material goods, and aspiring to become a boss.

Nowadays, on account of chain migration and the "demonstration effect" of returning migrants, villagers widely perceive labor migration to be the most feasible strategy for obtaining the resources needed to achieve goals. This book has examined the different strategies that social actors (migrants, nonmigrants, returned migrants, and the local state) use in acquiring and deploying the resources generated by migration. These strategies affect many dimensions of the rural society and economy. Examples include changing inequalities in the distribution of resources; changes in the spending goals of individuals and households and in the values and social practices that underpin these goals; and growth and diversification of the rural business sector.

9.1 RESOURCE DISTRIBUTION

Migration provides rural households with access to off-farm earning opportunities that lie beyond the limited resource base and patronage networks of the home areas. The relative ease of entry into urban labor markets enables any household with sufficient adult labor to participate in migration. In contrast, access to local off-farm employment generally requires political contacts or traditional family skills. The amount of resources that a household can obtain depends on its labor supply. In my survey, the better-off households tend to have at least two migrants, and the wealthiest have both migrants and local off-farm workers. Migration improves the situation of poorer households while allowing some richer and better-connected households to maintain their advantage.

Although labor supply determines the capacity to obtain resources through migration, some households incur losses for two reasons. First, not all migrants make money in the cities: unemployment, poor working conditions, injury, and illness commonly afflict migrant workers. Second, some households are adversely affected by the ways in which resources and burdens are distributed within the family. Households that include elderly parents sometimes incur an increased work burden without receiving sufficient remittances. This is because migrant children are caught between obligations to their family in the village and preparations for setting up their own households. Spouses remaining in the village with children may also suffer from an increased work burden and inadequate remittances as well as emotional hardship. In situations where the wife is farming only her husband's land, she may lack a fallback position from which to bargain for resources and pursue her goals.

Conflict over resources is an enduring feature of family dynamics throughout the world; by producing new resources, earners, values, and goals, migration intensifies these tensions. This leads individuals and families to pursue new strategies that affect resource allocation. For example, some individuals try to avoid the claims of other family members on their earnings. Another strategy pursued by elderly parents or spouses who lack remittances involves either migrating or threatening to migrate. In this case, knowledge of migration is a resource that enables physically healthy social actors to challenge the distributional mechanisms of the family. A further strategy, pursued at the family level, involves directing resources toward common goals – for example, building a house. This kind of collective spending benefits everyone by providing good shelter and enhancing social prestige, and it ameliorates the tensions engendered by expenditure on individual goals.

Finally, migration precipitates land transfers and affects the distribution of the incomes and burdens associated with agriculture. Informal transfers of land occur within families and between unrelated households. By cultivating absentees' land, some farmers can increase their earnings by an amount comparable with the average remittances from one migrant. Households with migrant members enjoy the benefits of increased land-to-person ratios: the grain allocations of the absentees can be sold or the plots of migrants can be leased to other households. However, the system of taxation in the villages means that farming households bear a greater burden of levies and local labor requisitions than households with nonagricultural income.

Migration in China is unique in that it is seldom a response to inequalities in the distribution of land and is not motivated by the goal of earning money to buy land in the village. This is because most rural migrants in China have access to land, the use of which is strictly confined to agriculture, and land-use rights cannot be bought or sold. As yet, migration has neither fueled inflation in local land markets nor led to a concentration of land in the hands of wealthy migrants or returnees.

Nevertheless, there are signs that remittances may stimulate inflation in rural property markets. As discussed in Chapter 7, returned migrants to Xinfeng and Yudu are using the emergence of an "invisible" (*yinxing*) land market in the areas surrounding towns and transport routes to gain collateral from local financial institutions for their business activities.

9.2 GOALS AND REMITTANCE USAGE

Overall, migration and return flows enable more villagers to obtain more cultural and economic resources, which they use to achieve goals such as securing a livelihood, reaching a higher level of physical comfort, maintaining self-respect, and participating in a changing social world. These urban resources are not sufficient to increase social prestige if deployed in the city, but when used at home, rural households are thereby able to demonstrate their socioeconomic advancement in tangible ways – for example, a modern house, a motorbike, or a small business located in the town. This enables them to enjoy improved access to local resources and to the social networks of the village.

Return flows of resources and exposure to new lifestyles in the city are nonetheless increasing the amount of resources needed to attain goals. Remittances feed into the cultural obligation to give gifts exceeding the value of those received. At the same time, remittances and exposure to modern commodities are raising the standard of a respectable house and bride price. In Chapter 4, I argued that a house and bride price are not only goals in themselves but in turn are resources needed to achieve the next generation of goals, which include a better standard of living, avoiding shame, and being able to marry. Thus houses and wedding goods are fundamental to the social reproduction of the rural household, and those without savings have no choice but to incur debt in order acquire them.

Although new values and resources are important in informing goals, they do not "modernize" the countryside. Rather, modern commodities are incorporated into the social practices of the village. This is illustrated by the filial son who brought Brand's Chicken Tonic home for his mother, by the migrants who remit money for fertilizer via the electronic banking system, and by parents who use photographs from city salons to arrange for the marriage of their children.

This incorporation of external values and resources into the internal values, practices, and distributional mechanisms of the village sometimes generates contradictory outcomes. One example, just mentioned, is the role of remittances: they alleviate the poverty of some households while contributing to the indebtedness of others by raising social standards of respectability. A further example is the role of migration in simultaneously depressing and stimulating investment in education.

Migrants who are forced to return home because of ill fortune in the cities or binding obligations in the village often feel frustrated because working in the cities has raised their expectations but has failed to provide the resources needed for meeting them. Furthermore, for many of these returnees, re-migration is not an option. This may affect women more adversely than men, because there are more opportunities for men to achieve their goals within the rural society and economy.

Despite the problems with rising social standards and aspirations, the impact of migration on the countryside is broadly positive because return flows increase the number of people who can achieve their goals. The resources generated by migration pay for school fees, the construction of better-quality housing, and the establishment of small businesses. Additionally, the injection of remittances increases the supply of loans for the creation of rural enterprises and substitutes for the limited availability of micro-credit among agricultural producers. Working in the cities informs goals and also acts as a valve for relieving the dissatisfaction that accumulates among the rural populace because of a lack of pathways to attain their goals locally.

9.3 RETURN MIGRANT ENTREPRENEURSHIP

The state is active in directing return flows toward strengthening rural infrastructure in ways that attract further gains from migration. The Chinese discussion on modernizing the rural populace is centered firmly on the following projects: transferring surplus rural labor from farms to factories, creating rural market towns, improving "population quality" in rural areas, expanding the market economy, and diffusing urban economic and cultural elements to the countryside.[1] The central state in China has designated a role for migrant remittances and returnee entrepreneurs in attaining these modernization goals.

As shown in Chapters 5–7, by establishing direct links between rural and urban areas, migration bypasses the slow core–periphery diffusion process envisioned by modernization theorists such as Skinner. I am not claiming that migration promotes modernization in the sense of accelerating any supposed "linear laws of development." Nor am I denying the resource endowments and innovative capacity of rural society. Rather, as I have argued throughout this book, labor mobility exposes rural people (both villagers and officials) to new values and possibilities while at the same time increasing the resources available to them for pursuing personal, family, business, and development goals.

In accordance with upper-level directives, the local states in Xinfeng and Yudu have been inventive in trying to implement national policies that channel return flows toward local economic development. The local state publicity campaigns appeal to values of loyalty to the family and native place and call on migrants to bring glory to their hometowns as soon as possible. Policy initiatives include offering entrepreneurial returnees preferential access to local resources such as credit, land near towns, and raw materials. Directing returnee resources toward local development projects also helps local state cadres increase tax revenue, enhance their legitimacy in the eyes of the rural populace, gain the approval of upper levels in the state hierarchy, and improve personal career prospects. Some of the goals of returned migrant entrepreneurs are compatible with those of cadres, but others bring petty commodity producers into conflict and bargaining with the local state.

The enthusiasm of the grass-roots officials for business creation means that returnees can use their urban resources to lobby for policy reforms and improved access to local resources. One example is returnees who advise local cadres of the liberal business policies of the coastal cities in order to protest against official extortion of their enterprises; another is the official–returnee reform consultation meetings held at Spring Festival. The imperatives to create businesses also lead to cadre–entrepreneur cooperation for circumventing the central state: for example, returnee manufacturers who use the seclusion of the countryside and the protection of township governments to pirate the brand-name products of the cities or to avoid paying taxes to higher levels.

Returnees to Xinfeng and Yudu pursue their goals of becoming independent bosses by combining skills, capital, information, and social contacts from their former place of work with resources and opportunities in the origin areas. The importance of the previous place of employment is revealed by the fact that over 90% of the returnee entrepreneurs in my survey have created businesses replicating the city ventures in which they had worked. This finding differs from the orthodox view in the migration literature, which recognizes the potential for returned migrants to innovate in agriculture but is skeptical of their capacity to establish off-farm ventures. The paucity of agricultural innovators encountered in my fieldwork may reflect the general disdain of returnees for farming. Similarly, my findings from Wanzai suggest that returnee or migrant households do not innovate in agriculture. In this case, the advantage to be gained by investing in farming innovations is limited by the high profile of government-run extension services and the dominance of the local state in planning agricultural production.

For most migrants, returning home and creating businesses is a pathway to related goals such as earning money, reuniting with loved ones, escaping oppression in the urban labor markets, and strengthening the standing of the native place within the broader political economy. For women in particular, migrating and then returning home to establish a business (usually a small service-sector entity) is a way of reworking relationships with family members and claiming an independent personal space; this is possible even when they have returned home at the behest of family.

Individual characteristics combine with the relative weighting of push–pull factors to determine a person's access to resources and hence his or her capacity to establish and pursue entrepreneurial goals. Those who set up large-scale factories or operate relatively successful enterprises tend to be men with higher levels of education who spend longer periods in the cities, experience greater occupational mobility, have better contacts at home, and return when they are older. Furthermore, these entrepreneurs have generally returned home because of "pull" factors. In contrast, the entrepreneurs who run into difficulties with their businesses or become individual owner–operators return home primarily because of "push" factors. Despite the differences among returnees in terms of their characteristics, all share the goals of escaping wage labor and earning money through self-reliance, and most also aspire to avoid farming.

Although women migrants have the same exposure to urban production techniques as men, patriarchal values and their own expectations of migration as an interim phase between middle school and marriage limit their involvement in entrepreneurship. Nonetheless migration gives these women control over resources, exposure to off-farm life, and the power to bargain for a change in their situation. Married women who are former migrants contribute capital and labor to the enterprises of their returnee husbands; compared with rural wives who have never migrated, fewer are involved in farming.

Return migrant entrepreneurship is by no means common to all the labor-exporting regions of China. Xinfeng and Yudu were selected for this study because of media praise for local government initiatives to encourage returnee participation in business. Although the support of local leaders goes a long way toward explaining the relative success of returnee entrepreneurship in these counties, there are other factors. Migrants return to Xinfeng and Yudu because of the attractions of natural timber resources and recent advancements in infrastructure and telecommunications. A further factor is that migration from Xinfeng and Yudu commenced in the early 1980s, so sufficient time has passed for a pattern of entrepreneurial return migration to form. In contrast, migration from Wanzai is too recent to produce a return flow of entrepreneurs.

A final factor is the occupational specialization of the migrants from the origin areas – in particular, whether they are mainly factory workers (as in Xinfeng and Yudu) or whether they are traders. For migrants to factories, setting up a business at home is a way of escaping labor discipline and subordination while reuniting with family and spouses. Work experience provides some returnees with the skills, exposure to urban production layouts, and contacts with factory bosses that are useful for entrepreneurship. In contrast, in localities that I visited where the majority of out-migrants work as traders (e.g., Fengxin and Fengcheng counties, and Licun township in Yudu county), the incidence of return migrant entrepreneurship is minimal. Traders seem less likely either to return or to acquire the extra skills needed for setting up workshops. Migrants in these localities tend rather to concentrate all of their energy and resources on their urban businesses. A further difference is that trading migrants generally leave their villages as couples, nuclear households, or joint families so they do not face the same emotional pressures to return home.

In encouraging returnees to contribute to national development projects such as rural town construction and modernization, various levels of the state administration have in mind the longer-term goal of transferring a large proportion of farmers permanently out of agriculture. Yet returnee entrepreneurs have played only a limited role in facilitating the permanent transfer of rural labor out of agriculture and villages. This is because most rural enterprise workers are unwilling to relinquish their land, which is central to the livelihood diversification of the rural household. Moreover, returnee entrepreneurs provide few jobs for the local nonmigrant population. Instead, by expanding the occupational structure of the native economy, returnee entrepreneurs have enabled other returning migrants with various kinds of urban work experience to earn a living at home. This helps to alleviate a shortage of skilled workers in rural areas and may eventually improve the capacity of the industrial and tertiary sectors of the countryside to provide earning opportunities for nonmigrants.

Although labor migration contributes to local development by bringing resources into origin areas, it nevertheless creates problems for welfare and stability in the countryside. These problems are linked with the loss of young and educated labor from the villages, the large number of returnees who are unable to readjust to rural life, and the insecurity of an entire generation of rural youths suspended between the city and the village. The legitimacy of the ruling Party depends upon the extent to which it can improve rural living standards, and it is no exaggeration to claim that this rests on the state's capacity to organize and orchestrate the absorption of surplus rural labor in the face of potential nationwide unrest. Evidence from Jiangxi suggests that the rising expectations of rural dwellers and the frustrations of failed returnees cause hardships for individuals and create dissatisfaction within rural society.

Some China scholars equate labor mobility and the rise of market forces in the countryside with the retreat of the state.[2] I argue that migration and return flows instead change the *functions* of the state, and this can be seen in local official responses to the problems that migration creates. Cadres try to monitor the behavior of home-town natives in the destination areas in order to ensure their continuing access to urban labor markets. This involves entrusting migrating cadres to act as mentors to their home-town fellows, establishing labor export offices in the destination areas, and incorporating the behavior of migrants into the rural household evaluation campaigns. Cadres represent their migrant constituents in compensation cases for injuries and deaths. Migration also forces local cadres to devise measures for collecting agricultural taxes, mobilizing labor for public works, raising school completion levels, and controlling the fertility of migrants.

9.4 CLOSING THOUGHTS

This book has shown how villagers in Jiangxi respond to socioeconomic transition and actively shape this transition. It has further demonstrated that social actors create their environment by using values and resources and that the outcomes of their strategies subsequently constrain and enable them as they establish and pursue further goals. This perspective challenges modernization and structuralist classifications of rural people as passive, backward, and traditional. The success of rural people is shown by the fact that they are much better off now than under Mao. However, factors other than migration also contribute to this – notably, the state's commitment to rural education, public investment in infrastructure, and poverty alleviation schemes. These state activities are important, and migration must not be seen as a substitute for them.

Without denying the human suffering associated with rural–urban migration, I have argued that, on balance, involvement in urban labor markets is improving conditions in the countryside by broadening perspectives and providing a pathway for more villagers to pursue their goals. Because migration and return flows are recent phenomena in contemporary China, the social, economic, and political ramifications are still unfolding.

Notes

INTRODUCTION

1. Bo Qiangzhong, "Employment: A Pressing Issue at the End of the Century."
2. Examples of important works on China include: Dorothy J. Solinger, *Contesting Citizenship in Urban China*; Delia Davin, *Internal Migration in Contemporary China* (esp. ch. 6, where Davin discusses the impact of migration on the countryside); Frank Pieke and Hein Mallee (Eds.), *Internal and International Migration*; Sally Sargeson, *Reworking China's Proletariat*; Thomas Scharping (Ed.), *Floating Population and Migration in China*.
3. These dates indicate when Maoist policies were influential, not when Mao was actually in power.
4. Arjan De Haan, "Livelihoods and Poverty," p. 22.
5. Allan F. Hershfield, Niels G. Rohling, Graham B. Kerr, and Gerald Hursh-César, "Fieldwork in Rural Areas."
6. Jan Breman, "The Partiality of Fieldwork in Rural India," pp. 25–6.
7. Ibid., p. 26.
8. See Nicole Constable, "At Home but Not at Home," and Constance Lever-Tracy, "Return Migration to Malta."
9. Some migration scholars have referred to the "structuration" theory of Anthony Giddens on agency–structure interactions (see Anthony Giddens, "Structuration Theory and Sociological Analysis"); they call for exploration of ways to use this in the study of migration. See Sylvia Chant and Sarah A. Radcliffe, "Migration and Development: The Importance of Gender," p. 19. See also Caroline Wright, "Gender Awareness in Migration Theory"; Ronald Skeldon, *Migration and Development,* p. 18; and Jon Goss and Bruce Lindquist, "Conceptualizing International Labor Migration: A Structuration Perspective." Although she does not use the term "structuration," Solinger (1999) focuses on the concepts of "agency" and "structure."

CHAPTER 1

1. Goss and Lindquist (1995), p. 314.
2. Christophe Z. Guilmoto, "Institutions and Migrations: Short-term versus Long-term Moves in Rural West Africa."
3. C. W. Wood, "Equilibrium and Historical-Structural Perspectives on Migration"; Michael Kearney, "From the Invisible Hand to Visible Feet"; Nanda R. Shrestha, "A Structural Perspective on Labor Migration in Underdeveloped Countries"; Calvin Goldscheider, "Migration and Social Structure"; Caroline Wright, "Gender Awareness in Migration Theory."

4. W. Arthur Lewis, "Economic Development with Unlimited Supplies of Labour."
5. J. Fei and Gustav Ranis, *Development of the Surplus Labor Economy*. Fei and Ranis pioneered the transfer of Lewisian concepts to the study of migration.
6. Michael Todaro, "A Model of Labor Migration and Urban Unemployment in Less Developed Countries"; Michael Todaro, "Income Expectations, Rural–Urban Migration and Employment in Africa."
7. Oded Stark and David Levhari, "On Migration and Risk in LDCs," p. 195.
8. John Harris and Michael Todaro, "Migration, Unemployment and Development"; Oded Stark and Robert E. B. Lucas, "Migration, Remittances and the Family."
9. Robert E. B. Lucas and Oded Stark, "Motivations to Remit."
10. This observation is also made by Graeme J. Hugo, "Circular Migration in Indonesia," p. 75; see also Sally Findley, *Rural Development and Migration*, p. 17. For first-hand examples of this approach, see W. J. House and H. Rempel, "The Determinants of Interregional Migration in Kenya," and the collection of articles in R. H. Sabot (Ed.), *Migration and the Labor Market in Developing Countries*.
11. John Kenneth Galbraith, *The Nature of Mass Poverty*, p. 96.
12. A. O'Connor, *The African City*; W. T. S. Gould, "Education and Internal Migration"; Tim Unwin, "Urban–Rural Interaction in Developing Countries"; Lorraine Corner, "Linkages, Reciprocity and Remittances"; *National Migration Survey of Thailand*, pp. 83–4; *Summary of World Broadcasts*, 5 July 1994; Zhonggong zhongyang zhengce yanjiushi nongcunzu (1994), p. 5.
13. Galbraith, *The Nature of Mass Poverty*, pp. 51, 120–39.
14. Lawrence A. Brown, *Place, Migration and Development in the Third World*, pp. 13–15.
15. See Katy Gardner, *Global Migrants, Local Lives*, pp. 10–13.
16. John Connell, Biplab Dasgupta, Roy Laishley, and Michael Lipton, *Migration from Rural Areas*, pp. 197, 200.
17. Graeme Hugo is one of the main pioneers of the study of "circulation"; see e.g. Graeme Hugo, *Population Mobility in West Java*. "Circulation" is used by people writing from a variety of theoretical perspectives.
18. Veena Thadani, "Social Relations and Geographic Mobility," p. 195; J. M. M. Van Amersfoort, "Migrant Workers, Circulation and Development," pp. 20–1.
19. Michael Lipton, "Migration from Rural Areas of Poor Countries," p. 14; John Connell, "Migration Remittances and Rural Development in the South Pacific."
20. Connell, "Migration Remittances," pp. 250–1; Connell et al. (1976), pp. 98–104, 209; Kearny, "From the Invisible Hand," pp. 345–7.
21. Connell et al. (1976), pp. 99, 209.
22. Hugo, "Circular Migration in Indonesia," p. 76.
23. Xu Zengwen, "The mobility of the rural labor force and the loss of agricultural labor."
24. Qin Hui, "The mobility of peasants and improved deployment of the factors of production."
25. Alan B. Simmons, "Migration and Rural Development," p. 170.
26. Zhou Pei, "Building a tripartite social structure is the strategic choice for promoting the orderly flow of the migrant worker tide," p. 122.
27. Michael J. Piore, *Birds of Passage*, pp. 116–19; Janet H. Momsen, "Gender Selectivity in Caribbean Migration," pp. 80–1; Simmons, "Migration"; K. Paerregaard, *Linking Separate Worlds*, p. 117; Samir Amin, "Modern Migrations in Western

Africa," pp. 103–5; Food and Agriculture Organization, "Migration and Rural Development."

28. Julian Laite, "Circulatory Migration and Social Differentiation in the Andes," p. 92; Francesco Cerase, "Nostalgia or Disenchantment."

29. Robert Rhoades, "Intra-European Migration and Rural Development."

30. George Gmelch, "Return Migration," p. 150; Robert Rhoades, "The Evolution of a Migratory System"; Russell King, "Return Migration: A Review of Some Case Studies from Southern Europe"; Russell King, Jill Mortimer, and Alan Strachan, "Return Migration and Tertiary Development"; Nora Ann Colton, "Homeward Bound."

31. Amin, "Modern Migrations," pp. 103–5.

32. A. S. Oberai, P. H. Pradash, and M. G. Sardana, *Determinants and Consequences of Internal Migration in India,* p. 151.

33. Christoph Reichert, "Labor Migration and Rural Development in Egypt"; Yuen-Fong Woon, "The Voluntary Sojourner among the Overseas Chinese."

34. Zhou Pei (1995).

35. The exception is Mike Parnwell, *Population Movements and the Third World* (p. 116), which mentions government initiatives to help returned migrants set up businesses in parts of rural Thailand.

36. Premachandra Athukorala, "International Contract Migration and the Reintegration of Return Migrants," p. 240.

37. See Colton, "Homeward Bound," pp. 880–1.

38. Reichert, "Labor Migration," p. 58.

39. Rosemarie Rogers, "Incentives to Return."

40. Nicholas Van Hear, "The Impact of the Involuntary Mass 'Return' to Jordan in the Wake of the Gulf Crisis," p. 364.

41. Goldscheider, "Migration and Social Structure," pp. 677–80.

42. Colton, "Homeward Bound," pp. 870–82.

43. Daniel Kubat and Hans-Joachim Hoffmann-Nowotny, "Migration," p. 326.

44. Ayse Kadioglu, "Migration Experiences of Turkish Women."

45. Ijaz Nabi, "Village-end Considerations in Rural–Urban Migration."

46. Goldscheider, "Migration and Social Structure," pp. 684–9.

47. Fe Caces, Fred Arnold, James T. Fawcett, and Robert W. Gardner, "Shadow Households and Competing Auspices," p. 9.

48. Robert E. Christiansen and Jonathan G. Kidd, "The Return of Malawian Labor from South Africa and Zimbabwe"; Jin Ho Choi, "Urban to Rural Migration in Korea."

49. R. Rhoda, "Rural Development and Urban Migration."

50. Veena Thandani and Michael Todaro, "Female Migration." This study finds that women are more responsive than men to the "push" of oppressive family relationships and "traditionally ascribed status."

51. Adrian J. Baily and Mark Ellis, "Going Home."

52. See e.g. Denise Hare, " 'Push' versus 'Pull' Factors in Migration Outflows and Returns."

53. Clyde J. Mitchell, "Towards a Situational Sociology of Wage–Labor Circulation." Mitchell attempts to overcome the micro–macro dichotomy by (a) using regional economic differences to explain the incidence and rate of migration while (b) using micro-level social factors to explain what triggers individuals to move in particular instances; see e.g. E. S. Lee, "A Theory of Migration." The concept of "intervening obstacles" (e.g., long distance and poor transport) is a theoretical innovation

attributed to Lee. See also Gordon F. De Jong and James T. Fawcett, "Motivations for Migration."

54. See the collection of articles in Guy Standing (Ed.), *Labour Circulation and the Labour Process.*

55. This point is made by Connell et al. (1976), pp. 16–17, 198–9, and in Thomas S. Weisner, "The Structure of Sociability," p. 201.

56. Kearny, "From the Invisible Hand," pp. 353–6.

57. Yuen-Fong Woon, "Circulatory Mobility in Post-Mao China"; Marc Howard Ross and Thomas S. Weisner, "The Rural–Urban Migrant Network in Kenya."

58. For an overview see Solinger, *Contesting Citizenship,* pp. 150–3.

59. For studies stressing the subjectivity and agency of migrants, see Heather Xiao-quan Zhang, "Female Migration and Urban Labor Markets in Tianjin," and Tamara Jacka, "My Life as a Migrant Worker."

60. Goldscheider, "Migration and Social Structure," pp. 686–7.

61. Roger Jeffery and Patricia Jeffery, *Population, Gender and Politics,* p. 79.

62. See A. M. Findlay and F. L. N Li, "An Autobiographical Approach to Understanding Migration."

63. This is also called the "tradition of migration." See Connell et al. (1976), pp. 38–9, 50.

64. Takeyuki Tsuda, "The Permanence of 'Temporary' Migration," pp. 713–14.

65. Findlay and Li (1997), pp. 34–44; Goss and Lindquist (1995), pp. 331–41; Daniel Gutting, "Narrative Identity and Residential History."

66. Caroline Bledsoe and Allan Hill, "Social Norms, Natural Fertility and the Resumption of Postpartum 'Contact' in the Gambia."

67. Lever-Tracy, "Return Migration to Malta."

68. Mary Beth Mills, "Contesting the Margins of Modernity."

69. Constable, "At Home."

70. Amartya Sen, "Poor, Relatively Speaking," cites the following authors: Peter Townsend (on p. 163), Adam Smith (p. 159), and John Rawls (pp. 163, 167).

71. Cited by Sen, "Poor," p. 159.

72. Amartya Sen, *Inequality Re-examined,* p. 116. Poverty is described as "capability failure."

73. Oded Stark, "Migration Decision-Making."

74. Manuela Reis and Joaquim Gil Nave, "Emigrating Peasants and Returning Emigrants," pp. 24–6.

75. De Haan, "Livelihoods and Poverty," p. 22.

76. This is also the approach adopted by Gardner, *Global Migrants, Local Lives,* p. 4.

77. George S. Dei, "The Re-integration and Rehabilitation of Migrant Workers into a Local Domestic Economy."

78. Hill Gates, *China's Motor: A Thousand Years of Petty Capitalism,* p. 29.

79. Penelope Franks, "From Peasant to Entrepreneur in Italy and Japan."

80. Janet W. Salaff, *Working Daughters of Hong Kong*; Susan Greenhalgh, "Intergenerational Contracts," pp. 42–4; John C. Caldwell and Pat Caldwell, "The Cultural Context of High Fertility in Sub-Saharan Africa."

81. Jennifer Lauby and Oded Stark, "Individual Migration as a Family Strategy."

82. Franks, "From Peasant to Entrepreneur," p. 703.

83. Gates, *China's Motor,* pp. 47–8.

84. Ibid., pp. 52–3.

85. Zhou Yi, *Zhongguo renkou yu ziyuan, huanjing, nongye kexu fazhan* [The Chinese Population and Resources, Environment, and the Sustainable Development of Agriculture], pp. 368–70; Liu Yingjie, "Tide of migrant workers: the thoughts of sociologists."

86. Standing, "Circulation and the Labour Process," p. 6.

87. Henry Bernstein, "Agrarian Structures and Change: Latin America," p. 45; Josef Gulger, "The Urban–Rural Interface and Migration," p. 80.

88. Murray Chapman and R. Mansell Prothero, "Themes on Circulation in the Third World," p. 25.

89. Frank Ellis, "Household Strategies and Rural Livelihood Diversification"; Karim Hussain and John Nelson, "Sustainable Livelihoods and Livelihood Diversification"; De Haan, "Livelihoods and Poverty."

90. See Kenneth D. Roberts, "China's Tidal Wave of Migrant Labor."

91. Colton, "Homeward Bound," pp. 870–82.

92. Other authors refer to a "return narrative" operating in the context of permanently postponed return as the "ideology of return" or the "myth of return"; see e.g. Russell King, *Return Migration and Regional Economic Problems*, p. 12. On the use of the return narrative to deal with inner conflict see Constable, "At Home," pp. 203–28.

93. Joan Nelson, "Sojourners versus New Urbanites"; see also Ronald Skeldon, *Population Mobility in Developing Countries*, p. 140. Skeldon says that a change in the nature of mining technology in a part of Peru meant that the company needed a stable and skilled workforce, so the employers started to provide good living and working facilities so that workers would remain.

94. Dennis A. Ahlburg and Richard P. C. Brown, "Migrants' Intentions to Return Home and Capital Transfers."

95. Graham E. Johnson, "Open for Business to the World."

96. Deborah Potts, "Shall We Go Home?"

97. Interviews in Jiangxi, September–December 2000. See Thomas R. Gottschang and Diana Lary, *Swallows and Settlers: The Great Migrations from North China*, pp. 80–3.

98. Reichert, "Labor Migration," p. 52.

CHAPTER 2

1. William G. Skinner, "Marketing and Social Structure in Rural China, Part 1"; William G. Skinner, "Marketing and Social Structure in Rural China, Part 2."

2. William G. Skinner, "Differential Development in Lingnan," p. 17.

3. Ibid.

4. Feng Chongyi, "Jiangxi in Reform," p. 252.

5. Sow-Theng Leong, *Migration and Ethnicity in Chinese History*, p. 121.

6. Ibid., pp. 26, 40–62.

7. Ibid., p. 121.

8. Ibid., pp. 121–36.

9. Bao Hongshen (Ed.), *Wanzai xianzhi* [Wanzai County Almanac], p. 302.

10. Wright, *Migration and Ethnicity*, p. 123.

11. Bao Hongshen, *Wanzai xianzhi*, p. 295.

12. Ibid., p. 298.

13. Here, I draw on the analysis of Woon and her findings for Kaifeng; see Yuen-Fong Woon, "The Voluntary Sojourner," p. 688.
14. Li Zhongdong (Ed.), *Yudu xianzhi* [Yudu County Almanac], p. 309.
15. Myron L. Cohen, "Cultural and Political Inventions in Modern China," pp. 161–5.
16. Woon, "The Voluntary Sojourner," p. 689.
17. Cohen, "Cultural and Political Inventions," pp. 155–6.
18. Ibid.
19. June Teufel Dreyer, *China's Political System*, pp. 180–2.
20. Michael R. Dutton, *Policing and Punishment in China*, p. 216.
21. For an excellent study of the *hukou*, see Hein Mallee, "China's Household Registration System under Reform"; see also Davin, *Internal Migration*, pp. 1–19.
22. Kam Wing Chan and Li Zhang, "The *hukou* system and rural–urban migration in China."
23. Solinger, *Contesting Citizenship*, pp. 42–4.
24. Jean Oi, *State and Peasant in Contemporary China*, pp. 29–31, 55.
25. Oi, *State and Peasant*, p. 1.
26. Solinger, *Contesting Citizenship*, pp. 38–42.
27. David Zweig, *Freeing China's Farmers*, p. 187.
28. See Solinger, *Contesting Citizenship*, pp. 40–2.
29. Zweig, *Freeing China's Farmers*, p. 253.
30. Li Zhongdong (Ed.), *Yudu xianzhi*, p. 309.
31. Jiangxi Committee of Xinfeng County (Eds.), *Xinfeng xianzhi* [Xinfeng County Almanac], p. 279.
32. This paragraph is informed by Zweig, *Freeing China's Farmers*, p. 188.
33. The description of village economies under Mao as "spinning tops" was used by Carl Riskin in a lecture at Murdoch University, 1992.
34. Feng Chongyi, "Jiangxi in Reform," p. 258.
35. Liu Feng and Wan Renrong, "The commercialization of agriculture"; He Lidong, "Nearly one hundred Yudu farmers study and return to the native home to become officials and bosses."
36. Feng Chongyi, "Jiangxi in Reform," p. 258.
37. Ellen R. Judd, *Gender and Power in Rural North China*, pp. xiv, 173–87. Judd cites Elisabeth Croll, "New Peasant Family Forms in Rural China."
38. Deng Shulin, "Sounding the Alarm on Population Growth."
39. See Zhonggong zhongyang zhengce yanjiushi nongcunzu (1994). The majority of migrants from Wanzai work in coastal cities.
40. *Jiangxi tongji nianjian* [Jiangxi Statistical Yearbook] (1999), pp. 442–3.
41. Ibid., pp. 322–3.
42. Ibid., pp. 376–7.
43. Yehua Dennis Wei, *Regional Development in China*, pp. 37, 44.
44. *Jiangxi tongji nianjian* (1999), pp. 322, 323, 376, 337, 442, 443.
45. Li Guoqiang, Wang Yuqi, and Huang Zhigang, "Deng Xiaoping's theory of development and the county economies of Jiangxi," p. 4; Chen Puhua, "Completely invigorate the economy of Yudu," p. 35.
46. Interview, Deputy County Head, December 2000.
47. Scholars at the Jiangxi Academy of Social Sciences cautioned that the reported figures are not entirely reliable. The income estimates given to me by county heads during fieldwork were considerably lower. In answering my income questions, the

officials were probably rounding off average estimates for the previous year to give a rough introduction to conditions in the locality. Although the income targets to be reached by villages and townships are supposed to be set from the bottom up, in practice the county commits itself to an income target set through complicated political negotiations with higher levels; it then imposes these targets on the administrative levels below. The lower levels must deliver the appropriate amount of tax to upper levels and may even take out loans in order to do so. Counties in different prefectures face different levels of pressure. I conducted fieldwork in a different county in October–December 2000, and the income figures reported in the *Jiangxi Statistical Yearbook* for that particular county were regarded as on the high side by the head of the county statistics bureau.

In *Zhongguo wushi nian de Jiangxi 1949–1999* [Fifty Years of Jiangxi 1949–1999] (p. 577), 1999 rural per-capita income for Yudu is 1,484 yuan. This is inconsistent with the 1997 figure of 1,851 yuan reported for Yudu in the 1999 *Jiangxi Statistical Yearbook*. In *Fifty Years of Jiangxi 1949–1999,* the 1999 rural per-capita incomes reported for Wanzai (p. 585), Xinfeng (p. 569), and Jiangxi province (p. 11) are 2,311 yuan, 2,232 yuan, and 2,129 yuan, respectively.

48. Duanwu township government working report on labor export, January 1996.
49. Wang Ben, "Appeals and strides toward reducing the farmer's burden," p. 36.
50. Chen Puhua (1996), p. 35. The official number of migrants from Yudu is 150,000, though the Yudu Labor Export officials suspect that the figure is closer to 180,000. The official figure for migrants from Xinfeng is 100,000.
51. Interviews: Deputy Head of the Yudu Labor Export Office, Yudu, 30 October 1997; Head of Xinfeng county, Ouyang Feng, 15 June 1997.
52. William G. Skinner, "Introduction," pp. 9–10.
53. Ruth Pearson, "Gender Matters in Development."
54. Yi Dangsheng and Shao Qin (Eds.), *Zhongguo renkou liudong taishi yu guanli* [The Trend and Management of Population Mobility in China], p. 167.
55. Woguo da chengshi xishou nongcun laodongli ketizu (1996), p. 8.
56. Chain migration is widely documented as a feature of labor mobility; see Connell et al. (1976), p. 28. See also Graeme J. Hugo, "Village–Community Ties, Village Norms, and Ethnic and Social Networks," p. 203.
57. Nongcun shengyu laodongli zhuanyi yu laodongli shichang keti zu (1995), p. 19.
58. Interview, Lai Jidong, Pudong Dajie docks, 20 December 1997.
59. *Yuduxian nianjian, 1986–1992* [Yudu County Yearbook, 1986–1992], p. 496.
60. Interview, Yichun District Labor Export Company, 9 February 1997.
61. Wen Jian, "Exactly how open is the city gate?" Also, conversation with Chinese economist Zuo Xuejin, Shanghai, 30 July 1998.
62. *Jingji ribao* [Economic Daily], 13 September 1995, p. 10.
63. *The West Australian,* 28 December 1995, p. 26.
64. Piore, *Birds of Passage,* p. 54.
65. *Wenhui bao* [Digest Newspaper], 12 December 1996, p. 2.
66. Gu Shengzu and Jian Xinhua, *Dangdai Zhongguo renkou liudong yu chengzhenhua* [Population Mobility and Urbanization in Contemporary China], p. 17; Sidney & Alice Goldstein, "Migration Motivations and Out-Comes."
67. See Zhao Shukai, "Peasant Mobility." Zhao asked 175 migrants: "Do you want to work long term in the city?" Over half replied that they did not want to (*bu xiang*) while a further 22% did not know. But this is not the whole story. Open-ended

interviewing by Zhao revealed that respondents who had said that they did not want to remain in the city actually meant that they thought they had no option but to return home (*xiang ye meiyong*). When Zhao asked the migrants what they would do if they earned 5–10 million yuan: 43% replied that they would return home and set up a business, 26% said that they would return home to enjoy a relaxed life, and only 17% answered that they would continue to work in the city.

68. Several returned migrant entrepreneurs later converted their *hukou* to nonagricultural and town or county seat status within the native place.

69. *Summary of World Broadcasts,* 30 March 1994.

70. *Summary of World Broadcasts,* 25 April 1995.

71. Interview, Zhu Chunsheng, Shanghai Municipal Labor Bureau, 22 October 1996.

72. Interview, Tian Weihua, Deputy Head of the Pudong Public Security Bureau, Shanghai, 31 July 1999; Fei Qiang, Yan Zhongde, Wu Dongping, Cheng Jian, Li Siqing, and Li Youwu, "The tide of migrant workers, the wind rises, the clouds swell for another year," p. 7.

73. Wailai nü laogong yanjiu keti zu (1995), p. 81.

74. Pudong Xinqu laowu guanli zhongxin [Pudong New District Labor Management Center], *Pudong Xinqu wailai wugong qingnian wenming shouce* [Pudong New District Civilization Manual for Migrant Working Youths], pp. 50–65.

75. Daniel Kelliher, "Chinese Communist Political Theory and the Rediscovery of the Peasantry."

76. Theodore W. Shultz, "Investing in People"; Naohiro Ogawa, Gavin W. Jones, and Jeffrey G. Williamson, "Introduction," p. 12; Yang Xi, "The two big hidden worries of social order in the countryside"; Nie Zhenbang, Wang Jian, and Wu Ahnan, *Woguo gongyehua zhongqi nongcun jingji wenti yanjiu* [Research on Problems of the Rural Economy during the Middle Period of China's Industrialization], pp. 98–106.

77. Zhou Yi (1997), pp. 366, 371.

78. Zhang Maolin, "Theoretical thoughts on the 'counterflow return' of the 'migrant tide'"; Zhang Shanyu and Yang Shaoyong, "The tide of migrant workers will bring forth a tide of return"; Chen Ru, "Analysis of the current phenomenon of returning rural youth," p. 29; Zhou Zhong, "On the hot issues of the Chinese economy"; Shang Guanfei, "Working for a boss."

79. Huang Chenxi, "The influence of the transfer and mobility of migrant workers on rural population quality and counter-measures"; Zhou Yi (1997), p. 366.

80. Interviews, Yudu Labor Export Company, Pudong Dajie, Shanghai, July 1997. A monthly magazine distributed to migrants in Shanghai, called *Dagongzu huakan* [Migrant Workers' Pictoral], is compiled under the direction of the Shanghai Judicial Bureau. These magazines have cartoons explaining how to queue, the importance of hygiene, and the need for social manners.

81. Fu Shaoping, "The ten main characteristics of behavioral change among farmers in our country."

82. Judd, *Gender and Power,* pp. 164–73.

83. Michael Palmer, "The Re-emergence of Family Law in Post-Mao China," p. 116.

84. Lin Han, "The walls of the marriage circle are breaking and changing"; Huang Chenxi (1995), pp. 114–16; *Renmin ribao,* 4 March 1997, p. 9; Yi Dangsheng and Shao Qin (1995), pp. 198–9. This eugenics folklore may be propelled by family planning imperatives: if a man waits until he is in the city to find a wife, he marries later than if he married the girl who lives nearby.

85. Interview, Lai Jidong, Head of the Yudu Labor Export Company in Shanghai, 12 August 1997.
86. Li Nairong, "Population quality and labor protection for female workers."
87. Interview, Yudu Labor Export Company, Pudong Dajie docks, Shanghai, 12 August 1997.
88. Meng Chaoyang, "Thoughts on the dislocation of workers by rural migrant workers."
89. Studies of migration in pre-liberation China include: William T. Rowe, *Hankow,* and Bryna Goodman, *Native Place, City and Nation.*
90. Kyung-Sup Chang, "The Peasant Family in the Transition from Maoist to Lewisian Rural Industrialization," p. 223.
91. Solinger, *Contesting Citizenship,* p. 155.
92. Gu Shengzu and Liu Chuanjiang, "Theoretical thoughts on China's population mobility and urbanization and policy choices," p. 2.
93. Zhao Min, "Urbanization, population mobility, and China's road to urbanization in the 21st century"; "Healthy Growth of Small Towns Vital."
94. Bernstein, "Agrarian Structures," p. 45; Gulger, "The Urban–Rural Interface," p. 80.
95. *China Daily,* 21 March 1994, p. 4; *Beijing Review,* 27 February–5 March 1995, p. 20.
96. Elisabeth Croll and Huang Ping, "Migration For and Against Agriculture in Eight Chinese Villages."
97. *Yudu nianjian, 1986–1992* [Yudu Almanac, 1986–1992], pp. 504–7.
98. Anhuisheng weiyuan zheng yan shi (1994), p. 54; Wang Youzhao, "Concerning the problem of interregional peasant mobility," p. 19; *Summary of World Broadcasts,* 25 April 1994.
99. Zhou Pei (1995).
100. Food and Agriculture Organization, "Part III: Rural Non-Farm Income in Developing Countries," document on the state of food and agriculture (1998), ⟨http://www.fao.org/docrep⟩, p. 16.
101. Zhou Yi (1997), pp. 319–24, 353–60.
102. Huang Chenxi (1995), p. 48.
103. Song Linfei, "The Flood of Migrant Job-Seekers to Urban Areas," p. 171.
104. Connell et al. (1976), p. 47; Kam Wing Chan, "Internal Migration in China"; Croll and Huang, "Migration For and Against."
105. Ellis, "Household Strategies"; Idriss Jazairy, Mohiuddin Alamgir, and Theresa Panuccio, *The State of World Rural Poverty,* pp. 79–80.
106. However, at the end of 1997 the prefecture granted permission for the restoration of a temple in the Wanzai county seat under the auspices of the Bureau for Tourism. This signifies not a religious revival but rather an attempt to attract overseas Chinese Buddhist pilgrims to the county. The crackdown on feudal superstitions and customs continues.
107. Skinner (1964), pp. 7–9.
108. Gates, *China's Motor,* pp. 62–83.
109. Graeme J. Hugo, "Road Transport, Population Mobility and Development in Indonesia," p. 380; Adrienne Kols, *Migration, Population Growth and Development,* p. 267.
110. Simmons, "Migration," p. 177.

111. Gu Shengzu and Jian Xinhua (1994), p. 17.
112. Chen Ru (1996), p. 28; Chen Ru, "Choice crossing the century," p. 5.
113. Liu Zhiping and Chen Yilun, "Record of migrant youths returning home and creating businesses in Wangtian town"; Wu Zhengbao, "Migrant youths have a future returning through the farm gate."

CHAPTER 3

1. Simmons, "Migration," pp. 156–83.
2. As an example of this approach, see A. Maude, "Population Mobility and Rural Households in North Kelantan, Malaysia."
3. Corner, "Linkages, Reciprocity," p. 121.
4. See King, *Return Migration,* pp. 1–37, and Parnwell, *Population Movements,* p. 112.
5. Kols, *Migration,* p. 263; Amin, "Modern Migrations," pp. 103–5; Lipton, "Migration"; Connell et al. (1976), pp. 103–4; Henry Rempel and Richard A. Lobdell, "The Role of Urban–Rural Remittances in Rural Development"; Connell, "Migration Remittances"; Richard Ulack, "Ties to Origin, Remittances, and Mobility," p. 339; Lipton, "Migration," p. 14; Janet H. Momsen, "Migration and Rural Development in the Caribbean," p. 57; A. Oberai and H. Singh, "Migration, Remittances and Rural Development"; Oberai et al. (1989), pp. 44–59; Maude, "Population Mobility."
6. Stark sees migration as a response to relative deprivation, so the poorer members migrate in order to improve their position and continue to evaluate their progress against the village standard. See Oded Stark, "Rural to Urban Migration in LDCs," and Oded Stark, "Migration Incentives and Migration Types."
7. Aside from the 138 households, a few households were randomly omitted because we were unable to find some people and because of the weariness of my long-suffering guides.
8. The actual figure is 1,843.87 yuan, but this average is based on very broad estimates of respondents, so it is not particularly meaningful to use such a specific figure.
9. Source: personal interviews, December 1996–September 1997.
10. Source: December 1996 census sheets. Many more people left the village after Spring Festival to return to the city and were not recorded as migrants on the census sheets.
11. Interview with officials of Gaocheng township government, 27 December 1996. In 1996, the annual product value for agriculture in the township was 56,010,000 yuan; for the same year, remittances totaled over 5 million yuan.
12. The problem of villagers avoiding tax by hiding livestock in the pens of out-migrants is discussed in *Yichun ribao,* 17 September 1997, p. 2.
13. Fieldnotes, 12 March 1997.
14. Jazairy et al. (1992), pp. 66–8.
15. For wealth groupings according to ownership of livestock, see Elisabeth Croll, *From Heaven to Earth,* pp. 83–4.
16. A. V. Chaianov, *A. V. Chayanov on the Theory of Peasant Economy.*
17. Rahman Atiur, *Peasants and Classes,* p. 37.
18. Jonathan Unger, "Rich Man, Poor Man," pp. 44–5.

19. Peter Nolan, *The Political Economy of Collective Farms.*
20. Anita Chan, Richard Madsen, and Jonathan Unger, *Chen Village under Deng and Mao,* pp. 219–20.
21. Jane L. Collins, "Migration and the Life Cycle of Households in Southern Peru."
22. Hein Mallee, "Rural Household Dynamics and Spatial Mobility in China."
23. Lipton, "Migration," p. 13. In his summary of migration case studies, Lipton observes that the propensity to migrate increases with the size of the nuclear family; see also Findley, *Rural Development,* pp. 56–8.
24. For the data in Graph 3.2, $\chi^2 = 30.35$, which is significant at the 5% level.
25. $\chi^2 = 2.52$, which is not significant at the 5% level ($p = 0.64$).
26. $\chi^2 = 10.59$, which is significant at the 5% level.
27. Fieldnotes, Qifeng, February 1997.
28. Collins, "Migration"; Weisner, "The Structure."
29. Fieldnotes, related by neighbors, Tuanjie, 8 September 1997.
30. Chen Hu, "Yichun city actively encourages migrants to return and set up businesses."
31. According to Cohen, brothers stress property disputes among their wives in order to deflect from the real disputes among themselves. Myron Cohen, *House United, House Divided,* p. 196; see also Lin Yueh-hwa, *The Golden Wing.*
32. Fieldnotes, Tuanjie, September 1997.
33. Louis Putterman, *Continuity and Change in China's Rural Development,* pp. 322, 348; Terry McKinley, *The Distribution of Wealth in Rural China,* p. 45; Christiansen Flemming, *The De-rustification of the Chinese Peasant*; Victoria Bernal, *Cultivating Workers*; Alan de Janvry, *The Agrarian Question and Reformism in Latin America.*
34. Ellis, "Household Strategies."
35. For a rigorous quantitative study on this in a north China village, see Sarah Cook, "Work, Wealth, and Power in Agriculture."
36. These figures refer to the "present" of my field study. Interview, head of Wanzai County Labor Bureau, 19 November 1996.
37. *Nongyou ribao* [Farmers' Friend Daily], 25 June 1997, p. 1.
38. Wang Hansheng, "Industrialization and changes in the structure of the business stratum in China's countryside since the reforms"; Chan et al. (1992), p. 278.
39. S. Rozelle, L. Guo, M. Shen, A. Hughart, and J. Giles, "Leaving China's Farms," p. 389. Findings from an extensive survey of 200 villages suggest that "the net education effect is either small or insignificant." However, it is worth noting that, as discussed in Chapter 4, some factories are starting to demand workers with higher levels of education.
40. Reichert, "Labor Migration," p. 48.
41. Wen Jian (1997).
42. Central Government Policy Research Office, "An analysis of the changing composition of the income of rural households," p. 6.
43. Although $\chi^2 = 6.69$ is not significant at the 5% level ($p = 0.153$), the relationship nonetheless looks persuasive.
44. $\chi^2 = 21.15$, which is significant at the 0.1% level.
45. $\chi^2 = 19.77$, which is significant at the 0.1% level.
46. For the data in bars E and F, $\chi^2 = 31.75$, which is significant at the 0.1% level. However, it is important to bear in mind that bar F represents only eight households.

47. Manuela Reis and Joaquim Gil Nave, "Emigrating Peasants and Returning Emigrants," pp. 24–5; Connell et al. (1976), pp. 93–4, 129.
48. Douglas S. Massey, Rafael Alarcón, Jorge Durand, and Humberto González, *Return to Aztlan*, pp. 236–41.
49. Ibid., p. 239.
50. Lipton, "Migration," p. 12 (study based on the same material as Connell et al. 1976).
51. Connell et al. (1976), p. 203.
52. Sucheng Chan, "European and Asian Immigration into the United States in Comparative Perspective."
53. Reichert, "Labor Migration," pp. 55–6.
54. Food and Agriculture Organization, "Migration and Rural Development," p. 200.
55. Rempel and Lobdell (1978), p. 335; T. O. Fadayomi, S. O. Titilola, B. Oni, and O. J. Fapohunda, "Migrations and Development Policies in Nigeria," p. 81; King, *Return Migration,* p. 26.
56. Oberai et al. (1989), pp. 60–73.
57. Stark and Lucas (1988), p. 467.
58. Meng Xianfan, "Chinese Rural Women in the Transfer of the Rural Labor Force," pp. 112–13.
59. Xu Zengwen (1995), p. 53.
60. Xu Rihui and Kuang Yingjian, "Realizing a transformation in the method of land usage."
61. This information is based on interviews conducted in 1997.
62. Amartya Sen, "Gender and Cooperative Conflicts."
63. Xu Ping, "Marriage mobility and the land usage rights of rural women."
64. Nici Nelson, "The Women Who Have Left and Those Who Have Stayed Behind," pp. 112, 126–7.
65. $r = 0.0966$.
66. For data in the <5 mu bracket, $\chi^2 = 1.688$, which is not significant ($p = 0.989$). For data comparing the below-middle, middle, and above economic categories for 5–7-mu households and households with <5 mu, $\chi^2 = 2.056$, which is not significant ($p = 0.152$).
67. McKinley, *The Distribution,* p. 30.
68. An adult requires 300 kg of unhusked grain per year for subsistence. Fieldnotes, Qifeng, January 1997.
69. Liu Feng and Wan Renrong (1996), p. 5.
70. Yi Kequn, "Research on deepening the reform of the rural land system," p. 34.
71. *Yudu nianjian, 1986–1992,* pp. 285–6.
72. *Tequ wenzhai* [Special Economic Zone Digest], 11 August 1997, p. 1.
73. *Jiangxi qingnianbao,* 3 April 1997, p. 2; Qin Hui, "The direction of development of the problem of the 'farmers' burden'," p. 61; Liu Feng and Wan Renrong (1996), p. 5; Li Guanghui and Yuan Chun, "Killing two birds with one stone with the 'two land system' in Zhaixia township"; *Funü zhi shengbao,* 6 March 1996, p. 8.
74. Wang Ben (1997), p. 36; *Yichun ribao,* 20 November 1996, p. 1.
75. Fieldnotes, Qifeng, February 1997.
76. Related to me by cadres in Qifeng, Tuanjie, Beihu village, Rongtang town, Fengcheng; Jiaocun village, Xinbei township, Yudu; and Zhaixia village, Songpu township, Fengxin county.
77. Qifeng, 9 January 1997.

78. These villages are all in Jiangxi province. They are Qifeng, Tuanjie, and Guyuan villages, all in Gaocheng township, Wanzai county; Beihu village in Rongtang township, Fengcheng county; Jiaocun village, Xinbei township, Yudu county; Gutian village, Zhenjiang township, Yudu county; and Zhaixia village, Songpu township, Fengxin county.

79. Qin Hui (1997), p. 87.

80. Han Jun and Li Jing, *Kua shiji de nanti – Zhongguo nongye laodongli zhuanyi* [Challenge on the Crossing of the Century – The Transfer of China's Agricultural Labor Force], pp. 7–8.

81. Liu Zhengqin, " 'Migrants' give 'birthday money' to the land in Tianbao township"; "Wai chu bu wang jia zhong shengchan, you qian bu gao tuchu xiaofei."

82. *Guangming ribao* [Guangming Daily], 9 March 1994, p. 6.

83. *Yichun ribao*, 11 January 1997; Kuang Qinglin, "Yangyu township guides farmers in spending money on production"; Wang Guang, "Moshan migrants return home to invest in the challenge of opening up orchards"; Qiu Shunyan, "Over one thousand migrant workers return home to farm the land"; *Yichun ribao*, 1 May 1997, p. 2.

84. Breakdown of the households by economic categories: poor, 4; lower-middle, 5; middle, 14; upper-middle, 6; rich, 2.

85. Oberai et al. (1989), p. 71. This survey in three Indian provinces finds that returnees invest more in agricultural production than do their migrant and nonmigrant counterparts, though this investment is measured in terms of farm machinery rather than fertilizer and piglets.

86. Fieldnotes, 13 March 1997.

CHAPTER 4

1. Lipton, "Migration," pp. 12–13; Rempel and Lobdell (1978); Oberai and Singh (1980; remittances in this study were not directed toward education); Mills, "Contesting the Margins"; Connell et al. (1976), pp. 98–101, 209; Fadayomi et al. (1992); Simmons, "Migration," p. 170; Hugo, "Circular Migration in Indonesia," pp. 60–1; Stark and Lucas (1988), pp. 465, 468; Hunan laodongli zhuanhua yu renkou liudong ketizu (1995; in this study, house building and education are the two main areas of remittance usage).

2. Goss and Lindquist (1995), p. 321.

3. R. Brown and John Connell, "The Global Flea Market," p. 616; Jorge Durand and Douglas S. Massey, "Mexican Migration to the United States," pp. 25–9.

4. Amin, "Modern Migrations," pp. 103–5; Diane Elson and Ruth Pearson, "The Subordination of Women and the Internationalisation of Factory Production."

5. Guy Standing, "Circulation," pp. 27–9.

6. Connell, "Migration Remittances."

7. Lipton, "Migration," p. 12.

8. Goldscheider, "Migration," pp. 677–8; Brown, *Place, Migration,* pp. 13–15.

9. Douglas Butterworth, *Latin American Urbanisation,* pp. 73–90; Piore, *Birds of Passage,* pp. 23–4, 117.

10. Gu Shengzu and Jian Xinhua (1994), pp. 5, 252, 360–1; Ji Enze, "Stealthy return flow of the tide of migrant workers."

11. Food and Agriculture Organization (1984), p. 6.

12. Sen, "Poor," p. 168. Sen describes having sufficient resources to achieve a life goal and satisfy a need which exists in absolute terms for that person as reaching an absolute level of "capability."
13. Ibid. Sen cites the following authors: Peter Townsend (on p. 163), Adam Smith (p. 159), and John Rawls (pp. 163, 167).
14. Philip Thomas, "Conspicuous Construction."
15. Graeme Hugo, "Structural Change and Labour Mobility in Rural Java," p. 81.
16. In Chinese studies, this theoretical position is associated with Siu. See Helen F. Siu, "Recycling Rituals," and Helen Siu, "Reconstituting Dowry and Bride-price in South China." See also Goodman, *Native Place,* pp. 305–14, and Yunxiang Yan, *The Flow of Gifts,* pp. 207–9.
17. Richard R. Wilk, "Houses as Consumer Goods."
18. Naila Kabeer, *Reversed Realities,* p. 113.
19. Qin Hui (1997), p. 56.
20. *Jiangxi ribao,* 3 January 1996, p. 1 ("Money? Children!").
21. Jan Breman, "Particularism and Scarcity," p. 275.
22. *World Bank Report: Poverty in China,* pp. 58–9; Rozelle et al. (1999), p. 389.
23. Hein Mallee, "In Defense of Migration."
24. For this data, $\chi^2 = 32.071$, which is significant at the 0.1% level.
25. Wanzai County News, 22.20 hrs, 8 March 1997.
26. Xiao Chiyuan, "Ought to curb the out-migration of minors."
27. The law says nine years of compulsory education, but in rural Jiangxi the norm is currently eight years.
28. This has been observed throughout the developing world. Caroline Harper and Rachel Marcus (Save the Children Fund), "Child Poverty," Development Studies Association Poverty Study Group Meeting on Children, Disability, Ageing and Poverty, 12 March 1999.
29. *Jingji cankao bao* [Economic Information Daily], 23 June 1997, p. 2; "Nongcun 'liushou hai' huanhu guanzhu"; Meng Zhaopu, "Troubled thoughts on education by the older generation in the countryside"; *Tequ qingnian bao* [Special Zone Youth], 15 July 1997, p. 8.
30. Ibid.
31. Gates, *China's Motor,* pp. 95–9.
32. Interview, Wanzai County Government Guesthouse, March 1997.
33. Interview, Yichun District Labor Export Company, 9 February 1997.
34. Interview, Gu Gengxin, Director of the Office of Adult Education of Pudong New Area, Shanghai, 9 December 1996.
35. Interview, Qifeng, 10 January 1997.
36. Interview, Tuanjie, March 1997.
37. *Jiangxi qingnianbao,* 21 January 1997, p. 1.
38. Guy Standing, "Circulation," p. 28; Hugo, "Structural Change," p. 81.
39. Dang Ming, "The huge transfer of 1.1 billion farmers," p. 5.
40. *Fengcheng qingnian* [Fengcheng Youth] 6 (1996), pp. 27–8 ("Return home").
41. Scott Wilson, "The Cash Nexus and Social Networks."
42. Wailai nü laogong yanjiu keti zu (1995), pp. 80–1.
43. Thomas, "Conspicuous Construction"; Josiah Heyman, "Changes in House Construction Materials in Border Mexico."
44. Heyman, "Changes in House Construction," pp. 136–7.

45. This practice is also common in Yudu.
46. Chant and Radcliffe (1992), p. 17.
47. Gao Xiaoxian, "Summary of research on rural women, 1991–1995," p. 15.
48. Chan et al. (1992), pp. 295–9.
49. Elisabeth Croll, "The Exchange of Women and Property"; Yunxiang Yan, *The Flow of Gifts,* pp. 200–3.
50. Siu, "Reconstituting Dowry," pp. 169–71.
51. Ibid.; Yunxiang Yan, *The Flow of Gifts,* pp. 176–209.
52. Judd (*Gender and Power,* p. 86) reports on the formation of this committee in one of her fieldwork villages in the late 1980s.
53. You Siqing, "New fashion in the love and marriage of young people in Huangcheng"; Zheng Yi, "It is not easy to ignore the phenomenon in the countryside of using marriage to extort wealth."
54. Connell et al. (1976), p. 101.
55. Thanks to Professor Tim Wright for this point.
56. Fieldnotes, Qifeng, 8 January 1997.
57. *Yichun ribao,* 2 November 1997, p. 2; Liang Gaochao, "Take practical measures to strengthen the ideological moral construction of out-migrants," p. 40.
58. Benjamin S. Orlove and Henry J. Rutz, "Thinking about Consumption," p. 42.
59. Wailai nü laogong yanjiu keti zu (1995), p. 75; *Renmin ribao,* 16 April 1997, p. 2.
60. Susan Mann, "Grooming a Daughter for Marriage," p. 204.
61. Li Zhiyang, "Several problems of working," p. 36.
62. Wang Yuzhao, "Chests full of warmth."
63. 3 December 1996, p. 4.
64. For an excellent discussion on the relationships between transport, labor mobility, and transformation in the origin areas in Indonesia, see Hugo, "Road Transport."
65. "Wanzai xian zuzhi zhuanche jiesong dagong renyuan."
66. Siu, "Recycling Rituals," p. 130.
67. Sen, "Poor," pp. 153–69.

CHAPTER 5

1. Chen Aisheng, "Migrant youths return home from the city."
2. Zhang Maolin (1996).
3. Chen Demei, "Rising and falling wave," p. 56. According to *Summary of World Broadcasts* (12 January 1996), most migrate from north to south Jiangsu; the total number of migrants to south Jiangsu is 1.2 million.
4. Zhang Maolin (1996), p. 54.
5. Ji Enze (1997), p. 13; Miu Xiaoqin, "The return flow of migrant workers, attracting people's attention"; Si Nan, "City-bound Workers Cannot Be Ignored." According to *China Daily* (30 January 1995, p. 4), there are 4 million surplus laborers in Jiangxi province, over half of whom have migrated. According to *China Daily* (29 July 1996, p. 4), there are over 5 million migrants from Sichuan – the most populous province of China, and also the largest labor exporter.
6. Zheng Ying, "Migrants Help, So Help Migrants."
7. Here is a small selection of references: *Summary of World Broadcasts,* 4 February 1994; *China Daily,* 15 July 1994, p. 15; *Renmin ribao,* 22 July 1994, p. 5; Xu Xiaogan, "Work and then return to set up big business"; Wang Xiaoping and Zhong

Yangping, "Happily seeing thousands of phoenixes returning to the nest"; *Jingji ribao* [Economic Daily], 30 October 1996, p. 1; *Yichun ribao,* 10 January 1997, p. 1; *Yichun ribao,* 24 January 1997, p. 3; *Yichun ribao,* 6 February 1997, p. 2; *Yichun ribao,* 20 February 1997, p. 1; Wu Zhengbao (1997); *Zhongguo qingnian bao,* 20 May 1997, p. 3; Chen Aisheng (1997); Liu Zhiping and Chen Yilun (1997); *Jiangxi qingnianbao,* 27 May 1997, p. 1; *Yichun ribao,* 5 June 1997, p. 1; Xu Nantie, "Topic of the century"; Wang Youcai, Zhan Shengsheng, and Xu Renhe, "Migrant youths return home and enrich the people of a village"; Wen Shi, "If you want to be a boss"; Chen Demei (1997); *Guangdong laodong bao,* 23 June 1997, p. 2; Zhang Shanyu and Yang Shaoyong (1996).

Wang Zhongzhou, "Bringing the road to prosperity home," states that over 100,000 migrants have returned to Linxu prefecture in Shandong province and that one third of these have set up over 600 businesses. Shao Suping, "Worked in the past," states that there are over 22,000 individual and private enterprises in the administrative district of Pingxiang (Jiangxi province), 75% of which have been established by returned migrants. According to Anhuisheng weiyuan zheng yan shi (1994), in Mengcheng county (Anhui province) there are about 12,000 rural enterprises, 57% of which have been established by returned migrants. According to Nongmin liudong yu xiangcun fazhan keti zu (1999), in two towns in Huantai county since 1986, returnees have set up 435 businesses while many other returned migrants have become small traders, transport operators, or specialist agricultural cultivators.

8. Government agencies sometimes exaggerate figures. In developed regions, exaggeration may be designed to diffuse the frustrations of migrants by redirecting their aspirations for social mobility from the cities toward home soil. Articles in the newspapers of interior provinces may be intended both to encourage return migration from provincial capitals and to urge rural governments within the province to welcome returnees.

9. Han Jun and Li Jing, "'The tide of migrant workers'," pp. 7–8; Zhonggong zhonyang zhengce yanjiushi nongcunzu (1994), p. 5.

10. Shao Suping (1997).

11. Yuen-Fong Woon, "Labor Migration in the 1990s." In contrast, highly educated migrants or those migrants who shared the cultural and linguistic background of the host society tended to obtain a blue-permit *hukou.* The destination area of the migrants in this study was towns in the Pearl Delta rather than large cities, so there may have been more opportunities for the migrants to integrate into the local society.

12. Laite, "Circulatory Migration," p. 92; Cerase, "Nostalgia."

13. King, *Return Migration,* p. 19.

14. Zhang Maolin (1996), p. 57; Zhang Shanyu and Yang Shaoyong (1996); Nongmin liudong yu xiangcun fazhan keti zu (1999), p. 65.

15. Gmelch, "Return Migration," p. 150.

16. William A. Byrd and Lin Qingsong, *China's Rural Industry,* p. 216.

17. See Table 5.1, note *c.*

18. King, *Return Migration,* p. 19; Rogers, "Incentives."

19. *Yudu nianjian, 1986–1992.*

20. Jean Oi, "Fiscal Reform and the Economic Foundations of Local State Corporatism"; Christine P. W. Wong, "Fiscal Reform and Local Industrialization."

21. Informal conversations in various locations in Jiangxi province with local leaders. Also, see Cha Yufeng, "Discussion of the problem of peasant burden"; Shi Jianmin

and Liu Fugui, "Stop the false wind of townships and villages"; Chen Zhongmin, "Country cadres difficult difficult difficult"; Liu Faming, "Problems in collecting village and township levies and countermeasures"; Zhang Dong, "Grasp the three barriers and walk out of the strange circle of reducing burden."

22. Wolfgang Taubman, "The Finance System and the Development of Small Towns in Rural China."
23. Liu Chunbin, "Small towns," p. 15.
24. *Dangfeng lianzheng* [Party-style Upright Government] 4 (1997), p. 32.
25. Interview, Deputy Director of the Yudu Labor Export Company, Yudu, 30 October 1997. Interview, Mr. Kang, Head of the Daa Town Labor Management Depot, Xinfeng, 15 June 1997.
26. Conversations with Yudu migrants at Shanghai docks. People in Yudu also mentioned the riots.
27. Gates, *China's Motor,* p. 41.
28. Ibid., p. 7.
29. Fieldnotes, Xinbei township, Yudu, 20 October 1997.
30. Lai Jidong is manager of the Yudu Labor Export Company in Shanghai, and Teng Huosheng is deputy. They are both Shanghainese who were sent to Yudu as youths and married while there. In their capacity as managers of the county government office in Shanghai, they have tried to contact former rusticated youths to encourage them to invest in Yudu, but without success. In Wanzai, similar attempts were made by government leaders to initiate links with Shanghainese who were rusticated to Wanzai. A teacher at the Shanghai Academy of Social Sciences said that the thought of Wanzai opened up too many wounds.
31. *Jiangxi tongji nianjian* (1996), table 18-3, pp. 568–9.
32. Fieldnotes, Qifeng, Wanzai, 1 September 1997.
33. Fieldnotes, Xinfeng, 15 June 1997.
34. Jingji ban xiaoshi [Half-hour economic update], Channel Two, 14.00 hrs, 12 November 1997.
35. Wen Jian (1997); Guangdong Satellite Television, Shehui zongheng [Social horizon], 21.00 hrs, 25 October 1997.
36. *Jiangxi qingnianbao,* 20 May 1997, p. 2. In a survey of migrants in 23 provinces and cities, 71.7% expressed the belief that it was more difficult to find employment than in the previous year.
37. Chen Hao, "The outflow of China's rural labor and rural development," p. 8.
38. Qifeng, Guyuan, and Tuanjie in Gaocheng township, Wanzai county; Jiaocun in Xinbei township, Yudu.
39. Shang Junfeng, "Strengthen the macro-level regulation of the floating population and give full play to the role of population mobility in urbanization," p. 31; Li Hongwei, "The return flow of rural labor"; Huang Zhigui and Zhong Yi, "Situation of the return of the rural labor force and strategies for transfer."
40. Jiangxi Funü Lianhehui, "Clash between city and village and marriage break-up."
41. *Jiangxi ribao,* 14 March 1997, p. 1. The provincial government formulated the following resolution: "Resolution concerning the organization, guidance, and encouragement of migrants returning to the countryside to establish enterprises."
42. Yang Shouyao, "Yujiang county adopts preferential policies to encourage migrant workers to return home and set up businesses"; *Jiangxi laodong* 6 (1995): p. 31 ("The expert's new explanation of the tide of migrant workers"); Zhu Yimin, "Survey of the outflow of labor from Yugan county"; Wang Xiaoping and Zhong Yangping

(1996); *Jiangxi ribao,* 19 August 1997, p. 1; Jin Xian, "Phoenix return!"; Xu Xiaogan (1996).

43. Duanwu Township Government, "Report on labor export from Duanwu township" (Duanwu township is in Yudu county); Yudu County Bureau of Statistics, "1993 survey of labor export"; *Xiangzhen jianshe,* 2 May 1997, p. 4; *Xiangzhen jianshe,* 14 March 1997, p. 4.

44. *Xinfeng bao* [Xinfeng News], 17 February 1997, p. 1.

45. Interview, Yan Jushang, Head of Xinfeng Bureau of Township and Village Enterprises, 9 June 1997. This slogan is used by counties that seek to encourage returnee business creation; e.g., cadres in Gaoan county in Jiangxi have also adopted the slogan in order to encourage returnees (*Yichun ribao,* 5 June 1997, p. 1).

46. Interview, Zhang Weidong, Office Director, Yudu County Government, 15 October 1997.

47. Xu Xiaogan (1996).

48. Interview, Zou Jinsheng, Youshan town, Xinfeng, 11 June 1997.

49. Interview, Lai Tianyang, Jinlong Furniture Factory, Xinfeng, 6 June 1997.

50. *Nongyou bao,* 18 February 1997; *Jiangxi qingnianbao,* 6 March 1997, p. 2; *Xiangzhen bao,* 14 March 1997, p. 4.

51. Some migrants reported such visits. Interview, Mr. Kang, Daa town, 15 July 1997; He Lidong, Head of Labor Management Depot, Geou township, Yudu, 9 October 1997.

52. Li Hedong (*Xinmin wanbao,* 20 July 1997, p. 22) discusses migrants from the Yudu Labor Export Company at the Pudong docks in Shanghai who return home to set up businesses and become village cadres. The following two articles recommend that local governments recruit returnees as village cadres or send cadres out to work in the cities for a couple of years: Zhang Rui, "Returnee migrants become village leaders"; Yu Xueqiang, "Send the cadre out to work."

53. *Jiangxi ribao,* 10 April 1997, p. 7.

54. Liu Yanguo, "Harbor schoolroom cradle"; Lai Jidong, "Strengthen the intensity of spiritual and cultural construction"; "Xinhua gang mingong guanli chang xin lu"; *Xinmin wanbao,* 20 July 1997, p. 22; interviews, Manager of the Shanghai branch of the Yudu Labor Export Company, Lai Jidong, August 1997.

55. "Dagongzai 'lulian' da Shanghai"; emphasis added.

56. Wang Linquan, "Daa has a 'migrant youth association'"; emphasis added.

57. Reichert, "Labor Migration"; Fadayomi et al. (1992), p. 82.

58. These brick factories are in Qifeng village, Gaocheng township, Wanzai county; Zhaixia village, Songpu township, Fengxin county; Manxiang village, Pingshi township, Xinfeng county; Zhengping township, Zhengping village, Xinfeng county; Tankou village, Zhengping township, Xinfeng county; Geou Township Brick Factory, Yudu county; and Xinbei Township Factory, Yudu county. A restauranteur (one of the interviewees for the Yudu service sector) pooled funds with seven other returnees to set up a brick factory on the outskirts of the county seat, and two brick factories are located in Chixing township, Wanzai county.

59. Interview, He Lidong, Head of the Labor Management Depot, Geou township, Yudu, 9 October 1997; interview, Land Management Bureau cadre of Xinbei township, Yudu, 20 October 1997; Luoe township, conversation with township guides, 15 October 1997; interview, Mr. Kang, Head of Daa town, Xinfeng, 15 June 1997; conversation with township guide, Youshan town, Xinfeng, 11 June 1997.

60. Conversation with Guo Guopeng, 20 October 1997.
61. Wu Huimin, *Zhongguo nongcun fangzhen zhengce* [Policy in Rural China], pp. 66–9.
62. Xinbei township branch of Agricultural Bank, 20 October 1997.
63. Wu Huimin, *Zhongguo nongcun.*
64. Interview, Head of the Land Management Office (*tuguan suo*) in Rongtang town, Fengcheng county, 15 April 1997.
65. Fieldnotes, Rongtang town, Fengcheng county, 18 April 1997.
66. For more on financial investment companies set up by county governments, see Jean Oi, "The Evolution of Local State Corporatism," p. 59.
67. Interview, Xiniu Township Steel Factory, Xinfeng, 16 June 1997.

CHAPTER 6

1. Antonius C. G. M. Robben, "Entrepreneurs and Scale."
2. The *small-scale* enterprises broadly correspond with the Chinese classification of "individual enterprise." A *large-scale* returnee enterprise broadly corresponds with a "private enterprise" in terms of both the number of employees and the tendency to engage in manufacturing (see the Note to Table 5.1, p. 128). The "private" classification of an enterprise is often ambiguous, and various forms of ownership and state–entrepreneur arrangements have produced an array of private businesses operating under the auspices of state registration. Recently a new criterion for separating "individual" and "private" enterprises has been advanced by the state: "private" enterprises would have at least 500,000 yuan in registration capital. The level of initial investment in the "large-scale" returnee enterprises is less than the private enterprise designation. This demonstrates that establishing factories in deprived economies requires less investment than the national standard.
3. Jazairy et al. (1992), p. 293.
4. Angela P. Cheater, *Social Anthropology*, pp. 100–1.
5. This average excludes the Yudu Woolen Sweater Company, which has 860 employees.
6. Ivan Bull and Gary E. Willard, "Towards a Theory of Entrepreneurship."
7. Rachel Murphy, "A Dependent Private Sector."
8. Xinfeng county's table for returnees who created businesses during 1995.
9. Jiangxi Satellite News, 08.00 hrs, 15 March 1997; *Jiangxi ribao,* 14 March 1997, p. 1.
10. Fieldnotes, Xinfeng Bureau of Township and Village Enterprises, 9 June 1997.
11. Cerase, "Nostalgia," p. 224, n. 13; Connell et al. (1976), p. 121.
12. Victor Nee, "Social Inequalities in Reforming State Socialism"; Jean Oi, "Fiscal Reform."
13. Interview, Xinfeng Textile Factory, 12 June 1997.
14. Interview, Xinfeng Bureau of Township and Village Enterprises, 9 June 1997.
15. Interview, Yudu, 11 October 1997.
16. Zhang Maolin (1996); Zhang Shanyu and Yang Shaoyong (1996).
17. These businesses are the Daa Furniture Factory and the Huaguang Leather Goods Factory.
18. The constitution says nine years but, in practice, eight years is the norm in the Jiangxi countryside.
19. King et al. (1984), p. 122; Frank Bovenkerk, *The Sociology of Return Migration,* p. 47; Cerase, "Nostalgia," pp. 227–8.

20. For the raw data presented in bars A and D of Graph 6.1, $t = 4.55$, which is significant at the 0.05% level.
21. For the raw data presented in bars B and C, $t = 1.245$ ($p = 0.219$).
22. For the raw data presented in bars A and D of Graph 6.2, $t = 5.364$, which is significant at the 0.0001% level.
23. Gary Sage, "Entrepreneurship as an Economic Development Strategy."
24. Hein Mallee, "In Defense of Migration," pp. 118–19.
25. Lin Yousu and Lincoln H. Day, "The Economic Adjustments of Migrants in Urban Areas"; Y. H. Zhao, "Labor Migration and Returns to Rural Education in China."
26. For this graph, $\chi^2 = 12.297$, which is significant at the 0.1% level.
27. Yudu County Bureau of Statistics (1994).
28. *Jiangxi tongji nianjian* (1996), table 7-23, p. 195.
29. The proportion of interviewees in the large manufacturing sector is less in Xinfeng than in Yudu, which may explain the lower percentage for Xinfeng.
30. Nongmin liudong yu xiangcun nongcun fazhan keti zu (1999), p. 64.
31. Interview, Hu Zhensheng, Youshan town, Xinfeng, 11 June 1997.
32. Gordon F. De Jong and Robert W. Gardner, "Introduction and Overview."
33. King et al. (1984), p. 117; Gmelch, "Return Migration," p. 141; Russell King, "Return Migration," p. 179.
34. Fieldnotes, Xinfeng, 7 June 1997.
35. Interviews in April 1997.
36. Interviews accompanied by Mr. Liang of Jiangxi Academy of Social Sciences, 1–10 July 1997.
37. In *Jiangxi qingnianbao,* 18 February 1997, p. 2, the journalist writes: "No matter how excellent you are working under somebody's hand, you still *dagong* ... his [the migrant's] heart's desire is to be a boss, even if it is the smallest boss in the world."
38. Interview, Xuehao Shoe Factory, Xinfeng, 10 June 1997.
39. Interview, Huadi Furniture Factory, Xinfeng, 5 June 1997.
40. Shanghai People's Radio Station, 23.15 hrs, 15 October 1996. This radio documentary describes business creation by returned migrants to Fengyang prefecture (Anhui province) and calls on Shanghai municipal authorities to provide resources that facilitate the historical transition from peasant to worker to entrepreneur. See also Wen Shi (1997) and Sun Chunyun, "The sound of roamers' footsteps," p. 7.
41. Fieldnotes, Jiaocun village, Xinbei township, Yudu, November 1997.
42. Interview, Luoe Township Paint Factory, Yudu, 19 October 1997.
43. Nongmin liudong yu xiangcun fazhan keti zu (1999), p. 63.
44. Interview, Xinbei Township Furniture Factory, Yudu, 19 October 1997.
45. Li Wensheng, "The influence of the Jing-Jiu Railway on urbanization in Jiangxi and countermeasures," p. 3.
46. Ibid.
47. *Xinfeng bao* [Xinfeng News], 17 February 1997, p. 1.
48. Interview, Xiniu Xiang Helmet Factory, Xinfeng, 16 June 1997.
49. See Judd, *Gender and Power,* pp. 120–3. This is a revision of Harrell's argument, which interprets the Chinese entrepreneurial ethic as a long-term one aimed at the enhancement of either a patrilineal estate or uterine family; see Stevan Harrell, "Why Do the Chinese Work So Hard?"
50. Interview, Xinbei township, Yudu, 20 October 1997.
51. Interview, Yudu Mattress and Furniture Factory, 10 November 1997.

52. Yudu County Bureau of Statistics (1994).

53. Daa, Xiniu, Youshan, and Da Tangbu.

54. Woon, "Labor Migration," note 36. Woon observes that, of those migrants who intend to create a business at home, most are men; she explains that this is to be expected because the "home community" is in fact the man's community.

55. Caroline Hoy told me that her women interviewees intended to return home to marry so that the money would be kept within the natal home (private conversation, July 1999).

56. Leann M. Tigges and Gary P. Green, "Small Business Success Among Men- and Women-Owned Firms in Rural Areas."

57. Interview, Geou Township Brick Factory, Yudu, 11 October 1997.

58. Interview, Duanwu Township Toy Factory, 23 October 1997.

59. Elson and Pearson, "The Subordination"; see also Haleh Afshar (Ed.), *Women, Work and Ideology in the Third World.*

60. Veronnika Bennholdt-Thomsen, "Subsistence Reproduction and Extended Reproduction."

61. Of all of the migrant women whom I have talked with in Wanzai, Yudu, Xinfeng, and Shanghai, I have only interviewed four who became managers – and these were all in lower-level supervisory positions except for one (a university graduate who contracted the Duanwu Township Toy Factory, Yudu).

62. This has been the case in all of the villages that I have visited.

63. In Tamara Jacka, *Women's Work in Rural China* (p. 132), the author is similarly informed by rural Chinese males that women are not suited to business because they cannot drink or smoke.

64. For a discussion on the influence of gender on networking in China, see Mayfair Mei-hui Yang, *Gifts, Favors and Banquets,* pp. 78–85, 312–17. The exclusion of women from public spheres of networking has strong parallels with the role of golf courses in the male-dominated business environment of Western nations.

65. Eggs are a source of nutrition to help convalescence.

66. Kellee S. Tsai, "Banquet Banking."

67. Constable, "At Home," p. 223.

68. Also known as "domestic sidelines"; see Tamara Jacka, "The Public/Private Dichotomy and the Gender Division of Rural Labour." Jacka finds that investigating the market and selling heavier goods are tasks carried out by the men. Women sell smaller items at the local market (e.g., chickens and vegetables) but the men sell the pigs because it is thought they are too heavy for women to carry. See also Croll, *From Heaven,* pp. 166–7, 178–9. Croll notes the important role of women in domestic sidelines as well as how, in some instances in richer localities, this income is more than that generated by the man, thereby increasing the status of the woman. However, in Xinfeng and Yudu, the activities of the women are confined to growing crops, raising chickens, and some handicrafts; a few also raise pigs. Ellen Judd argues that women prefer the courtyard economy because they have more freedom in the household than in the male-dominated public domain – for example, in rural industries.

69. Ernestine Friedl, *Women and Men,* pp. 35–7, 134–7; Michelle Rosaldo, "Women, Culture and Society," p. 41.

70. Lydia Kung, *Factory Women in Taiwan,* pp. 7–16; Gates, *China's Motor,* pp. 95–9; Susan Greenhalgh, "Sexual Stratification."

71. Interview, Fei Yangcheng Garment Factory, Xinfeng, 10 June 1997.
72. Thanks to Tim Wright for this point.
73. Interview, Da Tangbu Town Clothing Factory, Xinfeng, 13 June 1997.
74. Nongmin liudong yu xiangcun fazhan keti zu (1999), p. 67.

CHAPTER 7

1. For an urban dimension, see: Dorothy J. Solinger, "China's Transients and the State"; Solinger, *Contesting Citizenship*; Xiang Biao, "Creating a Non-State Space through Migration and Marketized Networks."
2. Research Group of the Yichun Prefecture Agricultural Bank Planning Research Group and Zhangshu City Agricultural Bank Planning and Science Federation, "The impact of labor export on rural financial markets"; interview with Manager of Yudu County Agricultural Bank, 25 October 1997.
3. Interview, Business Service Center, Xinfeng county, 17 June 1997. Originally this interviewee had wanted to set up a plastics factory, but he encountered so many bureaucratic obstacles that he was forced to abandon the plan.
4. Interview, 11 October 1997.
5. Zhang Shanyu and Yang Shaoyong (1996); Nongmin liudong yu xiangcun fazhan keti zu (1999).
6. *Guangdong laodong bao,* 23 June 1997, p. 2; Zhang Shanyu and Yang Shaoyong (1996, p. 46) recommend that local governments curtail incursions on the legal and property rights of returned migrants.
7. Jin Xian (1995), p. 36.
8. Interview, 8 January 1997.
9. Fieldnotes, Yudu Labor Export Company, dock workers in Shanghai, Pudong, 10 August 1997.
10. Fieldnotes, Wanzai, 7 March 1997.
11. Fieldnotes, Yudu, 5 October 1997.
12. Open letter circulated to migrants and those returning for Spring Festival (Yudu County Party Committee, Yudu County People's Government, 18 January 1995).
13. Enyinna Chuta and Carl Liedholm, "Rural Small-Scale Industry," p. 330.
14. There were factories in Yudu – and one in the administrative district of Yichun city (also established by a returnee) – that were unable to recruit sufficient labor.
15. Fieldnotes, Qifeng, Wanzai, 2 January 1997. Initially Mr. Long set up his factory in a room in Qifeng with an investment of 3,000 yuan, which was saved up during his time in the city.
16. Duanwu Township Government (1996).
17. Interview, Xinbei Furniture Factory, Yudu, 19 October 1997.
18. Joint investment, cooperative, and foreign investment enterprises.
19. Interview, Xinfeng Bureau of TVEs, Xinfeng, 9 June 1997.
20. Zhang Shanyu and Yang Shaoyong (1996), p. 46.
21. In the Chinese media there are many articles that credit returnees with introducing new fashions, songs, and consumer trends and with setting up disco halls and music bands in their home town. These actions are said to improve the cultural quality of the rural populace. See Ji Enze, "Phoenixes"; Yang Xiaoyong, "The mobility of migrant workers and the economic development of city and country," pp. 28–9; *Renmin ribao,* 16 April 1997; *Yichun ribao,* 3 May 1997, p. 3.

22. Conversation with women in Dawei village, Daa town, Xinfeng, 19 June 1997.
23. Fieldnotes, Daa town, Xinfeng, 15 June 1997.
24. Elson and Pearson (1984).
25. Zhou Pei (1995).
26. Interview, Huaguang Leather Company, Xinfeng, 8 June 1997.
27. Interview, Yudu Wig and Eyelash Company, 14 October 1997.
28. Douglass North, *Institutions, Institutional Change and Economic Performance,* p. 107, cited in Jean Oi, "The Role of the Local State in China's Transitional Economy," p. 171.
29. Gu Shengzu and Jian Xinhua (1994), p. 5.
30. Chen Hao (1996); Liu Yingjie, "Peasant workers," p. 13.
31. Liu Xinping, "A working life is also magnificent," p. 14; Wailai nongmingong keti zu, "The situation of migrant peasant workers in the Pearl River Delta," p. 103; Zhang Maolin (1996), p. 54.
32. Xin Zhiming, "Healthy Growth of Small Towns Vital."
33. Interviews, October–November 2000.
34. For more on this policy, see Delia Davin, "Never Mind If It's a Girl."

CHAPTER 8

1. Chen Hao (1996), pp. 1–7.
2. Oberai and Singh (1980).
3. Philip Guest, *Labor Allocation and Rural Development,* p. 12.
4. *Zhong wai jingji baokan wenzhai* [Chinese and Overseas Economic Readers' Digest] 20 (1996), p. 7 ("How is surplus rural labor to be transferred?").
5. Fieldnotes, Tuanjie, Wanzai county, 6 September 1997.
6. You Xiaowu, "Not one migrant from Liugongmiao township has committed a crime."
7. "Falu yu daode" [Law and morality], Dongfang dianshitai [Eastern television station], 18.00 hrs, 27 February 1997.
8. Liang Gaochao (1997).
9. Drugs Prevention address by Guo Senjiu, deputy secretary of the county, Xinfeng County Television, 22.10 hrs, 7 June 1997.
10. Yang Shanqing " 'Agricultural blindness' in the Chinese countryside."
11. Piore, *Birds of Passage,* p. 58.
12. When in Yudu (but more so in Wanzai), I availed myself of their services to go between the township and the village.
13. Interview, Tuanjie, 19 March 1997.
14. Thadani, "Social Relations," p. 195.
15. Kabeer, *Reversed Realities,* p. 146.
16. Wang Zehuan, "The behavioral characteristics, direction of mobility, and management of migrant workers," p. 161.
17. "Chao piao, xiang shou ai ni bu rongyi" [Money, wanting to say I love you is not easy], p. 33.
18. Interview, Yudu Labor Export Company, Shanghai, 10 August 1997.
19. Mou Wenjian, "Who will protect the rights of rural peasant workers?"
20. Fieldnotes, Duanwu township, Yudu county, 24 October 1997.
21. *Yichun ribao,* 3 March 1997, p. 1.

22. Informal conversation with a woman from the neighboring mountain village of Guyuan who married into Tuanjie, March 1997.
23. The work permit card is needed in order to be a legal temporary resident in the cities; otherwise, the migrant becomes a "three without" migrant (see Chapter 2).
24. In a township guest room in a county in Jiangxi, a wall calendar (printed by the township family planning office) listed various family planning regulations, some pertaining to migrants.
25. Sen, "Gender."
26. Ibid.; Zhu Jialiang and Wu Minyi, "Comparison of the transition of rural labor in different regions of China."
27. Wu Liangjie, "Love, marriage, and family among the floating population," p. 19.
28. Chen Yingtao, "The attitude of migrant women workers toward love and marriage," p. 44.
29. Zhou Qingfu, "Eighty thousand women of Wanzai become 'key fighters' in escaping poverty and prospering."
30. Interview, Qifeng, 19 January 1997.
31. Interview, Qifeng, 20 January 1997.
32. Interview, Wanzai county seat, March 1997.
33. Interview, Qifeng, 20 January 1997. This woman worked for six months in Nanhai, returned home for Spring Festival, then went to Xiamen.
34. Robert N. Kearney and Barbara Diane Miller, *Internal Migration in Sri Lanka and Its Social Consequences,* pp. 66–7, 84–6.
35. Lijia MacLeod, "The Dying Fields." A study by the World Bank, the World Health Organization, and Harvard University finds that 56.6% of female suicides occur in China, yet only 21% of the world's women live there.
36. Fieldnotes, Qifeng, February 1997. The sense of abandonment felt by women such as Lin is the subject of studies by the Women's Federation as well as reportage literature. See *Funü zhi shengbao,* 14 November 1996, p. 5; Zhang Yong, "Women of rural households holding up half the sky"; Tao Xiaoping, "Wives left on the yellow land"; Gu Chuan, "Peasant migrant workers – don't let your wife's tears soak the front of her garment."
37. Fieldnotes, Qifeng, 8 January 1997.
38. See also *Zhongguo funü bao* [China Women's News], 3 June 1997, p. 3.
39. Ibid.; Lu Bian, "The 'women left behind' in the countryside."
40. *Funü zhi shengbao,* 14 November 1996, p. 5; *Tequ qingnian bao* [Special Zone Youth], 2 May 1997, p. 8.
41. Li Naiqun, "Cases of divorce among migrant workers."
42. Colin Murray, "Migrant Labour and Changing Family Structure in the Rural Periphery of Southern Africa," pp. 150, 156; Nelson, "The Women Who Have Left," p. 135; Hemalata C. Dandekar, *Men to Bombay, Women at Home,* p. 225.
43. See also Gu Chuan (1997), p. 57; Sun Shuqing, "Research on the market economy and population mobility of females," p. 44.
44. Jiangxi Funü Lianhehui (1997).
45. Interview, Tuanjie, 9 March 1997.
46. The objection of returnees to rural latrines is mentioned in Delia Davin, "Migration, Women and Gender Issues in Contemporary China."
47. This occurred in February 1997. One village telephone was finally installed in Qifeng in December 1997. However, by November 2000 there were over a hundred telephones in the village.

48. Interview, Qifeng, 8 January 1997.
49. This observation is based on my long winter evenings of rustication. A line-up might include the national news, county news, a speech by a county leader, information on current agricultural chores, and then a soap opera.
50. The same observation is made in Skinner, "Differential Development."
51. See the discussion on dialect as "a classical experience of mobility" in Raymond Williams, *The Country and the City,* p. 201.

CHAPTER 9

1. Wang Dagao, "The situation of the quality of the rural labor force at the current stage and avenues for its improvement"; Chen Jiyuan, *Zhongguo nongye laodongli zhuanyi* [The Transfer of China's Agricultural Labor], pp. 222–8; Shang Junfeng (1996); Chen Hao (1996).
2. William Hinton, *The Privatization of China*; Kate Xiao Zhou, *How the Farmers Changed China.*

Bibliography

ENGLISH-LANGUAGE PRIMARY MATERIAL

I have consulted numerous English-language media articles dated between January 1995 and December 1997. The three main sources are: *China Daily, Inside China Mainland,* and *Summary of World Broadcasts.*

ENGLISH-LANGUAGE BOOKS AND JOURNAL ARTICLES

Afshar, Haleh (Ed.). *Women, Work and Ideology in the Third World* (London: Tavistock, 1985).

Ahlburg, Dennis A., and Richard P. C. Brown. "Migrants' Intentions to Return Home and Capital Transfers: A Study of Tongans and Samoans in Australia," *Journal of Development Studies* 35 (December 1998): 125–51.

Amin, Samir. "Modern Migrations in Western Africa," in Samir Amin (Ed.), *Modern Migrations in Western Africa* (Oxford University Press, 1974), pp. 65–124.

Athukorala, Premachandra. "International Contract Migration and the Reintegration of Return Migrants: The Experience of Sri Lanka," *International Migration Review* 24 (Summer 1990): 323–6.

Atiur, Rahman. *Peasants and Classes: Peasant Differentiation in Bangladesh* (London: Zed, 1986).

Baily, Adrian J., and Mark Ellis. "Going Home: The Migration of Puerto Rican-born Women from the United States to Puerto Rico," *Professional Geographer* 45 (1993): 148–58.

Bennholdt-Thomsen, Veronnika. "Subsistence Reproduction and Extended Reproduction," in Kate Young, Carol Wolkowitz, and Roslyn McCullagh (Eds.), *Of Marriage and the Market: Women's Subordination Internationally and Its Lessons* (London: Routledge, 1981), pp. 41–54.

Bernal, Victoria. *Cultivating Workers* (Oxford: Columbia University Press, 1991).

Bernstein, Henry. "Agrarian Structures and Change: Latin America," in Henry Bernstein, Ben Crow, and Hazel Johnson (Eds.), *Rural Livelihoods: Crises and Responses* (Oxford University Press, 1992), pp. 27–50.

Bledsoe, Caroline, and Allan Hill. "Social Norms, Natural Fertility and the Resumption of Postpartum 'Contact' in the Gambia," in Alaka Malwade Basu and Peter Aaby (Eds.), *The Methods and Uses of Anthropological Demography* (Oxford: Clarendon Press, 1998), pp. 268–97.

Bovenkerk, Frank. *The Sociology of Return Migration: A Bibliographic Essay* (The Hague: Martinus Nijhoff, 1974).

Breman, Jan. "The Partiality of Fieldwork in Rural India," *Journal of Peasant Studies* 21 (1985): 5–35.

Breman, Jan. "Particularism and Scarcity: Urban Labour Markets and Social Classes," in Hamza Alavi and John Harris (Eds.), *Sociology of Developing Societies: South Asia* (London: Macmillan, 1989), pp. 268–75.

Bromley, Ray. "Circulation with Systems of Periodic and Daily Markets: The Case of Central Highland Ecuador," in Chapman and Prothero (1985), pp. 325–50.

Brown, Lawrence A. *Place, Migration and Development in the Third World: An Alternative View* (London: Routledge, 1991).

Brown, R., and John Connell. "The Global Flea Market: Migration, Remittances and the Informal Economy in Tonga," *Development and Change* 24 (1993): 611–47.

Brydon, Lynne. "Ghanaian Women in the Migration Process," in Chant and Radcliffe (1992), pp. 91–108.

Bull, Ivan, and Gary E. Willard. "Towards a Theory of Entrepreneurship," *Journal of Business Venturing* 8 (May 1993): 189–90.

Butterworth, Douglas. *Latin American Urbanisation* (Cambridge University Press, 1981).

Byrd, William A., and Lin Qingsong. *China's Rural Industry* (Oxford University Press, 1990).

Caces, Fe, Fred Arnold, James T. Fawcett, and Robert W. Gardner. "Shadow Households and Competing Auspices: Migration Behavior in the Philippines," *Journal of Development Economics* 17 (1985): 7–25.

Caldwell, John C., and Pat Caldwell. "The Cultural Context of High Fertility in Sub-Saharan Africa," *Population and Development Review* 13 (September 1987): 409–37.

Cerase, Francesco. "Nostalgia or Disenchantment: Considerations on Return Migration," in H. Bernstein, B. Crow, and H. Johnson (Eds.), *The Italian Experience in the United States* (New York: Center for Migration Studies, 1970), pp. 217–39.

Chaianov, A.V. *A. V. Chayanov on the Theory of Peasant Economy* (Madison: University of Wisconsin Press, 1986).

Chan, Anita, Richard Madsen, and Jonathan Unger. *Chen Village under Deng and Mao* (Oxford: University of California Press, 1992).

Chan, Kam Wing. "Internal Migration in China: A Dualist Approach," in Frank Pieke and Hein Mallee (Eds.), *Internal and International Migration* (Surrey: Curzon, 1999), pp. 49–72.

Chan, Kam Wing and Li Zhang. "The *Hukou* System and Rural–Urban Migration in China: Processes and Changes," *China Quarterly* 160 (December 1999): 818–55.

Chan, Sucheng. "European and Asian Immigration into the United States in Comparative Perspective, 1820s to 1920s," in Virginia Yans-McLaughlin (Ed.), *Immigration Reconsidered: History, Sociology and Politics* (Oxford University Press, 1990), pp. 37–75.

Chang, Kyung-Sup. "The Peasant Family in the Transition from Maoist to Lewisian Rural Industrialization," *Journal of Development Studies* 29 (1993): 220–45.

Chant, Sylvia, and Sarah A. Radcliffe. "Migration and Development: The Importance of Gender," in Chant and Radcliffe (1992), pp. 1–29.

Chant, Sylvia, and Sarah A. Radcliffe (Eds.). *Gender and Migration in Developing Countries* (London: Belhaven, 1992).

Chapman, Murray, and R. Mansell Prothero (Eds.). *Circulation in Population Movement: Substance and Concepts* (London: Routledge, 1985).

Chapman, Murray, and R. Mansell Prothero. "Themes on Circulation in the Third World," in Chapman and Prothero (1985), pp. 1–27.

Cheater, Angela P. *Social Anthropology: An Alternative Introduction* (London: Routledge, 1989).

Choi, Jin Ho. "Urban to Rural Migration in Korea," in C. Goldscheider (Ed.), *Rural Migration in Developing Nations* (London: Westview, 1984), pp. 121–98.

Christiansen, Robert E., and Jonathan G. Kidd. "The Return of Malawian Labor from South Africa and Zimbabwe," *Journal of Modern African Studies* 21(2) (1983): 311–26.

Chuta, Enyinna, and Carl Liedholm. "Rural Small-Scale Industry: Empirical Evidence and Policy Issues," in C. Goldscheider (Ed.), *Agricultural Development in the Third World* (London: John Hopkins University Press, 1984), pp. 327–41.

Cohen, Myron L. "Cultural and Political Inventions in Modern China: The Case of the Chinese 'Peasant'," *Daedalus* 122 (1993): 151–70.

Cohen, Myron L. "Family Management and Family Division in Contemporary Rural China," *China Quarterly* 130 (1992): 357–77.

Cohen, Myron L. *House United, House Divided: The Chinese Family in Taiwan* (London: Columbia University Press, 1976).

Collins, Jane L. "Migration and the Life Cycle of Households in Southern Peru," *Urban Anthropology* 14 (1985): 279–99.

Colton, Nora Ann. "Homeward Bound: Yemeni Return Migration," *International Migration Review* 38 (Winter 1993): 870–82.

Connell, John. "Migration Remittances and Rural Development in the South Pacific," in Jones and Richter (1981), pp. 229–56.

Connell, John, Biplab Dasgupta, Roy Laishley, and Michael Lipton. *Migration from Rural Areas: The Evidence from Village Studies* (Oxford University Press, 1976).

Constable, Nicole. "At Home but Not at Home," *Cultural Anthropology* 14(2) (1999): 203–28.

Cook, Sarah. "Work, Wealth, and Power in Agriculture: Do Political Connections Affect the Returns to Household Labor?" in Walder (1998), pp. 157–83.

Corner, Lorraine. "Linkages, Reciprocity and Remittances: The Impact of Rural Outmigration on Malaysian Rice Villages," in Jones and Richter (1981), pp. 117–33.

Croll, Elisabeth. "The Exchange of Women and Property: Marriage in Post-Revolutionary China," in Renée Hirschon (Ed.), *Women and Property – Women as Property* (London: Croom Helm, 1984), pp. 44–61.

Croll, Elisabeth. *From Heaven to Earth: Images and Experiences of Development in China* (London: Routledge, 1994).

Croll, Elisabeth. "New Peasant Family Forms in Rural China," *Journal of Peasant Studies* 14 (July 1987): 469–99.

Croll, Elisabeth, and Huang Ping. "Migration For and Against Agriculture in Eight Chinese Villages," *China Quarterly* 149 (March 1997): 128–46.

Dandekar, Hemalata C. *Men to Bombay, Women at Home: Urban Influence on Sugao Village, Deccan Maharashtra, 1942–1982* (Ann Arbor: University of Michigan Press, 1986).

Davin, Delia. *Internal Migration in Contemporary China* (New York: St. Martin's, 1999).

Davin, Delia. "Migration, Women and Gender Issues in Contemporary China," in Scharping (1997), pp. 297–314.

Davin, Delia. "Never Mind If It's a Girl, You Can Have Another Try," in Jorgen Del-man, Clemens Ostergaard, and Flemming Christiansen (Eds.), *Remaking Peasant China* (Denmark: Aarhus University Press, 1988), pp. 81–91.

Day, Lincoln, and Ma Xia (Eds.). *Migration and Urbanization in China* (New York: M.E. Sharpe, 1994).

De Haan, Arjan. "Livelihoods and Poverty: The Role of Migration – A Critical Review of the Migration Literature," *Journal of Development Studies* 36 (December 1999): 1–47.

de Janvry, Alan. *The Agrarian Question and Reformism in Latin America* (London: John Hopkins University Press, 1981).

De Jong, Gordon F., and James T. Fawcett. "Motivations for Migration: An Assessment and Value-Expectancy Model," in De Jong and Gardner (1981), pp. 13–57.

De Jong, Gordon F., and Robert W. Gardner. "Introduction and Overview," in De Jong and Gardner (1981), pp. 1–6.

De Jong, Gordon F., and Robert W. Gardner (Eds.). *Migration Decision Making* (Oxford: Pergamon, 1981).

Dei, George J. S. "The Re-integration and Rehabilitation of Migrant Workers into a Local Domestic Economy: Lessons for 'Endogenous' Development," *Human Organization* 50(4) (1991): 327–35.

Deng Shulin. "Sounding the Alarm on Population Growth," *China Reconstructs* (July 1989): 30–3.

Dreyer, June Teufel. *China's Political System: Modernization and Tradition* (London: Macmillan, 1993).

Duncan, James S. "From Container of Women to Status Symbol: The Impact of Social Structure on the Meaning of the House," in James S. Duncan (Ed.), *Housing and Identity* (London: Croom Helm, 1981), pp. 36–59.

Durand, Jorge, and Douglas S. Massey, "Mexican Migration to the United States: A Critical Review," *Latin American Research Review* 27 (1992): 3–42.

Dutton, Michael R. *Policing and Punishment in China* (Cambridge University Press, 1992).

Ellis, Frank. "Household Strategies and Rural Livelihood Diversification," *Journal of Development Studies* 35 (1998): 1–38.

Elson, Diane, and Ruth Pearson. "The Subordination of Women and the International-isation of Factory Production," in Kate Young, Carol Wolkowitz, and Roslyn Mc-Cullagh (Eds.), *Of Marriage and the Market* (London: Routledge, 1984), pp. 23–7.

Fadayomi, T. O., S. O. Titilola, B. Oni, and O. J. Fapohunda. "Migrations and Development Policies in Nigeria," in Moriba Toure and T. O. Fadoyomi (Eds.), *Migrations, Development and Urbanization Policies in Sub-Saharan Africa* (London: Codesria, 1992), pp. 51–111.

Fei, J., and Gustav Ranis. *Development of the Surplus Labor Economy* (Homewood, IL: Irwin, 1964).

Feng Chongyi, "Jiangxi in Reform: The Fear of Exclusion and the Search for a New Identity," in Hans Hendrischke and Feng Chongyi (Eds.), *The Political Economy of China's Provinces* (London: Routledge, 1999), pp. 249–76.

Findlay, A. M., and F. L. N. Li, "An Autobiographical Approach to Understanding Migration: The Case of Hong Kong Emigrants," *Area* 29(1) (1997): 34–44.

Findlay, Christopher, Andrew Watson, and Harry X. Wu (Eds.). *Rural Enterprises in China* (London: Macmillan, 1994).

Findley, Sally. *Rural Development and Migration: A Study of Family Choices in the Philippines* (Boulder, CO: Westview, 1987).

Flemming, Christiansen. *The De-rustification of the Chinese Peasant?: Peasant Household Reactions to the Rural Reforms in China since 1978* (Leiden University, 1990).

Food and Agriculture Organization, United Nations. "Migration and Rural Development," in *Population Distribution, Migration and Development. Proceedings of the Expert Group on Population Distribution, Migration and Development. Hammamet (Tunisia), 21–25 March 1983* (New York: United Nations, 1984), pp. 193–208.

Franks, Penelope. "From Peasant to Entrepreneur in Italy and Japan," *Journal of Peasant Studies* 22 (July 1995): 699–709.

Friedl, Ernestine. *Women and Men: An Anthropologist's View* (New York: Holt, Rinehart & Winston, 1975).

Galbraith, John Kenneth. *The Nature of Mass Poverty* (Harmondsworth: Penguin, 1980).

Gardner, Katy. *Global Migrants, Local Lives: Travel and Transformation in Rural Bangladesh* (Oxford: Clarendon Press, 1995).

Gates, Hill. *China's Motor: A Thousand Years of Petty Capitalism* (London: Cornell University Press, 1996).

Giddens, Anthony. "Structuration Theory and Sociological Analysis," in J. Clarke, C. Modgil, and S. Modgil (Eds.), *Anthony Giddens: Consensus and Controversy* (New York: Palmer, 1990), pp. 297–315.

Gmelch, G. "Return Migration," *Annual Review of Anthropology* 9 (1980): 135–59.

Goldscheider, Calvin. "Migration and Social Structure: Analytic Issues and Comparative Perspectives in Developing Nations," *Sociological Forum* 2 (1987): 674–96.

Goldstein, Alice, and Sidney Goldstein. "Migration in China: Methodological and Policy Challenges," *Social Science History* 11 (1987): 85–104.

Goldstein Sidney, and Alice Goldstein. "Migration Motivations and Out-Comes: Permanent and Temporary Migrants Compared," in Alice Goldstein and Wang Feng (Eds.), *China: The Many Facets of Demographic Change* (Boulder, CO: Westview, 1996), pp. 187–212.

Goodman, Bryna. *Native Place, City and Nation: Regional Networks and Identities in Shanghai* (Berkeley: University of California Press, 1995).

Goss, Jon, and Bruce Lindquist. "Conceptualizing International Labor Migration: A Structuration Perspective," *International Migration Review* 29(2) (1995): 317–51.

Gottschang, Thomas R., and Diana Lary. *Swallows and Settlers: The Great Migration from North China to Manchuria* (Ann Arbor: University of Michigan Press, 2000).

Gould, W. T. S. "Education and Internal Migration: A Review and Report," *International Journal of Educational Development* 1 (1982): 103–12.

Greenhalgh, Susan. "Intergenerational Contracts: Familial Roots of Sexual Stratification in Taiwan," in Daisy Dwyer and Judith Bruce (Eds.), *A Home Divided: Women and Income in the Third World* (Stanford, CA: Stanford University Press, 1988), pp. 30–70.

Greenhalgh, Susan. "Sexual Stratification: The Other Side of Growth Equity in East Asia," *Population and Development Review* 11 (1985): 265–314.

Gu Shengzu. "Ideas and Policies for Solving the Problem of Surplus Rural Labor in China," *Social Sciences in China* (Winter 1995): 20–8.

Guest, Philip. *Labor Allocation and Rural Development: Migration in Four Javanese Villages* (Boulder, CO: Westview, 1989).

Guilmoto, Christophe Z. "Institutions and Migrations: Short-term versus Long-term Moves in Rural West Africa," *Population Studies* 52(1) (1998): 85–103.

Gulger, Josef. "Migrating to Urban Centres of Unemployment in Tropical Africa," in Anthony H. Richmond and Daniel Kubat (Eds.), *Internal Migration: The New World and the Third World* (London: Sage, 1976), pp. 184–204.

Gulger, Josef. "The Urban–Rural Interface and Migration," in A. Gilbert and J. Gulger (Eds.), *Cities, Poverty and Development: Urbanisation in the Third World* (Oxford University Press, 1992), pp. 62–79.

Gutting, Daniel. "Narrative Identity and Residential History," *Area* 28(4) (1996): 482–90.

Halfacree, Keith H., and Paul J. Boyle. "The Challenge Facing Migration Research: The Case For a Biographical Approach," *Progress in Human Geography* 17(3) (1993): 333–48.

Hare, Denise. " 'Push' versus 'Pull' Factors in Migration Outflows and Returns: Determinants of Migration Status and Spell Duration among China's Rural Population," *Journal of Development Studies* 35 (February 1999): 45–72.

Harrell, Stevan. "Why Do the Chinese Work So Hard? Reflections on an Entrepreneurial Ethic," *Modern China* 11 (1985): 203–25.

Harris, John, and Michael Todaro. "Migration, Unemployment and Development: A Two-Sector Analysis," *American Economic Review* 60 (1970): 126–42.

"Healthy Growth of Small Towns Vital," ⟨http://chinadaily.com.cn/cndydb/2000/11/d4-1town.b27.html⟩ (downloaded 31 April 2001).

Hershfield, Allan F., Niels G. Rohling, Graham B. Kerr, and Gerald Hursh-César. "Fieldwork in Rural Areas," in Martin Bulmer and Donald P. Warwick (Eds.), *Social Research in Developing Countries* (Chichester: Wiley, 1983), pp. 241–71.

Heyman, Josiah. "Changes in House Construction Materials in Border Mexico: Four Research Propositions about Commoditization," *Human Organization* 53 (1994): 132–42.

Hinton, William. *The Privatization of China: The Great Reversal* (London: Earthscan, 1991).

House, W. J., and H. Rempel. "The Determinants of Interregional Migration in Kenya," *World Development* 8 (1980): 25–35.

Hugo, Graeme J. "Circular Migration in Indonesia," *Population and Development Review* 8 (1982): 59–83.

Hugo, Graeme J. "Circulation in West Java, Indonesia," in Chapman and Prothero (1985), pp. 75–99.

Hugo, Graeme J. *Population Mobility in West Java* (Yogyagarta: Gadjah Mada University Press, 1978).

Hugo, Graeme J. "Road Transport, Population Mobility and Development in Indonesia," in Jones and Richter (1981), pp. 335–86.

Hugo, Graeme J. "Structural Change and Labour Mobility in Rural Java," in Standing (1985), pp. 46–88.

Hugo, Graeme J. "Village–Community Ties, Village Norms, and Ethnic and Social Networks: A Review of Evidence from the Third World," in De Jong and Gardner (1981), pp. 186–222.

Hussain, Karim, and John Nelson. "Sustainable Livelihoods and Livelihood Diversification," IDS Working Paper no. 69 (May 1998), Sussex, U.K.

Jacka, Tamara. "My Life as a Migrant Worker: Women in Rural–Urban Migration in Contemporary China," *Intersections* 4 (September 2000), ⟨www://sshe.murdoch.edu.au/intersections⟩.

Jacka, Tamara. "The Public/Private Dichotomy and the Gender Division of Rural Labour," in Andrew Watson (Ed.), *Economic Reform and Social Change in China* (London: Routledge, 1992), pp. 128–32.

Jacka, Tamara. *Women's Work in Rural China* (Cambridge University Press, 1997).

Jazairy, Idriss, Mohiuddin Alamgir, and Theresa Panuccio. *The State of World Rural Poverty* (London: International Fund for Agricultural Development, 1992).

Jeffery, Roger, and Patricia Jeffery. *Population, Gender and Politics* (Cambridge University Press, 1997).

Johnson, Graham E. "Open for Business to the World: Consequences of Global Incorporation in Guangdong and the Pearl Delta," in Thomas P. Lyons and Victor Nee (Eds.), *The Economic Transformation of South China: Reform and Development in the Post-Mao Era* (Ithaca, NY: East Asia Program, Cornell University, 1994), pp. 55–88.

Jones, G. W., and H. V. Richter (Eds.). *Population Mobility and Development: South-east Asia and the Pacific* (Canberra: Development Studies Centre, Australian National University, 1981).

Judd, Ellen R. *Gender and Power in Rural North China* (Stanford, CA: Stanford University Press, 1994).

Kabeer, Naila. *Reversed Realities: Gender Hierarchies in Gender and Development Thought* (London: Verso, 1994).

Kadioglu, Ayse. "Migration Experiences of Turkish Women: Notes from a Researcher's Diary," *International Migration* 35(4) (1997): 537–57.

Kearney, Michael. "From the Invisible Hand to Visible Feet: Anthropological Studies of Migration and Development," *Annual Review of Anthropology* 15 (1986): 331–61.

Kearney, Robert N., and Barbara Diane Miller. *Internal Migration in Sri Lanka and Its Social Consequences* (London: Westview, 1987).

Kelliher, Daniel. "Chinese Communist Political Theory and the Rediscovery of the Peasantry," *Modern China* 20 (1994): 387–411.

King, Russell. "Return Migration: A Neglected Aspect of Population Geography," *Area* 10 (1978): 175–82.

King, Russell. "Return Migration: A Review of Some Case Studies from Southern Europe," *Mediterranean Studies* 1 (1979): 3–30.

King, Russell. *Return Migration and Regional Economic Problems* (London: Croom Helm, 1985).

King, Russell, Jill Mortimer, and Alan Strachan. "Return Migration and Tertiary Development: A Calabrian Case Study," *Anthropological Quarterly* 57 (1984): 112–23.

Kols, Adrienne. *Migration, Population Growth and Development* (Baltimore: John Hopkins University Press, 1983).

Kubat, Daniel, and Hans-Joachim Hoffmann-Nowotny. "Migration: Towards a New Paradigm," *International Social Science Journal* 33(2) (1981): 307–29.

Kung, Lydia. *Factory Women in Taiwan* (Essex: Bowker, 1983).

Laite, Julian. "Circulatory Migration and Social Differentiation in the Andes," in Standing (1985), pp. 89–119.

Lauby, Jennifer, and Oded Stark. "Individual Migration as a Family Strategy: Young Women in the Philippines," *Population Studies* 42 (November 1988): 473–86.

Lee, E. S. "A Theory of Migration," *Demography* 3(1) (1966): 47–57.

Leong, Sow-Theng. *Migration and Ethnicity in Chinese History: Hakkas, Pengmin, and their Neighbors,* edited by Tim Wright (Stanford, CA: Stanford University Press, 1997).

Lever-Tracy, Constance. "Return Migration to Malta: Neither Failed Immigrants nor Successful Guestworkers," *Australia and New Zealand Journal of Sociology* 25(3) (1989): 428–50.

Lewis, W. Arthur. "Economic Development with Unlimited Supplies of Labour," in A. N. Agarwala and S. P. Singh (Eds.), *The Economics of Underdevelopment* (Oxford University Press, 1958), pp. 400–49.

Lin Yousu and Lincoln H. Day. "The Economic Adjustments of Migrants in Urban Areas," in Day and Xia (1994), pp. 164–5.

Lin Yueh-hwa. *The Golden Wing: A Sociological Study of Chinese Familism* (London: Routledge, 1998).

Lipton, Michael. "Migration from Rural Areas of Poor Countries: The Impact on Rural Productivity and Income Distribution," *World Development* 8 (1980): 1–24.

Lucas, Robert E. B., and Oded Stark. "Motivations to Remit: Evidence from Botswana," *Journal of Political Economy* 93 (1985): 901–18.

MacLeod, Lijia. "The Dying Fields," *Far Eastern Economic Review* (23 April 1998): 62–3.

Mallee, Hein. "China's Household Registration System under Reform," *Development and Change* 26 (1995): 1–29.

Mallee, Hein. "In Defense of Migration: Recent Chinese Studies on Rural Population Mobility," *China Information* 10 (1996): 108–40.

Mallee, Hein. "Rural Household Dynamics and Spatial Mobility in China," in Scharping (1997), pp. 264–77.

Mann, Susan. "Grooming a Daughter for Marriage: Brides and Wives in the Mid-Ch'ing Period," in Watson and Ebrey (1991), pp. 204–30.

Massey, Douglas S., Rafael Alarcón, Jorge Durand, and Humberto González. *Return to Aztlan: The Social Process of International Migration from Western Mexico* (Berkeley: University California Press, 1987).

Maude, A. "Population Mobility and Rural Households in North Kelantan, Malaysia," in Jones and Richter (1981), pp. 93–116.

McKinley, Terry. *The Distribution of Wealth in Rural China* (London: M.E. Sharpe, 1996).

Meng Xianfan. "Chinese Rural Women in the Transfer of the Rural Labor Force," *Social Sciences in China* (Spring 1994): 109–18.

Mills, Mary Beth. "Contesting the Margins of Modernity: Women, Migration and Consumption in Thailand," *American Ethnologist* 24 (1997): 37–61.

Miracle, M. P., and S. S. Berry. "Migrant Labour and Economic Development," *Oxford Economic Papers* 22 (1970): 86–108.

Mitchell, Clyde J. "Towards a Situational Sociology of Wage–Labour Circulation," in Chapman and Prothero (1985), pp. 30–53.

Momsen, Janet H. "Gender Selectivity in Caribbean Migration," in Chant and Radcliffe (1992), pp. 73–90.

Momsen, Janet H. "Migration and Rural Development in the Caribbean," *Tijdschrift voor Economische en Sociale Geografie* 77 (1986): 50–8.

Murphy, Rachel. "A Dependent Private Sector: No Prospects For Civil Society in China," Working Paper no. 62 (Asia Research Centre, Murdoch University, Perth, April 1996).

Murphy, Rachel. "The Impact of Labour Migration on the Well-Being and Agency of Rural Chinese Women," in Tamara Jacka and Adrienne Gaetano (Eds.), *On the*

Move: Women in Rural–Urban Migration in Contemporary China (New York: Columbia University Press, forthcoming).

Murray, Colin. "Migrant Labour and Changing Family Structure in the Rural Periphery of Southern Africa," *Journal of Southern African Studies* 6 (1980): 139–56.

Nabi, Ijaz. "Village-end Considerations in Rural–Urban Migration," *Journal of Development Economics* 14 (1984): 129–45.

National Migration Survey of Thailand (Nakonpathom, Thailand: Institute for Population and Social Research, Mahidol University, 1995).

Nee, Victor. "Social Inequalities in Reforming State Socialism: Between Redistribution and Markets in China," *American Sociological Review* 56 (1991): 267–82.

Nelson, Joan M. *Access to Power: Politics and the Urban Poor in Developing Nations* (Princeton, NJ: Princeton University Press, 1979).

Nelson, Joan M. "Sojourners versus New Urbanites: Causes and Consequences of Temporary versus Permanent Cityward Migration in Developing Countries," *Economic Development and Cultural Change* 24 (1976): 721–59.

Nelson, Nici. "The Women Who Have Left and Those Who Have Stayed Behind: Rural–Urban Migration in Central and Western Kenya," in Chant and Radcliffe (1992), pp. 109–38.

Nolan, Peter. "Economic Reform, Poverty and Migration in China," *Economic and Political Weekly* 28 (1993): 1369–77.

Nolan, Peter. *The Political Economy of Collective Farms: An Analysis of China's Post-Mao Rural Reforms* (Cambridge: Polity, 1988).

North, Douglass. *Institutions, Institutional Change and Economic Performance* (Cambridge University Press, 1990).

Oberai, A. S., P. H. Pradash, and M. G. Sardana. *Determinants and Consequences of Internal Migration in India* (Delhi: Oxford University Press, 1989).

Oberai, A., and H. Singh. "Migration, Remittances and Rural Development: Findings of a Case Study in the Indian Punjab," *International Labour Review* 119 (1980): 229–41.

O'Connor, A. *The African City* (London: Hutchinson, 1983).

Ogawa, Naohiro, Gavin W. Jones, and Jeffrey G. Williamson. "Introduction," in *Human Resources in Development along the Asia-Pacific Rim* (Oxford University Press, 1993), pp. 1–17.

Oi, Jean. "The Evolution of Local State Corporatism," in Walder (1998), pp. 35–61.

Oi, Jean. "Fiscal Reform and the Economic Foundations of Local State Corporatism," *World Politics* 45 (1992): 99–126.

Oi, Jean. "The Role of the Local State in China's Transitional Economy," in Andrew G. Walder (Ed.), *China's Transitional Economy* (Oxford University Press, 1996), pp. 170–87.

Oi, Jean. *State and Peasant in Contemporary China: The Political Economy of Village Government* (Berkeley: University of California Press, 1989).

Orlove, Benjamin S., and Henry J. Rutz. "Thinking about Consumption: A Social Economy Approach" in Rutz and Orlove (1989), pp. 1–83.

Paerregaard, K. *Linking Separate Worlds: Urban Migrants and Rural Lives in Peru* (Oxford: Berg, 1997).

Palmer, Michael. "The Re-emergence of Family Law in Post-Mao China: Marriage, Divorce and Reproduction," *China Quarterly* 141 (1995): 110–34.

Parish, William L., and Martin King Whyte. *Village and Family in Contemporary China* (University of Chicago Press, 1978).

Parnwell, Mike. *Population Movements and the Third World* (London: Routledge, 1993).

Pearson, Ruth. "Gender Matters in Development," in Tim Allen and Alan Thomas (Eds.), *Poverty and Development in the 1990s* (Oxford University Press & Open University, 1992), pp. 597–613.

Pieke, Frank, and Hein Mallee (Eds.). *Internal and International Migration* (Surrey: Curzon, 1999).

Piore, Michael J. *Birds of Passage* (Cambridge University Press, 1979).

Potts, Deborah. "Shall We Go Home? Increasing Urban Poverty in African Cities and Migration Processes," *Geographical Journal* 161 (November 1995): 245–64.

Putterman, Louis. *Continuity and Change in China's Rural Development: Collective and Reform Eras in Perspective* (Oxford University Press, 1993).

Reichert, Christoph. "Labor Migration and Rural Development in Egypt: A Study of Return Migration in Six Villages," *Sociologica Ruralis* 33 (1993): 42–60.

Reis, Manuela, and Joaquim Gil Nave. "Emigrating Peasants and Returning Emigrants: Emigration with Return in a Portuguese Village," *Rural Sociology* 26(1) (1986): 20–35.

Rempel, Henry, and Richard A. Lobdell. "The Role of Urban–Rural Remittances in Rural Development," *Journal of Development Studies* 14 (1978): 324–42.

Rhoades, Robert. "The Evolution of a Migratory System," *American Ethnologist* 5 (1978): 553–73.

Rhoades, Robert. "Intra-European Migration and Rural Development: Lessons from the Spanish Case," *Human Organization* 32 (1976): 136–47.

Rhoda, R. "Rural Development and Urban Migration: Can We Keep Them Down on the Farm?" *International Migration Review* 17 (1983): 34–64.

Robben, Antonius C. G. M. "Entrepreneurs and Scale: Interactional and Institutional Constraints on the Growth of Small Scale Enterprises in Brazil," *Anthropological Quarterly* 53 (1984): 125–38.

Roberts, Kenneth D. "China's Tidal Wave of Migrant Labor: What Can We Learn from Mexican Undocumented Migration to the United States?" *International Migration Review* 31 (Summer 1997): 249–93.

Rogers, Rosemarie. "Incentives to Return: Patterns of Policies and Migrants' Responses," in M. M. Kritz (Ed.), *Global Trends in Migration: Theory and Research on International Population Movements* (New York: Center for Migration Studies, 1981), pp. 338–64.

Rosaldo, Michelle. "Women, Culture and Society: A Theoretical Overview," in Michelle Rosaldo and Louise Lamphere (Eds.), *Women, Culture and Society* (Stanford, CA: Stanford University Press, 1974).

Ross, Marc Howard, and Thomas S. Weisner. "The Rural–Urban Migrant Network in Kenya: Some General Implications," *American Ethnologist* 4 (1979): 359–75.

Rowe, William T. *Hankow: Commerce and Society in a Chinese City, 1796–1889* (Stanford, CA: Stanford University Press, 1984).

Rozelle, Scott, Li Guo, Mingao Shen, Amelia Hughart, and John Giles, "Leaving China's Farms: Survey Results of New Paths and Remaining Hurdles to Rural Migration," *China Quarterly* 158 (1999): 367–93.

Rutz, Henry J., and Benjamin S. Orlove (Eds.). *The Social Economy of Consumption* (Lanham, MD: University Press of America, 1989).

Sabot, R. H. (Ed.). *Migration and the Labor Market in Developing Countries* (Boulder, CO: Westview, 1982).

Sage, Gary. "Entrepreneurship as an Economic Development Strategy," *Economic Development Review* 11 (1993): 65–7.

Salaff, Janet W. *Working Daughters of Hong Kong: Filial Piety or Power in the Family* (Cambridge University Press, 1981).

Sargeson, Sally. *Reworking China's Proletariat* (Basingstoke: Macmillan, 1999).

Scharping, Thomas (Ed.). *Floating Population and Migration in China* (Hamburg: Mitteilung des Instituts für Asienkunde, 1997).

Sen, Amartya. "Gender and Cooperative Conflicts," in Irene Tinker (Ed.), *Persistent Inequalities: Women and World Development* (Oxford University Press, 1991), pp. 123–49.

Sen, Amartya. *Inequality Re-examined* (Oxford: Clarendon Press, 1992).

Sen, Amartya. "Poor, Relatively Speaking," *Oxford Economic Papers* 35 (1983): 153–69.

Shrestha, Nanda R. "A Structural Perspective on Labor Migration in Underdeveloped Countries," *Progress in Human Geography* 12 (1988): 179–207.

Shue, Vivienne. "The Fate of the Commune," *Modern China* 10 (1984): 259–83.

Shultz, Theodore W. "Investing in People," in Carl K. Eicher and John M. Staaz (Eds.), *Agricultural Development in the Third World* (London: Johns Hopkins University Press, 1990), pp. 280–9.

Si Nan. "City-bound Workers Cannot Be Ignored," *China Daily,* 6 March 1997, p. 4.

Simmons, Alan. B. "Migration and Rural Development: Conceptual Approaches, Research Findings and Policy Issues," in *Population Distribution, Migration and Development. Proceedings of the Expert Group on Population Distribution, Migration and Development. Hammamet (Tunisia), 21–25 March 1983* (New York: United Nations, 1984), pp. 156–83.

Siu, Helen F. "Reconstituting Dowry and Bride-price in South China," in Deborah Davis and Stevan Harrell (Eds.), *Chinese Families in the Post-Mao Era* (Berkeley: University of California Press, 1993), pp. 165–88.

Siu, Helen F. "Recycling Rituals: Politics and Popular Culture in Contemporary China," in Perry Link, Richard Madsen, and Paul G. Pickowicz (Eds.), *Unofficial China: Popular Culture and Thought in the People's Republic* (Boulder, CO: Westview, 1989), pp. 121–35.

Skeldon, Ronald. *Migration and Development: A Global Perspective* (Harlow: Longman, 1997).

Skeldon, Ronald. *Population Mobility in Developing Countries* (London: Belhaven, 1990).

Skinner, William G. "Differential Development in Lingnan," in Thomas P. Lyons and Victor Nee (Eds.), *The Economic Transformation of South China: Reform and Development in the Post-Mao Era* (Ithaca, NY: East Asia Program, Cornell University, 1994), pp. 17–54.

Skinner, William G. "Introduction," in Leong (1997), pp. 1–18.

Skinner, William G. "Marketing and Social Structure in Rural China, Part 1," *Journal of Asian Studies* 24(1) (1964): 3–43.

Skinner, William G. "Marketing and Social Structure in Rural China, Part 2," *Journal of Asian Studies* 24(2) (1965): 195–228.

Solinger, Dorothy J. "China's Transients and the State: A Form of Civil Society?" *Politics and Society* 20 (1993): 91–122.

Solinger, Dorothy J. *Contesting Citizenship in Urban China: Peasant Migrants, the State and the Logic of the Market* (Berkeley: University of California Press, 1999).

Song Linfei. "The Flood of Migrant Job-Seekers to Urban Areas: Its Formation, Trends and Countermeasures," *Social Sciences in China* 1 (1997): 170–6.

Standing, Guy. "Circulation and the Labour Process," in Standing (1985), pp. 1–45.

Standing, Guy (Ed.). *Labour Circulation and the Labour Process* (London: Croom Helm, 1985).

Stark, Oded. "Migration Decision-Making: A Review Essay," *Journal of Development Economics* 14 (1984): 251–9.

Stark, Oded. "Migration Incentives and Migration Types – The Role of Relative Deprivation," *Economic Journal* 101 (1991): 1163–78.

Stark, Oded. "Rural to Urban Migration in LDCs – A Relative Deprivation Approach," *Economic Development and Cultural Change* 32 (1984): 475–86.

Stark, Oded, and David Levhari. "On Migration and Risk in LDCs," *Economic Development and Cultural Change* 31 (1982): 192–6.

Stark, Oded and Robert E. B. Lucas. "Migration, Remittances and the Family," *Economic Development and Cultural Change* 36 (April 1988): 465–82.

Taubman, Wolfgang. "The Finance System and the Development of Small Towns in Rural China," in Flemming Christiansen and Zhang Junzuo (Eds.), *Village Inc: Chinese Rural Society in the 1990s* (Surrey: Curzon, 1998).

Thadani, Veena. "Social Relations and Geographic Mobility: Male and Female Migration in Kenya," in Standing (1985), pp. 182–218.

Thadani, Veena, and Michael Todaro. "Female Migration: A Conceptual Framework," in James Fawcett, Siew-Ean Khoo, and Peter C. Smith (Eds.), *Women in the Cities of Asia: Migration and Urban Adaptation* (Boulder, CO: Westview, 1984), pp. 36–59.

Thomas, Philip. "Conspicuous Construction: Houses, Consumption and 'Relocalization' in Manambondro, Southeast Madagascar," *Journal of the Royal Institute of Anthropology* 4 (1998): 425–46.

Tigges, Leann M., and Gary P. Green. "Small Business Success Among Men- and Women-Owned Firms in Rural Areas," *Rural Sociology* 59 (1994): 289–304.

Todaro, Michael. "Income Expectations, Rural–Urban Migration and Employment in Africa," *International Labour Review* 104 (1971): 387–413.

Todaro, Michael. "A Model of Labor Migration and Urban Unemployment in Less Developed Countries," *American Economic Review* 59 (1969): 138–48.

Tsai, Kellee S. "Banquet Banking: Gender and Rotating Savings and Credit Associations in South China," *China Quarterly* 115 (Summer 2000): 201–25.

Tsuda, Takeyuki. "The Permanence of 'Temporary' Migration: The 'Structural Embeddedness' of Japanese-Brazilian Immigrant Workers in Japan," *Journal of Asian Studies* 58 (August 1999): 687–722.

Ulack, Richard. "Ties to Origin, Remittances, and Mobility: Evidence from Rural and Urban Areas in the Philippines," *Journal of Developing Areas* 20 (1986): 339–56.

Unger, Jonathan. "Rich Man, Poor Man: The Making of New Classes in the Countryside," in David S. G. Goodman and Beverley Hooper (Eds.), *China's Quiet Revolution: New Interactions between State and Society* (New York: Longman Cheshire, 1994), pp. 43–63.

Unwin, Tim. "Urban–Rural Interaction in Developing Countries: A Theoretical Perspective," in Robert B. Potter and Tim Unwin (Eds.), *The Geography of Urban–Rural Interaction in Developing Countries* (London: Routledge, 1989), pp. 11–32.

Van Amersfoort, J. M. M. "Migrant Workers, Circulation and Development," *Tijdschrift voor Economische en Sociale Geografie* 69 (1978): 17–26.

Van Hear, Nicholas. "The Impact of the Involuntary Mass 'Return' to Jordan in the Wake of the Gulf Crisis," *International Migration Review* 29 (Summer 1995): 352–74.

Walder, Andrew W. (Ed.). *Zouping in Transition* (Cambridge, MA: Harvard University Press, 1998).

Watson, Rubie. "Afterword: Marriage and Gender Inequality," in Watson and Ebrey (1991), pp. 347–65.

Watson, Rubie, and Patricia Buckley Ebrey (Eds.). *Marriage and Inequality in Chinese Society* (Berkeley: University of California Press, 1991).

Wei, Yehua Dennis. *Regional Development in China* (London: Routledge, 2000).

Weisner, Thomas S. "The Structure of Sociability: Urban Migration and Urban–Rural Ties in Kenya," *Urban Anthropology* 5 (1976): 199–225.

Wilk, Richard R. "Houses as Consumer Goods: Social Processes and Allocation Decisions," in Rutz and Orlove (1989), pp. 297–321.

Williams, Raymond. *The Country and the City* (London: Hogarth, 1985).

Wilson, Scott. "The Cash Nexus and Social Networks: Mutual Aid and Gifts in Contemporary Shanghai Villages," *China Journal* 37 (January 1997): 91–112.

Wolpert, J. "Behavioural Aspects of the Decision to Migrate," *Papers, Regional Science Association* 15 (1965): 159–72.

Wong, Christine P. W. "Fiscal Reform and Local Industrialization: The Problems of Sequencing Reform in Post-Mao China," *Modern China* 18 (1992): 197–227.

Wood, C. W. "Equilibrium and Historical-Structural Perspectives on Migration," *International Migration Review* 16 (1982): 298–319.

Woon, Yuen-Fong. "Circulatory Mobility in Post-Mao China: Temporary Migrants in Kaiping County, Pearl River Delta Region," *International Migration Review* 27 (1993): 578–604.

Woon, Yuen-Fong. "International Links and the Socio-economic Development of Rural China," *Modern China* 16 (1990): 139–66.

Woon, Yuen-Fong. "Labor Migration in the 1990s: Homeward Orientation of Migrants in the Pearl Delta Region and Its Implications for Interior China," *Modern China* 25 (October 1999): 475–512.

Woon, Yuen-Fong. "The Voluntary Sojourner among the Overseas Chinese: Myth or Reality," *Pacific Affairs* 56 (Winter 1983/84): 673–90.

"Workers Return from Coast to Invest in Inland Towns," *China Daily Business Weekly* (supplement), 16 June 1997, p. 5.

World Bank Report: Poverty in China (New York: World Bank, 1990).

Wright, Caroline. "Gender Awareness in Migration Theory: Synthesizing Actor and Structure in Southern Africa," *Development and Change* 26 (1995): 771–91.

Xiang Biao. "Creating a Non-State Space through Migration and Marketized Networks," in Pieke and Mallee (1999), pp. 215–50.

Xin Zhiming. "Healthy Growth of Small Towns Vital," *China Daily,* 27 November 2000.

Yan, Yunxiang. *The Flow of Gifts: Reciprocity and Social Networks in a Chinese Village* (Stanford, CA: Stanford University Press, 1996).

Yang, Mayfair Mei-hui. *Gifts, Favors and Banquets: The Art of Social Relationships in China* (London: Cornell University Press, 1994).

Yang, Xiushi. "Household Registration, Economic Reform and Migration," *International Migration Review* 27 (1993): 796–818.

Zhang, Heather Xiaoquan. "Female Migration and Urban Labor Markets in Tianjin," *Development and Change* 30 (1999): 21–41.

Zhao, Y. H. "Labor Migration and Returns to Rural Education in China," *American Journal of Agricultural Economics* 4 (1997): 1278–87.

Zheng Ying, "Migrants Help, So Help Migrants," *China Daily,* 2 November 2000, ⟨http://www.chinadaily.com.cn⟩.

Zhou, Kate Xiao. *How the Farmers Changed China* (Boulder, CO: Westview, 1996).

Zweig, David. *Freeing China's Farmers: Rural Restructuring in the Reform Era* (London: M.E. Sharpe, 1997).

CHINESE NEWSPAPERS

I have consulted a vast number of newspaper articles between October 1995 and December 1997. The newspapers that I have consulted most frequently are:

Funü zhi sheng bao	Voice of Women News (Jiangxi Women's Federation)
Jiangxi qingnian bao	Jiangxi Youth News
Jiangxi ribao	Jiangxi Daily
Renmin ribao	People's Daily
Xiangzhen bao	Township News (Ganzhou prefecture)
Xinmin wanbao	Xinmin Evening News (Shanghai)
Yichun ribao	Yichun Daily

Other periodicals cited in the Bibliography include the following:

Banyue tan	Bi-monthly Discussion
Chushe zhi chu	Start in Life
Dangdai qingnian	Modern Youth
Duzhe	Readers
Foshan wenyi	Foshan Literature
Funü yanjiu	Research on Women
Funü yanjiu lunzong	Journal of Women's Studies
Gaige	Reform
Gaige yu lilun	Reform and Theory
Guangdong laodong bao	Guangdong Labor News
Huangjin shidai	Golden Age
Hunyin jiating yanjiu	Research on Marriage and Family
Hunyin yu jiating	Marriage and Family
Jiangxi huabao	Jiangxi Pictorial
Jiangxi jianshe	Jiangxi Construction
Jiangxi laodong	Jiangxi Labor
Jiangxi qingnian luntan	Jiangxi Youth Tribune
Jiangxi shehui kexue	Jiangxi Social Science
Jiangxi zhengbao	Jiangxi Government Report
Jiating yu shenghuo	Family and Life
Jingji canzheng bao	Economic Information Daily
Jingji wenti	Economic Problems
Jingji yanjiu	Economic Research
Liaowang zhoukan	Outlook Weekly
Meizhou wenzhai	Weekly Digest
Nanfang renkou	Southern Population
Nanjing shehui kexue	Nanjing Social Science
Nongcun jingji	Rural Economy
Nongcun jingji daokan	Guide to the Rural Economy

Nongcun jingji guancha	Rural Economic Survey
Nongcun shehui jingji xue kan	Journal of Rural Society and Economic Study
Nongmin wenzhai	Farmer's Digest
Nongye jingji wenti	Problems of the Agricultural Economy
Nongyou bao	Farmers' News
Renkou xue	Demography
Renkou yanjiu	Population Research
Renkou yu jingji	Population and Economics
Renmin luntan	People's Forum
Shanqu kaifa	The Development of Mountain Regions
Shehui	Society
Shehui kexuebao	Social Sciences Weekly
Shehui xue	Sociology
Shehuixue yanjiu	Sociological Research
Shijian yu tansuo	Practice and Exploration
Tuopin zhifu	Escaping Poverty and Prospering
Wailaigong	Migrant Worker
Xiangzhen jianshe	Township Construction
Xiangzhen luntan	Township Tribune
Zhengce guangjiao	Wide Angle on Policy
Zhongguo funü	Women of China
Zhongguo haiyuan	Seamen of China
Zhongguo jiuye	China Employment
Zhongguo nongcun guancha	Survey of Rural China
Zhongguo nongcun jingji	Chinese Rural Economy
Zhongguo nongmin	Chinese Peasantry
Zhongguo qingnian bao	China Youth News
Zhongguo renkou kexue	China Population Science
Zhongguo shehui kexue jikan	China Social Sciences Quarterly

CHINESE BOOKS

Chen Jiyuan. *Zhongguo nongye laodongli zhuanyi* [The Transfer of China's Agricultural Labor] (Beijing: People's Publishing House, 1993).

Gu Shengzu and Jian Xinhua. *Dangdai Zhongguo renkou liudong yu chengzhenhua* [Population Mobility and Urbanization in Contemporary China] (Wuhan: Wuhan daxue chubanshe, 1994).

Han Jun and Li Jing. *Kua shiji de nanti – Zhongguo nongye laodongli zhuanyi* [Challenge on the Crossing of the Century – The Transfer of China's Agricultural Labor Force] (Taiyuan: Shanxi jingji chubanshe, 1994).

Nie Zhenbang, Wang Jian, and Wu Ahnan. *Woguo gongyehua zhongqi nongcun jingji wenti yanjiu* [Research on Problems of the Rural Economy during the Middle Period of China's Industrialization] (Beijing: Zhongguo jihua chubanshe, 1996).

Pudong Xinqu laowu guanli zhongxin [Pudong New District Labor Management Center]. *Pudong Xinqu wailai wugong qingnian wenming shouce* [Pudong New District Civilization Manual for Migrant Working Youths] (Shanghai: Baijia chubanshe, 1995).

Wu Huimin. *Zhongguo nongcun fangzhen zhengce* [Policy in Rural China] (Nanchang: Jiangxi kexue jishu chubanshe, 1996).

Wu Tianran. *Zhongguo nongcun gongyehua lun* [Debate on the Industrialization of the Chinese Countryside] (Shanghai: Shanghai chubanshe, 1996).

Yang Yunyan. *Zhongguo renkou qianyi yu fazhan de changqi zhanlüe* [Internal Migration and Long-Term Development Strategy of China] (Wuhan: Wuhan chubanshe, 1994).

Yi Dangsheng and Shao Qin (Eds.). *Zhongguo renkou liudong shitai yu guanli* [The Trend and Management of Population Mobility in China] (Beijing: Zhongguo renkou chubanshe, 1995).

Zhou Yi. *Zhongguo renkou yu ziyuan, huanjing, nongye kexu fazhan* [The Chinese Population and Resources, Environment, and the Sustainable Development of Agriculture] (Taiyuan: Shanxi jingji chubanshe, 1997).

CHINESE JOURNAL ARTICLES, GOVERNMENT REPORTS, AND NEWSPAPER ARTICLES

Anhuisheng weiyuan zheng yan shi [Policy Research Office of the Anhui Provincial Committee], "Guanyu Anhuisheng 'mingongchao' de diaocha yu duice jianyi" [Survey on the "tide of migrant workers" from Anhui province and suggestions for countermeasures], *Zhongguo nongcun jingji* 1 (1994): 53–7.

"Ba qian 'dagongzai' huixiang chuangye pu fu lu" [Eight thousand "migrant workers" return home and establish businesses laying a road to prosperity], *Yichun ribao,* 14 January 1997, p. 4.

Bao Hongshen (Ed.). *Wanzai xianzhi* [Wanzai County Almanac] (Nanchang: Jiangxi renmin chubanshe, 1988).

Bo Qiangzhong, "Employment: A pressing issue at the end of the century," *Renmin luntan,* 8 May 1997, translated in *Summary of World Broadcasts,* 9 August 1997, FE/2993 S1/1.

Central Government Policy Research Office, Ministry of Agriculture. "Nonghu shouru jiegou biange fenxi" [An analysis of the changing composition of the income of rural households], *Zhongguo nongcun guancha* 6 (1997): 1–7.

Cha Yufeng. "Nongmin fudan wenti tanxi" [Discussion of the problem of peasant burden], *Jiangxi zhengbao* 7 (1996): 31.

"Chao piao, xiang shou ai ni bu rongyi – wailaigong xiaofei zhuangkuang diaocha fenxi" [Money, wanting to say I love you is not easy – analysis of a survey on the consumption situation of migrant workers], *Wailaigong* 7 (1996): 32–5.

Chen Aisheng. "Jincheng wugong qingnian huigui jiayuan" [Migrant youths return home from the city], *Jiangxi qingnianbao,* 20 May 1997, p. 3.

Chen Demei. "Chaoqi chaoluo: kan mingong fanxiang chuangye" [Rising and falling wave: a look at migrant workers returning to the countryside and starting businesses], *Zhongguo nongmin* 3 (1997): 56–7.

Chen Hao. "Zhongguo nongcun laodongli wailiu yu nongcun fazhan" [The outflow of China's rural labor and rural development], *Renkou yanjiu* 20(4) (1996): 1–11.

Chen Hu. "Yichunshi jiji yindao zai wai dagong renyuan huixiang ban shiye" [Yichun city actively encourages migrants to return and set up businesses], *Yichun ribao,* 28 February 1997, p. 2.

Chen Liliao. "Dagong bu wei qian" [Migrant working is not for the money], *Jiangxi qingnianbao,* 20 May 1997, p. 3.

Chen Puhua. "Quanmian zhenxing Yudu jingji" [Completely invigorate the Yudu economy], *Jiangxi zhengbao* 13 (1996): 35–9.

Chen Ru. "Dangqian qingnian nongmin huiliu xianxiang tanxi" [Analysis of the current phenomenon of returning rural youth], *Nongye jingji wenti* 10 (1996): 26–30.

Chen Ru. "Kua shiji de jueze – dui dangqian nongmin 'huiliu' xianxiang de kaocha" [Choice crossing the century – investigation of the current "return flow" of peasants], *Shehui* 10 (1996): 4–6.

Chen Yingtao. "Dagongmei de hunlian guannian ji qi kunrao – lai zi Guangdong sheng de diaocha baogao" [The attitude of migrant women workers toward love and marriage and the problems – an investigative report from Guangdong], *Renkou yanjiu* 21(2) (1997): 39–44.

Chen Zhongmin. "Xiangzhen ganbu nan nan nan" [Country cadres difficult difficult difficult], *Xiangzhen luntan* 8 (1997): 9.

"Dagongzai 'lulian' da Shanghai" [Migrant workers "make an appearance" in big Shanghai], *Jiangxi ribao*, 23 July 1997, p. 2.

Dai Ziming. "Nongcun gongzuo zhong 'nong zhuan fei' de xianxiang" [The phenomenon of the transfer from farming to nonfarming in village work], *Xiangzhen luntan* 4 (1994): 20.

Dang Ming. "Yi wan nongmin da zhuanyi" [The huge transfer of 1.1 billion farmers], *Tuopin zhifu* 2 (1996): 5–8.

Duanwu Township Government. "Duanwu xiang laowu shuchu fenxi baogao" [Report on labor export from Duanwu township], in *Xiang zhengfu gongzuo zongjie* [Summary of the Work of the Township Government]. Internal government document, January 1996.

Fei Qiang, Yan Zhongde, Wu Dongping, Cheng Jian, Li Siqing, and Li Youwu. "Mingongchao feng qi yun yong you yi nian" [The tide of migrant workers, the wind rises, the clouds swell for another year], *Liaowang zhoukan,* 22 February 1993, pp. 4–10.

Fu Shaoping. "Woguo nongmin xingwei bianhua de shi da tedian" [The ten main characteristics of behavioral change among farmers in our country], *Nongcun jingji daokan* 11 (1997): 47–8.

Gan Shuqing. "Mingtian, shei lai zhongtian?" [Tomorrow, who will farm the land?], *Yichun ribao,* 25 March 1997, p. 3.

Gao Xiaoxian. "Nongcun funü yanjiu zongshu (1991–1995 nian)" [Summary of research on rural women, 1991–1995], *Funü yanjiu lunzong* 2 (1997): 13–18.

Gao Yinghua. "Dagong san zheng" [Three certificates for migrant working], *Wailaigong* 4(47) (1997): 12–14.

Gu Chuan. "Nongmin dagongzhe – mo rang xifu liu man jin" [Peasant migrant workers – don't let your wife's tears soak the front of her garment], *Dangdai qingnian* 3 (1997): 57.

Gu Shengzu and Liu Chuanjiang. "Zhongguo renkou liudong yu chengzhenhua de lilun sikao he zhengce xuanze" [Theoretical thoughts on China's population mobility and urbanization and policy choices], *Renkou yanjiu* 20(3) (1996): 1–6.

Guo Xiaosheng. "Waichu renkou xiangcun you yi nan" [Out-migration, another difficulty for the countryside], *Xiangzhen luntan* 8 (1997): 25.

Han Jun and Li Jing. " 'Mingongchao': Zhongguo kua shiji de keti – 'mingongchao' xianxiang taolunhui shuyao" ["The tide of migrant workers": the topic as China crosses the century – summary of the discussion forum on the phenomenon of the "tide of migrant workers"], *Zhongguo nongcun jingji* 5 (1994): 3–15.

He Lidong, "Lu Gan kaishi dianzi kuaihui wangluo, dagongzhe huikuan bu zai shang naojin" [The establishment of an express electronic remittance network between

Shanghai and Jiangxi, migrant workers no longer worry about remitting their money], *Xinmin wanbao,* 25 May 1997, p. 22.

He Lidong. "Yudu nongmin xue cheng fan gu li jin bai ren dang 'guan' zuo laoban" [Nearly one hundred Yudu farmers study and return to the natal home to become officials and bosses], *Xinmin wanbao,* 20 July 1997, p. 22.

Hu Nengcan. "Nongcun 'liu shou hai' huhuan guanzhu" [Call for attention to the "children left behind" in the countryside], *Jingji canzheng bao,* 23 June 1997, p. 2.

Huang Chenxi. "Mingong qianliu dui nongcun renkou suzhi de yingxiang ji duice" [The influence of the transfer and mobility of migrant workers on rural population quality and countermeasures], *Shehui* 10 (1995): 26–7, 48.

Huang Fengting and Fu Chengsheng. "Gaoan waichu dagongzhe huixiang ban qiye fanbu gutu" [Gaoan migrants return home and set up businesses giving back to home soil], *Yichun ribao,* 5 June 1997, p. 1.

Huang Zhigui and Zhong Yi. "Nongcun huiliu laodongli de shitai ji zhuanyi celüe" [Situation of the return of the rural labor force and strategies for transfer], *Nongcun jingji* 6 (1990): 27–38.

Hunan laodongli zhuanhua yu renkou liudong ketizu [Research Group on the Transfer of Labor in Hunan and Population Mobility]. "Hunan sheng laodongli de zhuanhua yu renkou liudong" [Transfer of labor in Hunan and population mobility], *Shehuixue yanjiu* 3 (1995): 75–85.

Ji Enze. "Feng huan wo – mingongchao huiliu xianxiang toushi" [Phoenixes returning to the nest – perspective on the phenomenon of the return flow of the tide of migrant workers], *Tuopin zhifu* 1 (1997): 31–2.

Ji Enze. "Qiaoran huiliu de mingongchao" [Stealthy return flow of the tide of migrant workers], *Xiangzhen luntan* 1 (1997): 13–14.

Jiangxi Committee of Xinfeng County. *Xinfeng xianzhi* [Xinfeng County Almanac] (Nanchang: Jiangxi renmin chubanshe, 1990).

Jiangxi Funü Lianhehui [Jiangxi Women's Federation]. "Chengxiang dui zhuangxia de hunyin liebian" [Clash between city and village and marriage break-up], *Funü zhisheng,* 25 September 1997, p. 4.

Jiangxi shelian ketizu [Jiangxi Social Sciences Federation Research Group]. "Houjin diqu zhanlüe yu kechixu fazhan" [Strategies for backward areas and sustainable development], *Jiangxi shehui kexue* 10 (1996): 7–12.

Jiangxi tongji nianjian [Jiangxi Statistical Yearbook] (Beijing: Zhongguo tongji chubanshe, various years).

Jin Xian. "Feng, guilai!' [Phoenix return!], *Jiangxi zhengbao* 7 (1995): 35–7.

Kuang Qinglin. "Yangyu xiang yindao nongmin ba qian hua zai shengchan shang" [Yangyu township guides farmers in spending money on production], *Yichun ribao,* 18 January 1997, p. 1.

Lai Jidong. "Jiaqiang jingshen wenming jianshe lidu, nuli tigao nongmingong duiwu suzhi" [Strengthen the intensity of spiritual and cultural construction, diligently improve the quality of the ranks of the rural migrant workers], *Shijian yu tansuo* 5 (1996): 43–4.

Li Guanghui and Yuan Chun. "Zhaixia xiang shixing 'liang tianzhi' yi ju liang de" [Killing two birds with one stone with the "two land system" in Zhaixia township], *Yichun ribao,* 21 January 1997, p. 2.

Li Guoqiang, Wang Yuqi, and Huang Zhigang. "Deng Xiaoping de fazhan lilun yu Jiangxi xianyu jingji" [Deng Xiaoping's theory of development and the county economies of Jiangxi], *Jiangxi shehui kexue* 11 (1996): 1–7.

Li Hongwei. "Nongcun laodongli huiliu" [The return flow of rural labor], *Nongcun jingji* 3 (1990): 9.

Li Naiqun. "Dagongchao zhong de lihun an" [Cases of divorce among migrant workers], *Hunyin yu jiating* 1 (1995): 31.

Li Nairong. "Renkou suzhi yu nügong laodong baohu" [Population quality and labor protection for female workers], *Renkou yu jingji* 4 (1996): 46–8.

Li Tao and Li Zhen. "Dagong mei: bianyuan ren de hunlian gushi" [Migrant girls: stories of the love and marriage of marginal people], *Zhongguo funü* 6 (1997): 16–17.

Li Wensheng. "Jingjiu tielu dui Jiangxi chengzhen fazhan de yingxiang yu duice" [The influence of the Jing-Jiu Railway on urbanization in Jiangxi and countermeasures], *Jiangxi shehui kexue* 5 (1997): 1–6.

Li Xianai and Li Wenlong. " 'Wailiu' dailai de fumian yingxiang" [The negative influences brought about by out-migration], *Xiangzhen luntan* 9 (1994).

Li Zhiyang. "Dagong ji he ti" [Several problems of working], *Foshan wenyi* 3 (1995): 36–41.

Li Zhongdong (Ed.). *Yudu xianzhi* [Yudu County Almanac] (Beijing: Xinhua chubanshe, 1991).

Liang Gaochao. "Qieshi jiaqiang waichu laowu renyuan de sixiang daode jianshe" [Take practical measures to strengthen the ideological moral construction of outmigrants], *Zhengce guangjiao* 3 (1997): 40–5.

Lin Han, "Lian hun weicheng dalie bian" [The walls of the marriage circle are breaking and changing], *Funü zhi shengbao,* 17 October 1996, p. 5.

Liu Chunbin, "Xiao chengzhen – Zhongguo huji zhidu gaige de qieru dian" [Small towns – point of entry for reforming China's household registration system], *Shehui* 1 (1997): 14–16.

Liu Faming. "Shouqu cun tiliu, xiang tongchou de wenti he duice" [Problems in collecting village and township levies and countermeasures], *Jiangxi zhengbao* 7 (1997): 67, 69.

Liu Feng and Wan Renrong. "Nongye qiyehua: nongye di er ci gaige yu fazhan de you yi tansuo" [The commercialization of agriculture: beneficial exploration of the second reform and development of agriculture], *Jiangxi shehui kexue* 8 (1996): 4–12.

Liu Sen. "Bixu nuli jiaqiang dui 'dagongzai' jinxing sixiang zhengzhi gongzuo" [Must diligently strengthen the ideological and political work carried out among migrant workers], *Jiangxi qingnian luntan* 2–3 (1995): 26–7.

Liu Wansheng. "Dui dangqian nongcun jian fang re de ji dian sikao" [Some thoughts on the current house-building craze in the countryside], *Yichun ribao,* 11 February 1997.

Liu Xiaohun. "Gaoanshi geti siying jingji shixian wu ge zhuanbian" [Five changes in the individual and private economy in Gaoan city], *Yichun ribao,* 20 February 1997, p. 4.

Liu Xinping. "Dagong de rensheng ye zhuangli" [A working life is also magnificent], *Zhongguo qingnian bao* 2 (1997): 12–21.

Liu Yanguo. "Gangwan ketang yaolan" [Harbor schoolroom cradle], *Zhongguo haiyuan* 5 (1995): 10–11.

Liu Yingjie. "Mingongchao: shehui xuezhe de sikao" [Tide of migrant workers: the thoughts of sociologists], *Liaowang zhoukan,* 18 April 1994, pp. 10–11.

Liu Yingjie. "Nongmin gongren: Zhongguo dute er maodun de shehui jieceng" [Peasant workers: China's unique and contradictory social stratum], *Zhongguo nongmin* 9 (1995): 10–15.

Liu Zhengqin. "Tianbao xiang 'dagongzai' gei tudi fa 'yasuiqian'" ["Migrants" give "birthday money" to the land in Tianbao township], *Yichun ribao*, 8 February 1996, p. 2.

Liu Zhiping and Chen Yilun. "Wangtian zhen dagong qingnian huixiang chuangye ji" [Record of migrant youths returning home and creating businesses in Wangtian town], *Jiangxi qingnianbao*, 20 May 1997, p. 2.

Lu Bian. "Nongcun 'liu shou nü' huhuan guanzhu" [The "women left behind" in the countryside calls for attention], *Zhongguo nongmin* 3 (1997): 62.

Meng Chaoyang. "Zhigong yu mingong cuowei de sikao" [Thoughts on the dislocation of workers by rural migrant workers], *Jiangxi jianshe* 5 (1995): 36.

Meng Zhaopu. "Nongcun gedai jiaoyu yousi" [Troubled thoughts on education by the older generation in the countryside], *Nongmin wenzhai* 4 (1997): 43.

Miu Xiaoqin. "Mingong huiliu, yin ren zhumu" [The return flow of migrant workers, attracting people's attention], *Jiangxi qingnianbao*, 18 February 1997, p. 2.

Mou Wenjian. "Shei lai baohu nongmingong liyi?" [Who will protect the rights of rural peasant workers?], *Banyue tan* 14 (1997): 10–12.

"Nongcun 'dagongchao' de beihou" [Behind the "migrant outflow" from the countryside], *Meizhou wenzhai* 751 (1997): 72.

"Nongcun 'liushou hai' huanhu guanzhu" [Calling attention to the "children left behind" in the countryside], *Funü zhi shengbao*, 10 July 1997, p. 3.

Nongcun shengyu laodongli zhuanyi yu laodongli shichang keti zu [Research Group on the Transition of Surplus Rural Labor and the Labor Market]. "28 ge xian (shi) nongcun laodongli kua quyu liudong de diaocha yanjiu" [Survey research on the interregional mobility of rural labor in 28 counties (cities)], *Zhongguo nongcun jingji* 4 (1995): 19–28.

Nongmin liudong yu xiangcun fazhan keti zu [Mobility and Rural Development Research Group]. "Nongmingong huiliu yu xiangcun fazhan: dui Shandongsheng Huantai xian 10 cun 737 min huixiang nongmingong de diaocha" [The return of migrant workers and rural development: a survey of 737 returned rural migrants in Huantai county, Shandong province], *Zhongguo nongcun jingji* 10 (1999): 63–7.

Nongye bu "mingongchao de genzong diaocha yu yanjiu" keti zu [Agricultural Ministry's Study Group of Continuous Survey and Research on the Tide of Migrant Workers]. "Jingji fazhan zhong de nongcun laodongli liudong" [The mobility of the rural labor force in economic development], *Zhongguo nongcun jingji* 1 (1995): 43–50.

Pi Yanbao, Tao Huoping, and Hu Qingning. "Dagong qingnian Liu Xiaoniu huicun chengbao gengdi 120 mu" [Migrant youth Liu Xiaoniu returns to the village to contract 120 mu of land], *Yichun ribao*, 20 March 1997, p. 1.

Qin Hui. "'Nongmin fudan' wenti de fazhan qushi" [The direction of development of the problem of the "farmers' burden"], *Gaige* 2 (1997): 57–62, 87.

Qin Hui. "Nongmin liudong yu jingji yaosu peizhi youhua" [The mobility of peasants and improved deployment of the factors of production], *Gaige* 3 (1996): 60–7.

Qiu Shunyan. "Huangchengzhen qianyu dagong renyuan fanxiang zhongdi" [Over one thousand migrant workers return home to farm the land], *Yichun ribao*, 28 February 1997, p. 2.

Rao Yingpeng and Luo Laixing. "Wai chu bu wang jiaxiang zhifu xinxi 'gualao'" [Going out but not forgetting the elderly of home], *Nongyou bao*, 18 February 1997, p. 4.

Rao Yingpeng and Luo Laixing. "Zhenqing qizhi shi wan" [Real feeling shown with ten thousand yuan], *Jiangxi qingnianbao*, 24 January 1997, p. 1.

Ren Jiping. "Mingong huanxiang, zhi lu xiao liao bu liu lei" [Migrant workers returning home, only show a smile and don't cry tears], *Zhongguo nongmin* 4 (1995): 19–21.

Research Group of the Yichun Prefecture Agricultural Bank Planning Research Group and Zhangshu City Agricultural Bank Planning and Science Federation. "Laowu shuchu dui nongcun jingrong de yingxiang" [The impact of labor export on rural financial markets], *Nongcun shehui jingji xue kan* 3 (1996): 40–3.

Shang Guanfei. "Dagong: yizhong xinxing de jiuye gainian" [Working for a boss: a new kind of employment concept], *Jiangxi qingnianbao,* 20 May 1997, p. 3.

Shang Junfeng. "Jiaqiang liudong renkou de hongguan tiaokong chongfen fahui liudong renkou zai chengshihua zhong de zuoyong" [Strengthen the macro-level regulation of the floating population and give full play to the role of the floating population in urbanization], *Zhongguo renkou kexue* 4 (1996): 27–39.

Shao Suping. "Xiri dagong, jin chao chuangye" [Worked in the past, create businesses today], *Jiangxi ribao,* 4 November 1997, p. 1.

Shi Jianmin and Liu Fugui. "Ezhi xiangcun 'xujia feng'" [Stop the false wind of townships and villages], *Xiangzhen luntan* 9 (1997): 19.

Sun Chunyun. "Liulangzhe de zuyin '97 hui an, tingting" [The sound of roamers' footsteps, '97 return to shore, have a listen], *Wailaigong* 12 (1997): 4–8.

Sun Shuqing. "Shichang jingji yu nüxing liudong renkou yanjiu" [Research on the market economy and population mobility of females], *Nanfang renkou* 4 (1996): 41–4.

Tao Xiaoping. "Liushou huangtudi de xifumen" [Wives left on the yellow land], *Shehui* 2 (1997): 4–6.

"Wai chu bu wang jia zhong shengchan, you qian bu gao tuchu xiaofei" [Migrate without forgetting production at home, not using money for conspicuous consumption], *Jiangxi qingnianbao,* 21 February 1997, p. 2.

Wailai nongmingong keti zu [Research Group on Migrant Peasant Workers]. "Zhujiang Sanjiaozhou wailai nongmingong zhuangkuang" [The situation of migrant peasant workers in the Pearl River Delta], *Zhongguo shehui kexue* 4 (1995): 92–104.

Wailai nü laogong yanjiu keti zu [Research Group on Migrant Female Labor]. "Wai chu da gong yu nongcun ji nongmin fazhan: Hunan sheng Jiamuxian Zhongshuicun diaocha" [Going outside to work and the development of the village and peasants: survey of Zhongshui village in Jiamu county, Hunan province], *Shehuixue yanjiu* 4 (1995): 75–85.

Wang Ben. "Tamen wei jianqing nongmin fudan huanhu, benzou" [Appeals and strides toward reducing the farmer's burden], *Zhongguo nongmin* 6 (1997): 34–9.

Wang Dagao. "Xian jieduan nongcun laodongli suzhi de zhuangkuang ji tigao de tujing" [The situation of the quality of the rural labor force at the current stage and avenues for its improvement], *Jingji wenti* 2 (1997): 17–21.

Wang Dingning. "Dagong fang zhi zhuixue ku chongfan xiaoyuan qin dushu" [Migrant worker who dropped out of school returns to the school yard to study hard], *Jiangxi qingnianbao,* 21 January 1997, p. 2.

Wang Guang. "Moshan dagongzai fanxiang touru guoyuan kaifa zhan" [Moshan migrants return home to invest in the challenge of opening up orchards], *Yichun ribao,* 6 February 1997, p. 2.

Wang Hansheng. "Gaige yilai Zhongguo nongcun de gongyehua yu nongcun jingying goucheng de bianhua" [Industrialization and changes in the structure of the business stratum in China's countryside since the reforms], *Zhongguo shehui kexue jikan* (Autumn 1994).

Wang Linquan. "Daa you ge 'wugong qingnian xiehui'" [Daa has a "migrant youth association"], *Jiangxi ribao,* 10 April 1997, p. 7.

Wang Qing and Zhong Xianwu. "Tiantai xiang chunji jihua shengyu gongzuo zhashi you xiao" [Effective grasp on spring family planning work in Tiantai township], *Yichun ribao,* 3 April 1997, p. 2.

Wang Xiaoping and Zhong Yangping. "Xikan wanqian 'feng' huan 'wo'" [Happily seeing thousands of phoenixes returning to the nest], *Jiangxi laodong* 4 (1996): 22.

Wang Yanbin. "Leguanzhe de kanfa: mingongchao hui zhubu huanjie" [View of the optimist: the migrant tide will gradually abate], *Zhongguo nongmin* 4 (1995): 28–9.

Wang Youcai, Zhan Shengsheng, and Xu Renhe. "Dagong qingnian huixiang fu le yi cun ren" [Migrant youths return home and enrich the people of a village], *Jiangxi qingnianbao,* 3 June 1997, p. 2.

Wang Youzhao. "Guanyu nongmin kua quyu liudong wenti" [Concerning the problem of interregional peasant mobility], *Zhongguo nongcun jingji* 12 (1994): 18–22.

Wang Yuzhao. "Man qiang reqing, guanxin nongmin de kuaquyu liudong" [Chests full of warmth, concern for the interregional mobility of farmers], *Zhongguo nongmin* 4 (1995): 25–7.

Wang Zehuan. "Wailai dagongzu de xingwei tezheng, liuxiang yu guanli" [The behavioral characteristics, direction of mobility, and management of migrant workers], *Shehuixue* 2 (1996): 160–5.

Wang Zhongzhou. "Ba zhifu zhi lu dai hui jiaxiang – waichu dagong licheng fanxiang chuangye xianxiang sikao" [Bringing the road to prosperity home – thoughts on the phenomenon of migrant workers returning home from the city], *Shehui kexuebao,* 29 May 1997, p. 4.

"Wanzai xian zuzhi zhuanche jiesong dagong renyuan" [Wanzai county organizes special vehicles to collect and send back migrant workers], *Yichun ribao,* 11 February 1997, p. 3.

Wen Jian. "Cheng men jiujing kai duo da?" [Exactly how open is the city gate?], *Banyue tan* (April 1997): 20–2.

Wen Shi. "Xiang dang laoban, xian da hao gong" [If you want to be a boss, first be a good migrant worker], *Huangjin shidai* 7 (1997): 30–1.

Woguo da chengshi xishou nongcun laodongli ketizu [Research Group on Absorbing Rural Labor in China's Big Cities]. "Jingji zhuangui, laodongli shichang fayu yu mingong liudong" [Economic transition, the development of a labor market, and the flow of migrant laborers], *Zhongguo nongcun guancha* 5 (1996): 1–13.

Wu Liangjie. "Liudong renkou zhong de lianai hunyin yu jiating" [Love, marriage, and family among the floating population], *Hunyin jiating yanjiu* 2 (1996): 18–23.

Wu Zhengbao. "Dagong qingnian, tiaohui nongmen you qiantu" [Migrant youths have a future returning through the farm gate], *Jiangxi qingnianbao,* 8 April 1997, p. 2.

Xiao Chiyuan. "Shaonian waichu dagong ying ji zhizhi" [Ought to curb the out-migration of minors], *Yichun ribao,* 11 March 1997, p. 3.

Xinfeng xian geti qiye xiehui [Xinfeng County Association of Individual Enterprises]. *Xinfeng xian jiuwu niandu waichu dagong renyuan huixiang ban qiye tongjibiao* [Xinfeng county's statistical table for people who migrate to work then return to set up businesses during the period of 1995].

Xing Ying. "Yi xi yi you de nongmin shouru" [The joy and worry of peasant income], *Zhongguo nongmin* 3 (1995): 50–3.

"Xinhua gang mingong guanli chuang xin lu" [Xinhua harbor creates a new road in managing migrant workers], *Xinmin wanbao,* 6 July 1997, p. 22.

Xu Nantie. "Shiji huati: dagong zhihou gan shenme?" [Topic of the century: what after being a migrant worker?], *Chushe zhi chu* 2 (1997): 4–7.

Xu Ping. "Hunyin liudong yu nongcun funü de tudi shiyong quanyi" [Marriage mobility and the land usage rights of rural women], *Funü yanjiu* 1 (1997): 29–34.

Xu Rihui and Kuang Yingjian. "Shixian tudi liyong fangshi de zhuanbian" [Realizing a transformation in the method of land usage], *Jiangxi zhengbao* 23(589) (1995): 39.

Xu Weigang and Gao Yuanzhong. "Chengli nan 'taojin' fanxiang xian shenshou" [It is difficult to "pan for gold" in the city, so return home and display one's skill], *Nongcun jingji* 6 (1990): 29–30.

Xu Xiaogan. "Dagong guilai chuang da ye" [Work and then return to set up big business], *Jiangxi huabao* 3(14) (1996): 18–19.

Xu Zengwen. "Nongcun laodongli de liudong yu nongye laodongli de liushu" [The mobility of the rural labor force and the loss of agricultural labor], *Zhongguo nongcun jingji* (January 1995): 51–3.

Yang Hongshan. "Zhujiang Sanjiao 'mingongchao' de diaocha yu fenxi" [Survey and analysis of the "tide of migrant workers" in the Pearl River Delta], *Renkou yanjiu* 19 (1995): 53–6.

Yang Shanqing. "Zhongguo xiangcun 'nong mang'" ["Agricultural blindness" in the Chinese countryside], *Jingji canzheng bao,* 26 March 1997, p. 1.

Yang Shouyao. "Yujiang xian caiqu youhui zhengce guli wailai dagong renyuan hui xiang ban qiye" [Yujiang county adopts preferential policies to encourage migrant workers to return home and set up businesses], *Jiangxi laodong* 7 (1996): 10.

Yang Xi. "Nongcun zhian de liang da yin huan" [The two big hidden worries of social order in the countryside], *Shehui* 5 (1995): 45–6.

Yang Xiaoyong. "Mingong liudong yu Zhongguo chengxiang jingji fazhan" [The mobility of migrant workers and the economic development of city and country], *Renkou yu jingji* 5 (1995): 26–32.

Yang Zheng. "Dagong, wo de qiu xue zhi lu" [Migrant working, my road to pursuing learning], *Dangdai qingnian* 6 (1997): 48–9.

Yi Kequn. "Nongcun tudi zhidu shenhua gaige moshi yanjiu" [Research on deepening the reform of the rural land system], *Gaige yu lilun* 11 (1996): 33–6.

You Siqing. "Huangcheng qingnian hunlian xin shishang" [New fashion in the love and marriage of young people in Huangcheng], *Yichun ribao,* 17 May 1997, p. 3.

You Xiaowu. "Liugongmiao xiang waichu wugong renyuan wu yi ren weifa fanzui" [Not one migrant from Liugongmiao township has committed a crime], *Yichun ribao,* 12 February 1997, p. 1.

Yu Aijiang. "Songpu dagongzai zhifu nongjia li dagong" [Migrant workers from Songpu create wealth for rural households], *Yichun ribao,* 6 February 1997, p. 2.

Yu Xueqiang. "Song ganbu qu dagong" [Send the cadre out to work], *Zhongguo nongmin* 7 (1996): 55–6.

Yudu County Bureau of Statistics. "1993 nian laowu shuchu diaocha baogao" [1993 survey of labor export]. Internal government document, January 1994.

Yudu nianjian, 1986–1992 [Yudu Almanac, 1986–1992] (Nanchang: Shehui kexue wenxian chubanshe, 1995).

Yuduxian nianjian, 1986–1992 [Yudu County Yearbook, 1986–1992] (Nanchang: Shehui kexue wenxian chubanshe, 1995).

Zao Wanhong. "Chuang ye zhi xing" [Stars of entrepreneurship], *Zhongguo nongmin* 3 (1996): 62–3.

Zhang Dashan and Wang Xiuyou. "Laowu fuwuzhan – wai chu dagongzhe de 'niangjia'" [Labor service center – a "maternal home" for migrant workers], *Zhongguo jiuye* 10 (1996): 20–3.

Zhang Dong. "Ba hao 'sanguan' zou chu jian fu guai quan" [Grasp the three barriers and walk out of the strange circle of reducing burden], *Jiangxi zhengbao* 6 (1997): 62.

Zhang Maolin. " 'Mingongchao' 'nichao huigui' xianxiang de lilun sikao" [Theoretical thoughts on the "counterflow return" of the "migrant tide"], *Jingji yanjiu* 7 (1996): 54–6, 66.

Zhang Rui. "Fanxiang mingong dang cunguan" [Returnee migrants become village leaders], *Xiangzhen luntan* 10 (1997): 13.

Zhang Shanyu and Yang Shaoyong. "Mingongchao jiang dailai hui xiang chuangye chao" [The tide of migrant workers will bring forth a tide of return], *Renkou yu jingji* 1 (1996): 43–7.

Zhang Yong, "Nongjia nü ding qi ban bian tian: guanyu 'liushou nüshi' de bei wenxue baogao" [Women of rural households holding up half the sky: regarding the reportage literature tragedies of "the women left behind"], *Jiating yu shenghuo* (April 1997): 51.

Zhao Min, "Chengshihua liudong renkou ji 21 shiji de Zhongguo chengshihua zhilu" [Urbanization, population mobility, and China's road to urbanization in the 21st century], Paper presented at Conference on the Future of Chinese Cities, Shanghai, 30 July 1999.

Zhao Shukai. "Nongmin liudong: neibu chengyin he shenghuo yuqi" [Peasant mobility: internal causes and effects and life expectations], *Nongye jingji wenti* 10 (1996): 22–6.

Zheng Yi. "Nongcun jie hun suo cai xianxiang bu rong hushi" [It is not easy to ignore the phenomenon in the countryside of using marriage to extort wealth], *Yichun ribao*, 13 June 1997, p. 2.

Zhonggong zhongyang zhengce yanjiushi nongcunzu [The Rural Group of the Policy Research Office of the Chinese Communist Central Committee]. "Guanyu nongcun laodongli kua quyu liudong wenti de chubu yanjiu" [Initial research on the problem of the interregional mobility of surplus rural labor], *Zhongguo nongcun jingji* 3 (1994): 3–7.

Zhongguo shehui kexueyuan jingji yanjiusuo, Zhongguo laodongli shichang he gongzi gaige keti zu. [Chinese Academy of Social Sciences, Economic Research Institute, Research Group on the Chinese Labor Market and Wage Reform]. "Woguo tizhi zhuanxing shiqi 'nongcun bing' ji qi zhili" [Rural sicknesses and their managment during the period of system transition in China], *Jingji yanjiu* 4 (1995): 60–6.

Zhongguo tongji nianjian [China Statistical Yearbook] (Beijing: Zhongguo tongji chubanshe, various years).

Zhongguo wushi nian de Jiangxi 1949–1999 [Fifty Years of Jiangxi 1949–1999] (Beijing: Zhongguo tongji chubanshe, 2000).

Zhou Pei. "Jianli sanyuan shehui jiegou cucheng 'mingongchao' you xu liudong de zhanlüe jueze" [Building a tripartite social structure is the strategic choice for the orderly flow of the migrant worker tide], *Nanjing shehui kexue* 10 (1995): 117–24; also published in *Shehui xue* 4 (1996): 117–22.

Zhou Qingfu. "Wanzai 8 wan funü chengwei tuopin zhifu 'zhugong shou'" [Eighty thousand women of Wanzai become "key fighters" in escaping poverty and prospering], *Yichun ribao*, 20 March 1997, p. 1.

Zhou Zhong. "Guanyu Zhongguo jingji de ji ge redian wenti – Li Yining tan Zhongguo jingji liu da redian" [On the hot issues of the Chinese economy – Li Yining talks about the six hot issues of the Chinese economy], *Duzhe* 3 (1997): 5.

Zhu Jialiang and Wu Minyi. "Zhongguo butong quyu nongye liudongli zhuanyi de texing ji qushi bijiao" [Comparison of the transition of rural labor in different regions of China], *Renkou xue* 1 (1993): 28–33.

Zhu Yimin. "Yugan xian nongcun laoli wailiu de diaocha" [Survey of the outflow of labor from Yugan county], *Jiangxi qingnian luntan* 1 (1995): 36.

Index

affines, 107, 108, 117
agency, 18, 20, 21, 175, 225n9
agricultural diversification, 36, 50, 84–5
agricultural extension, 50, 51, 85, 212, 221
agriculture
  impact of migration on, 52, 72, 73
  innovations, 73, 84–5, 221
  investment in, 110
  mechanization of, 73, 84
  modernization of, 73
  plowing, 40, 48
  returnee investment in, 71, 82, 84–5
  rice prices, 73, 77, 79, 87, 193
  specialized production, 144, 149–50, 161,
    163, 168–9, 185–9, 197
  transferring labor out of, 45, 84, 193, 195,
    220, 223
  see also farm inputs; remittances
altruism, 12
Anhui, 125
  Fenyang, Anhui, 34, 189

basic needs, 89, 114
Beijing, 39
betrothal, 92, 105, 109
  "hot water money," 105, 108–9
boredom, 212
boss, 164–6, 221
bride price, 63, 107–10
brides, 66, 92, 109
brothers, 63
burdens, 52, 63, 72, 80–1, 86, 218
business policies, 180–4, 221

cadres, xv, 150
  evaluations of, 131
  laying off, 131
  work style, 85
campaigns, 142
cash, 73, 74, 81, 83, 89, 112, 114, 180
Census, First Chinese National Agricultural, 55
census sheets, 55–6
cha fang (inspecting the house), 105
chain migration, 19, 20, 40–1, 69, 93, 197, 198,
  217

Chayanov, 57–9, 65
Chen Hao, 193
Chen Village, 58, 108
chickens, 55
child care, 64, 65, 202–3, 206
children, 37, 58, 59, 63, 64, 71, 96
China Poverty Relief Foundation, 125
China Rural Development Research Center,
  125
China Telecom, 116
chuzu, 76
  see also renting
circulation, 13, 14, 20, 24, 25, 88, 200
cities: *see* destination area conditions
city experience, 97
civilizing campaigns, 45
clans, 32, 45, 74, 117
clothing factories, 128, 147, 167, 178, 184
Cohen, Myron L., 31, 32, 235n31
collective enterprises, xv, 145, 150, 152, 188,
  189, 197
collectives, 32, 34, 35
  false, 151–2
collectivization, 28, 32
commodity consciousness, 45
communes, 32, 58
commuting, 135
compensation, 196, 214, 223
compensation cases, 201–2
conflict
  "cooperative conflict," 204
  within families/households, 21, 52, 57,
    65–7, 80–1, 85–6, 91, 105, 175, 204,
    213–14, 218
  see also fallback position; household/s,
    bargaining
Constable, Nicole, 173
constraints, structural, 8, 28, 42–4, 46, 51, 176
consumer goods, 22, 58, 66, 81, 88, 89, 103,
  107, 108, 111–18, 213
  livelihood goods, 91, 115, 190–1
  modern appliances, 115–16
  popular cultural products, 115–16
consumerism, 109, 114–17, 190–1
contacts, 145, 155, 166, 175, 189, 221

cooperatives, 34
core, 12, 17, 29
    diffusion process, 220
    dualism/dichotomy, 17, 18, 20
    interactions, 13
    of macro-regions, 30
corruption, 17, 132, 212
county government, 129, 133
county town, 49, 129, 131, 137, 148, 154, 188,
    192, 193, 199
credit cooperative, 66–7
credit rotation societies, 173, 177, 180
crime, 135, 196, 198
crops, 36
Cultural Revolution, 33, 56, 93, 133
culture of migration, 21

dagong, xv, 165, 188
dagong zu (working generation), 211
dam construction, 26
daughter migrant communities, 25
daughters, 174
    and domestic chores, 155
    and education, 93, 96, 97, 107, 155
    and marriage, 107
    and remittances, 59, 63, 66, 93, 97
debt
    of local government, 131–2
    of rural households, 23, 91, 110, 111, 112, 219
decision-making, 19, 20
decollectivization, 26, 34, 35, 68, 96, 135, 200
demonstration effect, 89, 136, 217
deposits, 178, 180
de-skilling, 14
    agricultural de-skilling, 199
destination area conditions, 1, 2, 18, 19, 42–4,
    47, 71, 163–4, 197, 200, 211, 213, 216
destination areas (for migrants from the
    fieldwork counties), 40
Development Research Office, 126
dialect, 213
diet, 57–8
disposable income, 37, 38, 191
dissatisfaction, 191, 207–8, 212
divorce, 76, 207, 210
dock workers, 4, 41, 201
Dongguan, 40, 117, 133, 198
dowry, 107–8, 113, 118
drugs, 198

economic figures, reporting of, 38, 129, 177–8,
    230–1n47
economic liberalization, 27, 102
education, 45, 46, 51, 57, 129
    demand for, 92
    drop-outs, 93–7
    figures for attainment among migrants,
        93–8, 157–60

general figures for attainment/progression,
    55, 93–8, 102, 118–23
impact of migration on, 92–103, 118
as an individual characteristic, 19, 88, 91,
    92–103, 125
investment of remittances in, 12, 88, 91, 97,
    99, 100, 102, 118, 219
Operation Hope, 92, 133
and propensity to migrate, 93, 157–8
sex differences in attainment, 95–6, 119–20
state policies on, 51, 92, 94–5, 224
see also remittances; return migrant
    entrepreneurship; schools
egalitarianism, 35, 59
Egypt, 73
elderly, the, 30, 37, 55, 58, 59, 63–5, 67, 77,
    79, 118, 211, 218
    see also conflict; grandparents
electronic cash transfers, 114–15, 219
eligibility, as a spouse, 43, 113, 105, 209–10
employment, 151, 184, 195
engagement, 205
environmental regulations, 37
equilibrium, 12, 13
eugenics, xv, 45
Europe, 35, 37
expectations, 219, 223
expenditure
    collective/family-based, 91, 105
    individual, 91, 105
    modern forms of, 118
    traditional forms of, 103, 118
export, 37, 147, 191
export-led development, 36

face, 103, 111, 130, 136, 165, 216
factory entrance deposit, 65
factory jumping, 65
failed migrants, 23, 65, 74, 86, 163, 200, 217,
    219
failed returnees, 14, 65, 142–3, 157, 196
fallback position, 76, 204, 215, 218
family, 20, 107
    as antithetical to modernization, 45–6
    businesses, 24, 145
    continuity, 103
    control, 216
    division, 24, 31, 35, 59–67, 105
    obligations, 91, 196, 217
    obligations and return, 203–11
    relationship to the household, 52, 105
    strategies, 12, 31
    workshops, 30, 31
    see also conflict; values
family planning, 42, 45, 46, 55, 65, 81, 129,
    130, 138, 149, 172, 194, 196, 202, 215, 223
family planning certificate, 42
    "proof of status" certificate, 203

family planning responsibility system, 203
farm inputs, 71–3, 74, 77, 79, 81–5, 88
"farmers without land," 74
female-headed households, 76
Fengcheng, 4, 148, 222
Fengxin, 4, 84, 141, 148, 164, 169, 222
fenjia: see family, division
feudal practices, 45, 49, 109
fieldwork
    interviews, 5
    researching inequality, 53, 55–7
    sites, 3, 4, 36, 37, 38, 39, 40, 41, 42
filial piety/obligations, 65, 66, 86, 174, 219
financial institutions, 142, 170, 178, 180, 218
fines, 65, 91, 132, 181, 202
firecrackers, 37, 40, 68, 69
fireworks, 30, 31, 39, 68
fiscal reforms, 130–2
foot binding, 24, 39
fuel, 58
Fujian, 30, 31
funerals, 45, 110, 111
"furniture city," 148
furniture workshops, 128, 147–8, 150, 167, 184,
    190
fuse paper, 30, 31

gambling, 45, 135
Gan Yanzi, 30
Ganzhou city, 39, 40
Ganzhou prefecture, 28, 36
Gaocheng, 37, 39, 54, 114
    off-farm employment in, 67–8
Gates, Hill, 23, 24, 49, 50, 132
GDP, 36, 38
gender
    imbalances, 110, 169
    relations, 18, 173
    and return, 207–8, 219–20
gendered division of labor, 39–40, 83, 96, 112,
    155, 174, 206, 214
    and returned migrants, 71, 200, 206–7
gendered networks, 172–3
generations, relationships between, 66, 204,
    213
gift giving, 103, 111, 172
gifts, 92, 108, 109, 110, 115, 181, 219
Gmelch, George, 126
goals
    and adaptation to possibilities, 43, 231–2n67
    as basic needs, 89, 117
    to be a boss, 136, 144, 154, 163, 164, 175,
        176, 217, 221
    defined/theoretical model, 6, 7, 10, 11, 16,
        18, 20, 27
    entrepreneurial, 147, 161, 176, 221
    familial, 168, 169
    formation of, 18, 21, 211, 216, 219, 220

higher life goals, 26, 102, 190, 205
    in/capability to attain, 118, 196, 207, 214
    and the life cycle, 88, 103–11
    through migration, 8, 26, 92, 141, 196, 216
    in narrative, 22
    new, 22, 89, 91, 100, 118
    pathways to, 217, 224
    personal, 25, 162
    physical/material, 21, 22, 89, 104, 219
    social, 89, 105, 136
    strategies to attain, 28
    traditional, 91, 117
    of women, 76, 190
grain procurement, 33
grain production quota, 55, 76, 130
grandchildren, 65, 96, 211
grandparents, 64, 65, 65, 71, 96, 211
grass linen, 30, 37, 40
Great Depression, 23
guahu: see collectives, false
Guangdong, 30, 31, 38, 40, 43, 108, 115, 133,
    164, 167, 183, 185
Guangdong Province Workers' Union, 201
Guangzhou, 39, 153, 161
Gulf (Jordan), returnees from, 17

Hainan Island, 141, 164
Hakka, 30, 31, 33, 34, 39
handicrafts, 23, 29, 30, 31, 34, 37
health, 40, 51
    see also ill health; infirm; medical expenses
hill country, 35
hills, 36, 84
hiring labor, 73, 77, 83
Honduras, 184
Hong Kong, 24, 128, 133, 153, 154, 178, 183
house, changing structure of, 112
house building, 64, 65, 66, 81, 91, 103–12,
    139–40, 142, 216
    banquets, 112
    brick factories, 139
    construction teams, 112
    roof beam, 112
    see also houses
house property certificate, 140
household/s, 11, 12, 13, 20, 34, 196
    bargaining, 76, 173, 204, 206, 208–11, 218
    categories, 57–8, 77
    characteristics and migration, 19
    data, 55–7
    definition, 35
    demographic composition, 19, 52, 57–67,
        69, 77, 79, 86
    developmental cycle, 57, 59, 65, 67, 86
    income, 22, 23, 56–62, 67–72, 74
    labor allocation, 47
    labor supply, 57, 69, 83, 86, 96, 217
    resources, 21, 197

household/s *(cont.)*
stem, 63, 66
see also conflict; fallback position; petty
commodity producers
household evaluation campaigns, 46, 55, 57–8,
68, 109, 129–30, 134, 198, 215, 223
household evaluation plaques, 55–6, 130
household resource distribution, 96, 217
see also conflict
household registration system *(hukou)*, xv, 32,
33, 43, 109
household responsibility system, 34, 35, 73,
96, 140, 196
houses, 22, 35, 57, 58, 59, 63, 89, 220
commodity housing, 132, 141
see also house building; *xiaokang lou*
Hubei, 125
Hugo, 89
hukou: see household registration system
human feeling, 172, 177, 188, 189
human resources
and household wealth, 68
impact of migration on, 13, 14, 48
and rural enterprise development, 127
Hunan province, 39

identity cards, 42, 44, 203
ideological education, 45, 130, 181, 211
see also household evaluation campaigns
ill health, 64, 65, 71, 200–2
income
agricultural, 67, 69, 70, 72, 74, 82–3, 86–7,
114
average per-capita, 37, 38, 39, 54
off-farm income, 37, 52, 67–72
rural, 38, 53
see also household/s
incubator organization, 147, 148, 175, 192
India, 73
individual operators, defined, 128
industrial product value, 128–9
industrialization, 2, 33, 34
inequality
caused by migration, 13
causing migration, 13
and household composition, 57–67
impact of migration and remittances on, 16,
53, 67, 69–72, 217
intravillage, 52
and off-farm income, 67–72
regional, 12, 13
rural–urban, 34
sectoral, 12, 13
state-endorsed, 59
structural, 25
and taxes, 80–1
see also land
infirm, the, 30, 37, 64, 77

informal small-scale producers, 145
information, 22, 41, 127, 138, 143, 148, 161,
175, 216, 221
feedback, 40, 74
see also networks
infrastructure, 51, 220, 224
defined, 192
farming, 18, 19, 47, 48
of towns, 124, 131, 143, 167, 177, 191–2, 195
inheritance, 13, 19, 63
injuries, 47, 65, 200–2, 217
inner conflict, 21, 22
innovation
in business creation, 126, 155, 183
failure of returnees, 14, 15, 16
failure of returnees in other countries, 16,
17
institution of return, 43
intergenerational contract, 66, 97
International Fund for Agricultural
Development, 57
international return migration, 17
Internet, 37
introductions to factory jobs, 40
investment
foreign, 201
from Guangzhou, 39
in returnee enterprises, 145, 177–80, 195
irrigation, 74, 81, 84, 110
Italy, 23, 24, 73

Japan, 23, 37
jia: see family
Jiangsu, 125
Jiangxi, 35
basic economic conditions, 36, 38, 50,
114–15, 167
Jiaocun, 191, 201
Jing-Jiu Railway, 39, 148, 167, 198
Jordan, 17
Judd, Ellen, 168

karaoke, 116, 149
kin, 20, 117
knowledge of urban labor markets, 209, 215,
218

labor brokers: *see* labor introduction agents
labor bureau, 41, 42, 102, 198
labor certificate, 44
labor costs, 194
labor discipline, 88, 161, 163, 214, 222
labor exchanges, 104, 112
labor export, 4, 39, 41–2, 48, 133, 201, 223
labor introduction agents, 40, 41–2, 65, 69,
97–9, 102, 132
labor market hierarchies, 199
labor market segmentation, 93

labor markets, 19, 43, 47, 59, 97, 100, 102, 134, 176
  and gender, 171
labor quality, 14, 15, 45, 89, 92
labor relations, 163, 165, 176
labor requisitions, 81, 87, 218
labor shortage, 14, 83, 108, 195, 211
laid-off migrant workers, 196–7, 214, 217
laid-off rural/county enterprise workers, 47, 147
laid-off workers, 50, 132, 134–5, 147, 165
land
  abandonment of, 79
  of absentees, 77, 79, 86, 218
  contracting of, 64, 71, 79–80
  division of, 35
  leases, 75
  markets, 72, 140, 218
  ownership, 140
  person-to-land ratios, 79, 218
  policies, 141
  purchasing, 72–3, 218
  redistribution, 32
  requisitioned, 74
  of returnee entrepreneurs, 193
  as a security net, 194, 195, 197, 216
  shortage, 74
  "two land system," 79
  use, 129
  use rights, 34, 72, 74, 75, 77, 79, 140, 218
land administration fees, 140
land allocations, 27, 36, 54, 55, 74
  adjustments to, 74, 75
  and farming innovation, 84
  and inequality, 19, 72, 73, 77–80
land distribution
  impact of migration on, 72
  and propensity to migrate, 72, 73, 74, 75, 218
land transfers, 72, 76–80, 86–7, 208, 209, 218
  policies on, 79–80
landlord, 32
laoban: see boss
Latin America, 26
legitimacy, state, 130, 134, 143, 220
Leong, S. T., 30
letters, 100, 113, 168, 198
Lewis, W. Arthur, 12, 14
Li Peng, 125
Li Tian, 30
Licun township, 40, 222
life-cycle events, 11, 13, 37
life cycle of the individual, 19
lily root, 36
lineage, family, 74, 112, 117
Lingnan, 30
links/linkages, 1, 11, 26, 42–4, 48, 127, 130, 133, 148, 150, 172, 195
"little peasant mentality," 142

livelihood diversification
  defined, 11
  and land, 74
  through local off-farm work, 67, 135
  through migration, 35, 37
  by petty commodity producers, 23, 25
  policies on, 25, 28, 48, 143
  and returnee entrepreneurs, 177, 185–7, 195
  and rural towns, 47–50, 191, 193, 211
livestock, 55, 57–8, 81–3
loans
  for collective enterprises, 151
  for entrepreneurs, 17, 142, 145, 171, 177–8, 195, 220
  informal, 110, 111, 145, 172
  of local government, 131, 171
  poverty alleviation, 149, 185
  with security, 140–1, 171, 180
local state, 129, 134, 150, 153, 196, 223
  defined, 124

macro-level, 18, 20, 216
macro-regions, 29, 30
management
  of enterprises, 151, 177, 188–9
  experience, 145, 155, 188–9
  methods, 147
  of migrant labor, 41
  modern, 151–4, 161, 188–9, 195
managers, 34, 127, 188–9
manufacturing
  in coastal areas and cities, 36, 40
  and problems, 178, 191–2
  and production layout, 151
  and returnee enterprises, 128–9, 145–8, 155–61
  in rural areas, 184–5
  see also clothing factories; furniture workshops
Mao Zedong
  countryside under, 32–5, 45, 58, 92, 140, 150
  markets under, 32–4
  see also rural industrialization
Mao-Deng-Jiang Thought, 35
marital problems, 201, 209, 211
market towns: *see* livelihood diversification; towns
marketing difficulties, 191–2
marketing structures, 20
markets, 23, 34, 49, 177, 190–2
marriage, 24, 59, 75, 88, 103, 105–10, 202
  arranged, 110, 113
  freedom in choice, 113, 205
  introductions, 113, 219, 204–6
  and return, 112, 169–70, 203–4
  urban residency through, 43, 108, 205
  see also marital problems

marriage market, 107, 113, 169
McKinley, Terry, 77
medical expenses, 65
Mexico, 25, 72
micro-credit, 83, 126, 220
micro-level, 18, 20, 53
migrant poets, xvii, 103, 228
Migrant Worker, survey, 201
migrant worker associations, 81
migrant youth society, 138
migration
    barriers to entry, 67, 69, 72
    figures, 2, 38–42, 54
    initial costs, 37, 67, 69, 216
Ming dynasty, 29, 30
model returnees, 136
modernization
    Chinese model for, 45–8, 193, 220
    as process and goal, 6, 16–19, 23, 25, 32, 50,
        88–92, 104, 112, 152
    returnees as emissaries of, 44–7, 50–1
    and towns, 28, 29, 50, 126, 143, 177, 223
modernization theory, 6, 11–19, 21, 24, 27–8,
    32, 46, 88–9, 118, 224
    Skinner's revision of, 29
mothers-in-law, 66
mutual aid, 18, 42, 103, 173

Nanchang, 39, 43, 108
Nanhai, 40, 198
Nankang, 148
nannies, 65
narrative, 22
narrative of return, 25, 26, 229n92
native place associations, 25
natural resources, 36, 37, 148, 167, 222
Nee, Victor, 152
neoclassical model, 12, 18
networks, 20, 52
    with cities, 133
    information, 20
    migrants, 20, 41
    political, 7
    social, 7, 26, 40, 216
    village, 86, 89
night school, 97, 160
North, Douglass, 192

off-farm employment, local, 54, 64, 67–72, 76,
    86, 135, 169, 185, 200, 211, 217
Oi, Jean, 152, 192
old-age care, 66
origin areas
    change in, 22
    characteristics of, 16, 18, 19
overseas Chinese, 26, 133
owner-operators, 23, 157

packaging, 166–7
paper making, 30
participant observation, 55
patriarchy, 24, 169
patronage, local, 52
periphery, 12, 17, 29, 176
    of macro-regions, 30
permanent migration, 26
permanent return, 2, 25, 26, 27
permits
    for business, 136, 153, 166, 181
    fees, 69
    for long-term urban residence, 43, 125, 165
    for migration, 42
    for temporary urban residence, 41, 42
    for town residence, 181, 193, 194
perspective, 6, 8, 21, 173, 174, 175, 215, 216, 224
petty commodity producers, 23, 24, 25, 28, 34,
    50–1
    defined, 23, 24, 25, 27
    state repression ("squeeze" of), 28, 50, 132
    struggle against officials, 35
    in Wanzai, 30, 31
photographs, 113, 190, 208
pigs/pork, 36, 55, 74, 81–3
place utility, 19, 162
political contacts, 67, 68, 71, 217
political elite, 52
population growth, 35
population quality, xv, 28, 44–7, 96, 138, 143,
    183, 211, 220
poverty, 22
    accommodation of, 13, 89
    due to illness, 202
    impact of migration on, 23
    and landlessness, 77
    and return migrant entrepreneurship, 125,
        133, 138
    the return to (*fanpin*), 111
    through social inflation, 114, 118
    and state legitimacy, 118
poverty alleviation
    through migration/remittances, 41, 48, 86,
        118, 219
    through rural enterprises and towns, 48
    and the state, 224
pregnancy, 196, 202–3
    premarital, 202
prestige, 218
    see also status
private entrepreneurs
    defined, 128
    government repression of, 152, 177, 181–2
    government support for, 37, 167, 177, 180–1
privatization, 152
production brigades, 32, 49
production difficulties, 191–2
production teams, 32

proletarianization, 24, 25, 88
prostitution, 45, 135
public security linkages, 198
public works, 81, 223
push–pull, 18–21, 25, 161–9, 176, 221–2

Qifeng, 37, 54, 77, 110
  farming in, 74
Qing dynasty, 29, 30, 31, 39
Qing Ming festival, 45

ramie, 30
ration, grain, 59
rationing system, 32
recruiters: *see* labor introduction agents
recruitment exams, 99–100
recruitment notices, 100–1
"red and white" committees, 109
regional development, uneven, 36
regional protectionism, 178
reintegration, 8, 208, 211–15, 223
relative deprivation, 22
remittances, 59, 71
  absence of, 65
  for agricultural investment, 2, 72–3, 75,
    81–7, 209, 219
  amount, 56, 77, 87
  for buying land, 75
  contribution to the household, 203–4, 217–18
  contribution to rural income, 38, 53, 54,
    114–15
  definition, 11
  for education, 64, 209
  family struggle over, 66
  for house building, 103–11, 142
  inadequate, 65
  and intention to return, 26
  for marriage, 103–11
  negative impact of, 14, 16
  secrecy about, 56, 85–6, 216
  and social gifts, 111
  usage, 7, 56, 81, 88–92
  see also consumer goods; consumerism;
    inequality; social inflation
renting, 76, 79
  see also chuzu
repatriation, 16, 33, 44
resources
  acquiring through migration, 23, 219
  defined/theoretical framework, 6, 7, 10, 11,
    20, 27
  endowments in origin, 23, 220
  local, 124, 162
  new, 216, 219
  reallocation/redistribution, 7, 17, 27, 52
  state harnessing, 28
respectability, 21, 22, 23, 66, 109, 111, 217, 219
  self-respect, 89, 103, 104, 110, 114, 118, 219

restrictions on mobility, 32–3, 43–4, 127
retirement and resettlement fund, 201
return migrant conferences, 137
return migrant entrepreneurship
  figures, 125, 127–9
  policies, 16, 17, 48, 50–1, 124, 127, 136, 166,
    177, 180–1, 184
  sign protection system, 182
  state support for, 8, 125–39, 141–3, 166, 177,
    178, 220
return migration, figures, 124–5
returnee enterprises
  investment sources, 146
  ownership, 144, 146, 150–2
  scale, 144–50
  type, 144–50
returnee entrepreneurs, 144, 221
  duration of absence, 144, 154–7
  level of education, 144, 154–5, 157–61
  reasons for return, 144, 154–5
  and state negotiations, 8, 132, 140, 143, 150,
    152, 153, 180–4, 192, 194–5, 221
returnee migrants, as consultants, 153
reverse chain migration, 161
revolutionary bases, 31, 33, 35
Rhoda, R., 19
risk, minimizing, 12, 23, 36
rural enterprises, 34, 37, 48, 50, 68, 84, 189
  contracting of, 138, 151–4
  defined, 47
  figures, 47–8
  and local officials, 68
  relocation of, 192–3
rural industrialization
  under Mao, 33–5, 47, 48
  policies, 47–8
rural industries, 37, 38, 47, 125–43
rural proletarian, 24, 48
rusticated youths, 33, 133

savings, 71, 83, 91, 111, 143, 145, 169, 171, 194,
  219
school, returning to, 102
school fees, 92–4, 96, 220
school students, migration of, 94–6
schools, 19, 43, 181, 194
seasonal migration, 19, 40, 64, 96
selection effect of migration, 14, 93
self-employment, 124
Sen, Amartya, 22, 204
separation of family members, 22, 47, 135,
  169, 209–10
service sector, 15, 16, 17, 34, 44, 47, 71, 84, 91,
  178, 221
  retail, 148–9
  and returnee enterprises, 126, 144, 145,
    148–9, 155, 161, 163, 170, 173, 175, 176
sexually transmitted diseases, 209–10

shame, 103, 200, 219
Shanghai, 38, 41, 45, 84, 100, 133, 138, 164, 201
shoes, 147, 148, 184, 190, 192
shuttling, 84
Sichuan, 125
Sierra Leone, 184
silk production, 24
Siu, Helen, 108
skilled migration, 162, 167
skills, 19, 22, 184
  acquired through migration, 71, 125–6, 143, 145, 147, 160–1, 176, 222
  handicrafts, 32
  national certificate system, 100
  off-farm, 39, 40
  and return migrant entrepreneurs, 157–61, 169
  shortage, 185–6
  traditional family skills, 67, 68, 217
  training, 16, 45, 160
Skinner, William G., 29, 30, 49, 143, 220
Smith, Adam, 22
social actors, 6, 18, 20, 103, 114
social inflation, 103, 109, 110, 111, 114, 118, 219
social reproduction, 103, 109, 214, 219
social stability, 134–5, 143, 196, 198, 223
socialization, 18, 21, 211
socializing, 213
socioeconomic mobility of migrants, 164, 189, 219
socioeconomic transition, 20, 23, 24, 27, 28, 96
sojourning, 39
Song dynasty, 24
sons, 59, 64, 96, 200
  and marriage, 107
  and property allocation, 63
  and remittances, 63, 66, 107
"speak bitterness" meetings, 32
special economic zones, in rural areas, 139, 141
spending patterns, 8, 88, 89
spouses left behind, 37, 112, 218
Spring Festival, 37, 40, 55, 81, 100, 104, 112, 137, 202, 205, 208–9, 212, 213
startup capital, 145, 173, 178
state-owned enterprises, 145, 150, 151, 152, 188, 197
status, 17, 92, 113, 163
  see also face; prestige; respectability; shame
strikes, 211
structuralist, 6, 11–16, 19, 20, 23, 24, 27, 88, 118, 145, 190, 200, 224
structuration, 225n9
subjectivity, 18, 20
sub-Saharan Africa, 24, 26
subsidies, farming, 77
subsistence, 13, 36, 53, 145, 197
sugar cane, 36

surplus rural labor
  absorption by returnee enterprises, 184–5
  absorption of, 47, 50, 125, 143, 223
  and China's political economy, 32, 34
  figures, 1, 47, 125
  in the neoclassical model, 12, 13
  in the structuralist model, 14

"taste transfer," 88
tax reforms, 131–2
taxes, 192, 220, 224, 225
  agricultural, 38, 52, 55, 72, 76, 81, 130, 131, 132, 178, 223
  on rural enterprises, 130–3, 143, 166, 177, 181–2, 183
tea, 36
technology, 34, 45, 93
  diesel-powered machines, 84
  farming, 19, 73, 84–5
  in rural enterprises, 126, 153, 161
telecommunications, 168, 192, 212, 222
telephones, 116, 168
television, 85, 92, 108, 114, 115, 135, 137, 198, 215
temporary return, 2, 55, 212
Thailand, 24
"three without" migrants, 44
tobacco, 31, 33, 34, 36, 37
Todaro, Michael, 12, 93
tools, 147, 178
"townization," 2
towns, 20, 29, 30, 31, 32, 47–50, 131–2, 135, 173, 174, 218
  building of, 139–43, 194, 223
  policies on development of, 47–8, 126–7, 191–5, 211
  and rural development, 47–50, 149, 211
township government, 129–31, 166, 192
township and village enterprises: *see* rural enterprises
townships, 49, 199
trade fairs, 37
trading/traders, 29, 30, 31, 35, 84, 141, 164, 169, 222–3
  in agricultural inputs, 68
tradition, 17, 18
traditional marriage, 204
transport, 20, 25, 34, 41, 47, 49, 69, 107, 111, 115–17
  costs, 29
  long-distance, 117
  minibuses, 117, 205
  motorbikes, 117, 168, 199, 200
  operators, 117
  roads, 19, 191
  ticket sales, 117
truancy, 93–5
Tsai, Kellee, 173

Tuanjie, 54, 110
  farming in, 74
  schooling in, 94–6

underemployment, 35, 197
unemployed returnees, 198, 199
unemployment
  during the Depression, 23
  and instability, 2, 43
  in urban areas, 41, 42, 50, 99
urban residency, 41–4
urban tastes, 85
urban wages, before return, 161–2
urban work experience, 145, 147, 157–61, 189, 222
urbanization, 34

values
  of collective welfare, 67, 88, 178
  defined/theoretical framework, 6, 7, 10, 11, 18, 20, 21, 27
  individualism, 88, 108, 190
  internalization of, 21, 217
  loyalty to family/home town, 8, 23, 24, 31, 112, 124, 136, 166, 168, 217, 220
  modern, 89, 91, 104, 118, 209
  moral, 134, 188, 190, 204
  in narrative, 22
  new, 92, 196, 211, 215, 216, 217, 219, 220
  patriarchal, 169
  and social customs, 111
  traditional, 88, 210
  urban, 89
  within rural society, 42, 89, 114, 118, 202
video, 149, 198, 213
village cadres, 80, 94, 134, 138, 203
village group leaders, 129
  see also zuzhang
visibility of labor, 204
vocational training, 100, 102, 118, 138, 160
  see also night school; skills, training

wage laborer, 24
wages, 167
  average of rural off-farm workers, 37, 38, 184
  delayed or unpaid, 163, 188–9, 198, 211
Wanzai, 3, 4
  basic economic conditions, 36, 38
  handicrafts, 37
  history, 28, 29, 30, 31, 32
  local off-farm employment, 68
  migration from, 39, 40
  returnee entrepreneurship in, 148, 182
weddings, 22, 45, 110, 115
welfare, 196
widows, 64, 65, 75, 80, 109
wives, 174
  as farmers, 83

and land allocation, 75–6
and remittances, 208–9, 211
women
  and agency, 175, 176, 206
  and the courtyard economy, 174
  and education, 97, 171–2
  as factory workers, 40, 96
  and family control, 24
  and family planning, 42
  as farmers, 74, 108, 174, 175, 208
  in firework production, 37
  and independence, 173, 174, 207
  and independent income, 24
  and labor quality, 171–2
  and marriage, 107–10, 205–9, 214
  as migrants, 18, 99, 153, 172
  and personal savings, 173
  and petty commodity production, 24, 108
  and pregnancy, 46
  as proportion of migrants, 39, 169–70
  as returnees, 71, 204, 214, 219–20
  and skills acquisition, 172
  and suicide, 207–8
  and working conditions, 46
  see also daughters; gender; gendered division of labor; wives
women returnee entrepreneurs, 144, 155, 169, 174, 221–2
  and family, 171–2, 174
  as large-scale manufacturing managers, 170–1
  and marriage, 171–2
women's enterprises, characteristics of, 170–1
women's labor, 108
Woon, Yuen-Fong, 125, 230n13
work permit card, 203
work points, 58
workers' protection, 201
working conditions, 1, 2, 43–4, 46–7, 100, 162–4, 188, 197, 200, 211, 214, 217
World Trade Organization, 77, 116

xiang, xv, 50
  see also townships
xiaokang, 104
xiaokang lou, xv, 104, 108, 110, 118
Xinfeng, 3, 4, 28, 29, 30, 31, 34
  basic economic conditions, 36, 38, 39, 132, 133
  migration from, 39, 40

Yan Yunxiang, 108, 109
Yichun city, 115
Yichun prefecture, 3, 4, 28
Yudu, 3, 4, 31
  basic economic conditions, 36, 38, 39, 132, 133

Yudu *(cont.)*
    government-organized labor export, 41, 42,
        138
    handicrafts, 37
    migration from, 39, 40
Yudu Labor Export Company, 4, 41, 42, 45, 46,
    138

"zero value" labor, 12, 14, 53
Zhejiang, 167–8
zhen, xv, 50
zhuanbao, 76
zhuanrang, 76
zuzhang, xvi
    see also village group leaders